OLD MEN FORGET

DUFF COOPER

Carroll & Graf Publishers, Inc.
New York

TO DIANA

Fear not, sweet love, what time can do;
Though silver dims the gold
Of your soft hair, believe that you
Can change but not grow old.

Though since we married thirty years
And four have flown away,
As bright your beauty still appears
As on our wedding day.

We will not weep that spring be past
And autumn shadows fall;
These years shall be, although the last,
The loveliest of all.

CONTENTS

FOREWORD

ALFRED DUFF COOPER, first Viscount Norwich, was a man of many and varied talents, the most conspicuous of which was a talent for life itself. From childhood he loved not wisely but too well, an amiable weakness that may have cost him something in worldly success but which earned him great happiness and the affection of innumerable friends.

No man can be called a failure who has served as Secretary of State for War, First Lord of the Admiralty, Minister of Information, Chancellor of the Duchy of Lancaster and Ambassador to France. In addition to all this Duff Cooper, in his life of Talleyrand, produced one of the most readable and yet academically sound of short biographies, a masterpiece of its kind which has stood up remarkably well to the half century that has passed since it was first published. His *Haig* lacked some of the panache of *Talleyrand* but was a lucid and gracefully written addition to that often spiritless genre, the official biography. He was an accomplished minor poet; wrote a successful novel, *Operation Heartbreak*; the acclaimed autobiography, to which this is the foreword; and much else besides. It was, by any standard, a formidable tally of achievement. Yet it was less than had been hoped for him, less than he had hoped for himself. With his ability and connections there had seemed no reason why he should not have filled one of greatest offices of state, perhaps even that of Prime Minister. That he failed to do so is attributable not so much to any lack of qualifications as to the quirks of his personality.

To call Duff Cooper idle would be to misjudge his nature. It was for him a question not of indolence but of priorities. He enjoyed playing backgammon with his cronies in White's, or talking to attractive and intelligent women, more than he did attending solemn meetings in Whitehall; he preferred reading poetry to White Papers; if the food, the wine and, above all, the conversation were good, he saw no reason why lunch should not be indefinitely prolonged, fading imperceptibly in due course into a rubber of bridge or a flirtation. Most of us would share his prejudices; Duff Cooper was unusual in that he acted on his inclinations. 'Writing in my sixty-fourth year,' he declares with barely concealed pride in his autobiography, 'I can truthfully say that since I reached the age of discretion I have consistently drunk more than most people would say was good for me. Nor do I regret it.' He might have said something similar about his affairs with women. Only in the most pressing instances was he prepared to sacrifice his pleasures to his duty; or perhaps more correctly he saw his pleasures as his duty and dutifully pursued them.

There were other more important reasons why Duff Cooper did not reach the very top. Integrity and moral courage are dangerous qualities in a politician, yet he possessed them to an extravagant degree. His resignation after Munich was the action of a brave and honourable man, but it was not calculated to ease his passage into Downing Street. He was not skilled in the arts of 'flesh-pressing' or those other techniques by which those seeking to get on in public life are supposed to ingratiate themselves with the electorate. 'Too reserved to win popularity and too proud to court it,' was Harold Nicolson's description of him. He could seem rude; could, indeed, *be* rude; but the victim was more likely to be his equal or hierarchic superior than some underling who could not answer back. He was neither cool nor temperate: when an undergraduate ventured some ill-formed criticism of Browning's poetry Duff Cooper berated him with the same outraged fury as he had shown when the Duke of Westminster was so ill-advised as to make an offensive remark in his presence about the Jews. His temper was terrible – 'veiners', his family would call it, when his face empurpled and he swelled out like a resentful bullfrog. It passed as quickly as it came and he bore no grudges, but the object of his fury was not invariably so ready to forgive and forget. In public life he collected a group of embittered enemies, a circumstance which played a more decisive part in his career than the fact that in private life he gained a far larger number of devoted friends.

The memoirs of statesmen and diplomats are often evasive and still more often pompous. *Old Men Forget* is neither. It is, on the contrary, admirably honest and written with an elegance and wit that are all too rarely met with in such works. There is no Rousseau-esque self-analysis, no titillating revelation about illicit loves – Duff Cooper abhorred vulgarity of any kind – but the author is always ready to denounce his own shortcomings with the same cheerful vigour as he metes out to others. His judgements of his contemporaries are always perceptive and have usually stood up well to the test of time. Neville Chamberlain had been 'a successful Lord Mayor of Birmingham, and for him the Dictators of Germany and Italy were like the Lord Mayors of different interests, but who must desire the welfare of humanity and be fundamentally reasonable, decent men like himself'. 'After spending more than half a century in the dehumanising profession of politics, Winston Churchill remains as human as a schoolboy. His friends are right and his enemies are wrong.' Ernest Bevin 'seemed to me to fulfil Pope's description of man as "a being darkly wise and rudely great" '. (Bevin had an equally high opinion of Duff Cooper. At a particularly protracted session of the Peace Conference in 1946 the Ambassador fell peacefully asleep. Bevin was much struck by this behaviour. 'Tell Duff I'll call 'im if anything 'appens,' he said, and added, ' 'E's the most sensible man in the room.')

Duff Cooper's love for his wife runs like a strong and vividly coloured thread throughout this book. Diana, in her idiosyncratic and inimitable way, was a superb complement to him in his career. Decorous she would never be, but she supplied the common touch that was so conspicuously absent in her husband. A talent for small talk with strangers was listed by Duff Cooper as among the first gifts an aspirant politician should possess. He knew that he lacked it, knew too that the talent required a genuine interest in his fellow men that he could neither feel nor simulate. 'Diana, on the other hand, is very soon at home in any company in which she finds herself, whether it be working women drinking tea in a mean street at Oldham, or French Cabinet Ministers sipping champagne at the Quai d'Orsay. She once found herself next to the Bey of Tunis at dinner. He spoke no word of any European language. Before the meal was over they were communicating by drawing little pictures on their menus, and were laughing happily together.' Duff regarded his wife with a baffled and loving admiration. He was as proud of her as she was of him. Through innumerable infidelities he remained in essentials faithful to the one woman who always meant far more to him than any passing fancy.

In spite of the vicissitudes of his career and a sometimes elegiac sadness as he surveys the glories of the past, *Old Men Forget* is the chronicle of a profoundly happy man. It was not Duff Cooper's way to regret the things he had done, only sometimes the things he had left undone. Of these there were few. He had performed a series of tasks that had interested and amused him; easily bored, he had married a woman in whose presence boredom was an impossibility; he had lived to see his son, whose birth he had described as 'the crown of happiness', thrive and exhibit many of the talents that he admired in others and enjoyed himself. 'Life had been good to me,' he concluded his autobiography, 'and I am grateful':

'My delight in it is as keen as ever and I will thankfully accept as many more years as may be granted. But I am fond of change and have welcomed it even when uncertain whether it would be for the better; so, although I am very glad to be where I am, I shall not be too distressed when the summons comes to go away. Autumn has always been my favourite season, and evening has been for me the pleasantest time of day. I love the sunlight but I cannot fear the coming of the dark.'

He died in 1954, within a year of his autobiography being published, leaving much which he wished to do undone and yet with much accomplished. He died as he had lived, with gallantry, humour and a resolute determination to enjoy whatever might be coming next.

Philip Ziegler
1986

CHAPTER ONE

CHILD AND BOY

1890–1907

Among the many things old men forget are the disadvantages of childhood. The benignity of time lays, sooner or later, upon the noses of most of us a pair of spectacles, and when we look through them towards the past a rosy colouring affects the lenses, so that the world in retrospect appears more beautiful than it does today. My memory, however, is still sufficiently retentive to assure me that childhood was not the happiest but the least happy period of my life.

I divide life by decades. The first covers childhood, the second boyhood, the third youth. Then for thirty years a man is middle-aged, until he hears the clock strike sixty and knows that old age has begun. Of those six decades I can say with truth that I enjoyed each one more than the one that went before, nor am I sure that old age would not be the happiest period of all, if it were not for consciousness of failing powers and occasional reminders of the time limit.

Let it not be thought, however, that I was badly treated as a child. I was, on the contrary, what is commonly called "spoilt." The youngest of my mother's five children, and my father's and mother's four—she had been married before—I was the first boy, so that my arrival was very welcome. Being a delicate and docile child, I could do no wrong in the eyes of the grown-up people, and if ever I erred it was said that I had been led away by one of my sisters. This secondary rôle in crime was one that I resented, but I repudiated it in vain.

The poet Wordsworth wrote that "delight and liberty" were the "simple creed of childhood." But in fact a child enjoys about as much liberty as a slave, and the delights of childhood are insipid and transitory, whereas its sorrows, also transitory, are fierce and desperate.

All children are snobs, and the aristocracy of childhood is age.

When the ten-year-old condescends to play with the seven-year-old the latter will cut his six-year-old friend on the playground. I was more than three years younger than the youngest of the three sisters with whom I was brought up, but she would be very kind to me when the two elder ones had no need of her.

This youngest sister I loved deeply and she had a great influence on my life. She was not an easy child to manage. She was wild and imaginative. She told me once that she was not my sister at all but that our parents had bought her out of a circus, a belief which I held for many years and which added romance to my affection.

As she became more unruly the decision was taken to carry out what had long been a threat and to send her to school. Girls were less frequently sent to school in those days, and my other sisters and most of their friends were educated at home by governesses. My youngest sister, Sybil, was therefore sent away to school at the age of twelve when I, aged nine, left for my first preparatory school at Westgate.

My sister returned from school for the summer holidays inspired by one of those excessive affections which girls conceive for a school-mistress, and also possessed with the belief, strange and new to me, that it was a very good thing to be clever, and that the easiest way to become so was to read books, whether you understood them or not. We started straight away with the plays of Shakespeare, distributing certain parts and taking the others alternately. We learnt duologues by heart—Brutus and Cassius, Romeo and Juliet, Hubert and Arthur, and the final meeting between Macbeth and Macduff. After we had recited this last one to my father we were told that we had better forget it. Among some strong language, it refers to the circum-stances of Macduff's birth, the result of a posthumous cæsarian opera-tion. Years afterwards, when we were both grown up and she was married, I asked her whether she remembered the day we gave our performance. "Perfectly," she said. "Father had a most terrible cough and went behind that screen in the drawing-room." "Has it ever occurred to you," I asked, "that he was roaring with laughter?" It never had.

My father was at that time a successful London surgeon. He had had a hard start in life, the youngest of four children whose father, a barrister, had died before he could make much provision for them. He was educated at the Merchant Taylors' School. His two elder brothers had, like their father and grandfather, been called to the Bar, but my father had chosen medicine as his profession. He was not, I think, scientifically distinguished, but he had beautiful hands, was a skilful operator and much loved by his patients. "Throw physic to the dogs" was one of his frequent quotations, and when he saw me swallowing some tonic, he would say, "What the boy really needs is a pint of champagne and a mutton chop."

His father had had literary as well as legal ambitions. He wrote three plays, one in verse, which acquired the dignity not only of print but also of performance at the Theatres Royal of King's Lynn and Norwich. Having tried to read them, I cannot be surprised that they never made the journey to London. He published also a slender volume containing a sketch of his elder brother Henry's life and of their father's. This elder brother seems to have been a more distinguished barrister than my grandfather, William. Of their father he writes, "He was Charles, now better known as Old Counsellor Cooper, a remarkable man, who, like the late William Cobbett, though of humble origin, possessed one of those minds that will and must, as they have ever done from the time of Deioces of Ecbatana (recorded by Herodotus) till now, elevate the possessor and compel the homage, while exciting the no small envy of inferior intellects." My grandfather certainly never acquired the simplicity of Cobbett's prose style.

This great-grandfather was admitted a member of Lincoln's Inn in 1782, when he was entered as "Charles Cooper of the City of Norwich, eldest son of Charles Cooper of the same place, merchant." In Norwich every member of the family, so far as I have record, including my father, was born, and when therefore I received the honour of a peerage I felt impelled by piety to take the name of that ancient and famous city.

My mother's family was more illustrious. The Scots take greater interest in genealogy than the English, and, their population being smaller, it is easier to trace relationships. The clan system also connects the humblest in the land with some great chieftain. Whether there ever was a clan Macduff is doubtful, as is the existence of the

Thane of Fife who slew Macbeth, and from whom my mother's family rashly claimed descent.

What is certain is that in the seventeenth century some people of the name of Duff in the neighbourhood of Aberdeen acquired wealth and land, that in the eighteenth century, after the Union, a member of that family sat in the British House of Commons, that he there rendered the sort of silent service which Sir Robert Walpole most appreciated and that he received as a reward for it an Irish earldom. Under the influence no doubt of the old legend, he took the name of Fife, although he owned not a square foot of territory in that county, nor did he ever visit Ireland or take his seat in the Irish House of Lords.

A century later further honour fell to the family, owing to Queen Victoria's affection for Scotland and to the fact that she bought Balmoral, where the Fifes, at Mar Lodge, were her near neighbours. The result was that my uncle, who had increased the wealth that he had inherited, married King Edward VII's daughter and was made a Duke—the last non-royal dukedom, so far, to be created.

What interested me more in my mother's descent than the Scottish noblemen was the fact that her grandmother was the daughter of Mrs. Jordan, one of the ten children that she bore to the Duke of Clarence, afterwards King William IV. Mrs. Jordan is an enchanting figure in the history of English comedy. Hazlitt wrote of her that "to hear her laugh was to drink nectar," and crabbed old Creevey when he found himself staying in the same house with her daughter Lady Erroll, my great-grandmother, described her as "playing and singing her mother's kind of songs in the evening—the merits inferior I must admit to the divine original—and yet certainly like her."

My sister and I were entirely devoted to the theatre at this time and had both decided that it was to be our profession. We were naturally glad therefore to discover that we had an actress and a dramatic author among our forebears.

My father, although he had no conception of the meaning of the word literature, had certain recitations at his command which his father had no doubt taught him. Every summer we spent in the Isle of Arran, where he owned a small house, and the 12th of August was a day to which we looked forward. He would have been out shooting over dogs all day with his elder brother. His sister, older still, would be staying in the house. It was her birthday. The children all came down to dinner to enjoy the first grouse. There was champagne, but whether in honour of the grouse or Aunt Aggie we never knew. After dinner there were games—dumb-crambo always, charades rarely—and my father would recite the dagger speech from *Macbeth*, the murder speech from *Othello*, and the famous speech from the tragedy of *Douglas*, beginning "My name is Norval."

I was now moving from the first into the second decade of life. Looking back, I think that my lack of enjoyment in childhood was very likely due to delicate health. I was nervous of other children, took no pleasure in outdoor games, preferring, until I could read to myself, to sit by the fire and be read to, or to look at pictures in books. Although I had probably hardly heard the word, I believe now that as a child I suffered, and that many children do suffer, from intolerable boredom.

But henceforth I had an overwhelming interest in life which centred itself upon the stage and which through the stage was to lead me further. It impelled my sister and myself to go in search of suitable subjects for recitation, so that not only on the annual occasion when my father took the floor, but on other evenings, which we sought to multiply, we could display our talents. In the search it was not surprising that we stumbled upon poetry. That great discovery, which most men never make, must be more precious to those who make it for themselves while they are groping through the forest of literature on an uncertain quest, than to those who are given a map, shown the road and perhaps led along it.

Rhetoric makes the first appeal to boys who have any literary bent. I was fortunate in finding Macaulay's *Lays of Ancient Rome* and Aytoun's *Lays of the Scottish Cavaliers*. Macaulay both in prose and verse is the greatest rhetorician in the language. And who will say that he does not come near to poetry in such a stanza as this?

> The harvests of Arretium,
> This year, old men shall reap;
> This year, young boys in Umbro
> Shall plunge the struggling sheep;

And in the vats of Luna,
   This year, the must shall foam
Round the white feet of laughing girls,
   Whose sires have marched to Rome.

I knew the whole of "Horatius" by heart, and of Aytoun I learnt "Charles Edward at Versailles" and "The Execution of Montrose." I think it likely that this early getting by heart of long passages of verse served me well by enriching my vocabulary and so helping me later in public speaking.

There is no poem that lends itself better to the art of recitation than Edgar Allan Poe's "The Raven," full as it is from beginning to end of dramatic effects. I was naturally led on from learning "The Raven" to reading the rest of the slim volume that contains his verse. I found not what I was looking for, but I found poetry, and by some happy chance I was able to recognise it as such. Poe's place in literature is still difficult to determine. His fellow-countrymen have shown little interest in him; to the English he is the author of "The Raven," "The Bells" and some strange stories; to the French he is one of the great masters whom Baudelaire was proud to serve. To me he gave the key that opened the door into the richest palace in the world.

It was during the Christmas holidays of 1900 that I paid my first visit to Paris, where my eldest sister was finishing her education in a French family. I travelled with my father and mother, my two younger sisters having remained in Scotland. The war in South Africa had been going on for a year. I took little interest in it, and did not, as most boys did, follow the campaign with maps and little flags. When I was given for Christmas a box of soldiers in khaki, which was then a novelty, I deplored the drab colour and exchanged them for some knights in armour, which I found in the toy department of the *Magasin du Louvre*.

That was my first trip abroad, and the recollection of it is very clearly stamped upon my mind. We stayed at a hotel in the Rue de Rivoli, and the windows of our rooms overlooked the gardens of the Tuileries. My interest in France and French history had already been aroused by *The Only Way* (a stage version of *A Tale of Two Cities*), so that I expected to meet a *sans-culotte* at every street corner.

I can still remember the restaurants we went to and how long my father studied the wine list. He was a fine judge of claret, but the delay exasperated my mother as much as it perplexed me. I was also appalled, as I suppose all children are, by the way in which grown-up people sit round the table talking when the meal is finished. One day I heard my father during one of these conversations discussing with a friend the great ill-will and even hatred that then existed between the English and the French. I was surprised, for I had seen no sign of it and everybody had been very kind to me. I was taken shortly afterwards to an entertainment which included what was called the American bioscope—forerunner of the cinematograph. When Kruger, the Boer President, appeared he was greeted with loud applause and enthusiastic cheers. To me he naturally represented the incarnation of evil. I tried to register my protest by booing and hissing and shaking my small fist. I felt how right the English were to hate the French, and I shared their hatred. Then my attention was caught by the tall figure of a bearded man standing beside me. There could be no doubt as to his nationality, but he was looking down at me with an expression of so much amusement and such sweet benevolence that all my hatred melted, and I returned his smile.

It is more than half a century ago, but I remember it all very distinctly. I fell in love with Paris then, and I have been faithful. I have loved London not less and I have never seen any reason why love should be exclusive or why fidelity cannot be shared. The events of my life bind me to these two cities. I have known them both in peace and war. I have looked from my window in St. James's Street down the length of Pall Mall while the first enemy bombs were falling on the town, and from the same window I have seen the President of the United States and the Marshal of France who had commanded the Allied armies driving by in the hour of victory. I have mixed with the hilarious crowd cheering the outbreak of war in 1914 and have felt my way through the black-out that fell upon the silent and awe-stricken masses on the eve of the declaration of war in 1939. I have known the rapture of arriving in Paris on leave from the front in the first war, and in the second war I visited Paris in the perfect June weather of 1940, a few days before the capital fell into the hands of the Germans. I have lived in London when every night from darkness till dawn the enemy was tearing her to pieces and slaughtering her children, and have seen her emerge haggard and grim and daunt-less from the ordeal. And I have been in Paris on the morrow of her liberation from four years of enslavement and seen the empty streets and bare shop-windows gradually putting on again their old gar-ments of gaiety. I have worked and played in both, yet at the sound of their names I seldom recall these historic memories of the past, but think rather of clear spring mornings in Paris, and misty autumn evenings in London, when I have walked through the streets with causeless exultation in my heart.

Those Christmas holidays of 1900 were, unlike most of my holi-days, full of events. On our return from Paris my mother and I went up to Arran to visit the two sisters who had stayed there. We found that they had had enough of that quiet life and were glad to travel back with us. On the morning of our departure the gardener, who came upstairs to carry down our luggage, told us that the Queen was dead. To us children it seemed a tremendous event. We could not have explained what we felt, nor could we know that it was in fact the end of a great epoch. Our minds were brought back to our own interests by the governess, who observed, perhaps spitefully, that all the theatres in London would be shut.

On account of my health I was first sent to school at Westgate for the bracing air, but after two years it was decided that the air was too strong for me and I was removed to Wixenford near Wokingham, which suited me better and where I was happier. But I have doubts about the preparatory school system. It seems a cruel thing to take a child of nine away from his home and the loving care of his mother. Boys between nine and thirteen have little to gain from each other's companionship. The influence of a good home must be better than that of the best school. I have known men who were spared the pre-paratory school or sent only to a day-school. I believe that they lost nothing and I know that they gained a few years of happiness.

In the life of an Englishman no period is more important than the years that he spends at a public school. He is a child when he goes there and he comes away a man. An older person takes him to the station when he sets forth for the first time, casting a regretful eye at the toy cupboard. When he comes back for good after four or five years he has a cigarette between his lips and the daily papers under his arm from which he has already culled the principal items of sporting or theatrical interest. He goes a grub, fearful of being trodden on. He returns a butterfly with wings spread for a flight.

I was not quite thirteen when I went to Eton, but in some ways I was old for my age. I read *The Mill on the Floss* during my first half and was deeply impressed by it. One of the reasons why Eton is the best school in the world is that every boy has a room to himself where he can indulge his own hobbies and read the books that he likes. Another reason is that eccentrics are tolerated. They are regarded with good-humoured amusement, but not with mistrust or contempt. A boy who has no aptitude for the recognised games nor much interest in them can never become a big figure in the school, but he can be perfectly happy. I detested football, lost interest in cricket as soon as my wicket had fallen, and regarded rowing merely as a convenient method of propelling a boat.

But I was very fond of fives and delighted in less orthodox games such as passage-football and stump-cricket in the yard. The happiest afternoons in the summer were spent on and in the river, and less respectable amusements included bridge, which was strictly forbidden, but which we combined with substantial teas in the back room of a shop in Windsor.

I was in an unruly house, the master of which was a man of science who spent most of his time in his laboratory, a habit of which the boys took full advantage. Smoking was indulged in almost openly and the captain of the house was not above taking an occasional bank at roulette. The abuse of toleration defeats its own end. A change of housemasters took place.

E. L. Churchill, the new broom, was determined to sweep clean and I narrowly escaped inclusion in the sweepings. But we came to know one another and to be the best of friends. He was a famous oar and naturally took an interest in coaching those who had taken up rowing. I had become a wet-bob in order to avoid cricket, but after an hour on the river in a "four," receiving advice from the bank through a megaphone, my waning enthusiasm for cricket revived, so that I became a dry-bob again. I was no longer a "junior," and not good enough to play for the house, so that my cricketing activities attracted no interest. I used to play on a ground called The

Triangle where would turn up a collection of boys whose approach to athletics was similar to my own. Two sides would be picked up, and the one that won the toss would spend a pleasant afternoon batting, but when they were all out the fielding side would often discover that one by one their opponents had slipped off to have their tea and that there was nobody left to bowl to them.

The volunteers in those days provided a good deal of fun. They really were voluntary, and were regarded with some contempt by quite a large proportion of the school, who referred to them as "the dog-potters." Field days, which always included a train journey and a picnic lunch, varied the monotony, and camp, which lasted only a couple of days at the end of the summer half, was most enjoyable. My final hours of Eton life were spent in camp, and I may be said to have left under a cloud because I assisted in putting a sheep into a master's tent on the last night. It was a harmless prank, but the authorities took an unfavourable view of it.

Let it not be thought, however, that my life at Eton was one of wild escapades. I was a serious boy and spent many hours in the school library. Had I devoted as much time to my school work as I did to promiscuous reading I might have obtained some scholastic distinction. But I had a stupid idea that hard work at given tasks was degrading. Brilliant success without undue application and, if possible, combined with dissipation was what I admired. I remember discovering and reading with delight Sir George Otto Trevelyan's *Early Life of Charles James Fox*. So Fox became my hero. He has much to answer for, he and others who came after, some even in our own days, who attained great fame without apparent drudgery, and sweetened rather than sullied it by amiable vices.

During my time at Eton my interest in acting faded, but another interest took its place. In every house there was a debating society. Membership was confined to the older boys and conferred some social distinction, so that although most boys thought the actual debating a bore they were glad to belong to the society. Debates took place on Saturday nights in the winter. To me they seemed to offer at last an opportunity of displaying some of those talents which I believed I possessed. I looked forward to them eagerly, and gave much thought to my speeches, but never wrote them down, for the excellent rule prevailed, as it does in the House of Commons, that speeches might not be read.

There was no opponent in our house who was worthy of my steel, and I am sure that I incurred a good deal of unpopularity by the ease with which I triumphed and the pleasure that I took in trouncing the other side. Yet I would lie awake for hours after the debates, over-excited, remembering points I had forgotten to make or thinking of additional ones.

Politics were never the subject of discussion. I think that, together with religion, they were excluded by the rules of the society. There can have been no desire to break such rules, for politics meant very little to any of us and we were probably all of the same way of thinking.

Yet these debates provided valuable political training. Every member was obliged to speak, and so to become accustomed to the sound of his own voice and to learn something of the procedure of a public meeting. The captain of the house was the chairman, and after the motion had been duly proposed and seconded and its rejection similarly moved and seconded he would call upon all members to speak in any order that seemed good to him. Questions, on the model of those in the House of Commons, could also be asked before business began, and during the debate boys would refer to one another as "Mr." or "the honourable member," forgetting for the time the opprobrious nicknames which came more readily to their lips.

While I was at Eton the General Election of 1905–6 took place and I threw myself heart and soul into the fight. Boys love any form of contest and are naturally partisan. At one of my private schools we were divided into two sects, "swallows" and "crusaders." Neither appellation had the slightest significance, but every boy on arrival enthusiastically embraced one side or the other. Matches took place between the two and colours were awarded.

In the same way, during the nineteenth century, as W. S. Gilbert wrote with truth, every child was born a little Liberal or a little Conservative. It so happened that I was born a little Conservative, and although in the course of my career I have occasionally had doubts as to the infallible wisdom of the Conservative Party, they have never been sufficient to induce me to contemplate joining any other.

In my home the subject of politics was as rarely mentioned as that of literature. It was assumed that Conservatives were always right and Liberals always wrong. So obvious a proposition no more admitted of argument than did the truth of revealed religion. There was therefore nothing more to be said about it. I remember the flags flying half-mast at the death of Mr. Gladstone, and my mother telling me that he was a very bad man but a very great one—neither of which views I now believe to be true. She never told me she had personally known Disraeli until, when I was grown up, I asked her. She had not thought it worth mentioning.

During the General Election in which I took so deep an interest, and in which the Conservative Party suffered the most overwhelming defeat in all its history, Sir Herbert Tree, with true showman's instinct, revived Ibsen's *An Enemy of the People*. There is a scene in it at a public meeting where the hero sustains on the platform the unpopular cause. He shouts against the jeers and hoots of the audience, "The majority is always in the wrong—the great liberal majority is always wrong." General elections in those times were not completed in one day, but were spread over three weeks. It was, however, usually known after the first few days which way the tide was flowing. Such a play was therefore well calculated to arouse excitement. A London theatre audience is predominantly Conservative, and we Conservatives at His Majesty's Theatre would loudly applaud the enunciation of such sentiments, which were received with hisses, whistles and catcalls by a powerful minority. I went more than once to enjoy the fun. So it was that rhetoric and drama, which had guided me to poetry, now led me into politics.

That election happened during the Christmas holidays, which I was spending in London. Holidays were not very gay now, for all my sisters were married before I was fifteen, the youngest committing that imprudence soon after her seventeenth birthday. My father had retired from practice and his health was failing, so that I usually found myself alone with my parents in some health resort. The last three winters of his life were spent in the South of France. The first time that I went there was during the Easter holidays, and I was quite unprepared for the difference from the English climate. I left London one bleak March morning, as foggy as November and as cold as

January, and I woke the next day in the radiant sunshine of the Riviera, where the hedges were already full of roses. Nobody had told me that it would be so, and I could hardly believe it. That was at Costebelle near Hyères. I never went there again.

During the last two years of my father's life we had a small villa at Menton, where he died in the spring of 1908. It was the first death-bed at which I had been present. I had never known him show any emotion, nor did he then. He had been used to encourage us to go to church and would always enquire as to the length of the sermon, but when my mother, who was sincerely religious, asked him on the last morning whether he would like to see a clergyman, he replied calmly, "Good God, no." He was quite conscious to the last, and when he could no longer see he asked whether I was still in the room. On being told that I was, he commented in his usual voice, "Rather an unpleasant sight for the boy." But I remained.

It was not a great sorrow. I had always been fond of him. He had always been kind to me. I had never heard an angry word from his lips. It would not have occurred to me to talk to him of any of the things that really interested me, and he would have been sorely puzzled if I had. He wrote to me dutifully every Sunday, giving me the events of his week and news of the family. Once while I was still at a preparatory school he asked in one of these letters what I wanted to be when I grew up, giving me a choice of professions. When I rejected them all and said that I was determined to be an actor, he thought it only a childish fancy, which it proved to be. He would have been more distressed if he had known that at the time of his death it was my ambition to become a poet.

For during my last years at Eton poetry became my chief interest. I read it in public and wrote it in private. The English approach to poetry is peculiar. Very few like it and those who do are rather ashamed of saying so, and yet it is the one art in which the English are supreme.

One day my division master, Hugh Macnaghten, who was the best teacher I ever knew, gave out as the subject for Latin verse the words "Hannibal peto pacem"—which can be translated "It is I, Hannibal, who am asking for peace." He added quite casually, "You can do it in English verse if you prefer." I thought that at last my chance had come and took more trouble over those English verses than I ever had over my Latin ones. The result cannot have been brilliant, but Macnaghten was very kind about it and gave me high praise.

I had loved books before I could read and would implore my nurse to read to me until she was hoarse. I had only to be told that a book was "too old" for me and I would fall upon it with enthusiasm, read it conscientiously to the end and maintain that I had thoroughly enjoyed it. Gibbon wrote that he would not exchange his love of reading for the treasures of India. Nor would I. The richness and variety of English literature are inexhaustible and it is a tremendous experience when a young man discovers the inheritance that is his. Nor is it unnatural that he should make some attempt to give expression to the feelings that such a discovery has stirred in him.

I became a member of the Essay Society during my last year at Eton and wrote for them two essays, one on Edgar Allan Poe and the other on Browning. I learnt by heart all the odes of Keats and most of his sonnets.

I sent a poem to one of those short-lived college magazines that appear like other ephemeræ in the summer months. It was accepted and I saw myself in print for the first time. It appeared over my initials. My tutor asked whether it was by me, and when I confessed he said that he had thought it too good to be mine. It was entitled "Invitation to Bathe before Breakfast." Not a line of it do I remember. Later I succeeded in getting a short poem into the *Saturday Review* with the zealous help, I must admit, of my youngest sister, who was a friend of the proprietor. I thought that my father would be impressed. After he had read it with some amazement, he reached for *Whitaker's Almanack* in order to find out what was the salary of the Poet Laureate. He decided that the appointment was not worth having. When I left Eton, I had written a canto of an epic on David and Bathsheba as well as a number of short poems and I had also unlocked my heart in a sequence of sonnets.

I had by this time given up my theatrical ambitions, and while I secretly hoped that my literary abilities might justify me in becoming a writer, I had reconciled myself to the prospect of a career in the diplomatic service. I was encouraged to do so by the example of Lord Lytton, who had been a viceroy, an ambassador and a poet.

It was therefore decided—I think I decided myself—that I should leave Eton early and spend a year abroad before going to the university. It was a wise decision. I was only seventeen but I had had the best of what Eton could give me. No athletic triumphs awaited me. I was captain of the house, and so had had some taste of the exercise of authority—a valuable experience. Although I greatly enjoyed Homer, Horace and Catullus, I could never become a scholar. My main interests were history and literature, which can be as well studied elsewhere as at Eton. In many ways I was precocious and had outgrown the society of boys.

Yet I was sad to go. Eton had meant much to me; how much I hardly knew at the time. I have met few Old Etonians who did not enjoy their time there and feel for the school a sentiment hard to express. It has little to do with the place itself, although it is beautiful, or with the teaching, although it is excellent, or with the tradition, although it is splendid. It has more to do with the friendships formed there, which are the first friendships and in happier times often prove the longest. In my case such friendships were hallowed, as they were brought, almost without exception, to an early end by death. Yet even such memories are insufficient to account for the emotion which Eton stirs in the hearts of her children and which can best be likened to love.

CHAPTER TWO

ADOLESCENT

1907–1913

IN the autumn of 1907 I arrived at Tours, where I was received into the household of Monsieur Suzanne. He was an elderly professor who had served in the Franco-Prussian War. He lived with his wife and his mother-in-law on two floors over an ironmonger's shop, and he found accommodation for three Englishmen. To each was allotted a bed-sittingroom. Monsieur Suzanne had no English and was therefore ill qualified for teaching French. Lessons usually consisted of dictations which he improvised. He would then carry away what had been written, often without correcting it, and the pupil would be lucky if he saw the result of his labours again, for these dictations were in fact the first drafts of articles that the professor was preparing for the local press.

The house was not very clean and the food was not very good. Neither Madame Suzanne nor her mother had any amiable qualities, but from the first evening of my arrival I was supremely happy. The life was so utterly different from anything I had known before. The two other Englishmen were older than I was, having both come down from the university. They had been at Tours already for some weeks and could give guidance about such pleasures as the town had to offer. They came respectively from Oxford and Cambridge, so that I was able to learn from them much about university life. The Cantab had edited the *Granta*, which conferred literary distinction in my eyes.

The distractions offered by a French provincial town are less than might be supposed. There was a theatre, visited at intervals by touring companies; there was a music hall which was little more than a café-concert and was the only establishment that stayed open after midnight except the station buffet, where we sometimes had gay supper parties when our means permitted.

Staying with another family was an Eton friend, and on Sundays the four of us would hire a car and go to one of the famous châteaux for which the Loire is celebrated. We made a few respectable friends in the surrounding country and a few less respectable ones in the town itself. Going to a café in the suburbs which had a tennis-court we discovered a young Englishman who was living there, writing his first novel before becoming a schoolmaster. He was Hugh Walpole, with whom we made friends, and who henceforth took part in our expeditions.

We were still in that delightful stage of development when subjects of conversation seem inexhaustible. Often we would sit talking in one of our rooms until four o'clock in the morning. I enjoyed these long talks and endless arguments. I enjoyed our Sunday drives to Blois and Amboise and Chambord and Loches. I enjoyed life in the cafés, and above all I enjoyed French literature, which I was reading for the first time.

Of the poets, Musset roused my greatest enthusiasm. He has been truly recognised by Maupassant as "le poète des tout jeunes gens . . . qui fut surtout un homme enivré de la vie, lâchant son ivresse en fanfares d'amours éclatantes et naïves, écho de tous les jeunes cœurs éperdus de désirs." Together with the high lyrical quality of his verse he combines dramatic appeal and romantic melancholy which enchant the heart of youth. I learnt "Les Nuits" and "Lucie" by heart and read "Rolla" again and again. The disorders of his life and the graver ones in the life of Verlaine further encouraged that foolish inclination towards dissipation which the career of Fox had inspired. At about the same time I read an essay by Cunninghame Graham which set forth the view that there was nothing so unattractive and vulgar as worldly success. In history, in literature and in life it was always the failures who were the most lovable and the most distinguished. I came to develop a kind of cult of failure. Ernest Dowson also, by precept and example, encouraged this tendency. I approved of his type of fidelity to Cynara. I longed with him to

> fling roses, roses riotously with the throng,
> Dancing, to put thy pale, lost lilies out of mind,

and like him to "call for madder music and for stronger wine." To write immortal verse in a disreputable café under the influence of absinthe seemed to me the summit of human achievement, but fortunately I had sufficient power of self-criticism to know that my verse, of which I wrote a great deal at that time, was not immortal; and perhaps it was equally fortunate that, at that age, I could not tolerate the taste of absinthe.

Any account of my life would be incomplete without mention of my friendship with John Manners. It began during my last year at Eton. He was nearly two years younger than I was. Imaginative boys of seventeen who read poetry demand some outlet for sentiment, and if they are surrounded during the greater part of the year by their own sex, as our public-school system decrees, and if the remainder of their time is spent in the narrow circle of their own family, as it was in my case, it is not surprising that masculine friendships should become infected or sublimated by a spirit of romance. It would be foolish to disregard the danger that attends such relationships, but it can easily be exaggerated. Normal young men with broad interests and healthy appetites can afford to gild their masculine friendships with a little of the gold they will lavish on their first love affairs, and there is nothing in my life upon which I look back with less remorse than the almost passionate affection I felt for my greatest friend.

John Manners combined personal beauty and athletic prowess with a love of literature, which I may have encouraged, but which existed before we met. He excelled at all forms of sport. In his last year at Eton he helped to win the most famous of all Eton and Harrow cricket matches by making 40 not out, and in the following week he played the part of Hamlet in a production arranged by himself before an Eton audience.

After that great innings he wrote to his father, who had warned him against allowing his head to be turned by success. He said that he would rather win the Grand National on his own horse, as his father had done, than make any number of runs at cricket. Lord Manners, who was the most modest of men, replied that he had no opinion as to which of the two forms of success might be the more desirable, but that he hoped that his son, unlike himself, would be remembered for something more important than either. No great career, however, awaited him. All that he did was to die for his country at the age of twenty-two.

It was owing to this friendship that I went to stay at Clovelly during the summer holidays of 1908. This visit was an important event in my life, for it opened to me a new world. My mother had few friends and no desire to make any. That she had been divorced from her first husband would, in those days, have closed many doors to her. She had, however, not the slightest wish to reopen them. She had a horror of strangers. It was a family failing. Her eldest sister was living in Paris at the time of our visit in 1900 and it was arranged that my sister and I should be taken to see her. At the last moment a manservant arrived with a present of money for both of us and a letter for my mother whom my aunt said she was looking forward to seeing, but she was not feeling well enough to welcome the children. I never saw Aunt Annie, though she lived for another twenty years and frequently sent me presents, usually in the form of prayer-books. She became a complete recluse and finally settled near Gloucester because her maid's relations lived in that town.

My mother's father had the same weakness. It is recounted of him that having invited guests to luncheon in Scotland, his desire to see them would wane as the hour for their arrival approached. He would then instruct the butler to say that he must have forgotten, as he had gone stalking, and he would retire to a spot on the hill whence he could spy the front door through his telescope, and would not come down until he had seen his friends drive away.

My father, on the other hand, was extremely social. He had a host of acquaintances, was generally popular and belonged to a number of clubs. He would often go away to shooting parties, but my mother never accompanied him. She saw hardly anybody except her relations, and not all of them, for she had quarrelled irreconcilably with her only brother. She had run away from her first husband—for those were the days when wives did run away—with the man whom I believe she loved best and to whom she was happily married for two or three years. He died, and she was a widow when she married my father, who had known and loved her before her first marriage and had sworn he would never marry anyone else. His fidelity was rewarded. She never talked to me of either of her former husbands, but the frequent presence in our house of the relations of both of them would have convinced me, had I had any doubts, that she had not been much to blame.

She had had one daughter by her first marriage, who after its collapse had been brought up by her paternal grandmother, whom she had solemnly promised that she would never enter my father's house. My father had been perfectly innocent of wrong-doing and the grandmother's objection had been based solely on his inferiority in rank. My mother remained on the best of terms with her eldest daughter and made her a generous allowance, but would not allow her to see her sisters and brother so long as she refused to come to their father's house. Finally the daughter gave way, saying that she was sure her grandmother would understand that times had changed. But I was eleven and my eldest full-sister was sixteen before we met our half-sister, Marie Hay. She was a very intelligent and attractive woman, the more attractive to me, as a boy, for having been so long shrouded in mystery. She wrote history and historical fiction. She married Herbert Hindenburg, a relation of the General, and having suffered greatly in the first World War, being regarded with suspicion in Germany while she was losing many of her English friends, died fortunately a year before the outbreak of the second.

At home I never met anyone except a very small circle of relations and connections by marriage, so that when I found myself for the first time in a large country house party, among a score of people of whom I knew only one, I was overcome by shyness, from which I suffered great misery for several years. I arrived, having taken the wrong train, at an inconvenient moment, just when the rest of the party had finished dinner and had, fortunately, left the dining-room. My hostess came out to greet me and for the moment set me completely at ease. Mrs. Hamlyn, to whom Clovelly belonged, was the sister of Lady Manners. She had been left a widow in middle age and had, I believe, decided to model the rest of her life upon that of Queen Victoria, whom a similar fate had befallen. She was always dressed entirely in black with a small lace cap on her white hair, so that she seemed to me a very old lady, although she cannot have been at that time much over fifty. She had an imperious and dominating manner which alarmed nobody. She was a tyrant whom nobody feared and many loved to tease. She had very strong political views and was a stern Tory, but she never allowed her opinions to interfere with her friendships, and both at her house and at that of Lady Manners in the New Forest, Mr. Asquith was as welcome as Mr. Balfour.

On that night of my first arrival, after she had left us, my friend took me into the deserted dining-room, where at one corner of a table laid for twenty I was served with the remnants of dinner. While he was giving me some account of the other guests, the door half-opened and one of the loveliest faces I ever saw looked round it, smiling, and asking whether we were coming to play some game or other. "She did that," said my friend, "because she wanted to see you before anyone else had." I then realised with horror, just as I was re-covering my self-composure, that he had been spreading such reports of my attractions that I was bound to cause grave disappointment.

The coast of North Devon invites romance, and in those days the atmosphere of Clovelly was heavy with it. To my confused memory it seems that the house party was composed of very distinguished old people and very attractive young ones. On one of the headlands, high above the sea, there is a cave called Gallantry Bower. Thither we would make pilgrimages, sometimes by moonlight. By day there were expeditions, with picnics, to beautiful parts of the country. After dinner there were games and charades. I was good at these. And when the elders had gone to bed there were occasionally midnight bathing parties, followed by clandestine suppers in the kitchen amid whispers and laughter. There was a great deal of singing and reading and repetition of poetry. We were all immensely interested in ourselves and in one another, and there was much courtship and innocent love-making.

On one occasion, some years later, a young lady persuaded me to read aloud after dinner a short story I had written. It was she who had looked into the dining-room on the night of my arrival. She explained to the others that it had been written by a friend of hers and she wanted to know what people thought of it. They were not slow to express their opinion. It was universally condemned for affectation and dullness. I think she suffered more than I did, although I tore the manuscript into shreds.

My visits to Clovelly became the focal point of my year. It is very pleasant to have a date to look forward to during eleven months. One year my visit was delightfully prolonged. This was the end of my last and John's first year at Oxford. Before going to Clovelly we stayed at Hartland, a few miles away, where lived Lady Stucley, who was Mrs. Hamlyn's eldest sister. It is a place of rare beauty, lying in a deep valley which leads to a wild strip of coast where the waves of the Atlantic are dashed against the savage rocks. A high tower stands on the cliff, from which the mother of King Harold is said to have watched for his returning ship.

It was good to rest in such surroundings after the effort and anxiety of final schools. We had both at that time a great enthusiasm for Ireland and all things Irish. The Abbey Theatre company from Dublin had visited Oxford during that summer term, and we had not only attended a supper-party that had been given for them, but had spent the rest of the night in a punt on the Cherwell with two members of the cast. There we had lain listening to Irish songs and Irish stories while the dawn broke. As a Conservative I was opposed to Home Rule, but Yeats and Synge and Maire O'Neill could convince me where the eloquence of all the Irish members of the House of Commons would have failed.

For six years in succession I went to Clovelly, and I was about to go for the seventh time in August 1914 when the war broke out which brought that happy epoch to an end.

It was due to my friendship with John Manners, to my going to Clovelly and to invitations to other country houses which followed, that I came to know that brilliant company of young men, most of them slightly older than myself, who had already made a stir in the University of Oxford. They were almost famous and their sayings were quoted. Those who knew them will remember their names always, but the next generation has already forgotten them. Posterity cannot be concerned with the inheritors of unfulfilled renown, however bright their promise may have been. Science may tell us that in the struggle for life it is the fittest who survive, but we who have lived through two great wars have seen with our eyes that it is the bravest, the noblest and the best who perish.

The contact with this shining galaxy of talent who greeted life with robust vigour and the determination to make the best of it went far to rid me of that lackadaisical admiration for failure into which I had fallen, and Oxford, whither I went in the autumn after my first visit to Clovelly, completed the cure.

One of the surprises that await a young man coming from a public school to the university is to find that there an entirely different scale of values prevails. Athletics are still regarded with a respect that outside England would be thought exaggerated, but they no longer form the sole criterion of merit. Young men are becoming interested in the agility of mind and brain as well as of limb and eye. Intellectual gifts and acquirements command admiration.

I had a good knowledge of English literature and knew something about French literature too. I had also a talent for public speaking. Such matters I had come to look upon as private peculiarities which could have little interest for anyone but myself. I was surprised to find that my attainments attracted attention, and glad when I discovered that among my contemporaries at New College I had a certain importance.

So completely had I given up my stage ambitions that I never joined the Oxford University Dramatic Society, but immediately became a member of the Union and of the college debating club. I made my first speech at the former on the 5th of November, which is usually a wild night at the university. I was torn between forming one of a riotous party and making my maiden speech on the reform of the House of Lords. I finally decided to combine the two and probably ended by spoiling both. At the time it seemed truly Foxlike behaviour to leave a gay party of roisterers in order to look in at the Union and deliver a speech that would convince all who heard it.

My first speech at the New College Twenty Club, as the debating society was called, was on a motion expressing no confidence in His Majesty's Government. I had made no preparation and as one speaker after another condemned the Liberal administration, I decided to defend it, and when my turn came I said that as a strong Conservative I supported all old English institutions, of which the Liberal Party was one, that we must allow them to hold office occasionally or they would disappear and we might get something worse in their place; that we ought to give them a fair chance and plenty of rope, relying upon them to make the right use of it at the proper time.

This speech, although it had a success, earned for me a reputation for frivolity which did me great harm among the extremely serious-minded young men who frequented such assemblies. I fear also that my general behaviour, following too closely the Fox tradition, strengthened this hostile opinion. I had had the ambition to become President of the Union, but when I stood for the junior post of Secretary I was bottom of the poll.

It was not only at debating societies that I spoke. The most prominent political question of the day was whether we should maintain our system of free trade or adopt one of protection. I joined the local branch of the Tariff Reform League and addressed meetings in the surrounding villages. This certainly afforded good practice for public life. Some self-assurance was needed to get up on a cart before an audience of sleepy Oxfordshire yokels and endeavour to persuade them that they would all be happier under a system of taxed imports which might include some articles of their diet.

Political economy was not and never became a subject of which I could feel that I had a firm grasp. At the time when I was explaining the advantages of Protection to the electorate I had to read an essay on the subject to my tutor, H. A. L. Fisher, who was a staunch Liberal and a leading light in the army of Free Traders. He made such mincemeat of my arguments from the start that I suggested I should not read out the rest of my essay, but he, with that grand courtesy that was natural to him, urged me to go on, saying that though he might have detected some confusion in the thought, the views that I held, and which were shared by many, could not be expressed more ably.

An athletic friend told me that after he had read his essay to Fisher one morning the conversation strayed on to sporting events and he was surprised to find that his tutor was as fully informed about them as he was himself. A few days later I noticed a volume of French verse lying on the table, and later Fisher, who had of course learned the direction of my tastes, asked me whether I was acquainted with the works of Albert Samain. I very soon found that he knew very much more about the French poets of the decadence than I did and that he had actually been in company with Verlaine.

Hitherto I had despised knowledge of subjects that did not interest me, but he set before me a higher standard of culture, and became my ideal of what the truly cultivated man must be. This was a friendship and an admiration that outlived my time at Oxford and I was glad, years later, that he happened to be the speaker who was called upon to follow my maiden speech in the House of Commons and to whom it therefore fell to offer the customary congratulations.

With the other authorities at New College my relations were not so happy. I became involved in an unfortunate bonfire, a foolish form of amusement in which undergraduates have always been inclined to indulge. On this occasion when the supplies of fuel were beginning to fail, it occurred to a friend of mine and to me that while we had burnt most of our own furniture, we had left untouched the property of the dons. We therefore invaded the Senior Common Room and, having removed from it some of the more portable objects, ransacked the rooms of one of the junior Fellows which looked out on the quadrangle where the fire was burning. It transpired afterwards that in the drawer of a small table which we burnt were some notes upon which he had been working for three weeks. I was overcome by remorse and wrote at once an abject and sincere apology. The innocent and much-wronged sufferer accepted my apology in the best possible spirit, but rumours spread throughout the university that I had destroyed the work of his lifetime, and that I had done it deliberately in some spirit of hatred or revenge. The punishment for this offence was banishment from college, so that I spent the remainder of my time at Oxford in lodgings.

Among those whom I not only liked but who also influenced my mind was Patrick Shaw-Stewart. He was the most brilliant of that brilliant group to which I have already referred. A scholar of Eton and Balliol, he had taken all the prizes which Eton and Oxford had to offer and had already, when I went up, taken his degree with the highest honours. He was then working for a fellowship at All Souls, which was duly awarded him. I was told that the answers he wrote in this examination might have been published as a volume of essays. His influence, however, strengthened what I have described as the Fox tradition, for he enjoyed to the full all the pleasures of life, and had more than once come into collision with the authorities during his dazzling scholastic career. He was determined to achieve success and was well on the way to doing so at the time of his death in action, having been promoted through sheer merit to a partnership in the firm of Baring before he was thirty.

At Eton I had made few friends, but at Oxford I made a great many. Looking back on those days across so many years, I believe that my character underwent a change at this period. I had been a nervous, delicate boy, not sharing in the pleasures that were natural to my age or enjoying the companionship of my fellows. I had come to think of myself as different from others and perhaps I took a pride in being so. I never threw myself into the life of any school, thinking possibly that my own life of books and dreams and poetry was more important. But at Oxford I found myself in surroundings that suited me. Love of literature was no longer considered an eccentricity, and talent for oratory was an asset. I could appreciate all the ordinary pleasures of adolescence. I delighted in gay dinner-parties where we believed our conversation to be brilliant and made efforts to render it so, and I enjoyed wild nights in London and late returns involving perilous climbs into college.

One June morning I was on my way to a lecture wearing my undergraduate gown when a motor-car drew up beside me, full of friends who were off to the Derby. I needed little pressing to join them, although they had no time to allow me to collect any belongings and we had to stop on the way to buy me a hat. The King's horse Minoru won and, as most of us had loyally backed it, we all went on to London to spend our winnings.

Although I never learnt to enjoy cricket or football, I took to riding at Oxford, which I had been taught as a child. I had not been happy in the football field and had come to think myself something of a coward, but I suffered from no such qualms on horseback, and although I could not afford a horse of my own I used to follow the drag on hirelings, and even rode in the New College Grind, which is the name given at Oxford to what is elsewhere called a point-to-point. I rode a horse that I had not seen before the day of the race. I was told afterwards that it was slightly lame when it started. It was certainly lame when it finished. My only aspiration was to complete the course. This I succeeded in doing, and I found, after the winner had been disqualified for going the wrong way, that I had secured the third place and, having backed myself each way, against all probability, had paid for the ride.

One of the many friends that I made at Oxford, and one of the very few who survived the war, was Sidney Herbert, who was my exact contemporary. He had been at Eton with me, but there we had hardly met although we had so much in common. Most of my friends despised the Union and the Tariff Reform League, but he, who had parliamentary ambitions, was a supporter of both. Driving with him one autumn day in a dog-cart to arrange a political meeting and at the same time to inspect a line for the drag, I felt that this might have been the Oxford life of a previous century and I savoured to the full every moment of it.

Another of my friends was Voltelin Heath, whom I had first met at Wixenford. He was an aesthete and devoted much of his time to making his rooms first in Magdalen and later at Micklem Hall as beautiful as possible. He was also the finest horseman in the university, Master of the Drag and President of the Bullingdon Club. One of my last days at Oxford was spent with him. It was the day of King George V's Coronation. We had both finished our final examinations and could have gone to London, but we preferred to go for a ride in Wytham woods, during which we solemnly discussed our careers. He was well-off and had political ambitions, but thought it well to go into the army first and then into business to get some practical experience, of which he had very little. Somewhat austere and ascetic, he was one of the most attractive of my generation. He joined the Blues and as a young officer at Windsor devoted his spare time to learning Italian. He died of wounds in September 1914.

In my second year I was elected to the New College essay society, which pleased me because it consisted of the more intellectual members of the college, mostly scholars of Winchester, few of whom I knew, and whose disapproval I was afraid I had incurred. I read them an essay on Rimbaud, of whom I doubt whether many of them at that time had heard. I wrote very little verse while I was at Oxford

but did not abandon my literary ambitions. Reading with a favourably prejudiced eye, I seem to detect some merit in the verse that I
have written from time to time, and I have wondered whether if my
life had been less fortunate it might not have been to the profit of my
muse. I enjoyed Oxford to the full, and apart from such sorrows as
are inseparable from human life I have certainly had more than my
share of good luck ever since. I cannot think that the muse thrives
upon ease and prosperity, but I would rather have been a happy man
than a famous poet.

I worked hard during my last year, and the news which reached
me at Clovelly that I had taken only a second class in history was a
severe blow. I could not, however, have received it in better surroundings, and the wound was soon healed. H. A. L. Fisher wrote
me a characteristically charming and sympathetic letter, explaining
that I had been on the border-line of the first class, which he admitted
was cold comfort. In the early autumn I set forth for Hanover to
prepare myself for the Foreign Office examination in the following
year.

What is now known as the Foreign Service was at that time divided
into two parts. These were the Foreign Office and the Diplomatic
Service. Candidates who presented themselves for the Diplomatic
Service had to guarantee before they took the examination that they
had £400 a year of their own, and it was known that at an expensive
post such as St. Petersburg or Vienna twice that amount was necessary to maintain the standard of living that was expected of any
member of the Embassy staff. Attachés received no salary during
their first year. During the second year they were paid £100, which
increased by £25 annually. There was no house allowance and it was
plainly impossible for any but wealthy young men to enter the service. Entrance into the Foreign Office, however, entailed no such
obligations. The salary was £200 a year from the beginning, and the
young clerk could live as inexpensively as in any other branch of the
Civil Service. Even at that date the supply of candidates with independent means was beginning to fail, and it was therefore inevitable
that competition for the Foreign Office should be much keener than
for the Diplomatic Service. Exchanges between the two were permitted, and there again the Foreign Office had the advantage, be-

cause there were always many who were glad to do a tour of duty at home, whereas those who wished to go abroad were few. There were usually about a score of candidates for the Foreign Office, and on the first occasion that I presented myself there was only one vacancy. Even if my total marks had been the highest, which they were not, I should not have been successful, as on that occasion I failed in German. A high standard in that language and in French was demanded, and although I had worked hard for many dull months in Hanover I had not come up to it.

I am sure that Hanover was in those days the least entertaining city in the world, and its inhabitants the plainest. It is without architectural or historical interest. Being tone-deaf, I am not qualified to give an opinion on the opera, which probably had merit, but the plays produced in the opera house and in the theatres were seldom of much interest. The house in which I stayed with other young men preparing for the same examination was comfortable, the old ladies who kept it were kindly and the food was good, but Hanover had nothing else to recommend it.

Among the Englishmen who were with me at Hanover was one whom I had known slightly at Eton, and who had subsequently been at Sandhurst. He had now abandoned the Army for the Diplomatic Service, but he never succeeded in passing the examination. He held very strong political and religious views, which led us into interminable discussions. He was a republican and an atheist and he assured me that the British monarchy was doomed. He was prepared to give it another twenty-five years. This argument ended in a bet which we solemnly set down and, in the youthful belief that stamps add validity to documents, we affixed German ones and had it witnessed by one of our companions, Maurice Peterson, who was to become Ambassador at Bagdad, Madrid, Ankara and Moscow. The document is still in my possession and entitles me to receive £1000 in the event of a monarchical form of government still prevailing in Great Britain in 1936.

In the course of the years that followed, the opinions of my republican friend underwent considerable change. He became first a Roman Catholic and then a Fascist, and having settled in Italy, he did so much to help the cause of the Axis during the war that he thought it wiser to disappear at the end of it, so that I have as little chance of ever seeing him again as I have of receiving the money he owes me.

I took little pleasure in learning German. The task was rendered the less agreeable for me by my failure to appreciate German literature. A man can only do himself harm by finding fault with great writers who have commanded wide admiration. When Tolstoy attacks Shakespeare it is Tolstoy who dwindles in stature, and when Bernard Shaw attacks him it is Shaw who appears a ridiculous pigmy shaking his fist at a mountain. I will therefore cautiously content myself with recording that Heine is the only German writer in whom I really delighted, and the only one to whom I return again and again with undiminished enjoyment.

Another handicap that I experienced in learning the language was that I was never so fortunate as to make a German friend of either sex. The fault no doubt was mine, but I believe that it might have proved easier in some other town than Hanover. There is a superstition in England—perhaps it dates from the dynasty—that it is in Hanover that the best German is spoken. Even if that were true it would not be in itself a sufficient reason for going there. Nobody can hope to speak a foreign language without accent unless it has been learnt thoroughly in childhood, and whether an Englishman speaks German with a slight Hanoverian or a slight Viennese accent is of no importance whatever. Unless he learns to speak it very well indeed his English accent will always predominate and conceal any local influence. I have often thought how much more pleasantly those dull months might have been passed in Vienna and of the charming Austrian friends I might have made there.

I did not return to Tours, but spent some time in Paris learning from that admirable teacher Jeanne de Hénaut, of whom Harold Nicolson has drawn so brilliant a portrait in *Some People* that there is little left to be said of her. The dominance of her personality was extraordinary. Unruly young men like myself, recalcitrant to discipline, never dared to infringe the unwritten laws of her establishment. Dinner was at seven. After a meagre repast conversation was always continued until nine, she herself doing most of the talking. Then the young men retired to their rooms, like monks to their cells, having been encouraged to work late. I was always deeply thankful that it was not upon me that Patrick Shaw-Stewart called one night after eleven o'clock. Not easily obtaining admittance, he kept his finger on the door-bell until the astonished maid-of-all-work rose from her bed and opened the door. He then walked down the passage calling out the names of two of his friends who were working there and whose scared faces appeared round their doors like startled rabbits imploring him to go quietly away. The incident became a saga of the establishment, a classic instance of ill-breeding and debauchery. When Jeanne was assured that the culprit was the most brilliant young man of the age, she was not impressed, and expressed the hope that he had no intention of going in for diplomacy.

For her no other career had any interest, and her year revolved round the examination. She kept all the papers and could quote the marks scored by her favourite candidates in various subjects. The victims of the day grew weary of oft-repeated anecdotes concerning their predecessors. Only those who had been successful were ever mentioned. Those who failed it was kinder to forget. She was not concerned with what became of them.

There was one exception to this rule, one bright star who had been well up to the level of her high standard and yet for some unaccountable reason had taken the examination three times, which was the limit, without success. Of that disaster she would say with the air of a queen in tragedy, "I shall carry the scar of that wound to my grave." I wish she could have lived to see the high position that he reached in another line, closely related to that of diplomacy.

The dreariest feature of the two years of preparation was due to the nature of the examination. It was necessary, in order to make up the total of marks demanded, to choose a very large number of subjects, and inevitably they included those which had already been taken at the university. Hours, therefore, which might have been devoted to acquiring new knowledge were spent in refurbishing what had already been learnt—a wearisome and profitless process. The examination could then be taken three times, between the ages of twenty-two and twenty-four. It seemed to me then, and seems now, that from those candidates with a university degree no special subjects, except languages, should be demanded, that they should be encouraged to live abroad after leaving the university and should perhaps be furnished with a list of recommended books to read, but that the examination should be of an entirely general nature, designed to test the breadth and accuracy of their information and their natural intelligence. A young man's time is obviously better spent in reading new books, or even in going to serious plays, operas and picture galleries, than in mugging up such subjects as English constitutional history, in which he has already proved his proficiency.

I was very much my own master during this period. My father was dead and my mother never interfered with my plans. I might easily have spent my time more pleasantly than I did, but I had learnt at Oxford to admire success and I was prepared to live laborious days in order to achieve it. Nor was I unduly discouraged by my first failure, although it entailed spending a longer period in Germany during the second year.

Old men forget and memory is capricious. My recollections of these two years of preparation are hazier than my recollections of Eton and Oxford. The background was composed of Hanover and Paris. In the latter my lodging was in the Rue de la Pompe, whence from my balcony at the corner of the top floor I could look into the Avenue du Bois and have a glimpse of the famous pink palace that Boni de Castellane had built there. Of one achievement I was very proud. Before I went up to take the examination for the second time I spent six summer weeks in Paris. I was twenty-three years old, and every single night I retired to work in my room after dinner. Jeanne allowed and indeed encouraged an outing on Saturday night. She held that what she termed "le petit week-end" gave needed distraction to the mind. She would be very coy about it on the following day. She would begin to ask questions and then check herself with feigned embarrassment, saying she feared she was being indiscreet. But during that last visit I refrained from availing myself of such indulgence, which in one so addicted to pleasure demanded a considerable effort of will.

When the examination was over I went to Venice, where one of my friends, George Vernon, had taken a palace and where were gathered that autumn nearly all the people whom I liked best. I have gone on visiting Venice ever since, except in those years when war has made it impossible, and I have come to feel an ever-increasing affection for the town, but to me it has never seemed quite so gay as in that September of 1913, when so many of my friends were there who never came again.

I came home at the end of the month, travelling with Denis Anson and stopping in Paris on the way. Our funds were very low when we reached England, and in order to economise we went to stay with his uncle, Sir William Anson, for thirty years Warden of All Souls and for long Member of Parliament for Oxford University.

Sir William had never married and lived at Pusey with his two sisters. It was a very Victorian household, and I was wondering one evening at dinner how long I should be able to endure it when I was handed a telegram. It was to tell me that I had passed the examination. It was the moment to which I had been looking forward for at least two years. I was longing to call for a magnum of champagne and to send telegrams to those whom I loved. All I could do was to inform the table of the news, and Sir William gravely offered me his congratulations, bowing to me over his glass of claret.

The next morning was perfect English autumn weather, which to me is the most beautiful in the world. We went out shooting, which is my favourite sport, and I shot well. Luncheon was served on a table under a tree, and Sir William told us interesting anecdotes of the past. I had good reason for returning to London now, and as I travelled back by train through the evening mist I knew that this had been one of the happiest days in my life.

CHAPTER THREE

THE FOREIGN OFFICE

1913–1917

IT was the 31st of December. I stood with two companions on the broad ledge which ran beneath the windows of my sitting-room in the Foreign Office. Two of the windows looked down upon the Horse Guards Parade, two across St. James's Park towards Buckingham Palace. Big Ben, accompanied by all the clocks of London, was striking midnight. As the solemn notes boomed out we drank glasses of port and wished each other happiness in the year to come—1914. One of my friends was John Manners, who had just joined the Grenadiers. He had eight months to live. The other was Eric Forbes-Adam, who had passed with me into the Foreign Office. He had a tragic end a few years later in Constantinople.

The reason for our presence there that night was that I had been compelled to accept the post of resident clerk and I was on duty. Eric, who was in the same position, was no doubt helping me with my work, and John had come to spend New Year's Eve in our company.

There were four resident clerks, and each was on duty for a week at a time. The amount of work varied according to the number of telegrams sent off by our representatives abroad and the hours of their arrival. From the closing of the office at about six o'clock until its opening the next morning at about eleven, and during the whole of Sunday, the resident clerk was a prisoner. If he went out to dinner for an hour he had to leave a telephone number that would find him. But he was advised to have his meals in his rooms. During his hours of duty he had to open the bags that arrived and distribute the contents. He had also to decypher the telegrams and make the required number of typewritten copies.

In return for these labours he was provided with splendid apartments. They were turned into offices in the war and have remained so. He had free fuel, lighting and telephone, which, for a man who would otherwise have had to find his own accommodation, was a very substantial economy. But to me, whose mother had a flat where I had been living very comfortably, it offered few advantages, and I had only accepted the appointment because I could not do otherwise. In those days I resented having to refuse invitations for seven evenings in a month and having to spend one Sunday out of four in London. For two years I had laboured to get into the Foreign Office and now, as Pope Alexander VI said of the Papacy, I meant to enjoy it. I sought therefore the first opportunity of handing over these advantages to another.

There had been, fortunately for me, four vacancies for the Foreign Office in 1913. I had taken the third place, Eric Forbes-Adam being first and Laurence Collier second. The fourth place should have fallen to Maurice Peterson, who had taken a first class at Oxford and whom I was surprised to have defeated. I also defeated Courtenay Forbes, who was placed above Peterson owing to the marks deducted from the latter's total on account of his handwriting, which was execrable. His father was Principal of McGill University, and although he was of Scottish descent he was considered a Canadian. It was rightly thought desirable to have a representative of Canada in the Foreign Service and it seemed hard to keep him out on account of bad handwriting, which in the age of the typewriter can hardly be considered a serious handicap. So after the long delays which are inevitable when dealing with government departments, a fifth vacancy was discovered and he was duly received into the fold. He had no home in London at that time, so willingly accepted the post of resident clerk, which I even more willingly surrendered.

Although, as I have said, this was the age of the typewriter, it was not yet, so far as the Foreign Office was concerned, the age of the typist. The young recruit, expecting to be initiated into the mysteries of diplomacy, found himself spending most of his time with a cypher book, and the rest of it in front of what the French call a writing machine, of which he was expected, self-taught, to acquire the mastery. I doubt if anybody ever got beyond the stage of typing with two fingers at less than half the pace at which he wrote in longhand.

Although I found it difficult to take much interest in such mechanical work, I was nevertheless very happy. I was pleased and proud to have passed into the Foreign Office. I had a large and increasing number of friends in London, and I thoroughly enjoyed all the pleasures that London had to offer.

It was early in this year that I met Winston Churchill for the first time. As a public figure he was probably more disliked by the Tories than any other member of the Government. That he had been elected first as a Conservative, that his language was as provocative as it was brilliant, and that he seemed to be on the left rather than on the right of his more respected colleagues, were the reasons, no doubt, combined with his innate pugnacity, why he had made so many enemies. While sharing the opinions of my party I was none the less very pleased to accept when I was invited to dine at Admiralty House by his young sister-in-law Miss Hozier, whom I had met and made friends with at country houses and dances.

Mr. McKenna, who was then Home Secretary, Mr. Illingworth, the Liberal Chief Whip, and a member of the Civil Service, were the men of the party, and after the ladies had left us they began to talk politics, assuming apparently that I thought as they did. I should have been too shy to set them right, although when Illingworth began to abuse Hilaire Belloc, whom I knew and loved, and Cecil Chesterton, I felt that I could understand some of the difficulties experienced by St. Peter in the house of Caiaphas. This led on to a discussion of the Marconi scandal, which was then fresh in people's memories, and I was delighted when Winston solemnly assured his colleagues that if that affair had been properly handled by the Opposition it might have brought down the Government. When Illingworth rejoined that the Tories had been too stupid to handle it properly, Winston said, "Some of them were too stupid and, frankly, some of them were too nice." Although he can be violently partisan, Winston Churchill has always been able to see the case for the other side, and justly to appreciate the strength of it.

After some months I was transferred to the Commercial Department of the Foreign Office, where I found the work hardly more interesting than in the cypher room. It is a department that no longer exists, its work having been taken over by the Department of Overseas Trade, which was brought into existence during the war. The

two other occupants of the third room (each department was divided
into three rooms, those of the Head, the Assistant, and the rest) were
two future Permanent Under-Secretaries of State, Alec Cadogan and
Orme Sargent. They set me an example of diligence and efficiency
which, I fear, I was slow to follow. That last, gay summer of a dying
age was the first full summer that I had known as a grown man living
in London, and as the fleeting months went by my heart and mind
were elsewhere than in the third room of the Commercial Department.

Yet over that summer two tragedies threw their shadow. During
the year there had appeared in London a young aviator of Swedish
origin, Gustav Hamel. He was handsome, brave and gay and, I believe, an excellent dancer. He became a close friend of many of my
friends, and to him I owed my first experiences of flying. There was
very little aviation before 1914, and the principal fliers commanded
much admiration, so that when one of them combined all the pleasant social gifts with courage, skill and professional fame it was natural
that he should be looked upon as a hero.

Then one day, when he was expected at some air demonstration, he
failed to appear, although it was known he had left the Continent in
his aeroplane. Neither he nor the machine was ever seen again. A
silk scarf, believed to belong to him, was picked up in the North Sea.
I wrote some verses on the subject and sent them to somebody who
had been very fond of him. They were sent on to the editor of The
Times and appeared in that newspaper over my initials. I had not
meant them to be published but I was pleased when they were,
and also somewhat alarmed. Many people did not connect me with
the initials, so that I sometimes heard the poem discussed unfavour-
ably in my presence. It was a long time since The Times had printed
verse of any sort and it therefore attracted attention. It was not a bad
poem.

The next tragedy in this sad year affected me more deeply. A party
of us had hired a launch for a night expedition on the Thames. We
had a band, supper and dancing. Denis Anson, who had recently inherited his uncle's baronetcy, was celebrated for acts of daring. It was
suggested that he should swim to shore, and he, ignorant of the cur-
rents in that part of the river, leapt in. He was soon seen to be in

difficulties. A member of the band and Constantine Benckendorf, the son of the Russian Ambassador, went to his help but they could do nothing. The bandsman was swept away too; Benckendorf, a very strong swimmer, succeeded in returning to the boat. I was very fond of Denis and this was the first great sorrow of my life. I had hardly emerged from it when the war broke out.

I was twenty-four years old when the war began; I had been eleven when the South African war ended. I had read about the British colonial wars of the previous century, about the Crimean War and the great war against the French Revolution and Napoleon. I had also read about the other wars started by the Germans against Denmark, Austria and France. None of those wars had interfered very much or for very long with the life of the civilian population, and I lacked the imagination to conceive that this war was likely to differ to any great extent from others, a lack of imagination that was shared by the vast majority of my compatriots.

It seemed perfectly natural to me that those of my friends who had just begun their careers, had gone into some business or been recently called to the Bar, should volunteer for commissions in the Army. I was glad that owing to being in the Foreign Office it was not in my power to do so, for I felt that, had I been free, I should have wished to go to the war, but that to have done so voluntarily at that time would have been very cruel to my mother, who was deeply devoted to me and whom I loved. Because I should have been glad to go I felt no shame at not going, and when I saw some of my civilian friends transformed overnight into officers, with plenty of leisure and the prospect of exciting adventure, I could only envy them while I returned to the Foreign Office, where at that time I was working twelve hours a day or longer.

For the first effect of the crisis upon the Foreign Office was to increase enormously, even before war was declared, the number of telegrams. All available help was demanded by the cypher room, where the whole work had hitherto been carried out by three clerks. Those like myself, who had recently been employed at this task and therefore retained some dexterity, were particularly welcome. We were arranged in shifts, and I worked from eight in the morning until four in the afternoon, when I went upstairs to begin my normal day's work in the Commercial Department. This arrangement was not, however, continued for long and I was soon released from the Commercial Department and put on the night shift in the cypher room, where I worked from midnight until eight.

Those first months of the war were the darkest ones for me. The country had gone into it in a mood of confidence and excitement. The night of the declaration was one of wild enthusiasm in London. Men remembered the relief of Mafeking and of Ladysmith and the victory of Omdurman. It was generally felt that war was a glorious affair and the British always won. Then came the tales of disaster, the long retreat and the casualties, and for me the report that John Manners was missing. The certain information that he had been killed came together with the news of the victory of the Marne, so that the latter could bring me little comfort. Those winter months were sad ones. I can remember walking home in the morning in fog and drizzle through St James's Park, having decyphered telegrams full of bad news all night, and feeling some satisfaction as I got into bed at the thought that I could go to sleep while for others another gloomy day was beginning. Afterwards I thought I had been fortunate to have got through the worst so early. One by one my friends were to be killed. Fresh blows were continually falling. But the first had been the cruellest, and although I suffered from the others I suffered less.

At the turn of the year, or perhaps earlier, there came an improvement in spirits. London during the first world war was very different from what it was during the second. From April 1915 I kept a diary. When I read it now I am surprised at the full and cheerful life that it depicts. The reason is obvious. There was in circulation through the town a perpetual stream of soldiers coming from and returning to the war. If anybody ever had a right to a good time it was they. These brief respites from intolerable tedium alternating with mortal danger had to be filled with all the gaiety that their friends could provide. Though there was some criticism of those who danced in wartime and they were taunted with heartlessness, they had a complete answer to their critics. Who would refuse any harmless pleasure to a young man who has come from the war and is going back there tomorrow? The theatres were all open. The danger from air-raids was considered negligible, as it proved to be.

There were raid warnings and I heard of people taking shelter in cellars, but it was a rare occurrence. As the war went on there were shortages. Sugar and butter were hard to come by, and taxi-cabs were rare. Owing to the lack of petrol there was a brief revival or that elegant but impractical conveyance the electric brougham.

My work in the Foreign Office during these years had little interest for me. I was kept for the greater part of the time at cyphering and spent most of it on the morning shift, working from eight to four. Although I disliked getting up early, I was glad to have so much of the afternoon to myself, and I missed this advantage when later I was transferred first to the Contraband and then once more to the Commercial Department. My heart was not in my work. I felt that either I should be allowed to join the Army, or else that I should be employed on work more worthy of what I believed to be my mental equipment. I had not learnt that a man can show his ability by the faultless performance of the humblest task, and that it is only by taking advantage of such opportunities that he can gain promotion.

My life outside the office absorbed my attention, and as I re-read my diaries I see that it was a life full of pleasure. Had I had any qualms about leading such a life in the middle of a terrible war—and I cannot find that I had—I should have stilled them by arguing that it is the first duty of a citizen in time of war to put his services at the disposal of the Government and to obey any orders he may receive. I had done so. If all the clerks of military age in the Foreign Office had insisted simultaneously on joining the colours, the administration would have been seriously embarrassed and the Army might have gained one platoon.

Although my functions at the Foreign Office were subordinate and my work might have been done by any half-educated man, young or old, I had the advantage of knowing what was happening at a time when what happened might prove decisive in the history of mankind. I had also the benefit of being behind the scenes and knowing how wrong the audience can often be in their distribution of applause.

In May 1915 the Germans sank the *Lusitania*, in which many American citizens lost their lives. A demand that the United States should declare war on Germany became vociferous both in America and Great Britain. We were then suffering from a grave shortage of munitions, which we were obtaining from America, and the official British view was that the entry of America into the war would be a disaster. I am not sure that the official view was right. I expressed it and my own reservations in my diary:

The feeling in America is so strong that they may be forced to go to war. If they do it will simply be playing into Germany's hands, and we are most anxious to prevent it. It is a pity that the mass of the people both here and in America don't seem to realise this, but our press is very restrained and sensible for once. Here is another instance of the truth that it is not statesmen and diplomats who are responsible for wars but the people themselves, a truth that the Left Wing refuses to recognise. And even I have my doubts. The disadvantage to us if America comes in will be immediate and military, but I cannot help feeling that in the long run neutral nations, and even the more thoughtful of the Germans, could not fail to be impressed by the spectacle of all the most civilised nations of the world joined in alliance against one enemy.

As for the manner in which I spent my leisure during this period, I could have said with truth that my time was always at the disposal of my friends in the Army. There were many of them; there were always some on leave; and over them all was hanging the shadow of death. How splendidly our youthful spirits resisted the gloom and terror which that shadow is wont to cast! It may well be that the near presence of death enables us to form a truer estimate of its importance. The nineteenth century had been, especially in England, a period of great security, and sudden death was so rare that it came to be regarded as the greatest of all calamities. These four years of war, with casualties more numerous than ever before or since, familiarised us with the spectre. We did not feel our losses the less because we wore our mourning more lightly. Among my own friends it became a point of honour never to show a sad face at the feast. And if we wept—as weep we did—we wept in secret.

I recently read a memoir of Professor Henry Jackson, O.M., at one time Regius Professor of Greek and Vice-Master of Trinity College, Cambridge. Born in 1839, he had long passed his seventieth year when the war began. During it he corresponded with his old friend Sir George Otto Trevelyan, to whom he wrote in May 1916, commenting on something he had been reading, "It has one of the qualities which war has bred in us: gaiety. We are learning on the one hand to take things seriously—very seriously; and at the same time to make the best of things however bad they may be. I am prouder to be an Englishman now than I ever was before the war. We have all learnt much." That was surely a noble tribute from an eminent Victorian to the younger generation, whom it had been the fashion among some of their elders to decry.

Although the society in which I moved was gay it was neither shallow nor entirely frivolous, and it was closely concerned with the conduct of the war. It was during these years that I became a friend of Edwin Montagu, who in 1915 married Venetia Stanley. Their home in Queen Anne's Gate and later their country house in Norfolk became and remained for me throughout their lives ever-open havens of hospitality. He was then Financial Secretary to the Treasury and became Chancellor of the Duchy of Lancaster and Minister of Munitions. He resigned when Asquith fell, but took office later under Lloyd George as Secretary of State for India. His tenure of that post was a fateful one in Indian history.

He was a man whose ugliness was obliterated by his charm. He had a huge, ungainly body, a deep soft voice and dark eyes that sparkled with humour and kindliness. He loved the open-air life—a rare thing in men of his race. He had a great knowledge of ornithology and was happiest shooting or merely watching wild birds on the Norfolk Broads. This taste was a link between him and Edward Grey, who was often in his house. He was very nervous and absurdly pessimistic. Whenever he talked about the future he would interject: "But I, of course, shall be dead by then," and he did die at the age of forty-five.

Two other intimate friends were Alan and Viola Parsons. A few years older than I, he was a scholar of Eton and Magdalen and had passed into the Civil Service, for which he was ill suited. The two interests of his life were English literature and the theatre. He had married Viola, the eldest daughter of Sir Herbert Tree, a rare and brilliant personality, who just failed both in singing and acting to achieve the success that always seemed to be awaiting her. The three Tree girls had long been friends with the three Manners girls. Their mothers, Lady Tree and the Duchess of Rutland, were friends also. And at this time Diana Manners was becoming, as she has remained, the most important person in my life. To see her was the main object of my every day, and I usually succeeded.

The age of the chaperone was passing, but it had not passed. An unmarried girl who had been well brought up was not expected to be seen in a public place alone with a man. This rule, like all rules that are not in accordance with the spirit of the age, was the cause of much deceit and prevarication. Young married women, broad-minded because they were young and adequate chaperones because they were married, found their services much in demand. To two young people who wanted to meet frequently the advantage of having two houses in London where they were always welcome was tremendous. At the Montagus' there was often a party. At the Parsons's it was usually only the four of us, and we all contributed towards the feast, for they were poor. Dinner at their house used to be followed by reading aloud—sometimes scenes from Shakespeare or other Elizabethan dramatists. Alan never read aloud himself but he was always full of suggestions as to what should be read. He was an authority on Pepys and he revelled in the comic passages of Shakespeare, which so many people fail to enjoy.

Once they gave a more ambitious entertainment than usual, and I have the record of it in my diary.

Viola and Alan had the Prime Minister [Mr. Asquith] and Edwin Montagu to dinner besides us. They were very nervous about the success of the evening and had taken great pains, bless their hearts. They had as a waiter one of the messengers from the Treasury who claimed to have studied the habits of Cabinet Ministers. There was special food and special wine, but at first Alan could only grunt from shyness and Viola only moan. However, contrary to their expectations, it proved a brilliant success. The food was excellent, the conversation never flagged and the P.M. was as happy as a sandboy. After dinner Edwin read aloud one of Chesterton's Father Brown stories, and then I read Max Beerbohm's essay on Switzerland, and then the P.M. read a sonnet of Keats so badly that it was hard not to laugh, and Diana said the ballad of Marie Hamilton.

Despite this irreverent comment I was full of admiration for Mr. Asquith and of affection for the members of his family. They showed me the greatest kindness and I was often invited to Downing Street and to The Wharf at Sutton Courtenay. I also went once or twice to stay at Walmer. Mr. Asquith was not Warden of the Cinque Ports. He told me that he regretted not having taken the post when it fell vacant, as Mr. Churchill was to do when he was Prime Minister. Lord Beauchamp, who then held it, put the house at the Prime Minister's disposal whenever he wished. The first time that I stayed there was in March 1916, and my visit coincided with one of the Prime Minister's visits to the war. I wrote in my diary

On Sunday after luncheon we motored over to Dover to see the P.M. off to France. Lloyd George, Grey and Kitchener met him there. They looked an odd lot. The P.M. wearing a very light brown overcoat, the collar turned up, his long white hair sticking out behind and his red face, was a striking, cheerful figure. Grey looked ominous with white face and black spectacles. Ll.G. looked untidy, ordinary and common. Kitchener looked like an officer who has got mixed up with a lot of strolling players and is trying to pretend he doesn't know them.

The impression of Mr. Asquith that remains with me is of a man of great dignity, somewhat aloof and Olympian. He belonged to the Victorian age. He would have thought it ill-bred to discuss current politics at the dinner-table, or to criticise other politicians. The guests who were staying in his house, especially those who claimed to know him best, would tell you what he was thinking, but his own conversation never gave a clue. I have an entry in my diary for June 25th 1916, when I was staying at The Wharf: "They say the Prime Minister is worried about having made Lloyd George Secretary of State for War. He thinks it is the mistake of his life." Perhaps it was.

The member of the Asquith family whom we knew and loved best was Raymond, the eldest son. He was acknowledged to be of that brilliant and witty family the most brilliant and the wittiest. In this year his son was born. He had already had two daughters. Diana and I were invited to be godparents and we attended the christening in St. Paul's Cathedral on June 5th. Dean Inge conducted the ceremony and Mrs. Asquith, who arrived a little late, felt bound to impart to him the news, which she brought hot from Downing Street, that Lord Kitchener with all his staff had been drowned in the North Sea. The Dean, accustomed to expect the worst, betrayed no emotion, slightly raising his eyebrows. She, disappointed at not having produced the effect she expected, and aware of his deafness, repeated her information louder, to be rewarded only by a slight inclination of the head. Finally she raised her voice to a pitch that took the whole congregation into her confidence, and the journalists present hastily left for the nearest telephone.

Raymond was not there that day. He had already returned to France. He had consented under pressure to take a staff job until the child was born, but afterwards he insisted on returning to his regiment, and was killed three months later on the Somme as a second lieutenant in the Grenadiers. To the many who knew and loved him his loss was irreparable. He had been the legend of his own generation, an earlier one than mine, and I cannot do better than quote what one of his contemporaries, John Buchan, wrote of him in his history of the war.

A scholar of the ripe Elizabethan type, a brilliant wit, an accomplished poet, a sound lawyer—these things were borne lightly, for his greatness was not in his attainments but in himself. He had always borne a curious aloofness towards mere worldly success. He loved the things of the mind for their own sake—good books, good talk, the company of friends—and the rewards of common ambition seemed to him too trivial for a man's care. He was of the spending type in life, giving freely of the riches of his nature, but asking nothing in return. His carelessness of personal gain, his inability to trim or truckle, and his aloofness from the facile acquaintances of the modern world made him incomprehensible to many, and his high fastidiousness gave him a certain air of coldness. Most noble in presence, and with every grace of voice and manner, he moved among men like a being of another race, scornfully detached from the common struggle; and only his friends knew the warmth and loyalty of his soul. At the outbreak of war he joined a Territorial battalion, from which he was later transferred to the Grenadiers. More than most men he hated the loud bellicosities of politics, and he had never done homage to the deities of the crowd. His critical sense made him chary of enthusiasm, and it was no sudden sentimental fervour that swept him into the army. He saw his duty, and though it meant the shattering of every taste and interest, he did it joyfully, and did it to the full. For a little he had a post on the Staff, but applied to be sent back to his battalion, since he wished no privileges. In our long roll of honour no nobler figure will find a place. He was of the type of his country at its best—shy of rhetorical professions, austerely self-respecting, one who hid his devotion under a mask of indifference, and, when the hour came, revealed it only in deeds. Many gave their all for the cause, but few had so much to give. He loved his youth, and his youth has become eternal. Debonair and brilliant and brave, he is now part of that immortal England which knows not age nor weariness nor defeat.

Earlier in the same year, on July 10th, I was present at a conversation which I thought at the time worth recording. Dinner was at Downing Street, and the only ladies present were Mrs. Asquith and her daughter Elizabeth. The men, besides the Prime Minister, were Lord Crewe and Lord Robert Cecil. I had doubtless been asked to make a four at bridge. When the ladies left the dining-room:

At first I felt very uncomfortable alone with three Cabinet Ministers, who I feared would wish to say things that I should not hear. But they seemed quite unaware of my presence. They talked about the campaign in Mesopotamia. The mismanagement, they said, was all due to the Government of India, especially to Sir Beauchamp Duff. Lord Curzon had always maintained against Lord Kitchener that it was a mistake to combine the two military offices in India, and experience had proved Lord Curzon right. The decision to attempt the capture of Bagdad was entirely due to the military experts. Kitchener had said we might take it but couldn't hold it. Even so he thought it worth doing from a political point of view. Curzon had said "Don't take it unless you can hold it."

The Prime Minister said he had only once seen Kitchener really rattled and that was when it had been settled to evacuate Gallipoli. Kitchener came to him one morning and said that he hadn't slept for two nights, thinking of the terrible casualties we were bound to suffer. He estimated them at 50,000, while other military experts put it at twice that figure. The P.M. likes quoting these instances of the miscalculations of military experts. He said that Kitchener originally proposed Rundle as commander of the Gallipoli expedition but afterwards he wouldn't consent to the recall of Ian Hamilton when everyone else wished it. Crewe said, and the P.M. agreed, that the failure of the Dardanelles expedition was entirely the failure of one man—Ian Hamilton. They all agreed in praising Archibald Hunter, whom the P.M. described as the most sensible soldier he had ever met. He said that Hunter won the Battle of Omdurman in spite of Kitchener and defended Ladysmith in spite of White. But he has fits of insanity.

The most dramatic story that the P.M. told was about the debate in the House of Commons on the reduction of Kitchener's salary. The P.M. made a speech defending and praising Kitchener. When he sat down, Bonar Law, who was beside him, said to him: "That was a very good speech. It will make it harder than ever to get rid of him." Four days afterwards Kitchener was dead. "Nobody will ever know that," the P.M. added. Apparently all the Cabinet were determined to get rid of him at the time of his death.

I recorded another conversation about Kitchener that I had with Lord Haldane in the previous October.

He [Haldane] says that all our failure in this war has been due to two things, the lack of public education and the lack of a General Staff. When he went to the War Office himself the first thing he did was to create a General Staff. It consisted of about eighty people, which was ample for the small army then existing. He also doubled Staff College. But all this was undone by Seely and partly by Asquith, who put Wolfe Murray at the head of it (the General Staff) because he was a suitable man to deal with the Ulster business, though otherwise he had no qualifications at all. Kitchener, finding a bad General Staff in existence, decided to do without one and do the whole work himself, which was madness. He thought that fighting against the German General Staff was the same thing as fighting against the Khalifa or the Mahdi. Haldane spoke with considerable bitterness about Kitchener and with the greatest contempt about Winston. He is intolerant of the people, whom he describes as uneducated.

We had been staying in the same country house, and travelled up to London together on Sunday afternoon. I record that "at Paddington we couldn't find a taxi so had to share a four-wheeler." Perhaps the acerbity of his views was intensified by the discomfort of the conveyance.

Augustine Birrell was another great friend of ours among the members of that memorable Government. Being a man of letters rather than a philosopher, he had some of the contempt for Haldane that Haldane felt for others. Once when he had been criticising him I dared to say that I supposed he would agree that Haldane had a very good mind. "Haldane's mind," he snorted, "is full of black slush." I have a record of an argument between him and Mr. Asquith on the subject of Shakespeare's sonnets, the Prime Minister taking the view that they were merely literary exercises addressed to nobody in particular. This has always seemed to me an untenable opinion and I have never ceased to wonder that it should have been held not only by such a clever man as Mr. Asquith but also by so true a poet at Hilaire Belloc.

We saw more of Birrell after his fall from power as the result of the abortive Irish rebellion of April 1916. I record in my diary on April 24th:

During the morning they brought us over a telegram which Birrell had received from Ireland and which he hadn't been able to decypher because his secretary was away and no one else knew where the cypher was! We decyphered it and it sounded rather exciting. It said that the man arrested at Tralee had made a full confession. That he had landed with Casement.

that the rising was to have begun that day, and that there was to have been an attack that day on Dublin Castle. It really seems amazing that when things of this kind are going on in Ireland Birrell should be unable to decypher his own telegrams because nobody in the Irish Office knows where the cypher is.

After Asquith had ceased to be Prime Minister we were discussing one day whether he had suffered from his fall. He was too grand, built too much "after the high Roman fashion," to show weakness or betray emotion, and somebody advanced the view that after a premiership of nearly ten years he was perhaps glad of a rest and that his fall had not hurt him. "Nonsense," growled Birrell, "of course it hurt him. I know how much it hurt me when I fell off my donkey, so I can imagine what he felt when he fell off his elephant."

Birrell, although at this time he was nearer seventy than sixty and we were all under thirty, inspired none of us with any awe and fitted perfectly into our parties. Here is the record of another one that took place in the small house in Chelsea where Alan and Viola lived.

It turned out a very successful evening. Diana was looking most beautiful. Birrell was in very good form. We had plenty of champagne supplied by me. After dinner we read aloud. First Viola read selections from Gosse's *Father and Son*, then Diana read a poem or two of Matthew Prior's. Then I read the close of *Urn Burial*. Then Birrell and Viola read *The Workhouse Ward* together excellently. Then Cynthia [Asquith] read "The Bishop Orders his Tomb". We ended up by Birrell and me reading Silence and Shallow—a very pleasant evening.

On one occasion we dined with Birrell. We were a party of eight. I do not appear to have enjoyed it, for I write:

I thought it a most unsuccessful evening. Old Birrell, charming as he is, doesn't know how to entertain. There wasn't enough to drink at dinner. Afterwards in a most uncomfortable room, badly lit, he read aloud part of "The Rape of the Lock" and "The Vision of Judgment." I said a bit of Browning. Lady Goonie [Lady Gwendeline Churchill] was looking, I thought, lovely, but Diana told me afterwards that she thought her not looking her best. Anyhow, it was a bad evening.

I was a close spectator of the events that led up to the formation of the Lloyd George Government in December 1916. Here are some extracts from my diary at the time.

December 3rd. After dinner I went on to 24 Queen Anne's Gate. On arriving I was almost shown into the dining-room, where Edwin, the

Prime Minister and Reading were waiting for Lord Crewe. I stopped the servant in time and went up to the drawing-room, where I found, sitting on cushions round the fire, Venetia, Lady Wimborne and Lady Goonie. They were all looking very pretty and were beautifully dressed. I liked the scene—lovely women warming themselves at the fire this bitter night while under their feet the fate of the empire was being decided. In the next room Margot, with a face as long as a book, was playing bridge with Francis McLaren, Oliver Stanley and Mrs. Henley. At last Edwin, Reading and the Prime Minister came up, the first two rather white and careworn, but the P.M. happier and less concerned than I have ever seen him. We played bridge, Venetia and I against the P.M. and Lady Goonie. . . . After they had gone we gathered from Edwin that the resignations of all the Cabinet are to be asked for tomorrow, as happened at the forming of the Coalition. Edwin seemed happy.

Alan Parsons, whom I was seeing daily at this time, was private secretary to Mr. McKenna, the Chancellor of the Exchequer.

December 4th. Alan told me that Lloyd George's scheme is himself at the Foreign Office, Carson at the War Office and Bonar Law at the Admiralty. He also told me that he had heard from Edwin that both Bonar Law and Ll.G. had refused to try to form a Government of their own.

6th. I saw Venetia before lunch and Alan after. It seems that the P.M. at first consented to Lloyd George's small War Council, of which the P.M. himself was not really to be a member, but that later, on the advice of his Liberal colleagues, especially McKenna and Runciman, he refused it. I gathered from the rather bitter way in which Venetia spoke of him that even his loyalest adherents are rather irritated at this last lamentable lack of decision. Alan had been packing up for McKenna at the Treasury all the morning. . . . The report now is that Lloyd George has resigned. If I were the P.M. I should accept his resignation, make Jellicoe and Robertson peers, and First Lord and Secretary of State for War respectively. I really believe that he might then carry on, especially if he got rid of Grey and made Hardinge or even Curzon Foreign Secretary.

While I was confiding to my diary these admirable schemes for the assistance of the Prime Minister, he resigned and the new Government took office. I wrote on December 8th:

Dined with Diana, Edwin and Venetia at Queen Anne's Gate. Edwin was in the depths of depression and could talk of nothing but the political situation. He is miserable that he had to resign and thinks he might have avoided it. I don't think he could have. He is very fond of Lloyd George and hates all the other Liberals. He was especially bitter about McKenna. He says that all might have been well if it hadn't been for McKenna and Margot on the one side dragging Asquith away from Lloyd George, and

Harmsworth and Hedley Le Bas on the other dragging Lloyd George away from Asquith.

That winter of 1916–17 was the longest and coldest that I remember, but the summer when it came, almost without a pause for spring, made up for it. Tied as we were to London, for she was working in the hospital that had been set up in her home in Arlington Street, Diana and I used sometimes to lunch in Kensington Gardens, bringing our supplies with us and supplementing them from the inadequately stocked refreshment-room. We also contrived to have picnic suppers on Coombe golf-course, having apparently received permission from the authorities of the club.

It seems to have been a gay summer, the laughter being continually caught by the throat and strangled into sobs. In the course of it we had to abandon all hope for Lord Elcho, who had married Ciana's sister, and who was very dear to us all. He had been missing for many months in the Middle East and reports had been received that he was a prisoner. It was only now that they were all proved to be false.

My own grief at that time was diminished by the hope, which gradually became a certainty, that I was about to be released from the Foreign Office for military service. A very strong press campaign had been carried on against the retention of men of military age in the Civil Service. The government departments were described as "the funk-holes of Whitehall" and the respectable Christian name of "Cuthbert" was applied to the younger Civil Servants, who were daily covered with vituperation for carrying on their duties according to the instructions they received. So far as I can remember I was in no way affected by these articles in the newspapers and there is no reference to them in my diary. The first mention of the possible change of employment is dated May 17th, 1917.

The Government want more men for the Army and we in the Foreign Office are all to be medically examined. I think they will have to let some of us go. If anyone is allowed to go I shall be, as I am the youngest of the permanent staff, unmarried and I should think perfectly fit. The thought fills me with exhilaration. I don't own to it, as people would think it was bluff, and I dare say that I shall very soon heartily wish myself back. But I am eager for change. I always wished to go to the war, though less now than I did at first. I envy the experience and adventure that everyone else has had. I am not afraid of death, though I love life and should hate to lose it. I don't think I should make a good officer. The only drawback is the terrible blow it would be to Mother. I don't know how I should dare to tell her. I think Diana too would mind.

When I told Diana she did mind, and minded especially that I should mind so little.

I explained to her that it was no nonsense about dying for my country or beating the Germans that made me glad to join, but simply the feeling I have had for so long that I am missing something, the vague regret that one feels when not invited to a ball even though it be a ball that one hardly would have hoped to enjoy.

I have sometimes remembered this entry when I have heard grave discussions as to why young men joined the Army and for what they fought and died, in this war or that. There are of course those who have to wrestle with their conscience before they take a decision, and to whom every action of free will presents a problem, but the normal young man joins the Army and goes to fight, with thrills if he is adventurous, with qualms if he is timid, but in both cases because it is plainly the decent thing to do, like giving up a seat to an old lady or taking off one's hat in a holy place.

I lacked the courage to break the news to my mother, who heard it from another source. The effect was as bad as I had feared—and worse, because I was accused, not altogether unjustly, of having deceived her. She made one pathetic request, which showed the extent of her withdrawal from the world. "Promise me, at least," she pleaded, "that you won't join the cavalry. I have always had such a horror of horses." Now, although she was not aware of it, a young man who voluntarily joined the cavalry in 1917 ran the risk of being handed a white feather, so faint appeared the prospects of that once formidable arm taking any important part in future hostilities.

On May 21st I called on the Regimental Adjutant of the Grenadier Guards at Wellington Barracks. He was a friend and he introduced me to Sir Henry Streatfeild, the Regimental Lieutenant-Colonel, who treated me with great courtesy. He was a Guardsman of the old school. He spoke to me of my mother, whom he had known years ago, and said he would put down my name and consider my request to join the regiment. After I had left, the Adjutant followed me, and told me I might consider it as practically settled.

It was not, however, until June 18th that I was told definitely that I could go.   On June 22nd:

I left the Foreign Office without a single regret. I went there in the morning but did not return after lunch. I love to think of the dreary files of papers that I shall not see again. Even if I survive the war I doubt whether I shall go back to the Foreign Office. I should hate to face that monotonous routine again.

That day was followed by a short period of leave which I enjoyed the more from a new-found sense of freedom from responsibility, and on July 5th I joined the Household Brigade Officers Cadet Battalion, which was then housed in what had been a large country hotel in Bushey Park.

CHAPTER FOUR

THE ARMY IN ENGLAND

1917–1918

OF the many fortunate things that have happened to me in life, one of the most fortunate was that in the summer of 1917 I joined the Army. It was not, like joining the Foreign Office or the House of Commons, of my own doing. And it might so easily not have happened. Had the shortage of man-power been a little less acute, had the press campaign been a little less violent or the Government's resistance a little more stubborn, the decision to transfer a few young men from the Civil Service to the armed forces might never have been taken.

Fortunate for me also was the timing of that decision. Had it been taken earlier—that is to say had I spent longer at the war—I might well have been killed. Had it been taken later, I might hardly have completed my training in England at the time of the armistice. This indeed was the fate of the next batch that were released from the Foreign Office.

None of these advantages was, however, apparent to me when I arrived at the Officers Cadet Battalion. I had expected a sort of Sandhurst designed for those of riper years and restricted to candidates for commissions in the Brigade of Guards. I thought that I was going to enjoy it, that instead of being shut up in an office I should spend the summer in the open air in pleasant surroundings and with congenial companions.

I was now twenty-seven. I had lived very comfortably all my life, and I had come not only to value comfort highly but even to insist upon having the best of everything. Some of my friends and I had made it a matter of principle never to accept the second best if the best were available. My feelings may then be imagined when I found that I was to lead the life of a private soldier, clean my own boots and equipment, make my own bed, sleep between blankets and take part with my comrades in swabbing the floor of the barrack-room. The great majority of the cadets were non-commissioned officers who had risen from the ranks. Combined with material miseries was the longing I felt for the life I had been leading and for the people, especially for one of them, whom I had left. I have seldom been more utterly wretched than during the first few days of my sojourn at Bushey Hall.

As the week drew to its close I discovered that it was possible to get leave of absence from mid-day Saturday to ten p.m. on Sunday, and immediately applied for it. To my surprise it was granted, but it was too late to make arrangements to be with those whom I most wanted to see. To get back to London, however, and to change out of my ill-fitting private's uniform and service boots gave me the sensation of escaping from prison. I spent a dull evening with a friend who was living in a villa at Tadworth, where he was quartered. Already, after those few days, an officer in the Brigade, which he happened to be, had assumed in my eyes almost god-like proportions. On Sunday it rained all day and I left in the early afternoon, so nervous did I feel of overstaying the hour of return. I could find nobody whom I knew in London. I went to dine alone at a club. "A great cloud of depression came upon me and I felt even more miserable than I had been at Bushey and without hope."

It was one of those great station-hotels of clubs where I knew nobody, but where in those days the food was simple and good, and the wine very cheap. Also it had a library. I ordered an imperial pint of champagne, that admirable measure which like so many good things has disappeared from the world, and I took *Alice Through the Looking-Glass* to accompany me during dinner. I wrote in my diary the next day:

As by enchantment my melancholy left me and I knew that I should not be unhappy again. Courage came back to me which I had lost and I despised myself for having done so. I went back to my flat, changed into my uniform, spoke to the Montagus, who had just returned, and motored down to Bushey feeling perfectly happy.

Whether it was the humour of Lewis Carroll or the sparkle of the widow Cliquot that had restored my spirits would be hard to say. I think it was the mating of the two. I have already made mention of the happiness I have derived throughout my life from literature, and I should here, perhaps, acknowledge the consolation I have never failed to find in the fermented juice of the grape. Writing in my sixty-fourth year, I can truthfully say that since I reached the age of discretion I have consistently drunk more than most people would say was good for me. Nor do I regret it. Wine has been to me a firm friend and a wise counsellor. Often, as on the occasion just related, wine has shown me matters in their true perspective, and has, as though by the touch of a magic wand, reduced great disasters to small inconveniences. Wine has lit up for me the pages of literature, and revealed in life romance lurking in the commonplace. Wine has made me bold but not foolish; has induced me to say silly things but not to do them. Under its influence words have often come too easily which had better not have been spoken, and letters have been written which had better not have been sent. But if such small indiscretions standing in the debit column of wine's account were added up, they would amount to nothing in comparison with the vast accumulation on the credit side.

I am proud that Belloc's great poem on wine should have been dedicated to me. I transcribe the first lines:

> To exalt, enthrone, establish and defend,
> To welcome home mankind's mysterious friend:
> Wine, true begetter of all arts that be;
> Wine, privilege of the completely free;
> Wine the recorder; Wine the sagely strong;
> Wine, bright avenger of sly-dealing wrong—
> Awake, Ausonian Muse, and sing the vineyard song!

This mysterious friend has proved a very loyal one to me, and to all those, I believe, who do not abuse friendship and who learn by experience that even between friends excessive and coarse familiarity cannot be permitted. Nor would I be thought, while paying the homage that I owe to wine, to exclude from their share of it those who, if they cannot aspire to the high dignity of friendship, do at least deserve the deep gratitude that is owed to trustworthy and faithful servants. I refer to beer and spirits, which belong to a different class from that of wine but are not upon that account to be less loved and honoured.

Class is a word that in this age stirs passions and provokes people to talk nonsense. There are even those who would, if they could, create a classless society. If such a society were possible it would be as useless as a rankless army and as dull as a wine-list that gave neither the names of the vineyards nor the dates of the vintages. Class is an inevitable adjunct of human nature. The aim of the lawgiver should be to render the relations between classes happy and to facilitate the passage from one class to another. When class, which is natural, degenerates into caste, which is against nature, it becomes an evil.

The man who finds himself suddenly thrown into another class is ill at ease, whether he be a peasant in a palace, or a prince in a pothouse. Part of my distress during the first days of my training at Bushey was due to finding myself in a room with six companions whose habits, interests and subjects of conversation differed so entirely from my own. This was really no very great hardship, but it was one to which I was not used. Fortified by the wisdom I had acquired during my solitary Sunday dinner, I returned in a mood to form a fairer judgment of my comrades and I wrote in my diary:

I am with six others. They are all ex-rankers except one who is a bank clerk and has somehow escaped military service hitherto. They are as follows. Clay, a shoemaker from Nottingham, a very nice friendly fellow who helps me a lot with my equipment and in other ways. All the men are really very nice and helpful. Schofield, a boy of nineteen who speaks broad Yorkshire and knows the whole of the drill-book by heart. He seldom talks on any other subject. Harris, a tall thin dark fellow, who before the war was a window-dresser in Sheffield. He is quite nice. Catley, a common fellow with waxed moustaches, who talks a lot, fancies himself, refers to the "fair sex," insinuating that he is one of their conquerors, and smokes Virginian cigarettes last thing at night and first thing in the morning. There is no harm in him. Durgan—not a bad fellow, uninteresting and sleeps in his shirt. Jones, a bank clerk, with a splendid cockney accent and a fund of filthy stories which sometimes shock the others but always amuse me.

I did not enjoy Bushey, but I was not unhappy. The regularity of the routine made the days pass quickly. The Commandant, Colonel Ebenezer Pike, and his wife, the well-known portrait-painter, Olive Snell, were very kind to me, as indeed were all the officers, although I was not a promising cadet. I found great difficulty in learning to drill others and when being drilled my attention would wander. Nor did I distinguish myself in the more intellectual aspects of the profession, such as map-reading—an accomplishment I have never been able to master.

The discomforts of the life there were greatly alleviated by the existence of a golf club at five minutes' walk from the Hall. Although I played golf seldom, getting all the exercise I needed from the work of the day, I became a regular frequenter of the club house, where those of us who were accustomed to better fare than the Hall could offer would forgather both before and after meals at which attendance was compulsory. Sometimes one or two of us would get permission to absent ourselves from dinner and would entertain one another, or friends from London, at the club, and sometimes we would invite an officer and hope thus to be excused what was called "private study," to which the hour before bedtime was by regulation devoted.

The course lasted four months. During five days of the week the work was strenuous. It ceased at eleven o'clock on Saturday morning, and until that moment it was uncertain whether the coveted thirty-four hours' leave would be granted. It usually was. More important still was the four days' leave that was accorded to all in the middle of the course.

One of the greatest friends that I had made at Oxford, and with whom my friendship had increased in the years that followed, was Edward Horner. He belonged to the generation of Patrick Shaw-Stewart rather than to mine, and I had not known him at Eton. He was handsome, brilliant and extravagant, and would have found the age of the Regent more sympathetic than his own. He telephoned to me at the outbreak of war that he did not intend to allow it to interfere with his life in any way, that we must all learn to be Martians and to dissociate ourselves from terrestrial affairs. A few days later he rang up again, quite oblivious of what he had said before, to tell me he had got a commission and to ask me what regiment I was joining. He was sure the war was going to be tremendous fun and he had just been ordering a special pair of boots for riding into Berlin. He was soon seriously wounded, but by 1917 he had recovered and was once more with his regiment in France. He was a Liberal, because his family had always been Liberals, Whigs and Roundheads, and it was his ancestor who had given rise to the nursery rhyme of

Little Jack Horner, the plum that he had pulled out of the Christmas pie being the estate of Mells in Somerset, which his family had acquired at the time of the dissolution of the monasteries.

It so happened that Edward's leave from France coincided with mine from Bushey and I was therefore able to spend it at Mells, which is among the most beautiful places in England. The weather was the best which September can give. We had a delightful day's shooting on Saturday and the guests were those whom I most wanted to see. I was perfectly happy and recorded in my diary how every minute of those four days was spent. Here is a brief extract:

Dinner on Sunday night was even pleasanter than the night before. There were two tables. Edward and Diana and I sat at the small one. She was looking royally beautiful, like a fairy-tale princess. Edward and I extolled her beauty and revelled in our little hour of happiness. After dinner we played bridge, and after that Edward, Michael Herbert, Tommy Bouch and I sat up arguing about religion until two o'clock. I enjoyed it.

The rapid transition from luxury to hardship, the vagueness of the future and the uncertainty of life itself stimulated the pleasures of that time but in no way rendered them hysterical. Among those present during those days at Mells was Edward's sister Katharine, who less than a year before had lost the husband she adored, Raymond Asquith. At other times and in other countries it might have seemed too soon for a widow to take part in a gay assembly. But such age-long conventions had been put aside. Her heart was broken but she did not wear black to prove it, and would have thought it wrong to cast the shadow of her comfortless sorrow over the fleeting moments of our gaiety.

The return to Bushey after that visit I describe as shattering, and the two months that followed were certainly no better than those that had gone before. The weather got worse. Discomfort is more easily borne in heat than in cold. And over us hung the menace of failing in the final examination, which would mean spending another month, the month of November, as a cadet. But after much anxiety which induced some hard work the danger was overcome, the examination was passed, and the most uncomfortable four months of my life were ended.

There were two principal houses on the Mells estate: the larger one, called the Park, which was let, and the smaller and older one, called the Manor, where the family were living. During the month of October the larger house was burnt to the ground. Edward was the only son and on account of the legal complications caused by this catastrophe, which necessitated the termination of leases and the signing of documents, he was granted special leave from the Army and was at home again when I left Bushey. I went there the next day and had a good day's shooting and a happy Sunday. The following Saturday I went there again. A few days later he was recalled to France although his leave was not yet at an end, and on November 21st he was killed. It was the heaviest blow I had received since John Manners had been killed three years before. I wrote in my diary:

Edward meant so much in my life. I loved no man better. His high courage and fine independence had so splendidly resisted the effects of the war that already he had begun to seem a glorious relic of the glorious past. By his death our little society loses one of the last assets which gave it distinction. And I think we have paid more than our share. To look back now on our Venice party, only four years ago, is to recall only the dead. The original four who motored out there together were Denny [Anson], Billy [Grenfell], George [Vernon] and Edward, of whom not one remains. The most precious guests, in fact the only ones that I can remember while I was there, were Raymond [Asquith] and Charles [Lister], both dead. Rottingdean, another high-water mark of our happiness, was practically the same except that we had Ego [Elcho] instead of Charles. Only Patrick and I remain. We can make no new friends worthy of the old ones. When one like Ivo Charteris appears promising he is immediately struck down. I had looked forward to years of happiness with Edward. He was the only companion with whom I was perfectly happy and whom I could always amuse. Patrick is more reliable in company and in every way, but I never have such fun alone with Patrick as I had with Edward. I begin to feel that the dance is already over and that it is time to go.

Two evenings later I was dining alone with Venetia Montagu when Patrick Shaw-Stewart telephoned to say that he had just arrived in England from Salonica.

He didn't know of Edward's death. Venetia told him on the telephone. He joined us at dinner. I felt very emotional on seeing him. He is almost the last of my friends. But I now find myself always comparing him with Edward in my mind and he suffers from the comparison. He isn't the joy to me that the other was, but no doubt he will be again. We agreed that there was so little left in life that we had lost all reluctance to dying.

I had picked up my former London life where I had left it, the only change being that I now spent my working hours at Chelsea Barracks instead of at the Foreign Office. I had rooms over the post office at the bottom of St. James's Street and had to make an early start, walking across the park to St. James's Tube Station, whence I travelled to Sloane Square. I continued to show little aptitude for drill and took longer than most young officers to "pass off the square."

Edwin Montagu, now Secretary of State for India, had gone there on that tour of inspection which was to produce the Montagu–Chelmsford report. He had taken Alan Parsons with him as private secretary, so that both the houses upon which Diana and I so largely relied for entertainment were temporarily widowed. Venetia Montagu, however, continued to entertain as generously as ever, and on Christmas Eve I record that I attended

a cheerful Christmas dinner at Queen Anne's Gate. Round the table were Venetia, Freyberg, John Lavery, Lady Constance Stewart-Richardson, myself, Geoffrey Howard, Hazel Lavery, Hugo Rumbold, Bruce Ottley, Baroness d'Erlanger and Mr. Birrell. The last named was in perfect form, very witty and very appreciative. Later we all went on to a party at the Fairbairns' which was also great fun. Finally I played chemin-de-fer until half-past four.

It sounds a light-hearted existence, but on December 31st I write: "So ends 1917 which has been, I think, the least happy year that I have lived." And I did not know when I was writing this that Patrick Shaw-Stewart had been killed in France on the previous day.

It was not until late on January 3rd that I was told the news. The next day was Friday and I was due to pay a visit to Taplow Court, where Lord and Lady Desborough lived. For many years before the war their house had been a celebrated centre of entertainment, and as their children grew up it was thrown open to the younger generation, who considered it the summit of all that was delightful. Their two elder sons, Julian, brilliant athlete and memorable poet, and Billy who equalled his brother in athletics and surpassed him in scholarship, had both been killed. Patrick, who came between them in age, had been a close friend of both, and had so loved their mother, his own parents being dead, that she had counted perhaps more than anybody in his life. She had loved him too, had helped him in his career and been proud of his success. There was no house in the country where his loss would be felt so much. A transcript from my diary of the following days shows how we had learnt at that time to cope with tragedy.

January 4th. The lines running in my head all day have been

> And there is nothing left remarkable
> Beneath the visiting moon.

I telegraphed the news to Diana. Michael Herbert came in the afternoon. We were going to Taplow but wondered whether we should and whether Lady Desborough would have heard the news. Phyllis came. [This was a young lady who had been in love with Patrick and with whom he had been on the eve of his departure less than three weeks before.] She was very white but quiet and sweet. We decided to go to Taplow and caught the 5.5. We travelled with Rosemary [Leveson-Gower], Casie [Lady Desborough's daughter] and Diana Wyndham. They were in high spirits and obviously hadn't heard. I told Rosemary when we got to Taplow station and she told the others. They all heard it quietly. There were no tiresome tears or exclamations. When we arrived we found that Lady Desborough was in her room and had already heard. Patrick's sister had telegraphed to her. She adored Patrick. I went to see her after tea. She was sitting by the fire, almost in the dark. She has been ill. She kissed me and I couldn't help crying a little. We sat and talked about Patrick until dinner. She is the most wonderful woman in the world, and the bravest. She didn't come to dinner that evening. . . . After dinner Rosemary made me read some chapters of *South Wind* aloud, which rather shocked Lord Desborough.

January 5th. Lady Desborough came down to breakfast and held the table as gallantly as ever. A pleasant morning spent playing with ponies and donkeys and sitting about. I went for a walk with Rosemary before tea— the same walk that we went only a month ago when we were lamenting Edward. We had not had time even to find new words for our new sorrow. I like her enormously. She is so sensible. This evening more guests arrived Michael, Rosemary, Diana and I played bridge until dinner. I sat between Lady Desborough and Ivo. We talked about the past. It is my favourite subject now. After dinner a little bridge and then Michael and I tried to do a stunt which wasn't funny. I sat with him and talked till late at night.

January 6th. I played tennis in the morning. Lord Revelstoke appeared at lunch. I wanted to talk to him about Patrick but didn't. . . . I felt more and more depressed as the day went on. I had enjoyed my visit and had felt happier in my misery than I thought possible. I had been like one with a bad wound in a hospital and I felt that I was leaving the hospital before the wound was healed. . . . I was indeed treated like an invalid these days —given the best of everything, sat in the best places, everyone being very kind to me. . . . I had to come back to London after dinner.

The medical metaphor seems to have influenced my .mind, for a few days later I find myself writing:

I think at times I am going to be ill. The extraordinary lethargy and lack of interest that I feel all the time may be due to some physical cause besides the cloud of sorrow that darkens all my days. I have felt more keenly wretched but never more unutterably sad.

But the human heart, especially in youth, is wonderfully resilient, and anyone reading the pages of my diary that follow might be excused for doubting the sincerity of my grief. Many cheerful evenings are described, including one of charades at Lady Gwendeline Churchill's. "We acted the trial of Bolo, Winston doing the judge, Michael Bolo and Rosemary Madame Caillaux."

There were a number of air raids at this time and I was occasionally on "air-raid duty." This entailed returning to barracks as soon as the warning went and remaining there until the All Clear. It is difficult, in the light of subsequent experience, to understand what can possibly have been the object of this manœuvre. The officer would probably have to make the journey to barracks on foot and would be exposed all the time to danger, while serving no purpose, and on arrival he went into the ante-room, where a large number of officers were collected together with no protection whatever. The bombers of 1918 were certainly treated with greater contempt than their successors. I recount going to a party in Chesterfield Gardens in a house which Lord and Lady Pembroke had taken. The Prince of Wales was among the guests.

The guns were booming when we arrived but Lord Pembroke told the nigger band to play on without a moment's pause until the guns stopped. So the band made a perfectly deafening din, far worse than any guns and quite drowning them. It was a good party.

Spring was coming and in March the Germans made their last great effort to win the war.

April 5th. I dined with Venetia at the Savoy. She had been lunching with Winston and Lloyd George, both of whom she said were pretty gloomy. They were prepared to lose Amiens. Gough's whole army had run away. Robertson and Wilson had always wanted to get rid of Gough, but Haig wouldn't and still won't.

These events produced the Conference of Doullens and the setting up of a unified command under Foch. Their repercussions were also felt in Chelsea Barracks, where young officers began to "pass off the square" more rapidly and to complete the courses that were considered necessary before they could be sent into battle. My lack of proficiency in drill had already put me behind some of my military contemporaries, and when these began to go to France and get killed I became impatient for my turn to come.

Easter fell early that year. I spent it in my eldest sister's house in Sussex with my mother and other relations. My eldest sister had lost her first husband before the war and had recently married again. Her second husband had been badly wounded in 1914. It was a cold and melancholy Easter, as my mother was much distressed by the prospect of my departure. But April was warm and fine and my spirits rose at the thought that this might be my last month in London. I have always thought that going away is far less sad than being left behind. So many of my friends had gone away, and now that it was my turn there was only one person whom I was really unhappy to leave behind.

So I enjoyed those warm April days in London. My duties grew lighter and finally ceased altogether. I had more time to spend with my friends and the fact that the time was limited lent a certain tang to every pleasure. The last night was the best of all. The draft, which consisted of four officers and some sixty men, paraded at Chelsea at 11.55 p.m. This gave ample time for a pleasant evening. We dined with another of my Liberal friends, Harold Baker. He had resigned from the Government with Asquith and was to become in the course of time Warden of Winchester. Diana, Venetia, my sister Sybil, Michael Herbert and Hugo Rumbold made up the party.

The atmosphere was a little strained at first, but under the influence of wine it all went well enough, I thought. We sat long at the table. Mother telephoned to say good-bye. We walked over to Venetia's, where we had a final bottle. I found that I had left my coat behind. Sybil volunteered to go and get it in a taxi. She returned with the wrong one. Diana and I then went for it and this made me late, so that our last drive together was marred by my worrying about the time. She dropped me at Chelsea. It was very dark on the square. The draft was already formed up. The Adjutant was there and only laughed at my being late. The officer in charge of the draft had arrived, but was in no state to march to Waterloo, and so had gone away again and was coming on by taxi. Teddie [the Adjutant] thought that I should probably be in the same state but I explained to him that I wasn't. As I was senior to the two other officers, I took charge and marched off the men, leading them, with the drums in front. The band played nearly all the way from Chelsea to Waterloo and I felt proud, romantic and exalted. There were a lot of people at the station, the Baroness [d'Erlanger], Hugo, Ivo, Gerard Brassey, Sybil, Venetia and Diana. Diana had changed her clothes or wrapped something round, I didn't notice which, but she appeared to be all in black, and her face so white, so white. We had some time to wait at the station though it seemed too short, and she and I found a dark deserted waiting-room where we exchanged our last embraces. . . . At last we left. The band struck up again as the train moved out of the station.

CHAPTER FIVE

THE ARMY IN FRANCE

1918

I LEFT England at the end of April and returned at the end of October. I thus spent six months on active service—the best months of the year and, as it proved, the most successful months of the war. After their great spring offensive the Germans were in fact defeated, as the British Commander-in-Chief, Sir Douglas Haig, had foretold that they would be, but as very few were convinced that they were. Although I did not know it and was the last to believe it, the tide had turned and was to turn no more. I was indeed lucky to go to the war when I did.

Exasperation, boredom and fear are the emotions which make up a soldier's life on active service, and the first two predominate. It was exasperating having been hurried off from England, where every day seemed precious, and having taken forty-eight hours to travel via Folkestone, Boulogne and Etaples to Havre, to find oneself stuck there, at the army base, for a fortnight with nothing to do. But I was not bored, because I was glad to be in France again after five years, and I could appreciate the simple pleasures offered by a French provincial town even in wartime. I was not, however, sorry to leave it and to join the Third Battalion of my regiment, which was then in the line.

Old men forget, but fortunately I still have the diary which I kept; and the letters which I wrote daily have been preserved. It is therefore better that I should describe the campaign, so far as possible, in the words of these original documents rather than seek new ones to convey vague and uncertifiable recollections.

On May 22nd I wrote in a letter from the trenches:

Yesterday evening after tea Gunther, another boy called Inglis-Jones, the Commanding Officer and myself set out on horseback for the trenches. A pleasant enough ride but rather too warm owing to the number of things one was carrying. As we got nearer the battle and the guns became louder my horse grew rather nervous and began shying at each shell-hole and I was terrified of falling off. At last we got off and left them with two grooms. We then had a few hundred yards to walk to the Battalion Headquarters. There we descended into the bowels or into one bowel of the earth, an incredibly deep dug-out with rather uneven steps down into it, which I thought most unsafe. At the bottom we found Harry Lascelles, who is Second in Command of this Battalion. He was looking extraordinarily elegant, and beautifully clean. I felt ashamed to be covered with perspiration, very untidy and wearing camouflage—i.e. a private's uniform. There was another elegant young man with him called Fitzgerald and the table was strewn with papers and periodicals like *Country Life* and the *Burlington Magazine*, which one associates with the comfortable houses of the rich.

I was led by a guide to my own Company, twenty minutes' walk over green fields, while the sun was beginning to set most beautifully. At last we arrived at a dug-out, an ordinary shallow one, and here I met my captain face to face—nobody more surprised than my captain, as he had expected someone else of the same name. It was then 8.15. He called for dinner for two, which was immediately produced. Quite good soup, hot fish tasting like sardines but larger—no one knew what they were— cold beef, pickles and peas, prunes and custard—plenty of whisky and port. It was still light when we finished and I was sent on to the very front line of all, in order that the officer there might come back and dine. The front line proved extraordinarily unalarming—and it was rather thrilling to think that there was nothing between oneself and the German Army.

In my diary I summed up my first tour of duty in the line as follows:

Altogether I was a fortnight in the line, alternating between the front line, support, reserve and rest. I didn't write in this book during that time and cannot now give an exact account of it. We had a good deal of excitement at night and were often severely shelled. I was glad to find that I was no more frightened than other people—and I really think rather less so— especially, I must confess, after dinner. The weather was wonderful; we had only one really wet day. . . .

We were heavily shelled one day in rest and Inglis-Jones, whose company was next to ours, was wounded. It was not a severe wound and I couldn't help envying his return to England. . . . Later when we were in reserve we had an unpleasant moment when they started sending over gas-shells in the early morning. I was asleep at the time and woke with a start and immediately smelt the gas. I had some difficulty in finding my gas-mask, which I had imprudently taken off to sleep. We had a sergeant killed that morning. His name was Shakespeare.

On the whole the line was not as bad as I expected. The dirt is the chief inconvenience and the difficulty of washing. I saw it of course under favourable circumstances, as it was fine and warm all the time.

I wrote my diary at intervals, but I wrote letters daily, and here are some further quotations from those I wrote during this first visit to the line:

May 23rd. I like both the officers who are with me, which is so lucky. They were discussing the American Civil War today and had a little argument as to which side Washington fought on or whether he was only President at the time. It is a marvel to me that men who don't care for reading can face this sort of life at all, unless they are able, as some are, to sleep whenever and as long as they want. I am reading *Doctor Thorne* now, the sequel to *Barchester Towers*. I'm not sure that you would like it as much as I do. I have discovered that the edition of Gibbon I have with me omits the indecent Latin quotations in the notes. Isn't that a shame? I hardly care to go on with it. . . . I have re-read this letter and am ashamed of it. I think, like Machiavelli, that one must be clean and comfortable and well dressed in order to write well.

This was the fourth year of trench warfare and, although the authorities may be criticised for having failed to find any way of ending it, they should at least be given credit for having mastered the technique of conducting it in the manner most conducive to the physical and mental well-being of the soldiers. I give in one of my letters a brief description of the system.

At the risk of boring you I'm afraid I must explain a little of our organisation. It will save time afterwards in making my movements clear to you. When we are "in the line"—which means front line, reserve, support, etc. i.e. our normal life, except when the whole division is withdrawn and is "out" which is rare—when we are "in the line," we have only three officers from each company "up" at a time. The remainder are left down at what is called (God knows why) "Details," where they are safe and comfortable. We are supposed to have six officers in each company and at present we have seven in ours.

I might have added that the battalion consisted of four companies and that each company spent two days in the front line, where clothes were never removed and where washing and shaving were hardly possible, two days in support, where conditions were little better, and two in reserve, where they improved considerably and where access to sleeping-bags and kit was usually possible.

This method was admirably designed so to vary the strain necessarily imposed upon soldiers at war as to reduce it to the minimum. Fear was lessened by the rarity of exposure to great danger, monotony was mitigated by perpetual change. Nearly always something was going to happen the day after tomorrow. Nerves are subject to wear and tear. The age-long belief that veteran troops are in all circumstances more reliable than those that have been recently recruited did not survive the test of the trenches. Shell-shock, although not always easy to distinguish from cowardice, became nevertheless a recognised malady for which the sufferer was held no more to blame than for concussion. But the men most subject to shell-shock were not the last arrivals but those who had been longest at the front.

It is plain from my letters and diary that my highest hope was a wound that would send me home. Therefore I was never unduly depressed by the prospect of going into the line. But I was none the less glad to come out of it, and to find myself once more in comparative safety, and, what I seem to have valued even more highly, comparative comfort. Here for instance is an entry after another long tour of duty in the line:

Today I was relieved and to my great joy and relief went down to Details. I really needed a rest. It was a lovely day and I had a pleasant ride down in the evening, arriving at Bailleulmont in time for dinner. I found the band playing in the rose-garden. It provides such a contrast to the line considering how near it is.

And on the following day I write:

After a lovely night's sleep followed by breakfast in bed at nine this morning, I did nothing all day but sit in a chair and read and play a little bridge. A good day.

I was doubtless excused all duties that day owing to having come so recently out of the line, for idleness was very seldom permitted. The life of a soldier in the Brigade of Guards when he was not actually engaged in fighting was similar to his life in peacetime. All his morning was occupied with parades, drill, musketry instruction and other forms of training; and these were sometimes but not usually followed by further duties in the afternoon. So that in many cases, certainly in mine, the pleasant sense of security was soon replaced by an acute sense of boredom.

For the greater part of the month of June the whole battalion was at rest. We were quartered in a vast farm; the battalion headquarters and the company in which I served occupied the principal house, which had served as the dwelling of the gentleman-farmer to whom the property belonged. Rather than share a bedroom in the house I lived in a tent, where I made myself fairly comfortable. I am not one who enjoys life under canvas but I have always preferred privacy to chance companionship.

Of the six months I spent in France this was the one I enjoyed the least. We did intensive training all the morning and played communal games such as football, which I always detested, in the afternoon. But even here there was variety.

June 14th. I am getting very bored here. The life is monotonous, the company unentertaining. . . .

June 15th. A route march this morning. I was sent on with two men as advance party, having had the route explained to me on the map. At one point I thought I had gone wrong, turned back in a panic—the band behind me turned too and stopped playing—there was a scene of great confusion and it turned out that I had been right all the time.

June 16th. After church parade we had to do revolver practice. A peaceful afternoon and a very good dinner, as Pilcher, who commands the Fourth Battalion, came to dinner. It consisted of caviare, soup, salmon mayonnaise (tinned), excellent beef with potatoes and peas, asparagus, a pudding, sardines on toast, strawberries and cream—not a bad menu for within a few miles of the front line. I sat next to Lascelles, whom I found a far pleasanter companion than anyone else in the mess. He is cultivated. We talked about wine, books, pedigrees and old houses. He has bought Chesterfield House in London. After dinner I played bridge and just before I was going to bed I was told that I was to proceed the next day to Hardelot for a week's course of bayonet-fighting and physical training. I was glad for every reason except that I shall miss my letters all that time. Diana's letters are my great abiding joy. Otherwise it is a pleasant prospect. I am tired of this place and Hardelot is quite close to Boulogne and civilisation.

June 17th. We left Saulty at 1 p.m. We got a carriage to ourselves, but the train went only as far as Doullens. There we stopped at about half-past three and were told to be back at the station at six. We strolled down into the town, which was very desolate and deserted. At the one hotel they refused to serve us with food, but sold us a bottle of champagne. When we got back into the train we thought we were there for the night, made ourselves as comfortable as we could and went to sleep. At midnight the train stopped at Abbeville and we learnt that it was going no further. The station was in complete darkness and there was not a soul about, as an air-raid was going on. Not knowing what to do or how to find our way to the town, which is always completely deserted now at night, we got back into the train and slept till morning.

June 18th. A lovely morning. We went down into the town and found the Officers' Club—a rather pleasant house, where we had a good wash and an excellent breakfast. The best new bread and butter that I have tasted for a long time. We went on from there at about 9.30. The train was crowded. We got into a large saloon carriage. All the other officers in the carriage were going to England, which stirred bitter envy. We reached Boulogne shortly before two and immediately dashed off to the Folkestone, where we had a good lunch. It was so pleasant to feel that one was back in the world again, the world of restaurants and shops and cabs and women. . . . We wandered about the town all the afternoon and spent some time at the barber's. I had a hot bath at the Folkestone before dinner and we dined there. We had a fellow to dinner who works in the censor's office here. He seemed an agreeable fellow. We all got fairly drunk and we set forth for Hardelot after dinner, hoping to be able to get there on passing lorries. It is about ten kilometres out. We were very successful and arrived there safely.

A change of this kind made a very welcome break in the monotony of that life. Under the hot sunshine we disported ourselves for some days on the broad sands of Hardelot, and I was able on the Saturday evening to get away to a hospital near St. Omer where Rosemary Leveson-Gower and Katharine Asquith were nursing.

The sun indeed was so hot that some of my companions became casualties from sunburn, and I myself became a minor casualty owing to one of them inadvertently thrusting his bayonet through my finger. My first thought was, would the wound be serious enough to send me home? But when the doctor dispelled any such hope and offered to send me to hospital in Boulogne, I rejected the suggestion, for it was towards the end of the week and I was already anxious to get back to the battalion, to my letters and to the line, where only could I get the kind of wound I wanted.

Soon after this we returned to the peaceful life in the large farm, where we spent another ten tedious days. It was, so far as I remember, a beautiful place, but I was very glad to leave it. I was ill adapted to the military profession and could not share the sentiment of one of the senior officers in my regiment who was reported to have said: "I shall be glad when this damned war is over and we can get back to real soldiering again."

At the beginning of July we went back to the line and remained there for the next six weeks. The latest tactical development had entirely changed the earlier system in which the front was held by an unbroken rank of soldiers standing in the trenches almost shoulder to shoulder. This had been replaced by a series of strong points divided from one another by as much as four or five hundred yards. I record in my diary that the front which our Company were holding at this time was of such a length that it took over two hours to walk along it. As officers were on duty for four hours at a time they were kept fully occupied if they sought to pay two visits to each post.

Night patrols were a form of activity to which the authorities attached great importance. An officer would set forth after dark accompanied by two or three reliable men and creep about in no-man's land between the trenches, getting as close as possible to the enemy so as to discover how and where his barbed wire was arranged, where his strong points were situated and other details. When enough information had been collected a raid might be carried out to take prisoners and find out which German regiments were holding which sector. These raids certainly added to the excitement of trench warfare and it is to be hoped that they furnished the Intelligence with valuable information. This is how I wrote of my first experience:

August 8th. I am going out on patrol tonight and feel elated and excited—and perhaps also a little bit frightened, but I'm not sure. I should be very disappointed if I were told now that I was not to go.

August 9th. It didn't after all prove very exciting. I went out with the Headquarters patrol men, none of whom I know, and I had to allow myself to be more or less guided by them. We went out to Observation Trench, whence I went on with two men to within about twenty yards of a German machine-gun post. We came in about three. I went back to Battalion Headquarters, where I had breakfast. Miz Churchill was there. He had been out on patrol on the right and had had a fight. He had had two casualties and thought he had killed a lot of Germans.

Gordon got a tap on the head with a piece of shell last night and so went down to Details today instead of me. The company went up into the front line. I went on in front in order to go out on patrol on the right with de Reuter. It was very cold but otherwise uneventful. We got back about 3.30. We were very heavily bombarded at dawn and had a few casualties from gas-shells.

August 10th. I had a good sleep all the morning and was on duty most of the afternoon. I went out on patrol at night with two sections. We wandered about a good deal and at one moment I had no idea where we were. But it was a starlight night and by marching north we found ourselves in our own lines sooner than we expected. We came in rather early, as there was a raid to take place at 3.15. De Geijer was to raid the machine-gun post in front of Observation Trench. When he got there he found neither gun nor Germans. They had all got out. I met him coming back.

August 11th. This afternoon I crawled out to Observation Trench to get de Geijer's respirator which he had dropped there. I found it and crawled on to the Sunken Road, where I found a skeleton stretching a gloved hand out of the earth. I went on to No. 10 post, which I got into without being seen by the sentry. It was rather a foolish thing to do but it showed how insecure No. 10 post is.

I was very proud of having possibly saved my life by my rudimentary knowledge of astronomy. As I have always told the story since, we were walking straight into the German trenches when I happened to look up at the heavens, and ordered an immediate about-turn. It may have been so. I had convinced myself it was so until I came to look into the diary, which makes no mention of such a dramatic incident. Old men forget, but they also, and more often perhaps, "remember with advantages what feats they did that day."

After another six weeks of duty in the line the battalion was suddenly withdrawn, and we guessed rightly that this was to give us a short rest before throwing us into the great advance about which there had been many rumours. I wrote my account of the battle immediately after it took place:

August 20th. At 9 a.m. the Commanding Officer gave us the last instructions about the battle. It seems to be a hazardous enterprise but I feel quite confident. I spent the rest of the morning superintending the men's baths. I wrote to Diana and tried to say how much I love her, but failed, failed.

We had a sort of high tea before we started. We got into motor lorries at about eight and drove to somewhere near Hendecourt. Here tea and biscuits were awaiting us. There was bright moonlight, but before we marched off a thick mist suddenly came down. We went on to the Red Line, where we were to spend the night. We reached there at about midnight. I stayed on duty till two, walking up and down the line. The men seemed very cheerful. At two I went and had something to eat and drink at Company Headquarters. The barrage was to come down at five and we were to start off twenty minutes after. I got into position with my platoon some time before. The barrage was terrific. I had never heard anything to touch it. We started off at the right time. The mist was so thick that you could see only about twenty yards. My platoon was on the left, but we never succeeded in getting in touch with the rest of the Company. The first people we met were the Headquarters of the 1st Battalion

Scots Guards. I saw Dudley Coats and Victor Mackenzie, their Commanding Officer. They directed me to our own front line, which we crossed and set out in what I hoped was the right direction. We met an officer in the Coldstream with a platoon. He said the Scots Guards had failed to get their objective, that everyone was lost and that the trench we were in was full of Germans. I said I would work down the trench, which I thought was Moyblain, our first objective, and clear it of the enemy. We went on, and presently I met Alec Robartes and Fryer. The latter was commanding No. 1 Company, which should have been in support of our No. 3 Company, but which had, although I did not know it at the time, already got in advance of it. After this I pressed on alone with my platoon, guiding myself roughly by the sound of our guns behind us. We were occasionally held up by machine-gun fire and we met one or two stray parties of Scots Guards without officers. Finally we met a fairly large party of the Shropshires, who I knew should be on our right. The officer with them did not know where he was, but we agreed to go on together. We ran into a small party of the enemy, of whom we shot six and took two prisoners, including an officer. We then learnt that we were on the outskirts of Courcelles. We had gone a great deal too far to the right. I tried to get back by going up a road to the left but could not get on owing to a machine-gun firing straight down the road. There were several dead men lying about this road, one particularly unpleasant one with his face shot away. These were the first sights of the kind I had seen and I was glad to find that they did not affect me at all. I had often feared that they might have some physical effect on me, as in ordinary life I hate and always avoid disgusting sights. I went back to the beginning of the road, where I found a tank which, like everyone else, had lost its way in the mist. It consented to go up the road in front of us, and we were not troubled further by the machine-gun. I got on to another road which led straight up to the Halte on the Arras–Albert railway. This was the right of the final objective of my Company. There was a ruined building there from which a few shots were fired. We lay down and returned their fire with rifles and Lewis guns. Six Germans ran out with their hands up. We took them prisoner. Almost at the same time a party of the Shropshires came round on the left of the building. There was a steep bank on the edge of the railway, along which I told my men to dig themselves fire-positions.

So we obtained our objective. Not only were we the first to do so but we were the only platoon in the Company who succeeded in doing so at all. I sent a report to the Commanding Officer and later in the day I got his reply—only two words—"Well done."

It was then 9 a.m. Not long afterwards I saw No. 1 Company coming over the hill behind us. Fryer came on to see me. We heard that No. 2 Company, which had come through No. 4, as No. 1 had through No. 3, was on our left, but there was a considerable gap between. Fryer and I started walking down the edge of the railway embankment towards No. 2. Suddenly we noticed an enemy machine-gun shooting through the hedge along which we were walking. It was just in front of us and we had almost walked into it. We hurried back and on the way were fired at by machine-guns from the other side of the railway cutting. Fryer told me to take a Lewis gun and a couple of sections and capture or knock out the machine-gun. It was rather an alarming thing to be told to do.

However, I got my Lewis gun up to within about eighty yards of it, creeping along the hedge. The Lewis gun fired away. When it stopped I rushed forward. Looking back I saw that I was not being followed. I learnt afterwards that the first two men behind me had been wounded and the third killed. The rest had not come on. One or two machine-guns from the other side of the railway were firing at us. I dropped a few yards away from the gun I was going for and crawled up to it. At first I saw no one there. Looking down I saw one man running away up the other side of the cutting. I had a shot at him with my revolver. Presently I saw two men moving cautiously below me. I called to them in what German I could at the moment remember to surrender and throw up their hands. They did so immediately. They obviously did not realise that I was alone. They came up the cutting with their hands up, followed, to my surprise, by others. There were eighteen or nineteen in all. If they had rushed me then they would have been perfectly safe, for I can never hit a haystack with a revolver and my own men were eighty yards away. However they came back with me like lambs, I crawling most of the way to avoid fire from the other side of the railway. Two of them who were Red Cross men proceeded to bind up my wounded. Fryer then sent in two platoons under Delacombe and Clough Taylor to fill up the gap.

I hardly ate anything all this day except an orange and a few biscuits. I lived chiefly on whisky and water. The mist had cleared off at about ten o'clock and been followed by brilliant sunshine. In the afternoon I went to a dug-out about 400 or 500 yards back where Fryer had his headquarters and had about an hour and a half's sleep. That evening at "stand to" the Commanding Officer came along the line of the railway. He said to me "The Major-General and the Brigadier are extremely pleased with the work of your platoon, and asked me to tell you so. You've done most awfully well."

After "stand down" I took my platoon back to the rest of the Company. They were in a steep bank some way back. It seemed almost like returning to safety, although it afterwards proved to be anything but safe. There I found Tuffy and Sally and after a little conversation went and lay down in a place about as long as a child's grave, where I could not stretch my legs but managed to get an hour or two's sleep.

August 22nd. I went on duty again at 2 a.m. Another lovely moonlight night and no mist this morning. Soon after four the enemy started a bombardment. Tuffy said it was the worst he had ever been in. It went on for nearly an hour and a half. We were expecting a counter-attack all the time. Apparently one was started but never reached our line owing to our retaliatory barrage. We had several casualties. Two men were killed close to me and a small piece of shrapnel from the shell that killed one of them hit me in the face, drawing a little blood and remaining in my cheek. At last it stopped and we had breakfast. There were some eggs, which they cooked for us, and very glad we were of them.

After breakfast I lay down and had two hours' refreshing sleep, the best sleep I had all through the battle. When I woke up a message came from Alan Adair, commanding No. 2 Company on our left front, saying there seemed a chance of a counter-attack on his front and asking for reinforcements. I was sent up with two platoons.

All that day, which was a very hot one, we sat under a shallow bank, and from 1.30 till 7 we were shelled continuously. We expected to be relieved that evening—had been told we were to be and lived on the hope. As the day went on the rumour changed, but it was not until nearly midnight that we learnt that we had to make another attack at 4 a.m. the next morning. The Commanding Officer came up and there was a terrible crowd in the small dug-out which had been No. 1 Company Headquarters. To add to the confusion a mail was distributed. Three beautiful letters for me from Diana. I had to try to read these, to get something to eat, to understand my instructions, all in a few minutes in the crowded, ill-lit dug-out. It was a miracle that we got the Company into position in time. They had been having casualties from shell-fire all the evening and when I went to my platoon a shell fell which knocked out five more. When we were eventually formed up for the attack I had only ten men, and the climax was reached when I discovered that my Platoon Sergeant, who had been excellent all the day before, was so drunk as to be useless. He started the attack with us but we never saw him again until the next day.

The attack itself was beautiful and thrilling—one of the most memorable moments of my life. The barrage came down at 4 a.m. A creeping barrage —we advanced behind it. We kept direction by means of a star, and a huge full moon shone on our right. I felt wild with excitement and glory and knew no fear. When we reached our objective, the enemy trench, I could hardly believe it; so quickly had the time passed it seemed like one moment. We found a lot of German dead there. The living surrendered.

It was light now and I felt exhausted. We found that our right was in the air—the Shropshires, who should have been there, had been unable to get on. We had to arrange our men to cover as much of the trench as we could.

Later at about 9.30 Tuffy told me to go with a few men as far down on our right as possible, to try to get into touch with someone and to try to deal with two machine-guns which were firing at us both from in front and behind. I never liked an order less. Courage is half a matter of health and energy and I was feeling worn out and not at all brave. The trench had been so knocked about by our barrage that in many places even crouching one was visible to the enemy machine-guns. However I went off, and although the incident was not one for which I got any particular credit it was the one for which I gave myself most.

We went down the trench pretty slowly with frequent halts, which were necessary, as we had to run and jump and crawl half the way. At eleven o'clock we had reached the furthest point we had set out for, when suddenly our guns behind put down a barrage not very far in front of us. Soon afterwards we saw our own men pouring over the ridge behind. It was a fine sight to see them come on in perfect formation as on a field day. There were tanks in front. Our only fear was lest they should mistake us for the enemy. We waited until they were close and then all stood up together and waved our hats and cheered. When they were in line with us we advanced with them for a few hundred yards. Germans were giving themselves up on all sides. We took about eighty prisoners, whom we brought back with us. The rest of the day was uneventful and we were relieved by the Scots Guards at nightfall—a blessed relief. We marched back to Ayette. I don't think I was ever so thirsty or so tired as when we arrived there. I drank gallons of hot cocoa and certainly never enjoyed a drink so much. We spent the night in a cellar, where I had only boards to lie on, but I managed to sleep pretty well.

August 24th. We were able to wash and shave this morning—a great pleasure. Our appearance was beginning to be too revolting. All the morning troops were passing through Ayette—cavalry and artillery. It was exhilarating to see them passing in perfect security through a village that had been in German hands two days before. In the afternoon we heard we were to go further back—to a spot between Ransart and Adinfer. We marched off at about 6 p.m.

We had to halt on the road, as our guide was not there. While we were halted the Commanding Officer rode by with the Brigadier and I heard the Commanding Officer say "That's Duff." The Brigadier stopped and congratulated me in words that made me thrill with pride, blush with pleasure and sweat with shyness.

It was glorious to get back to our new quarters. Very peaceful they seemed—not a gun to be heard, though two days before they were in the support line. Our kits met us there—and the final joy was to get off one's clothes, put on one's pyjamas and creep into one's sleeping-bag. George Godman met us and I shared a hut with him.

August 25th. A late rise, a glorious morning, a delicious breakfast out of doors, a tremendous feeling of well-being. After lunch the Brigadier turned up and talked to me again—very flatteringly. I went down to Ransart before tea and had a bath. After tea we all listened to the band. Champagne for dinner, after which Sally and I went up to No. 1 Company, where we all sat round drinking port and talking about the battle.

August 26th. We tried to parade in the morning but it was too showery. Tuffy went down to Details in the afternoon and Billakin came up. We had another pleasant champagne dinner and went early to bed.

August 27th. We paraded in the morning. After lunch I came down to Details, which have moved from Bailleulmont to Berles au Bois. I was a little sorry to leave the Company but it is nice to live in a house again for a few days.

August 28th. Life here is a complete rest. There are no duties whatever. Today I saw the Commanding Officer's account of the battle. He ends by a summary of the outstanding features, of which he mentions as No. 1. Splendid leading of No. 10 Platoon by Lt. Duff Cooper. I have really won more praise than I deserve for I was very lucky.

I was indeed more fortunate than the narrative indicates, for all my life I have lacked sense of direction. In a familiar countryside and among streets where I have lived for years I frequently get lost, and only a little before, as already recounted, I had almost led the whole battalion astray. Yet on this particular occasion, when in the thick mist everything depended on sense of direction, I had succeeded in finding the way when everybody else lost it. I have always been a gambler, and up to the period of which I am writing I had been a most unlucky one. I had already lost a great deal of the small capital my father had left me. These losses had been a source of sorrow to those who were fond of me, and I had frequently promised to give up the evil habit and had as often fallen into it again. I had received and merited many reproaches. Writing to Diana after the battle, having boasted of my prowess, I added:

But to tell the truth my success was very largely due to the favours of that fickle goddess whose smiles I have so often courted at the green table where she has so often withheld them, biding her time for this even more valuable occasion.

And she replied:

Strange that such an eventuality never occurred to me before. I set no value on hope so didn't hope; yet now it seems this is what's made me happiest since you left. Such luck (forgive me, darling) is so seldom touchable by us that our whole strength of hope is negatively directed, and "not death" is all our prayer.

Perhaps I put your triumph too much on luck. I really in my heart think it is all your due, but in a strange kind of defence for the others I find myself declaring for chance. In valour weren't they all Herculeses? But they had little to flaunt.

It was a timely reminder of those many friends of ours who were all heroes and who had fallen, having won no more glorious decoration than the wooden cross that marked a soldier's grave.

On the 1st of September our Commanding Officer, Colonel Andrew Thorne, left, having been promoted to the command of a brigade. Harry Lascelles succeeded him. I wrote:

I used to want this but, like so many things one wants, as soon as it happens one regrets having ever wanted it. He [Thorne] was a man who had no thoughts except for soldiering, and the energy which he displayed and expected was very tiresome in our hours of ease. But he had the great quality of a commander, the power of inspiring confidence. Everyone felt tafe when he was there, or at least certain that the best would be done for them. Also I had presumably just won his approval. Lascelles is far more human and I get on very well with him, but one feels that on the day of battle he would be of less help. It is the difference between the professional and the amateur.

September 18th. We learnt this morning that our Company are to do an attack on the 24th. Tuffy is leaving us and Jaggers will take the Company over and I should think he would do it well.

September 20th. Every afternoon I play chess with Carroll and dominoes with him and Sydney. This evening we had a large dinner-party at our place—the installation of Jaggers. We were eight. Jaggers, self, Carroll, Alan, Sydney, Bunbury, Fryer. It was quite fun. We played vingt-et-un afterwards. I won. Just before dinner some port and sherry and foie gras arrived for me very opportunely.

I remember, although I find hardly any reference to it in the diary, that I felt greater apprehension before this attack than I had felt previously. The reason may have been that I was anxious to enjoy a little longer the credit that I had gained, or, as Diana would have said, to "flaunt" my medal; it may have been that as the result of our four months' daily correspondence our marriage seemed more possible than it had seemed before, and that the future was brighter with promise than it had ever been. Or it may have been that escape from danger of death increases the appetite for life, a phenomenon that I have noticed on other occasions.

Whatever the reason, I certainly had some nights of disquietude before I went into battle again. I explained it to myself at the time as being the instinctive animal reaction to danger; the fear of death implanted by nature for the preservation of the species.

The victorious advance of the Allies continued. In front of the Guards Division lay the Canal du Nord, and the Germans were firmly entrenched before it. In the coming battle only one company of the Third Battalion was engaged, the one in which I was serving, and one platoon of another company was attached to us. We had plenty of time to study beforehand exactly what we had to do, and we had a complete picture of the trenches occupied by the enemy, to which we gave our own names and which, while studying the operation, we reproduced by white tape stretched out on the ground. We went so far as to select the German dug-out where we proposed to have luncheon; and told our servants to meet us there with what would be required.

September 22nd. Sydney and I had to go to Legnicourt to attend the court martial of those sergeants we put under arrest at Berles au Bois. Afterwards we went to Vaux Vraucourt to lunch at the Officers' Club. The food was bad but we had some good Château Yquem, two bottles followed by brandy. We got rather drunk. We managed to get a lift back—spent the rest of the day playing dominoes. . . . He and Carroll stayed to dinner. We go up to the line tomorrow. We don't know when the push is to be but understand it is to be the biggest battle of the war.

September 23rd. We played some final dominoes in the afternoon. We marched off at 7.15—a long and very tiring march. I slept a good deal in the night.

24th. Was on duty from 4.30 to 8.30, when I had an excellent breakfast and slept again. It was a warm and lovely morning. We are living in a very deep dug-out—very cold. On duty from 1.30 to 7.30. Then had dinner—a little sleep and duty from 10.45 to 2.30. The night was quiet.

25th. A terrific enemy bombardment began at about 9 a.m. I had to go up to the front line in the midst of it. My runner was wounded on the way. I found that at one post we had three men, including a sergeant, killed. They were terribly knocked about. Stayed on duty till 1.30, when I came back and had a good lunch—wrote to Mother and Diana, from both of whom I had heard last night. We hear that the attack will not be until the day after tomorrow, which is a bore. The sooner the better. On duty from 8 to 11.30. Came back and found two bottles of port had arrived—most opportune—drank some and slept well.

26th. On duty 7 to 10.30. Came back and was resting, when I was called out by the Commanding Officer, and there was the Major-General, whom I had never seen before. I had to explain to him our plan of attack. Claud Sykes was with him.

I was on duty from 5 to 8.30, and put up notices at the various places in the trench where the different parties were to form up for attack. Jaggers relieved me. It took some time to get back to the dug-out as the trenches were full of troops moving up. I had dinner with Madox Gunther, who is in charge of the platoon of No. 4 Company which are attached to us for the attack. I felt perfectly calm, cheerful and confident, although during the past week I had several times felt fear. The nearer we came to the battle the less uneasy I felt. After dinner I lay down meaning only to rest but I slept soundly until past three.

27th. We had some breakfast before we started and I drank some port and had a mouthful of rum. It had been raining hard in the night but had stopped when we left the dug-out at about four. It was very dark. Zero was at 5.30, and we went over the top simultaneously with the beginning of the barrage. I was just scrambling up the parapet when two of our own trench-mortar shells fell almost among us, wounding two men. The rest scrambled back into the trench. I waited half a minute and then went on again. We were well up to our barrage but had no further casualties from it. We attacked in three parties. I was leading the centre platoon, Gibbon was on the right, Madox on the left. I got too much to the left but met Jaggers, who put me right. Nearly all the enemy we came in contact with surrendered at once. I soon got right down to the Canal du Nord. Here I was very nearly hit by a bomb which a small party of Germans threw before running away. It landed just behind me and hit my runner. It was light by now and a beautiful morning. We were soon in touch with the H.L.I., who were attacking on our left. The Germans tried to counter-attack on the right and three times they advanced over the ridge, but there was no heart in it and a little Lewis-gun fire sent them back each time. Machine-guns continued to fire in front for some time, but before mid-day all was quiet and the battle had rolled away from us.

We lunched in a German dug-out where we had told our servants to meet us and spent the afternoon watching from a slag-heap the distant battle and the large batches of German prisoners coming in. In the evening we were relieved and marched back to near Doignies. We found a good hot meal awaiting us and although we were very crowded we made our-selves pretty comfortable and had a good night's sleep. Our kits came up in time for us to sleep in our sleeping-bags. On the whole it was a good battle.

I should have been happier still that evening if I had known that for me the war was at an end. I was to spend another month in France, ten days of which were to be passed in Paris, but I was not to take part in any further attacks, and I was to miss, by being on leave in England, the last advance in which the battalion was engaged, when Madox Gunther was killed going to the help of Carroll Carstairs, who was badly wounded and crippled for life.

It was with Carroll that I went on Paris leave, and I could not have chosen a better companion. He knew the town as well as, or better than, I did. His father was a partner in the firm of Knoedler's, the celebrated picture-dealers. He himself, although entirely American, had joined the British Army on the outbreak of war and had already won the Military Cross. He had published some verse and later was to write *A Generation Missing*, a book of war memories which contains an account of this visit to Paris. We had many tastes in common, including literature, cards and chess.

In one respect leave in Paris was even more enjoyable than going home. It was pleasure with no attendant duties. There were no elderly relations who expected visits, no justified claimants on consideration, no feelings of others to be respected. The young soldier, from waking in the morning to going to bed the next morning, had nothing to think of but his own amusement.

It was during these days in Paris that I paid my first visit to the British Embassy. Lord Derby was Ambassador and his daughter Lady Victoria, whose first husband, Neil Primrose, had been killed, was staying with him. It was doubtless owing to her, whom I knew, that I was invited, or to Lord and Lady Pembroke, who were also there. I dined there twice, and when I left, Lord Derby, who had been a Grenadier, told me to let it be known that any members of the regiment who found themselves in Paris had only to telephone to the Embassy and announce themselves for luncheon or dinner, or both, and they would always be welcome. His hospitality was princely.

When I wrote that I had no duties in Paris I had forgotten one which I am glad to say that I then remembered—to pay a call on my old French teacher, Jeanne de Hénaut.

She fell on my neck with love and gratitude for my visit. I could hardly see how old she looked, for the room was dark and she sat with her back to what light there was, but she must begin to be very old.

When I came back to Paris in the following summer on my honeymoon she was dead.

CHAPTER SIX

MARRIAGE

1918–1922

WITHIN a fortnight of my return from Paris I was lucky enough to be granted leave to England. I arrived in London on the 31st of October and found everything there as I had been hoping and dreaming it would be. I passed the first Sunday at Taplow and the second at Breccles, the house in Norfolk which the Edwin Montagus had recently bought. I had not been there before. When we came in from shooting on Saturday evening we learnt that the Kaiser had abdicated, and as we travelled to London on Monday morning we saw increasing signs of rejoicing at every town and village that we went through. It was past eleven o'clock when we reached Liverpool Street, the armistice had been signed and the town was in an uproar. As we drove from the station I felt unable to take part in the enthusiasm. This was the moment to which I had looked forward for four years, and now that it had arrived I was overcome by melancholy. Amid the dancing, the cheering, the waving of flags, I could think only of my friends who were dead.

My inability to share in the high spirits of the crowd had doubtless physical as well as mental causes. I was not feeling well. I struggled to a gay dinner-party that evening, as it seemed an occasion that I could not miss, but had to leave before it was over and go to bed, where I remained for a week with a sharp attack of influenza. As I lay in bed that night listening to the cheers of the crowd, I thought that it would be a cruel irony of fate if I had survived the war only to die of flu during the armistice.

Nor were my fears without foundation, for the scourge was never more dangerous than during that year, and in the following month my eldest sister died of it. I wrote in my diary at the time:

These last four years have so inured me to death that I cannot feel it deeply. I was very fond of Steffie and never quarrelled with her in my life. Our relationship was ideal. We were always glad to see each other and never went out of our way to do so. I had no irksome feeling of duty towards her. For months at a time we didn't meet but I always knew that if I went to see her or proposed myself at the Priory [her country house in Sussex] she would be delighted to see me and wouldn't ask why I hadn't been before. She was content with her own life, and I think she had been very happy the last year or two. She was not clever but she was the only member of the family, except myself, with any sound sense.

My short illness served me in good stead, for had I been well I should have been obliged to return to the battalion a few days after the armistice and to take part in the march into Germany, during which they suffered more from fatigue, discomfort and privation than at any previous period. It was also uncertain how long I should have had to remain with the army of occupation before the slowly-turning wheels of government departments set me free. But under the protection of a medical certificate I had time to speed up the machinery, so that the Foreign Office put in their claim for my return without delay and the War Office granted me extension of leave until a decision was reached.

While I had been in France, Diana had made a new friend, Lord Beaverbrook, whom I was anxious to meet. My first impressions of him were favourable, but I doubt if they were reciprocated. He rightly admired Diana and rightly thought that I was unworthy of her. We both spent Saturday to Monday with him at Cherkley during the General Election, where Lloyd George came to luncheon on Sunday. I wrote in my diary:

I had never met the Prime Minister before, beyond once shaking hands with him in a box at the theatre. There is something very remarkable about him. He creates the impression of a great man and he does it without seeming theatrical and without seeming sincere. We sat for some time over lunch after the women had gone and he talked of nothing but the election—of what cries went down with the electorate and what did not—and speculated what the results would be. He is a great contrast to Mr. Asquith, who prefers to talk of nothing nearer home than Thucydides. At one moment he was eloquent, saying how the English people had long memories, how they remembered the fires of Smithfield and the hungry forties, and that one should never rouse those memories because it was a dreadful thing to fight against ghosts.

It would seem from the diary that I took little interest in that election. I have wondered since that my political opinions should have remained uninfluenced by my many distinguished Liberal friends. I knew nobody of similar importance in the Conservative Party and yet I never leaned towards Liberalism. There is a letter written from France in which I say, "I feel so very strongly sometimes about politics, and I don't find myself in agreement with anybody. . . . The *Morning Post*'s silly reactionary jingoism irritates me only a little less than the silly contemptible pacifism of —— [one of our friends]." So far as the Liberal Party was concerned I was strongly on the side of those who had been loyal to Mr. Asquith and against those who followed Lloyd George, and I could feel little enthusiasm for the Coalition of which the latter was the head. My opinion of it sank still lower when the failure of the ignoble Black-and-Tans experiment in Ireland, an attempt to suppress gangsterdom by gangsters in uniform, was followed by the still more ignoble surrender to a campaign of murder. But these events, far from impelling me towards the remaining Liberals of the true faith, turned me rather towards the die-hard Conservatives, who seemed to stand for principle, and who sought to chase the renegade Liberals from the Conservative camp.

A matter, however, more intimate and more important than politics was occupying my mind as the year 1918 drew to its close. As a result of the daily correspondence which Diana and I had carried on during the six months of my absence it had gradually come to be agreed between us that we should be married if all went well. All had gone well, the war was over and we saw no further reason to wait. We knew, however, that we were bound to meet with strong opposition from her parents, opposition with which it was difficult for me not to feel some sympathy.

The most beautiful of her generation, she had acquired, owing to her position, her talents, her friends and her enemies, such celebrity as no other young lady has ever enjoyed. The least worldly of parents would have been justified in hoping that she would marry somebody whose great name, whose vast possessions or whose splendid achievements would seem to justify her choice. I had none of these things, nor any prospect of acquiring them. My salary as a clerk in the Foreign Office was about £300 a year and I had as much again of my own. If I married, my mother, always ready to deny herself anything, was prepared to make me an annual allowance of a few more hundreds, which she could ill afford. Nor can I suppose that my reputation, that of a wild young man who played too high and drank too deep, was likely to recommend me. I was nevertheless surprised—more surprised perhaps than I should have been—at the shock which the announcement caused my future mother-in-law, and by the violence and obstinacy of her opposition. After a fruitless and distressing interview, which took place during a ball at the Albert Hall, held to celebrate the victory, she told me that I had better consult Diana's father if I had anything further to say. I thought that he had no very strong feelings on the subject and I hoped that I might make some impression on him, but when the interview took place I found that he had received his orders and he faithfully carried them out.

At twelve o'clock I went to see the Duke. There was something grotesquely old-fashioned about the solemn interview with the heavy father. He received me very civilly, listened to all that I had to say, complimented me on the way I had said it, added that he had always liked me, and concluded by saying that he could not possibly allow the marriage and preferred not to discuss it. I asked him if he could give me any reason for his attitude and he refused to. I asked, was it money? He practically said it was not. I asked whether he had heard anything against me. He said he had heard nothing. I tried to make him see the silly unreasonableness of his attitude and hinted that it could only drive one to take the law into one's own hands, but he would say nothing except "I am sorry I can say no more." We were both very polite and parted with every civility.

We became, indeed we remained, the best of friends. I thought him foolish at the time, but looking back on it I consider his handling of the situation was masterly. He told me long after that Disraeli, who was his father's greatest friend, said to him when he was a very young man, "My dear Henry, never explain."

Early in the new year this attitude was changed and it was agreed that if we would wait for a year no obstacle would be put in the way of our marriage, but that there was to be no engagement in the meanwhile. Diana was more reluctant than I was to accept this compromise, as her heart was set upon being married in the spring or early summer, and she disliked the idea of a winter wedding. My diary fails to make plain whether we agreed to this proposal. In any case we continued to behave, and our friends to treat us, as though we were engaged. Seeing this and understanding, I suppose, that further opposition was hopeless, Diana's mother told her towards the end of April that if she would speak to her father he might relent.

April 30th. In the evening Diana had her interview with her father. I met her afterwards at the Ritz. They have given in completely and are willing for us to be married as soon as we wish. It seems too wonderful, and hard to realise. The Duke, she says, was perfect and gave away the whole case by saying to her after the interview, which lasted only about ten minutes, "Don't go upstairs for a little. I don't want your mother to think I gave in at once."

May 1st. At 6.30 I went to see the Duke, fortified with whisky but feeling almost as nervous as on the occasion of our last interview. He was extremely charming, could not possibly have been nicer or made it easier. He said a word or two about settlements. . . . Our interview only lasted about twenty minutes, for half of which he succeeded in talking about other things such as the growth of Bolshevism and the future of the Territorials.

I remember also that he said the sooner the wedding took place the better, as he was going away for Whitsun and wanted to travel before the trains were too crowded.

Meanwhile I had returned, before the end of 1918, to the Foreign Off ce and I was once more in the Commercial Department. I found myself much happier in my work there than I had been before, and I did it better because I took more interest in it. The Army had taught me a great deal. Not only shall I always be glad that I served in it and very proud to have been a Grenadier, but I shall also feel that I learnt, while serving, lessons that I might otherwise have missed. I learnt the importance of efficiency, which is the first quality of an officer, and I learnt that the effort to acquire efficiency lends interest to the dullest task. My superiors were not slow to notice the improvement in my work and to wonder at it, supposing that eighteen months spent with the brutal, licentious soldiery would have bred idleness rather than application to duty.

We were married on the 2nd of June 1919 and spent our honeymoon in Paris, Florence, Rome and a beautiful villa in the south of Italy. Honeymoons are better to remember than to recount. I kept a careful record of mine and wrote at the end of it, "A lovelier honeymoon man never had." We had no home to come back to because we had been unable to find a house that suited us before we left. We stayed first with one friend and then another and finally with Diana's parents in Arlington Street. It was not until the following March that we were able to move into our own house in Gower Street, where we lived happily for seventeen years.

On the 19th of July we watched from Carlton House Terrace the peace procession, in which I thought Foch was the most impressive figure. That evening we went to dine with friends in a house in Mayfair in order to see the firework display. On account of the crowds in the streets and the impossibility of getting transport we arrived very late and dinner was finished. We were helping ourselves to what remained of it when it was reported that the fireworks were beginning and Diana, ever enthusiastic, led the procession to the roof. I was bringing up the rear, had reached the top floor and was about to climb the ladder that led up from it, when I heard the sound of shattered glass followed, after what seemed to me a long interval, by the sound of a falling body. I opened a door from behind which the noise seemed to come and looked into a narrow box-room, on the floor of which Diana was lying. She had fallen through a skylight about twenty-five feet from the floor. The opening was so narrow that the large hat she was wearing remained on the roof. She had broken her thigh.

This was not an auspicious beginning to our married life. We had still no home and this accident made it more difficult for us to look for one. We had very little money and the spectre of doctors' bills was alarming. Recovery was bound to be slow and painful. Yet we survived this misfortune, and it may even have had a good side to it. For the next few months we, who had grown accustomed to a life of excitement, had one of rigorous routine imposed on us. I had had a month's leave for my honeymoon and was probably hoping to get away again before the summer was over. Any such hope was now banished and with it any such desire. I settled down to hard work at the Foreign Office and had no more leave until the following February, when we were both able to go to Paris for a week. When I was not at work I was by Diana's bedside until she was able to come out in a chair which I wheeled. The first occasion was on Sunday September 28th, when we went down Piccadilly as far as Hyde Park Corner and back to lunch at the Ritz, where I wheeled the chair into the restaurant. After that we went out frequently in the evening. I enjoyed wheeling the chair through the streets and into theatres and restaurants. At about the same time my chief in the Foreign Office fell ill so that I was left in charge. I congratulated myself, when he returned and Diana could walk again, that during the six weeks interim I had neither committed any gross error in the conduct of the Commercial Department, nor upset the wheeled chair in the course of our nightly peregrinations.

We were distressed at this time by the ill-feeling which had arisen between two of our friends, Max Beaverbrook and Winston Churchill. The latter was Secretary of State for War and was identified with the policy of supporting the parties in Russia who were fighting against the Bolshevik Government. For several months he had been attacked violently in the columns of the *Daily Express*. I wrote in my diary at the beginning of September:

First Beaverbrook and then Edwin [Montagu] came to see Diana this evening. She talked to the former about his attacks on Winston. Later we discussed with Edwin the cause of these, and he believes it to be an argument which Max and Winston had one night in Paris when Winston coined the phrase "The press is easier squashed than squared." Edwin thinks Max never forgave this. It seems an absurdly trivial cause for such a procedure. Max himself told us he had received a very strong letter from Bonar Law [then leader of the House of Commons and of the Conservative Party] on the subject of these attacks. He had merely replied that he did not control the articles in the *Express* and that he had forwarded the letter to Blumenfeld [the editor].

Diana, being very fond of both and ever active in the cause of peace, sought to effect a reconciliation. We were living then in Arlington Street, where the large back drawing-room served us as a bed-sittingroom. It was a long, high room looking out on to the Green Park. The bed was at one end and in the middle was a narrow refectory table where we had our meals and sometimes entertained our friends. On November 4th I wrote:

This evening we had a memorable dinner-party—Winston, Beaverbrook, Nellie Romilly and the Montagus. It was the first time that Winston and Max had met for several months. From the point of view of the dinner-party it was a tremendous success. Winston arrived first, then Nellie, then Max. The two shook hands. They were both obviously nervous, Max more so than Winston. Then the Montagus arrived. We had dinner in the bedroom as usual. The table is very narrow, which I think promotes conversation. The food was excellent, the champagne circulated freely and the conversation never flagged. It started on general subjects such as the Douglas–Pennant enquiry, on which everyone was agreed, and gradually veered round to politics and Russia. Winston was at his very best, witty, courteous, eloquent. Max was less at his ease. He is never at his best elsewhere than in his own house. I several times feared disaster but it was always avoided. Edwin took a fairly neutral middle line and acted rather as arbitrator. They ended perfectly good friends and both said they had enjoyed themselves tremendously. I think they had.

I am under the impression that this dinner-party produced results and that the press campaign against the Secretary of State for War was abandoned, but old men forget and I have not consulted the files of the *Daily Express* to refresh my memory.

Meanwhile the life of the old Commercial Department of the Foreign Office was coming to an end. It was being swallowed up by the Department of Overseas Trade, and I narrowly escaped being swallowed up with it. As a result of my protests, for I was not interested in commerce and I was interested in politics, I was transferred early in 1920 to the Egyptian Department of the Foreign Office, which was also a wartime product. The head of it was John Murray, who had spent fourteen years in the Egyptian Civil Service and had come to the Foreign Office in 1919 to inaugurate the new department. He was a man of great ability and became a regular member of the Diplomatic Service. He died young when serving as Minister in Mexico.

It was a small department. We were never more than three and we all sat in what had been my private sitting-room when I was resident clerk. The years that I spent in this department were the most interesting in my time at the Foreign Office and the most useful to me. They were important years in the history of Egypt and it was possible for the humble Civil Servant to feel that he was exercising some influence on national policy. Murray, being an expert on the subject, was little interfered with by the higher authorities, who were inclined to accept his opinion, and he would discuss every problem with me and give weight to what I had to say, in spite of my complete lack of first-hand knowledge of the subject.

Many of the failures of British statesmanship have been due to the reluctance of Ministers to deal with a problem so long as postponement was possible. Too often have we been forced in the end to accept an unsatisfactory and even a humiliating solution because we have refused at the beginning to agree to a far better one. Too often have we conceded grudgingly and too late much more than would have been accepted gladly and gratefully at an earlier date.

When the war broke out in 1914 the Khedive of Egypt happened to be in Constantinople, and he immediately threw in his lot with the enemies of Great Britain. For many centuries Turkey had exercised a shadowy suzerainty over Egypt. We were now at war with Turkey and we therefore declared that suzerainty at an end, set up a British protectorate, deposed the Khedive and installed another member of his family in his place. These were obviously war measures and abundantly justified as such, but the Egyptians expected that when the war was over the situation would be reconsidered.

Soon after the armistice Zaghlul, the leader of the nationalist movement, appeared at the British Residency at the head of a delegation and demanded the independence of Egypt. As it was not within the power of the High Commissioner to give any satisfactory reply, Zaghlul asked to be allowed to go with his delegation to England and lay his demands before His Majesty's Government. The request was referred to the Foreign Office and refused. It was, however, followed by a similar request put forward by the Prime Minister of Egypt, Rushdi Pasha, and his distinguished colleague, Adly Pasha. Although this request was strongly supported by the High Commissioner, Sir Reginald Wingate, it met with an equally blunt refusal from the Foreign Office. Mr. Balfour was then Secretary of State and he ought to have known better. It was one thing to turn down a demand made by a mob-leader, for such Zaghlul might have been, not quite justly, considered; it was quite another thing to refuse even to receive two moderate and respected statesmen holding the highest positions in the administration of their country. It was worse than inept, it was discourteous. By discrediting the moderates it strengthened the extremists, and under the insult the two Ministers resigned. The field was thus left open to Zaghlul, who promoted agitation until, after having been warned, he was arrested and deported. Disorder broke out. British and other Europeans, for whose safety we were responsible, were murdered, until the state of anarchy was suppressed by firm military measures. This was the condition to which the British Coalition Government had brought the country when in March 1919 Lord Allenby arrived in Cairo as High Commissioner.

He had been sent there in the belief that he was the kind of tough soldier, known to the army as "the Bull," who would stand no nonsense, but the first thing that he did after his arrival was to insist on the release of Zaghlul. It was not the first nor the last time that politicians have been disappointed in their belief that soldiers are stupid creatures who understand nothing but the use of force.

Allenby would have been the last to deny that force is necessary to restore order, but it had been judiciously used by General Bulfin before his arrival and order had been restored. He believed therefore that this was the moment, in an atmosphere of calm and when the proof of strength had been given, to make generous concessions. But the British Government thought differently. It was the moment in their opinion to send out a Mission of Enquiry. They chose Lord Milner as the head of this Mission, and they could have chosen nobody with more experience and wisdom. But once again they disregarded the factor of time. They had refused to receive Rushdi and Adly when they had wanted to come. They had invited them when it was too late. They appointed Lord Milner in April. His Mission arrived in Egypt in December. Meanwhile the position had deteriorated. Zaghlul had not spent eight months patiently awaiting the arrival of the Mission. He had been stirring up opposition against it on the grounds that its terms of reference included the maintenance of the protectorate, so that when it arrived nobody of importance in Egypt dared be known to have any dealings with it. After seeing enough of the country to form some estimate of the state of public opinion, and after holding some very secret conversations with one or two prominent people, the Mission returned to England in February 1920.

This was the state of affairs when I joined the Egyptian Department, and one of the first successes that we had, for which I can claim no credit whatever, was that Zaghlul, who had refused to see Lord Milner or any member of his Mission in Egypt, consented to hold conversations with him in London. Zaghlul and his party arrived in June. Negotiations with Lord Milner were opened at once and continued until the end of the summer.

Soon after their arrival we stayed from Saturday to Monday at Highclere, where Lord Carnarvon had arranged a large house-party in honour of the Egyptians. I think this was my only meeting with Zaghlul, who seemed a benevolent old gentleman with a twinkling eye. Adly, Mohammed Mahmoud and Lufti were also there. They were taken to inspect their host's racehorses on Sunday afternoon. Half-way through the inspection it was noticed that Zaghlul was missing. After a hasty search he was discovered reclining at full length on a bundle of hay in an empty loose-box. He had been overcome by fatigue and possibly by tedium, for although he was a great gambler at the poker table he took no interest in horseflesh.

Milner, as the result of negotiations, was willing to make wise and extensive concessions to Egyptian nationalist sentiment, but his manner of handling the affair in its final stages showed a strange lack of technical skill. On August 23rd I wrote:

The Times this morning publishes a more or less correct account of the results of Milner's conversations with Zaghlul. The situation is still very unsatisfactory as nobody, neither the Egyptians nor ourselves, is in any way bound by the agreement. The Cabinet have never considered it. Before the terms were telegraphed to Egypt they were shown to Curzon and Bonar Law, to both of whom they came as a shock. I wonder that Milner didn't get some measure of Cabinet concurrence before going so far.

I had returned that day from a month's leave and Murray had left the day before, so that I have no record of the final stages of the negotiations, but there was in fact no agreement, because Zaghlul made it plain that he could not commit himself until he had ascertained the views of the Egyptian people on Lord Milner's proposals.

When Murray and Lord Curzon returned from leave at the beginning of October the department were required to state their views with regard to the Milner plan, the main lines of which were that the protectorate should be replaced by a treaty which would recognise the independence of Egypt whilst retaining some British control over administration. Murray and I were strongly in favour of a settlement on these lines and we doubtless said so. But there was deep division in the Cabinet.

On November 4th we dined with the Winston Churchills.

The Montagus and Laverys were there, Jack and Goonie, and Michael. Winston was in his best form, ragging Edwin about Gandhi, who he said ought to be laid, bound hand and foot, at the gates of Delhi and then trampled on by an enormous elephant with the new Viceroy seated on its back. He believes firmly that there is a world-wide movement of reaction in progress at the present time and he is optimistic of the future. Edwin of course is pessimistic and mutters of the revolution that is to come. He tells me that in the Cabinet Winston is the chief opponent of Milner's Egyptian schemes which they were discussing this morning. There was a debate on the subject in the Lords this afternoon where the Opposition, Salisbury and Selborne, was satisfactorily disposed of by Curzon and Milner.

Early in the New Year, 1921, the Government decided to publish the Milner report, the main features of which were already known, to reserve their own decision upon it until it could be submitted to the Imperial Cabinet, and meanwhile to invite the Sultan, as the Khedive's successor was called, to send over a delegation in the spring to discuss the problem.

Early in April an effort was made by Adly to persuade Zaghlul to work with him and to accompany him to England, but Zaghlul, full of the self-importance bred by popular support, refused to accept any post in the delegation except that of leader, which it was impossible for Adly, as Prime Minister, to yield to him. It was also difficult for Adly to collect a truly representative Egyptian delegation which did not include Zaghlul. While bickerings were going on between the two I met Winston at dinner on May 3rd and wrote:

Had a long argument with Winston about Egypt, he pointing triumphantly to the apparent failure of our policy. He was very bad at details but good in general. His great line was that you could only make concessions to people you had beaten. He instanced the success of this in South Africa.

A few days later, however, Adly decided to disregard Zaghlul's opposition, to form the strongest delegation that he could, and to bring it to England. Two months later, at the beginning of July, they arrived. A few days before their arrival I wrote:

July 7th. We had a hard day at the Foreign Office. I didn't leave till 8.20. The explanation was that Curzon in the Cabinet was taunted by Massey, the Prime Minister of New Zealand, with not knowing his own mind [about Egypt], whereupon he replied that not only did he know it but that he had ready in the Foreign Office two alternative draft treaties which he would circulate to the Cabinet. He then came across to the office and told us to prepare the treaties forthwith.

July 9th. Saturday. As I was sitting in the office about four, thinking of going, the telephone rang and Crowe asked for Murray who was at Lord's [watching the Eton v. Harrow cricket match] and had so far as I was aware no intention of returning. Crowe said that Curzon particularly wanted to talk about Egypt. Lindsay had gone. It was an awkward moment. While I was still speaking to Crowe, Murray to my intense delight reappeared. Then we had a most hectic afternoon. Murray and Crowe came out from Curzon at five with a treaty in scraps and fragments which with the aid of the last typist in the Foreign Office I was able to present in a respectable form by a quarter to six. They took it across to Carlton House Terrace [where Curzon lived], and I went home but couldn't leave London till I heard the result in case my services were further needed. Not until eight did Murray telephone to say I could go. Then off we started in the car for Monkey Island. It was a heavenly evening after a grilling day. The drive was delightful and all went well. We arrived there soon after 9.30 and found everything ready for us. It was still broad daylight. We had dinner of cold salmon and duck in our little temple and two bottles of champagne. It was as beautiful and as romantic as could be. Mr. Tinker, the proprietor, was very genial and rather drunk. His daughter waited on us admirably. We went to bed soon after dinner and slept well.

July 10th. A heavenly day—the hottest in the year. We lay in the shade all the morning reading. I bathed before luncheon, which we had in our temple. We slept afterwards and then some of the Taplow party came over to see us. . . . After they had gone we went on the river and rowed round the island. Then we tied up the boat under some trees and read aloud *A Group of Noble Dames*. We dined in the temple and motored up to London after dinner, arriving about 10.30. It was a perfect day of perfect and memorable peace.

On the following day the Egyptian delegation arrived and on the day after:

July 12th. This afternoon Adly had his first interview with Lord Curzon. They were alone and got on fairly well. Curzon asked him what the delegation wanted. Adly replied the Milner report plus the Zaghlul reservations. Curzon was apparently surprised at this and said it was deplorable. But of course Adly must ask for the maximum to start with. The first full-dress meeting is to take place tomorrow.

The following is the brief account I gave of the meeting:

There were seven of them. We were five—Lord Curzon, Vansittart [then Curzon's Private Secretary], Lindsay, Murray and I. We had to write hard all the time taking notes of what occurred. We were in there from 3 to 6 and then I had to dictate the minutes, which took me till 8.30. I didn't think Curzon was good as a negotiator. He was too much the parliamentarian, too argumentative and anxious to score. I thought Adly was good. Only he, Rushdi and Curzon spoke. They, the Egyptians, seemed on the whole fairly reasonable.

July 26th. The Egyptians let us have their formula today, which contained nothing new and no sign of concession. Negotiations may now break down on the military question but I don't think they will. The delegation will certainly want to prolong them over the holidays.

I was right. We continued to negotiate until the middle of August, when the Egyptians scattered to various pleasant places in Europe, where they no doubt enjoyed their holidays at their Government's expense. I also took a month's leave, and when I returned Murray had gone to Scotland, so that I found myself in charge of the department.

October 2nd. Allenby charged into my room this morning very much in the manner of a bull. Confronted with a whipper-snapper like myself he expected, I am sure, that I should spring to attention and prepare to receive words of command. When I calmly held out my hand, said good morning and asked him to sit down, he looked both astonished and amused. His aide-de-camp, standing behind him, looked only astonished. His visit was most opportune, for Crowe had just said that he wanted to see him.

October 3rd. Murray returned today. I am sorry he's back, though in some ways it is a relief. I have no longer any responsibility, which I was beginning to enjoy.

October 12th. Murray and I are coming round to the view that it is worth making far greater concessions than have yet been contemplated in order to secure an agreement with Egypt.

October 21st. The Prime Minister says it is time he put his foot down somewhere, and he has chosen Egypt for the operation. A sub-committee of the Cabinet has been formed consisting of Winston, Austen Chamberlain, Worthington-Evans, Fisher and Curzon. Allenby's return to Egypt which was fixed for tomorrow has, much to his rage, been put off.

November 4th. Apparently the Prime Minister refused to make any concessions whatever to the Egyptians beyond what the Cabinet agreed to originally before the delegation arrived. Allenby thinks this is disastrous. It is largely his fault for not having spoken up to the Cabinet in favour of concessions. A Cabinet has been called for five this afternoon and Allenby told to attend. If they put off his journey again it will be the limit.

November 5th. Diana and I went down to Breccles after lunch by the 2.30. We had to change at Ely and wait there half an hour. We walked to the cathedral, which was looking most beautiful. It stands so well and the surroundings are so lovely. There was a service going on and the interior was very dim. Outside it was a perfect autumn evening—the trees all russet brown and frost in the air. . . .

At Breccles they were letting off fireworks when we arrived, which was fun. The party, consisting of Freyberg and Barbara McLaren, was enlivened after dinner by the arrival of Winston. We had a tremendous Egyptian argument, Edwin supporting me warmly. They were only agreed in their contempt for Allenby, who had apparently been very weak in the Cabinet. Winston said that if he had charge of Egypt the first thing he would do would be to get rid of Allenby and Zaghlul. Edwin said that if Winston had charge he would come to an agreement with Adly in three months, giving him more than anybody had yet proposed to do.

On November 15th the Egyptian delegation presented their final reply to the proposals that had been made to them and as it was plain that there was no hope of an agreement they returned to Egypt.

December 6th. A long telegram from Allenby today suggesting that we should at once put into force the terms of the treaty which Egypt rejected, i.e. abolish the protectorate, grant them control of foreign affairs etc. It seems to me a foolish suggestion. Why give for nothing whatever in return all that the Cabinet were persuaded with great difficulty to offer in the hope of settling the Egyptian question. We have put up a minute to this effect.

My first reaction to this proposal was not unnatural. Others were to share it, but I soon changed my mind. Adly had now resigned. The failure of the negotiations had naturally reduced his prestige in the country and increased that of Zaghlul proportionately. The country was without a Government and the agitators were taking advantage of the situation to produce a state of anarchy. Shortly before Christmas Allenby boldly arrested Zaghlul and five of his followers and had them deported to the Seychelles. Disorders followed, but he was able to keep the situation in hand and we, at home, were surprised by the mildness of the resentment aroused.

January 13th, 1922. We were met this morning at the Foreign Office by a batch of telegrams from Allenby. Sarwat is prepared to form a Government and can do so on certain conditions which Allenby wishes to offer him and for which he wants H.M.G.'s approval. The situation looks really hopeful and a possible solution of the Egyptian question seems in sight. It is unlucky that Curzon should be at Cannes at this moment. Briand resigned yesterday—a blow to the Entente. The Cannes conference is over.

January 18th. There was a Cabinet on Egypt today when they failed miserably to come to any conclusion, and they have merely telegraphed to Allenby to send someone home—Amos and Clayton are suggested—to give them further information Lindsay thinks this won't matter, and that the whole thing will remain in cold storage for the time being. Murray thinks it will be disastrous, and that the delay will destroy the possibility of Sarwat forming a Ministry.

January 21st. A reply from Allenby—unless his advice is accepted he will resign. He refuses to send home Amos and Clayton but suggests that the Cabinet should hear Selby, who will be back tomorrow. Allenby knows that Curzon is supporting him. The question is, will Curzon, if Allenby's resignation is accepted, resign too? He clearly should. Or on the other hand will Winston and the Cabinet give way? I believe they will. Murray doesn't. Curzon is to see the Prime Minister this morning.

I went to Buck's for lunch, where I met Edwin for a moment and informed him of Allenby's threatened resignation. He was much interested. He said that he himself hadn't supported Curzon because he thought we were giving away everything and gaining nothing.

I went back to the office and spent the afternoon jawing with Murray about the situation. Curzon ought to resign if his advice is rejected. Will he?

January 22nd, Sunday. A thick fog. We lunched with the Laverys. We went there in the tube and could hardly grope our way from the station to their house. Hazel had had Winston and Michael Collins to dinner the night before and was very full of them and of their delight with themselves at having come to an agreement with Craig.

I had to go to the Foreign Office in the afternoon to get out some papers which the Prime Minister wanted, and then I had to go to Victoria to meet Selby, as he may have to appear before the Cabinet tomorrow and nobody knows his address. I missed him in the crowd and fog, so I accosted another with Cairo-labelled luggage and asked him if he knew Selby. By great luck he did and knew that he had been on the train and thought he was staying at the station hotel. I then tried the Grosvenor, where I found him. He insisted on telling me all the woes of Egypt at once. He feels very strongly. Is prepared to resign himself if Allenby does. . . . He showed me a telegram he had got from Allenby at Marseilles saying all the advisers would resign too.

January 23rd. Edwin lunched with Diana and me and we discussed the Egyptian question the whole time, Edwin's great point being that if you give away the protectorate without getting a treaty in return you have no legal justification for remaining in Egypt at all. He went to see Curzon after lunch, who no doubt intended to appeal for his help. The Cabinet met at five. They decided that a Cabinet Committee should on the following day endeavour to draw up a draft which should provide an acceptable compromise.

January 24th. The Cabinet Committee produced a telegram to Allenby asking him not to resign and offering to ask Parliament to say that when agreement has been reached on certain other points the protectorate should be abolished. This is quite useless. It amounts to saying that if a treaty is ever arrived at we promise to carry out our side of it.

January 26th. There was a Cabinet on Egypt this evening consequent on a further telegram from Allenby asking to have his resignation submitted to the King. I saw Edwin in the evening. Apparently when he lunched with us the other day he was really in agreement with me about Egypt and only took the other side in order to fortify himself with my arguments. He went straight to Curzon and said he was prepared to back him, but found that he was already climbing down and had drafted a telegram to Cairo which was subsequently sent.

January 28th. We have sent a very insulting telegram to Allenby, refusing to accept his resignation and telling him to come home. He has been ill-treated. We had a busy afternoon at the office preparing a Blue Book.

January 30th. Diana in bed in the evening with a tickle in her throat. I dined in her room. Edwin came in after dinner full of wrath against Winston for a speech he had made about the Indians in Kenya. Edwin is full of the wickedness of the Government.

February 2nd. Diana's cold bad again. She went to bed in the evening instead of coming to dinner with Goonie. I went. Edwin and Winston were there and the Ned Grosvenors. Winston said at the beginning of dinner that we mustn't discuss Egypt or Kenya, and we didn't. It was really a very pleasant evening.

February 3rd. Allenby left Cairo today and appears to have had a great send-off from all parties and nationalities. Northcliffe has been staying with him and has obviously espoused his cause, seeing in it, no doubt, a good weapon with which to attack the Government. *Tant mieux.*

The day that Lord Allenby left Egypt I left the Egyptian Department, so that I played no part, not even from behind the scenes, in the last act of this drama. I was not present when the Field-Marshal arrived, flanked by his two advisers, Sir Gilbert Clayton and Sir Sheldon Amos, armed with the despatch which was his answer to the insulting telegram, and determined not to argue, but to get his way or to resign. That despatch was such a shattering document that Lord Curzon was afraid to circulate it to his colleagues, but was obliged to give way when Allenby insisted on its circulation.

At the interview which took place between them Curzon soon discovered that Allenby could be neither cajoled nor bullied out of his determination, and the task was therefore transferred to the Prime Minister. It was a quarter of a century later, when I read Lord

Wavell's life of Allenby, that I first learnt what took place at that interview.

Allenby was accompanied by his advisers and stuck to his policy of refusing to argue, but Amos, provoked by a remark of the Prime Minister's, felt impelled to protest, and an argument was beginning when Allenby checked it, saying that it was useless to dispute. "I have told you what I think is necessary. You won't have it, and it is none of my business to force you to. I have waited five weeks for a decision, and I can't wait any longer. I shall tell Lady Allenby to come home." Lloyd George knew that he was beaten. How could he, a Liberal Prime Minister, go down to the House of Commons and explain that he was less liberal-minded than the stern soldier whom he had sent out to govern Egypt? He knew also how to accept defeat. Gently laying his hand on the Field-Marshal's arm he said, "You have waited five weeks, Lord Allenby, wait five more minutes"—and he went on to explain that he would accept the entire scheme with a few minor amendments. These proved, on examination by the advisers, to be of a purely drafting character, designed doubtless to save the faces of those who had denounced the scheme as unacceptable.

Although I knew nothing of what had taken place at these interviews I was of course well aware that the Government had given in and that Lord Allenby's proposals had been accepted. It was therefore with some astonishment that I heard Austen Chamberlain assure the House of Commons a month later that it was Lord Allenby who had surrendered, and who when the Government's views had been explained to him "face to face" had gladly accepted them. The days of Lloyd George's ascendancy and those of his discredited Coalition were numbered. To such subterfuges were he and his colleagues reduced in order to maintain the tottering fabric.

CHAPTER SEVEN

PRIVATE SECRETARY

1922–1924

ALTHOUGH I was sorry to leave the Egyptian Department at such a dramatic moment in the history of Egypt, I was very pleased with my new post, which was that of Private Secretary to the Parliamentary Under-Secretary of State. I had never ceased to cherish the hope of sometime becoming a Member of Parliament. As the years passed the hope grew. On November 30th, 1922, I wrote in my diary:

All these days our minds, Diana's and mine, have been absorbingly occupied with one subject, which we call "the plan." Briefly it is that we should go to America in order that she may in a few years make a large fortune on the films. It involves my giving up the Foreign Office. The idea is that when we come back I should stand for Parliament. To many it would appear that I had decided to give up working and live on my wife. I should therefore have to work very hard and endeavour to write my book about Talleyrand. It is the only way in which I can get into Parliament, the only way in which either of us can ever travel, which we both long to do. I feel sure it is right, though I naturally hesitate to give up a profession at which I have worked for nearly ten years and which I like. It will be a great adventure and infinitely better than sinking into a secure rut.

Lack of money had been one of our difficulties from the beginning and we had striven energetically to cope with it. Even before we were married, Lord Beaverbrook had kindly commissioned six well-paid articles for his new journalistic venture, the *Sunday Express*. We worked at the articles together and they appeared under Diana's name. They were sufficiently successful to be followed by orders from the *Express* and other papers, sometimes to report public events, sometimes to contribute to a discussion that was occupying the mind of newspaper readers. Shortly after marriage Diana accepted the nominal editorship of a new monthly called *Femina*. Her work was limited to a lengthy leading article for each number. The magazine was short-lived.

More important than these essays in journalism were two films in which Diana performed and which occupied a great deal of her time while I was dealing with Adly and Zaghlul. They were among the first of the coloured films. They were produced in England with an English cast and they were both historical. The first dealt with the reign of Charles II and included the Plague and the Fire of London. The second was of the days of Elizabeth I, and Diana was most inappropriately cast for the rôle of the Queen. I have never cared for historical films, perhaps because I know a little history, but I thought these two were quite good of their kind and found the colour surprisingly satisfactory. They were not great successes, but no doubt those interested in the trade received information that Diana could act, and this produced results later.

One of the reasons why I was pleased with my new post was that as a Private Secretary I received an additional £150 a year—not a large sum, but it counted in those days. But far more important to me was the fact that I was now in close contact with the House of Commons. As the Secretary of State, Lord Curzon, was in the House of Lords, all the House of Commons work fell upon the Under-Secretary, whose Private Secretary had to be present in the seats reserved for Civil Servants "under the gallery" at question time, and at every debate when foreign affairs could come under discussion. Here for a young man who aspired to a political career was a wonderful opportunity of studying the procedure, the methods and the moods of the House of Commons.

During the two years that I held this post I served three masters, a Liberal, a Conservative and a Labour member. I am glad to think that I got on very well with all three, and have equally pleasant memories of each of them.

Of these, Cecil Harmsworth was the first. He had sat as a Liberal member throughout his parliamentary career and had doubtless owed his latest advancement to the friendship between his brother, Lord Northcliffe, and the Prime Minister. But Lloyd George's friendships were not always lasting, and the friends of yesterday sometimes became the bitter enemies of tomorrow. His relations with Northcliffe gave an example of this love turning to hatred, and support to violent opposition. The position of poor Cecil Harmsworth between these "mighty opposites" was most unenviable. He was a kind of love-token, an evidence of former affection, a pledge which had been neither reclaimed nor rejected. I wrote in my diary on May 10th:

I found a note from Mr. Harmsworth saying he hoped to be back on Monday and adding that Wickham Steed, Northcliffe and *The Times* were making his position *vis-à-vis* the Prime Minister intolerable, and that he was very depressed about it. I hope he won't resign.

I had no reason to desire a change of masters. He was kind and considerate, making the minimum demand on the services of his secretary. Not only would he never ask me to help in anything that was not part of his Foreign Office duties, but he would never dictate to the typist, with whom the Foreign Office provided him, any letter to a constituent or one that concerned his private affairs. Nor would he allow such a letter to be written on Foreign Office stationery. He had his own private secretary, who came daily from his home to attend to such matters. Few Ministers maintain so high a standard of integrity. I cannot claim that I later maintained it myself.

A political event which occurred soon after I had taken over my new post was the resignation of my friend Edwin Montagu. He had authorised a statement in the press, without consulting the Cabinet, that in the view of the Government of India it was essential, on account of Moslem feeling, that certain territories, including Constantinople, Thrace and Smyrna, should be restored to Turkey. On the afternoon of the day in which this announcement appeared, Austen Chamberlain, then Leader of the House, stated that the Secretary of State for India had resigned, a statement which was received with vociferous cheers by the Tory Party. I wrote, "What possessed Edwin to do it nobody can explain. Whether it was because he knew he would have to go anyhow and thought this a good way of doing it, or whether it was a pure loss of head, or whether a mixture of both, I can't say." Despite his personal charm he was not a popular member, and it looked at that time as though the Coalition had thrown him to the pack of Conservative wolves who were already thirsting for their blood. If so the sacrifice only served, as such sacrifices usually do, to secure a temporary respite. The incident gave proof of the greater importance of personalities than of principles in politics, for here were the Conservatives, traditionally pro-Turk and pro-Moslem, rejoicing at the overthrow of one who was fighting for that cause against the traditionally Liberal pro-Greek policy which was known to have the support of the Prime Minister.

On the ground that questions of foreign affairs were involved I contrived to be present in the House of Commons when he delivered his speech of resignation, the first of many such occasions that I have attended. I thought that he should have devoted himself more to public policy than to private conduct. He sought to justify his authorisation of publication without Cabinet approval, which was unjustifiable. He should rather have argued that his policy was right, as it proved to be, and that, faced by the refusal of his colleagues to accept it, he had sought to force their hands by publication. It would have been a bold attitude and would have facilitated his return, but he was not one who loved bold attitudes and there was to be for him, alas, no return.

How right Edwin Montagu's estimate of the situation had been was shown by the events in the Near East which followed. The victories of Mustapha Kemal restored to Turkey all the territories which he had thought should be ceded to her, and six of the leading politicians of Greece, all former Prime Ministers, who had been led to believe they could rely upon British support in withstanding Turkish claims, had to face a firing squad. In the course of these events Great Britain found herself on the verge of war with Turkey, and it was even rumoured that there were Ministers who favoured war as the best means of prolonging the life of the Coalition. It was generally believed in the Foreign Office that Curzon was not in the inner ring of Ministers at this time and that important decisions were taken without consulting him, as the Prime Minister had, from experience, formed the opinion that in no circumstances would he offer his resignation.

When I returned from my summer holiday in Venice the crisis was at its height.

September 19th. Mr. Harmsworth returned unexpectedly this afternoon on account of the war scare and because Curzon has gone to Paris. I can't believe that we shall be involved in any fighting.

September 20th. Curzon's first conversation with Poincaré today was fairly satisfactory. They have agreed on the necessity of a conference.

Meanwhile instructions have been sent to the Naval Commander-in-Chief in the Mediterranean to take any action that may be necessary to prevent Kemal's forces crossing the straits. This might lead to an incident like Navarino or Copenhagen.

September 22nd. Reports from Constantinople say that Kemal is determined to advance on Constantinople and Chanak. This will mean war. There is an amusing telegram from Curzon this morning recounting interviews with the Serbians and Roumanians in Paris and the stupid obstinacy of Pasitch. Curzon is a master of the art of modestly giving himself the *beau rôle* in conversations. The Second Battalion of Grenadiers and one battalion of Coldstream are going out.

September 24th. Curzon has agreed with Poincaré and Sforza on the terms of the invitation to be addressed to Kemal. It did not look as though he would be able to do so and it is a great triumph for him that he has succeeded. It looks now as though all will be well. I think we have been very rash and are lucky to have got so well out of it. I disagree with most people in that I think the French were right to withdraw from Chanak. The troops there were serving no practical purpose and were a provocation to Kemal's victorious army, especially after our bellicose declaration of September 16th (which Lord Curzon did not see before it was published). Had Kemal attacked and annihilated them, which it appears he might easily have done, we should have been irrevocably committed to a long, costly and unnecessary war. I think England and Lloyd George have lost prestige while France and Curzon have gained it. There was an extraordinary scene at the interview on Friday when Poincaré lost all control and stormed at Curzon to such an extent that he left the room in protest. Poincaré had to come out after him and apologise to get him back.

During these days there had appeared in some newspaper column devoted to what is called society gossip a statement that Diana and I were purchasing a palace in Venice for our use during the summer months. The result was:

October 9th. In the afternoon Bland sent for me and said that Curzon's first action on returning in glory from Paris and settling the fate of nations was to ring up Crowe and say he thought I was having too much leave. I told Bland what leave I had had and by slightly diminishing the Easter and Whitsun episodes proved that I had had less than my due. I also told him that I was proposing to go away that day for three days shooting at Belvoir. Crowe then sent a minute in to Curzon, saying what leave I had had, that he understood I was intending to go away for three days and he saw no reason for preventing me.

I accordingly went, and on my return I wrote:

October 13th. This morning Bland showed me Curzon's minute on the statement Crowe sent him about my leave. "It is not so much his ordinary leave to which I object as his ability while performing his duties to enjoy an amount of social relaxation unclaimed by his fellow workers." Such utterly meaningless drivel I never read. I said so and Bland agreed. He told me that Crowe's comment had been that this was just the kind of incident which made it impossible to have any respect for the Secretary of State.

Cecil Harmsworth's reaction was even stronger. He was, after all, my master, and the amount of leave I had was primarily his concern. When the House was not sitting and he was away there was very little for his Private Secretary to do.

October 16th. I told Harmsworth of my incident with Lord Curzon. He was outraged, said it was infernal cheek on Curzon's part, swore he would "put it right." I don't know what he will do.

He had not time to do much, for three days later:

October 19th. This is a day of great events. Chamberlain was defeated at the Carlton Club in the morning. The Prime Minister resigned in the afternoon. As I write this I am awaiting the return of Harmsworth, who has gone over to No. 10. . . . He found the Prime Minister extremely cheerful but wondering what he was going to say at Leeds on Saturday.

A few days later Harmsworth took his leave of the Secretary of State.

He said after seeing Curzon that he thought he had "put my matter all right," that he had "spoken very strongly" and that Curzon had been extremely nice.

Some time before he had told me that he did not intend to stand for Parliament again. He had been much affected by the death, following a mental breakdown, of Lord Northcliffe, which had occurred in August. He told me that he thought it was a warning that men of his family should not work too hard after a certain age. I was gently amused, for I doubted whether excessive devotion to hard work had ever been Cecil Harmsworth's failing, and a man less like his dynamic brother could hardly be imagined. He was born to lead the quiet life of a country gentleman, to contribute letters to the *Field* and to write, as he did, a delightful brochure on fly-fishing. Owing to his wise decision not to strain his mental faculties unduly I am glad to say that he lived for another twenty-six years.

Bonar Law became Prime Minister, Curzon remained Foreign

Secretary and after a short delay Ronald McNeill was appointed Under-Secretary and became my second master. He was an Ulsterman, an intimate friend of Edward Carson and of H. A. Gwynne, the editor of the *Morning Post*. He was a strong Tory and one who many years before had thrown a book at Winston Churchill across the floor of the House of Commons. They later became firm friends and served together as Chancellor of the Exchequer and Financial Secretary to the Treasury respectively, a very strong partnership.

I did not meet my new chief for some time, as the Government, having no independent majority, had to appeal immediately to the country and McNeill had already gone to his constituency, Canterbury, where he remained until after the election. In the course of this contest I committed a grave imprudence.

November 9th. Motored down to Bethnal Green to a political meeting. On the way down Scatters [Sir MathewWilson, the sitting member] asked me to speak. I have of course no right to do so, but there seemed little chance of its ever being heard of, so I said I would. It was a very noisy meeting, full of Communists, who hardly allowed one to get a hearing, but I managed to speak for some time, a thing I haven't done since I left Oxford, and I thoroughly enjoyed it.

Civil Servants are rightly forbidden to take any part in party politics and it was therefore a foolish risk to take, for had it been discovered I should have got into serious trouble. It shows how strongly at that time I felt the desire for public life. I am sorry to say that my candidate lost his seat, though I cannot think that my speech contributed to his defeat.

I soon established very friendly relations with Ronald McNeill, whose only fault I found to be an extraordinary reluctance to go out to luncheon. He was not a young man, it was his first ministerial post and he was determined to work hard at it. He therefore developed what I considered a detestable habit of bringing sandwiches to the office and remaining there until he went to the House of Commons.

I was compelled therefore occasionally to suit my habits to his, although it went against my principles. I had been much impressed by a remark once made to me by an older official in the Foreign Office whom I had seen one afternoon looking dejected. I asked him if anything were wrong and he replied that there was something very wrong—he had had a bad luncheon. When I seemed prepared to make light of his misfortune, he said, "Remember, the number of luncheons we are going to have is limited. Therefore it is a sad thing to have a bad one." I have done my best to avoid falling into that error ever since.

The job that I now had was certainly one of the more agreeable in the Foreign Office. Unlike most Civil Service employment it was not monotonous. When the House was sitting it was extremely strenuous, when the House was up the amount of work depended on the activities of the master, who, however energetic he might be, was forced to spend a good deal of time in his constituency, where he passed out of the ken of his Foreign Office Private Secretary.

Parliamentary questions were the bane of the Private Secretary's life. They had to be printed and circulated forty-eight hours before they were to be answered, but the period was all too short to follow them through the labyrinths they were bound to traverse. From the Central Registry the question was sent to the department concerned, who very often attempted to pass it on to another branch. When it was settled who was to answer, some research was probably required and it had to pass through the three rooms of the department before being sent on to the Under-Secretary, who duly sent it on to the Permanent Under-Secretary. From him it came to the Parliamentary Under-Secretary, my master, who, having approved or altered the answer, sent it on to the Secretary of State. Often questions would fall by the wayside, get lost among the pile of papers on somebody's desk, and then it would be my duty to hunt them, following them from one covert to another. I knew that if I could get them to Lord Curzon before midnight, or later, they would be back on my desk the following morning with his final decision. He was a late worker and I should think never left a paper on his table at night that he had not read. But on the following morning the approach was less easy, and although House of Commons questions had a very high priority, the difficulty of getting any paper to his lordship's notice before luncheon cost me many anxious hours. It was not that he rose late or was ever unwilling to attend to business, but that his mornings were so filled with other claims on his attention with which his own secretaries hesitated to interfere.

The private notice question was another thorn in the side of the Private Secretary. Such a question could, with the Speaker's permission, be sent to the Minister on the morning of the day it had to be answered, and the inconvenience imposed by the cumbrous method of the Foreign Office in answering questions may be imagined. Even when the final form of the answer had been approved, the Private Secretary's responsibility was not at an end, for the Minister might in anticipation of supplementary questions require additional information at the last minute, and it was desirable that the Private Secretary should be present in the House to supply it. These labours, combined with attendance throughout debates on foreign affairs which might continue until late hours, rendered the Private Secretary's life extremely busy, but when the House rose on Friday afternoon his labours were at an end and unlike his master no importunate constituents claimed his attention.

March 6th. Debate on the Ruhr this afternoon. Curzon made a great fuss yesterday because nobody in the Office knew it was coming. There was no reason why they should, as the Prime Minister was dealing with it. Curzon, however, got one of the P.M.'s private secretaries to say he would like assistance from us, with the result that he was able to make the wretched department draw up a lot of memoranda which of course the P.M. never looked at. Curzon also wrote a rather rude letter to McNeill about it, full of caustic remarks about "your Private Secretary." It was a dull debate, over at 8.15.

May 15th. Diana has received an offer to go and play *The Miracle* in New York next winter.

This offer, upon which I made no comment at the time, was to have a great effect upon our future and to provide the answer to what we had called "the plan." Morris Gest, the American impresario who was responsible for the production of *The Miracle* and whose idea it had been that Diana should play the leading part, arrived later in the summer, and in the course of our holidays we went to Salzburg to stay with Max Reinhardt, in order that he might see her and satisfy himself that she was suitable.

Leopoldskron, where Reinhardt lived, was a beautiful house which had formerly, I believe, been the Archbishop's country residence. Reinhardt was a man of exquisite taste, and the decoration of the house was perfect, but I had the feeling that he himself did not belong there and that his attractive shyness showed that he knew it. Each room, admirably arranged, was too like a stage setting, and my feeling of being in the theatre was confirmed when at dinner a white-whiskered major-domo, worthy of an archbishop or an archduke, bore in a bottle wrapped in a napkin and containing, one supposed, either the best champagne or imperial tokay, and proceeded to pour out of it some indifferent beer which was the only liquor provided with a meagre repast.

But I liked Reinhardt, although I was ashamed to find that I had so far forgotten my German that I was unable to carry on an intelligent conversation with him. He became and remained a close friend of Diana's, and before we left Salzburg all arrangements were made for her to take part in the production of *The Miracle* in New York at the end of the year. The salary was to be such as would render my leaving the Foreign Office a more practicable proposition, provided the production was a success.

Earlier in the year, during the Whitsun recess, we had made a pilgrimage to Saint Sauveur in the Pyrenees, where I left Diana to do a cure and where she was joined after I had gone by our dear friend Katharine Asquith. As they passed through Lourdes on their return journey they both offered up a prayer, Diana that she might bear a child, Katharine that she might be converted to the Roman Catholic faith. In the fullness of time both prayers were granted.

It was while we were making this journey that Bonar Law resigned and was succeeded by Mr. Baldwin. The change did not affect me, as Lord Curzon, who had hoped for the Premiership, was left at the Foreign Office, and McNeill, who had feared that he might be promoted to the Ministry of Health, remained, to his own satisfaction, where he was.

In the autumn our plans for going to America became more definite and it was doubtless owing to my declining interest in my Foreign Office career that I formed the design, although my leave for the year was exhausted, of accompanying Diana on her journey and returning to England by the same ship. This meant an absence from duty of three weeks, but the proposal was rendered more acceptable by the imminence of a General Election which would keep McNeill away from the office for about the same period. He put no difficulties in the way and in due course we sailed for New York in the *Aquitania*. I enjoyed that voyage as I have enjoyed all subsequent crossings of the Atlantic. We knew nobody on board, but we were sufficient to ourselves and for both of us the journey was a novelty.

My first impressions of America were not very happy, for those were the days when life was rendered miserable for visiting Europeans by the disastrous experiment of Prohibition. It was worse for them than for Americans, the majority of whom are not accustomed to drink wine with their meals. Those who happened to have formed the habit had no doubt stocked their cellars before the blow fell. The well-organised speakeasies, which later formed a delightful alternative to observation of the law, were not yet developed. There were many restaurants where doubtful liquor could be had at high prices, but it was most unpleasant for a law-abiding foreigner, who felt that the law should be more binding on him as a guest of the country than it would be at home, to be obliged to get what he wanted by a wink and a nudge to the waiter, with whom he felt he was conniving in crime.

The calamitous results of Prohibition, which need not be here catalogued, should serve as a warning to all future legislatures never to pass a law which respectable citizens feel bound to break. From the President himself, from Judges of the Supreme Court downwards, there was nobody who was superior to the violation of the Eighteenth Amendment, although there were doubtless many lifelong total abstainers who had no difficulty in observing it and rejoiced at the suffering they were inflicting on their fellow-countrymen.

Let it not be thought, however, that the most hospitable people in the world allowed me to go short for a moment of anything they could supply. On the very afternoon of our arrival a gift of whisky was delivered at our hotel, the despatch and acceptance of which constituted in themselves breaches of the constitution, and on the following morning my old friend and brother officer Carroll Carstairs took me to his club, where he not only made me a member but also presented me with the key of his locker, well stocked with spirits, to which he begged me to help myself whenever I felt in need of refreshment.

After six days I sailed sadly home, sadly because it was the beginning of our first long separation. I arrived at the end of the second General Election of 1923, which had been caused by Mr. Baldwin's decision to demand a mandate for a policy of Protection. The result had been that the Conservatives had lost their independent majority, and while they remained the largest party in the House, it became possible for Labour with Liberal support to form a Government. Mr. Baldwin decided to meet Parliament in the New Year with a programme from which protective measures had been dropped, and to leave to the Liberal Party the decision as to who should govern. My own life was temporarily unaffected because the Conservatives of Canterbury had reaffirmed their confidence in Ronald McNeill. At the end of the year, however, I was promoted to the rank of First Secretary, and as such I was no longer eligible for the post I was holding. I spent Christmas with my mother in the south of France and I wrote in my diary on the 31st of December:

This has been a wonderfully happy year for me with an amount of leave and foreign travel rare in the life of a hard-working Civil Servant. I can hardly hope that the next one will be as good.

Mr. Asquith always held that the Liberals were wise to put Labour into office in 1924. The act of doing so dealt a death-blow to the Liberal Party, which few if any Liberals understood at the time, but which, even if they had, should not have deterred them from acting in the national interest. I did not then think they were doing so, but in the light of subsequent events I have changed my opinion.

It is easier to remember events than to recall emotions. During the period that immediately followed the first World War there was in Great Britain a widespread fear of revolution. Because the revolution never happened, all its aims having since been accomplished by constitutional methods, the fear of it has been forgotten. Great profits had been made out of the war, and many of those who had made them had succeeded in getting into the first post-war House of Commons, those "hard-faced men who had done well out of the war." There was a trade boom and there was a general feeling that the war had produced not poverty, as had been expected, but plenty; but that while it had enriched the few, there was no improvement in the condition of the many. The first General Election of 1923 had been a vote of censure on the defunct Coalition Government, the second was a rebuff to the Conservative Party. Although some Conservatives lost their seats to Liberals, the outstanding feature of this second election was the success of Labour, and for the first time it became apparent that to Labour had passed the great inheritance of the Whig and Liberal Parties.

If, in these circumstances, the two older parties had combined to deny the spoil to the victors, although they might quite legitimately have done so, not only would they have deeply embittered those whom they were depriving of their first chance to try their hands at the great task of government, but they would also have given to the electorate the impression that wealth and privilege had combined together to rob the working classes of an opportunity of winning their spurs. Many would have felt that the young party—and youth is always attractive—had not been given a fair deal. Nor can there be any doubt that the members of the Labour Party learnt many invaluable lessons during their first short period of office. Nothing can enlighten a theorist so quickly as the task of dealing with a practical problem; nothing can sober an agitator so completely as the weight of responsibility.

January 8th. I went to the Albert Hall to see what was called the Labour Victory Demonstration. It was a very tame show. It struck no note of revolution but rather of respectable middle-class nonconformity. They sang hymns between the speeches, which were all about God.

I ought to have been pleased, but I fear I was disappointed.

On January 15th took place the opening of Parliament. I was there until the House adjourned after the Prime Minister's speech at 7.30. Ramsay MacDonald spoke rather well, Lloyd George rather badly, Baldwin very badly. . . . This was the eve of Diana's first night and I got all the people where I was dining to send her a telegram. I had already sent her one myself. We went to the Embassy [the popular night-club of the time] where were a lot of friends. I got another telegram sent to Diana. I spent most of the following day in the House but left in time to dine with Goonie. She had Winston and Clemmie, the Spearses, Birrell, Juliet [Duff] and a young Australian journalist called Bracken. It was a very enjoyable evening. I had some heated argument with Winston [who had lost his seat at the first election of 1923 and had failed again at the second]. He is very anxious to prevent at all cost a Labour Government from coming into power.

January 21st. I had a long journey to London this morning, as a railway strike broke out last night. The train took three hours and a half. There was a great rush of work at the office and I didn't get my luncheon until three. I spent the rest of the day in the House watching the death-agonies of the Government. It was a very interesting scene. Baldwin spoke well and so did Hogg. The Liberals looked thoroughly ashamed of themselves.

January 22nd. In the afternoon I took a sad farewell of McNeill. I am truly sorry to lose him.

January 24th. I was rather late arriving at the office this morning and found that my new master, Arthur Ponsonby, had been there some time before me. Considering his detestable principles, he seems a decent enough fellow. He was in the Office twenty years ago and had a row with Sanderson, whose last words to him were, "If ever you want to get back you won't be able to." I lunched at Arlington Street with the Duke and Letty. I thought he seemed very old. Most of the afternoon was spent piloting Ponsonby round the office introducing him to people.

January 25th. Had a very busy day with Ponsonby. They wanted him to take Ingram as my successor. He inspected Ingram but didn't like him, thought he seemed too old, preferred Butler and insisted on having him. I don't know what's to become of me. Bland said at first that I was to take Ingram's place. I pointed out that that would be a queer kind of promotion, as it would amount to going back to what I was doing four years ago. He said that Murray is away, which is true, but he is coming back.

January 28th. I had three letters from Diana this morning with accounts of her first night. It seems to have been a wonderful success.

January 29th. For the first time I succeeded in arriving at the office before Ponsonby at a quarter to ten. I was kept very busy all day until seven. A telegram from C. B. Cochran this morning saying "Wife's performance exquisitely beautiful unquestionably work of sensitive artist with many individual subtleties the result of thought and complete mastery of rare resources."

It is interesting to watch the new administration grappling with the Foreign Office, but I am glad that I am giving up my private secretarial job. It is impossible to dislike Ponsonby, but the people that he sees and that are his friends and the views he holds are equally distasteful to me. The Prime Minister [who was also Foreign Secretary] makes a lot of use of him and practically employs him as a Private Secretary. They go through all papers together and in the Prime Minister's absence it is Ponsonby who decides everything. But already they are getting into difficulties with their own supporters, who are impatient for the recognition of Russia and cannot understand why there should be an hour's delay. This afternoon Ponsonby had to have an interview with a man who was organising a demonstration on the subject. He was persuaded to put it off. Already they say that the Daily Herald is "getting out of hand." Already they begin to adopt the official point of view.

The attitude of a Civil Servant towards party politicians should be "a plague on both your houses" and he should do his best to stifle any sympathy he feels with one side or the other. But not only did I then hold strong political opinions but I was contemplating plunging into the fray. When, therefore, owing to the importance of the part played by the new Under-Secretary for Foreign Affairs, which was very different from that of his two predecessors, I frequently saw highly confidential papers not closely connected with the work of the department, I had the uneasy feeling that I was having access to secrets that I had no business to know.

Ramsay MacDonald had indeed a hard task to perform. Neither he nor any of his Cabinet, with the exception of Lord Haldane, who accepted the Woolsack, had ever held office before and it was not unnatural that they should regard the Civil Service with suspicion. Some of his more ardent and impetuous supporters expected that important posts in the Civil Service would be awarded to Socialist sympathisers, and judging from the number of applications for jobs that Arthur Ponsonby received I can form an estimate of the number addressed to the Prime Minister. Among that multitude were some from former members of the Foreign Service who had been obliged to leave it for one reason or another and who now applied to have their cases reopened on the ground that they had been victimised for holding advanced political opinions.

I remember bringing Arthur Ponsonby a letter which he could see was very lengthy. "Does he want a job?" he groaned. "No," I said, "he expressly says he doesn't want one but that in the interests of the country he is willing to overcome his natural inclination and to accept anything that's going."

The firmness with which these appeals were resisted was altogether admirable. The right candidate cannot always be selected but I do not recall a case during his first or second administration when Ramsay MacDonald made a really bad appointment on account of political pressure.

Although I was glad to quit the post of Private Secretary I was sorry to leave Arthur Ponsonby, with whom I remained on the best of terms, even when we were sitting on opposite sides of the House of Commons. He never did himself justice in that assembly. Although his political opinions were very far to the left he remained an aristocrat. He hated bad manners. The crude interruptions to which all speakers are subjected in the House made him angry, while the views which he expressed, coming from one who had enjoyed his advantages, angered the Tories more than they would have from one of humbler origin, and the result was unfortunate. It was a strange irony of fate that led so sincere a Socialist into the House of Lords. His party were wise to send him there, where he proved as successful as he had proved unsuccessful in the Lower House. The atmosphere suited him, Their Lordships liked him, he was at home.

With Philip Snowden exactly the reverse occurred. To him the interruptions of his opponents while he was speaking were as the flick of the whip or the prick of the spur to a racehorse. They stirred him to further effort, they roused him to put forth all his powers. A master of taunts and jeers, he loved to goad his audience to fury and would smile with grim satisfaction when his thrusts went home. Faced by the calm complacency of the Upper House he was lost. When his cruellest quips, his most bitter sneers were received in silence, with perhaps the raising of a few eyebrows, he realised that he had met with a form of resistance against which he was powerless.

Outside the House of Commons Arthur Ponsonby had a keen sense of humour. He sat for the Brightside division of Sheffield, among the safest Labour seats in the country. He told me that he was one of three candidates for the seat who were invited to appear before the selection board. The other two were working-class men and he was therefore surprised that he was chosen. Afterwards he consulted a member of the board, who told him that his "college accent" had of course gone against him, but that they had had unfortunate experiences with working-class members, who when they returned from Westminster would say that the Tories weren't so bad after all, and even that some of them were very decent chaps. The Tories of course had made fools of them. "Now you," he said to Ponsonby, "have known those people all your life. They won't be able to make a fool of you." The incident delighted him, for he, of course, had many life-long friends who were Conservatives.

February 13th. I was told this evening that I was to become Head of the Communications Department. It is a damned-fool job but slack and easy, and one is one's own master, so I don't much mind. It makes me more than ever determined not to stay in the Foreign Office. Bland was very apologetic when he told me and said it would be only for a year.

The Communications Department was a wartime development. Before 1914 the whole work of cyphering and decyphering telegrams, typing and distributing them and when necessary writing paraphrases, was carried out by the three most junior clerks, of whom during my first six months in the office I had been one. These duties were now performed by two shifts of about a dozen workers each who were on duty for eight hours at a time, none of whom had ever to touch a typewriter, as they had a whole room of typists at their disposal. My job henceforth was simply to superintend their labours, to read through the telegrams they produced and to draw attention to errors, to adjudicate on their disputes when they arose and to grant them leave when they deserved it. I had a room to myself and was master of my own hours of arrival and departure.

The only problem that I can remember arising concerned a cypher-machine which a former member of the service had invented and wished to sell to His Majesty's Government. Nobody in the office felt qualified to give an opinion as to the usefulness of this machine, and it was still more difficult to assess its pecuniary value. For obvious reasons of security it was undesirable to submit these questions to extraneous enquiry and advice. The result was a series of lengthy minutes and puzzled conferences, and the problem remained unsolved when I quitted the service.

In March took place the by-election for the Abbey division of Westminster when Winston Churchill stood as a "Constitutionalist" against the official candidate of the Conservative Party. On the morning of March 20th the result was announced, and at a quarter to one I read on the Foreign Office tape "Mr. Churchill returned." I sent him an enthusiastic telegram of congratulations and went out to luncheon. When I came back the result had been reversed, there had been a recount and he was defeated by some fifty votes. I wrote to him apologising for my error and in the course of my letter I said that I hoped to serve under him when he became leader of the Conservative Party. Eighteen years later my hope was fulfilled.

In May I granted myself a month's leave and took advantage of it to travel to New York, where I spent a fortnight, and brought Diana home with me. The winter theatrical season was over and she was free until the play started again in the autumn. I enjoyed this second visit to America very much more than the first one. The spring weather was delightful and I made many new friends.

On my return, although I continued to perform, I hope conscientiously, my exiguous duties at the Foreign Office, my mind was elsewhere. Ronald McNeill had kindly recommended me to the Central Office of the Conservative Party and with their assistance I was busily engaged in hunting for a constituency.

July 12th. Today I burnt my boats and sent in my resignation. It seemed a terrible step, giving up a profession I had worked at for nearly eleven years, but I leave it without one pang of regret.

CHAPTER EIGHT

CANDIDATE

1924

ONE summer afternoon I travelled down to Stroud in Gloucestershire, where faith in the Conservative Party was reputed strong enough to survive any political vicissitude. The Member was not going to stand again and I was one of three between whom the local party authorities had to choose. I had imagined having to answer some searching questions about Bills then before the House of Commons, with the details of which I should be ill-acquainted, and I had even equipped myself with a few facts about agriculture, a great subject of which I was woefully ignorant. I was therefore relieved when the small party who received me, some six or seven ladies and gentlemen, only enquired concerning my health, my religion and the amount I was prepared to contribute to local expenses. When I say that they enquired concerning my religion I should make it plain that they wanted only to be assured that I was not a Roman Catholic. For the majority of English people there are only two religions, Roman Catholic, which is wrong, and the rest, which don't matter. I was able to give the required assurances concerning health and religion and I undertook to contribute £300 a year to the local association, which I hoped I should be able to do out of my parliamentary salary. They were very polite, and as I travelled back to London that evening I thought, with characteristic optimism, as I looked out of the carriage window, how well I should get to know that journey in the days to come. I did not have long to cherish the illusion, nor did I ever make the same journey again. Two days later I learnt that an older, possibly wiser and certainly much richer candidate had been selected.

It would have made a great difference to my life if I had become Member of Parliament for Stroud. There is no more beautiful part of England than the country that lies around it. We should certainly have bought a house there, and there we should probably be living to this day. I should not have lost my seat in 1929 and missed two years of the House of Commons, two precious years of opposition, nor should I have been able to avail myself of that interval to write a book. The literary side of my life would have suffered, the political side would have gained. What happened was probably for the best, but I sometimes miss that grey stone manor house in the Cotswolds.

My next and more successful venture was in a very different part of the country. The borough of Oldham is within half an hour of Manchester and forms part of that vast industrial district which covers the southern part of Lancashire. It is a cotton town and was enfranchised by the Reform Bill of 1832. William Cobbett was one of its first members and it was the first constituency of Winston Churchill. It returned two members to Parliament, and as such double-barrelled seats have now been abolished it may be well to explain the system under which they worked. Two members were elected by one electorate and each elector had two votes. If therefore in the days of three parties each party was represented by two candidates the strongest party would obviously win. But if two of the parties ran one candidate each while the third party ran two candidates, then the two single candidates, if there existed some measure of agreement between their parties, could count on support from two parties and had obviously a great advantage over the couple running in double harness with only one party behind them.

The members returned in 1923 were Labour and Liberal. Mr. Baldwin's programme of Protection had been ill-received in Lancashire, the traditional home of Free Trade. Labour had run only one candidate, both the other parties had run two, and the two Conservatives had been bottom of the poll. The successful Liberal, Sir Edward Grigg, was only a few hundred votes behind the Labour Member, who headed the list. Grigg was a powerful candidate. He had already distinguished himself in journalism, had served in the Grenadiers during the war and had acted as Private Secretary to the Prime Minister and as Military Secretary to the Prince of Wales. When I consulted him he told me that if the Conservative and Liberal parties ran one candidate each they would probably both get in. He would certainly advise the Liberals to do so but he could not promise that they would take his advice. He doubted whether they would, and he gave me little encouragement.

But time was passing. The Government was living on sufferance and there was talk of an early General Election. I had become a man of leisure with scanty means of self-support, while my wife was earning a large income. Having been rejected by Stroud I had no immediate alternative but Oldham, which the Central Office, who were willing to pay a large part of my election expenses, wanted me to accept. Having met the chairman of the association in London I consented to do so and I paid my first visit to the constituency on July 31st.

I arrived at Manchester at about half-past six, where I was met by Mr. Howcroft, the chairman of the Conservative Association, and Mr. Greenwood, the Member for Stockport. With them I drove to Oldham, to the house of the doctor with whom I was to stay the night. The household consisted of my host, his very aged wife and his daughter. Dinner at 7.15 was an ordeal. I was feeling none too well, as though only champagne could revive me, which the doctor's very sweet Graves was quite powerless to do. I further found it impossible to join in the conversation, so that they must have thought me very dull. At the meeting which followed, however, I acquitted myself adequately and was unanimously adopted as candidate. I felt a little nervous before speaking but was reassured by the sound of my own voice. Nothing could have been better calculated to make one nervous. They all assembled and started the meeting while I waited in another room. Then I was asked to step forward, and found myself in a small room where there were about thirty people seated round the wall. There was a table in the middle at which the chairman sat, and one chair at his side for me. There I sat while they all stared at me and the chairman talked about me; and then I had to get up and give them my views. This, however, I succeeded in doing to their satisfaction.

This was the beginning of my political career. As I read again this entry in my diary two comments occur to me in the light of later experience. I say that I was not feeling well. Many years afterwards I noticed that I never felt well before making an important speech, and it was by a process of deduction that I at last discovered that this malaise was a form of suppressed nervousness.

I say also that I was unable to join in the conversation. That inability was to prove a serious handicap. A talent for small talk with strangers should come high on the list of the gifts which the life of a politician in a democracy demands. I have never possessed it. Diana, on the other hand, is very soon at home in any company in which she finds herself, whether it be working women drinking tea in a mean street at Oldham or French Cabinet Ministers sipping champagne at the Quai d'Orsay. She once found herself next to the Bey of Tunis at dinner. He spoke no word of any European language. Before the meal was over they were communicating by drawing little pictures on their menus, and were laughing happily together.

I paid one more visit to Oldham in the following week and spoke to as many members of the association as cared to turn up at the Central Conservative Club. I thought that my second speech was better than the first and was glad to think that I was already making progress. It was probably because of the larger and more congenial audience. In the success or failure of any speech the audience plays a great part.

No longer obliged to count the days of my leave and distribute them carefully across the calendar, I now proceeded to enjoy my new-found freedom. Diana had to return to New York for the re-opening of *The Miracle* and I, having arranged to visit my constituency in October, had no reason for remaining in England and therefore accompanied her. I thus crossed the Atlantic for the fifth time within nine months.

We sailed in the *Berengaria*. The Prince of Wales was on board. He was travelling with the Mountbattens and was going to watch the Anglo-American polo matches. Dicky Mountbatten with his wonted energy persuaded us to form a tug-of-war team and to challenge the Americans. When it was objected that we were none of us either very heavy or very muscular, he assured us that it all depended upon learning to pull in the right way and that under his instruction we should prove invincible. After some practice we took on a team of the ship's crew, who certainly appeared much heavier and stronger than we were, but after a tough struggle we succeeded in defeating them. In our elation it never occurred to us that our opponents had probably received strict orders on no account to pull over the Prince of Wales's team. We learnt later that our victory had been witnessed by other eyes, that an agent of the enemy had watched it from a place of concealment and had spread alarm in the American camp by tales of our prowess. The result was that they hastily sought fresh recruits

and enlisted all the most powerful and heaviest Americans on board.
Nor when we met these giants in contest were their efforts restrained
by any respect for the person of the Heir Apparent. They pulled us
over so easily that they must have thought for a moment, as they
lay on their backs, that the rope had broken. And the second tug
was as humiliating as the first.

The defeat of the British in the international polo matches was almost as complete as the defeat of the royal team in the tug-of-war, but
it was a gay season in New York and on Long Island, and we enjoyed
the splendid parties which were given in the Prince's honour. At the
end of three weeks I returned alone and sorrowing to England to
keep the appointments I had made at Oldham for the beginning of
October.

On this and on all future visits to my constituency I stayed at the
Midland Hotel, Manchester, which became a second home to me
during my connection with Oldham. The first night that I returned
there after attending three meetings at Oldham the hour was late and
I wondered, in my ignorance, whether it would still be possible to
get some supper before going to bed. In reply to my anxious enquiry
I was told that if I wanted music and dancing there was the Trafford
gallery but that if I preferred quiet I could go to the French grill
room. On entering the latter I found it full of familiar faces and I was
soon sitting with George Grossmith, Dorothy Dickson and Cicely
Debenham, and on the following evening I entertained there Martin
Harvey and his wife, having in the afternoon seen *The Only Way* for
the last time, a quarter of a century after I saw it first.

The best plays and revues were always being tried out in Manchester, the best touring companies were often visiting it, the leading
politicians came there to make speeches, and it was surrounded by so
many constituencies that the Midland Hotel became the hub of an
active theatrical and political world. Supper there made a good end
to a tiring evening's work in the constituency.

There was little to do in Oldham during the day, for the whole
population was at work. Visits to cotton-mills and to cotton machinery factories filled up some of the time, and here again I discovered a failing in my political equipment that I have never been
able to overcome. Mechanics make no appeal to me and I have never

derived the slightest satisfaction from studying the process of manufacture. How often has my heart sunk at a cordial invitation to come and see over the works. Not only do factories fail to interest me but they embarrass me, for I feel that I should ask intelligent questions and I fear that if I try to do so I shall betray not only laughable ignorance but also inattention to something that has just been explained. If, however, I had to name my favourite form of factory I should certainly select a cotton-mill. It has many advantages. The noise is such as to preclude conversation, the temperature is warm, the smell is pleasant and the rosy faces of the girls whose complexion has benefited from the soft, damp air of Lancashire turn the drab factory precincts into a garden of flowers.

My evenings were mainly occupied in visiting the clubs. I learnt a great deal in Oldham. I had no idea before I went there that in every ward of a great industrial city there were working men's clubs devoted to each of the three political parties. There were eleven Conservative clubs in Oldham and each had to be visited at least once a year. It was possible to crowd three visits into an evening, but it was better to limit them to two. A visit entailed conversation, a glass or two and a speech. The chairman of the club would speak too, and others might, but seldom did, feel inclined to take part in the discussion. I usually found the speech easier than the conversation.

October 9th. I went down to Oldham by an early train and was taken by Shepherd, our agent, to Greenwood's cotton-mill. Greenwood met us there and showed us all over. A cotton-mill is much pleasanter than a machinery factory and I rather enjoyed seeing it. He motored me back to Manchester so that I caught the 12.26 and arrived in London about half-past four. There I was met with the news that Parliament was dissolved and that the General Election was to be on October 29th. This is at least ten days earlier than I ever expected, and leaves me very little time. I telegraphed at once to Diana urging her to sail the day after tomorrow in the *Homeric*. I then went to Buck's, which this evening had all the appearance of a political club. There were so many ex-Members and candidates and nobody talking of anything but the election. I was so glad to be in it and no longer an onlooker.

October 10th. I went down to the Central Office in the morning in order to get them to give me one of the leaders to come and speak for me. All was pandemonium there but very exciting. I only succeeded in getting my name put on a list which already seemed pretty long. I walked back to White's and taking my courage in my hands wrote to Lord Derby asking him to come and help me. I lunched with Sibbie at the Carlton Grill and after lunch I wrote also to Ronald McNeill and Philip Lloyd-Greame. I caught the five o'clock train to Wilton, where I found a telegram from Lord Derby saying he would come any day I liked, except one.

I shall never forget Lord Derby's kindness on this occasion. My only claim to his acquaintance was the hospitality he had already shown me at the Embassy in Paris. After this prompt reply it was arranged that he should speak at an afternoon meeting. There was no ex-Cabinet Minister in England whom the people of Oldham would have been more pleased to see. He told me to arrange a luncheon party at the Midland Hotel before the meeting and to invite my principal supporters. When the election was over I gladly paid my three-weeks' hotel bill without examining the details. Some time later I had a letter from Lord Derby saying he had been "horrified" to discover that I had paid for this luncheon; he had found out from the hotel what it had cost and enclosed a cheque for the amount. It was a shining example of how a great patrician can behave to somebody of no importance, and show not only generosity but thoughtfulness.

October 11th. Ned Grigg rang me up after dinner to say that he had, with great difficulty, persuaded his Liberals to run only one candidate. This is the best of news.

It was indeed, for although I hardly believed it at the time it made the result a certainty.

Diana returned at the end of the week and I went down to London to meet her. We had arranged before I left New York that she should be allowed to come in these circumstances. We returned to Oldham together for the final fortnight of the election. Many friends and relations came to help us. Maurice Baring, with his happy gift for making friends quickly, was invaluable as a canvasser, especially with the important Roman Catholic section of the community.

There are people who enjoy elections. I am not one of them. The combination of anxiety and tedium is very trying. The solitary subject of conversation, to which, however hard one may try to avoid it, one always returns, the good ideas which suddenly strike one's supporters, their hopes and fears and petty quarrels, the rumours of one's opponents' successes, the one thing that should have been done and has been forgotten, the great mistake that has been made and that it is too late to rectify, the vast accumulation of daily annoyances culminating in the evening's speeches, which are followed by sleepless nights of pondering over possibly unwise utterances, all these build up an atmosphere of nightmare through which the distant polling day shines with promise of deliverance. It came at last, and with it victory. I was at the head of the poll with a few hundred more votes than Grigg and a majority of 13,000 over Labour.

The votes were counted the same night, and the counting was followed by a great meeting to celebrate the victory. The next morning we left by car for Belvoir, stopping for luncheon at Haddon on the way. It was a beautiful autumn day—the 30th of October. The storm and stress of the election were over, a new life full of adventure lay ahead. I was a Member of Parliament; a long-cherished ambition was fulfilled. The House was not to meet for a month, so that no urgent duties beset me. I was going to shoot on the morrow in pleasant surroundings. How lovely the country looked as I drove through it with well-earned leisure in prospect and the sweet taste of success in the mouth.

CHAPTER NINE

MEMBER OF PARLIAMENT

1924–1926

THE House of Commons that was elected at the end of 1924 contained a larger Conservative majority than had been expected. The publication a few days before the election of a letter supposedly signed by Zinoviev, then one of the Communist leaders in Russia, later one of Stalin's countless victims, was supposed to have had a great effect on the result. I never thought so, nor did I make any reference to the letter in my campaign. The letter proved only that the Russians were engaged in Communist propaganda in Great Britain and that the Labour Government knew it. To me these facts were already so patent that it seemed everybody must be aware of them, and I saw no reason why they should influence anybody's vote.

There were other sufficient reasons for the Conservative majority. The country was tired of elections; this was the third within two years. The Labour Government had done nothing during their nine months of office to prove efficiency or to gain popularity. The Liberal Party, still divided, had increased rather than diminished their discredit by putting the Socialists rather than the numerically stronger Conservatives into power, and therefore shared some of the Government's unpopularity. The policy of Protection which had ruined their chances at the last election had been abandoned by the Conservative Party, to whom the electorate now turned as offering the best chance of the peace and quietness which everybody wanted.

The Liberal Party, as has been said, was still divided, but in the Conservative Party also there existed a certain lack of harmony among the leaders. Lloyd George's Coalition had been overthrown eighteen months earlier by a vote cast in the Carlton Club against a motion proposed by Austen Chamberlain, who was himself considered, together with Birkenhead and Winston Churchill, to be one of the Prime Minister's most stalwart lieutenants. The principal opponent of Austen Chamberlain on that occasion had been Stanley

Baldwin, who was now once more Prime Minister and in whose previous short-lived Government none of those three had served. Until the last election Winston Churchill had not stood for Parliament as a Conservative for just on a quarter of a century, and there was therefore some speculation in the party as to how the Prime Minister would deal with these distinguished men when he came to form his new Government.

Stanley Baldwin's decision was as wise as it was magnanimous. He did not receive them back into the fold on sufferance, nor offer them minor offices which it would have been beneath their dignity to accept. The Exchequer went to Winston Churchill, the Foreign Office to Austen Chamberlain and Lord Birkenhead became Secretary of State for India. Winston Churchill told me himself that he was surprised, and when the offer was made to him verbally he thought for a second that the Prime Minister was speaking of the Chancellorship of the Duchy of Lancaster.

I thought it might be to my advantage to attach myself to the Cabinet Minister whom I knew the best.

November 11th. We have been trying these days to get me the job of Parliamentary Private Secretary to Winston. Sidney [Herbert, who was himself Parliamentary Private Secretary to the Prime Minister] first proposed it. This morning Winston sent for me to the Treasury and we had a long conversation. He said he was very flattered at my wanting the job and that he was prepared to give it to me, but he strongly dissuaded me from taking it. He said that I ought to get on by making speeches and that having a job of that sort could only hinder me. The experience that it gave of government offices etc. was just the experience I already had. We left it open, but I am sure he is right.

He was indeed, and I took his advice. The House met early in December for a very short session before Christmas and was then to adjourn until the 10th of February. I made up my mind to make my maiden speech in the course of the debate on the Address, that is to say during the first few days of the session. Diana had been obliged to return to her work in America and my daily letters to her furnish the best record of my doings at this time.

Here is one of my first impressions, dated December 11th.

Have you ever been to the opening of Parliament? If not you mustn't miss it next time. The scene in the House of Lords is the most delightful thing in the world, the most like a fairy story. The King and Queen sitting on their thrones with their crowns on, the King reading the speech extremely well, the Prince of Wales on a smaller throne in the robes of the Garter, looking most like a fairy prince, his pink face and golden hair rising out of ermine, beautiful as an angel, the Peers looking like chessmen, F.E. looking very fine standing on the left of the throne carrying the sword of office, never moving a muscle—and best of all, saintly Bob Cecil wearing some wonderful robes and carrying something, standing on the right of the throne and looking incredibly wicked and scheming, like the evil counsellor in the fairy tale, or the bad uncle of a mediaeval king.

I had thought of speaking on December 10th and wrote:

All the afternoon I had to hang about in a fever of excitement and uncertainty. I went through the ordeal of standing up to catch the Speaker's eye and saw it hovering over me. I could have spoken in the dinner hour when the House was empty but I was strongly advised not to. Sidney was very kind to me and took me to dine at the St. Stephen's Club. When we came back the House was still empty and I finally decided not to speak. The Speaker has practically promised to put me on on Monday next, which in many ways will be a better day for me, as it will be especially devoted to the discussion of Egypt. I am glad now that I didn't speak. I think I can improve what I was going to say.

I spent the week-end at Hatfield. Lord Salisbury was one of those who had kindly come to speak for me at Oldham. I passed some hours in the library, which is one of the most agreeable rooms in that beautiful house, and which would prove, I thought, with its great traditions, an inspiring workroom for the preparation of a parliamentary speech. There I wrote out all that I was going to say and although, when I came to say it, I looked neither at the script nor at notes, I have no doubt that my speech was the better for the work I did there.

I returned to London on Monday December 15th, and on the following day I wrote:

All the afternoon I waited anxiously. Trevelyan spoke first, then Austen Chamberlain spoke for an hour and a half. I thought he would never stop. Then Ramsay MacDonald spoke. I had got a good place by then and towards the end of his speech I saw Curzon (Mary's husband, who is now a Whip) nodding at me from behind the Speaker's chair, so I realised that I was probably going to be put on next, and yet I could hardly believe it when I heard my name called. I felt really nervous and a thing happened to me which has never happened before: my mouth became perfectly dry. However, the sound of my own voice encouraged me and I gathered confidence. What was still more encouraging was that as I went on people kept dribbling in instead of dribbling out, as usually happens. It was a wonderfully fortunate moment to get put on, as Ministers and ex-Ministers hadn't left the House. Ramsay was one of the few who left while I was speaking. Lloyd George was there throughout and so was Baldwin. Austen came in after I had been going about five minutes and I heard him say to Baldwin as he sat down, "I hear he's very good." H. A. L. Fisher, who spoke after me, congratulated me on "a really brilliant and successful maiden speech, perfect in form and distinguished by liberality and generosity of spirit and by a width of outlook that the whole House has appreciated." Arthur Ponsonby spoke next and said it "was one of the most brilliant maiden speeches he had heard in the House." Lady Astor, who was sitting near me, said it was the best she had ever heard and asked for your address to telegraph to you. I hope she did. Sidney said he would too. I had a letter of congratulation from the Speaker, which I gather is rather an unusual honour—and also one from Winston and one from Archie Sinclair. All the evening people whom I didn't know were coming up to me and congratulating me, including members of the Labour Party, and finally Philip Sassoon asked me what I was doing for Christmas.

It was a great triumph. The press was kind to me next morning. *The Times* had a headline "A Maiden Speech" and even the Liberal *Daily News* was friendly. I had many letters of congratulation, including four pages in his own hand from Lord Curzon.

Lord President of the Council

> 1, *Carlton House Terrace,*
> *S.W.*1.
> *Dec.* 17, 1924.

Dear Duff Cooper,
        Will you allow me to be among those who congratulate you on your brilliant achievement in the House of Commons.

For a maiden speech to be pronounced good is or may be a concession to courtesy, for it to be universally described as brilliant is as rare as it is gratifying.

It adds to my pleasure that the success has been achieved by one who leaped straight from the F.O. to St. Stephen's and whose experience of Egyptian affairs was partially acquired in events in which I was a participator. I refer to our long and abortive conversations with Adly, Rushdi, Sidki and that genial but slippery crowd.

> Yours sincerely,
> CURZON.

Another letter of congratulation came from one whom I did not know by sight, a Labour member whose name I had heard because in the recent election he had defeated Mr. Asquith at Paisley.

House of Commons Library,
15th December 1924.

Dear Mr. Duff Cooper,

Will you allow another new member—and an opponent—to add his voice to the chorus of congratulation which has arisen on account of your speech today? I was told that the House listened only to the peculiar and irritating style, known as the House of Commons manner, which is made up of hesitation, eh-ahing and a crowd of clichés of the "venture to suggest", "make bold to say" sort. Now you have proved that what I was told is untrue. You were direct, fluent, a wee bit rhetorical at times, but above all things courageous, for much that you said was at complete variance from the opinions expressed by your friends in earlier speeches. Now, what was the result? Except for breaks for meals, I have sat in the House all the time since Parliament met. Yours is the first speech that has gripped the House. You perhaps didn't notice it, but no one went out, there was no conversation, no moving about.

It is a delight to see a man do a job well, and you were first rate. I am sure that your wife feels, as I know mine would have felt, rightly comforted by her husband's success.

My ordeal is yet to come!

Yours very truly,
E. Rosslyn Mitchell
Paisley.

Triumph is often corrected by grief. I spent that Christmas quietly with my mother at Cimiez. Our only excursion was a visit to the circus. She enjoyed it with the enthusiasm of a child, although she was over seventy. Within a fortnight she was dead. I loved her very dearly. It was a profound sorrow which I had to bear alone.

After the Christmas recess the House of Commons reassembled on the 10th of February. I became a member of a group of Conservatives who dined together about once a fortnight, when they would invite a Cabinet Minister to give an informal talk after dinner, which was followed by a general discussion. When no Cabinet Minister was available the members of the group would discuss some subject among themselves. Not only were they all of the same party but they were most of them friends apart from politics. Our much-loved chairman was Bertie Spender-Clay. I was pleased to be invited to join this group, which contained some who were already and many who became my friends. It was recruited rather on a social than on a political basis, and there was no intention that it should represent one trend of political thought within the party more than another. I think, however, it would be true to say that it leant rather towards the left than towards the right.

I have already mentioned the inclination that I felt at one time in the direction of the extreme right, or die-hard wing of the Tory Party. It had been due to my dislike of the Coalition, my disapproval of the Irish treaty and my belief that the Die-hards stood for principle rather than expediency. Oldham had taught me something and the House of Commons taught me more. In Oldham I had had a glimpse of the condition of the people and had realised that a man's head must be as wrong as his heart who denied the need of social reform. In the House of Commons I soon discovered that the Die-hards were not the stern, unbending Tories of my imagination, the descendants of those who had supported Pitt against Fox, Wellington against Grey, and Disraeli against Gladstone. They were mostly business men who had recently made fortunes, often by methods that did not invite close scrutiny. Some of their more ribald critics within the party would refer to them as "the forty thieves."

The question that was principally occupying the minds of the Conservative Party at the beginning of 1925 was the decision which would have to be taken with regard to the political levy. There were two views within the party with regard to it and there was uncertainty as to which would prevail.

Within the Trade Unions it was the custom to deduct from every member's subscription a certain percentage towards a fund which was employed for political purposes. In practice this meant that the sum so collected went straight into the coffers of the Labour Party. Although each man's contribution was small, the total, on account of the number of Trade Unionists in the country, was very large, and formed a most important item in the annual assets of the party.

Any Trade Unionist could prevent his money from being used for this purpose by writing to the authorities of his Union and saying that he objected. The commonly used words to denote such action were "to contract out." But when there is an effort to be made and a letter to be written, men, and especially working men, and still more especially English working men, are inclined to postpone action and, the amount of money being very small, in a great majority of cases action was never taken. There was no doubt therefore that the Labour

Party were receiving large sums of money from men who were not supporters of their movement, even from some who were definitely opposed to it.

The proposal for remedying this state of affairs was, upon the face of it, perfectly equitable. It was proposed that men should be required to write to say that they did want to contribute to the political fund rather than to write to say that they did not. No part of their contribution should be deducted for political purposes until they had given their written authority for its deduction. This was to be known as the system of "contracting in." Small as the difference appeared to be in principle, it was evident that in practice the effect would be considerable and the difference to the revenue of the Labour Party might be very large.

I have forgotten all the arguments that were used on either side at the time, but I remember that many Conservatives, of whom I was one, felt that the hour of victory was not the time to deal an additional blow to the defeated, and that there were better ways of celebrating our triumph than by piercing a hole in our opponents' money-bags.

The matter was brought to a head early in the new parliament by Mr. Macquisten, a Scottish lawyer, who was fortunate in the ballot for private members' bills and who announced his intention of bringing in a bill which would alter the system in the manner desired by the right wing of the Conservative Party. When I visited Oldham I found that feeling on the subject was very strongly in favour of Macquisten's bill, and letters I received on the subject were in the same sense. I am glad that I did not allow such pressure to alter my opinion.

February 24th. I dined in the House with a dozen other members who are all opposed to the political levy bill. Feeling on the subject is running quite high. Mr. Bardsley, who came up from Oldham today, is strongly in favour of it. We still don't know what line the Government will take. I should like to speak on the subject but I expect there will be tremendous competition.

February 25th. After Questions about twenty of us went on a deputation to the Prime Minister. Skelton stated our case, briefly and well. Clifton-Brown, Hudson, Colfox, Lloyd spoke. The Prime Minister replied that he regretted the division in the party, but there it was and it had to be faced. One side would have to be disappointed, and that was all he could say at present. Later some of us went to see Jackson and Blair at the Central Office, who confessed crudely that their object was to deplete the funds of the Labour Party.

February 26th. At five I attended a meeting of the League of Nations Committee at the House, at which Ramsay MacDonald was to have spoken but he didn't turn up. Fisher spoke instead and I spoke too, against the Geneva Protocol. My speech had a good deal of success I went on to a private members' committee where they were discussing the political levy bill—a large majority in favour of it. I dined in the House with the Compatriots Club. Ormsby-Gore addressed us on British East Africa.

February 27th. I went to the House in the morning—a private member's bill on workmen's compensation, introduced by a Labour member. I thought the opposition to it was feeble and asserted my independence by voting for it, although the Government was against it. I lunched with Frank Meyer at Buck's and dined with Malcolm Bullock before the Speaker's levée. He had a party of twelve. We had a good dinner and I went on with Edward [Stanley] to the levée. Winston talked to me there and urged me to speak next Friday. I should like to but I doubt whether I shall get the chance. I went on to Wimborne House to pick up Diana. I took a heavy fall there, tripping over my sword on the parquet, and hurt my hand.

A little later I wrote:

I find it impossible to keep my diary these days. I haven't a minute to spare. I have hardly time to deal with my correspondence in the morning, and the rest of the day I am in the House. I have had two disappointments this week. I hoped to speak on Thursday on the Geneva Protocol, but there was a row about Kirkwood, the whole Labour Party left the Chamber and Ramsay MacDonald never spoke. What I particularly wished to do was to show how all his criticisms of the Treaty of Mutual Assistance applied with equal force to the Geneva Protocol. [The Labour Government had rejected the Treaty and the Labour Opposition was now blaming us for rejecting the Protocol.] In the circumstances I didn't think it worth while speaking. On Friday I wanted to speak on the political levy but there were so many on our side that I never got in. The Prime Minister's speech had a wonderful effect on the House. It was vague and rather off the point, and although I liked it myself I was afraid it wouldn't impress other people. But it did; and completely silenced all those who were most vehement for the bill. I saw a member sitting near me with a carefully prepared speech on many sheets of paper, tearing it into little pieces and throwing them angrily on the floor.

Mr. Baldwin had come down on our side and no more was heard of the political levy until after the General Strike.

March 14th. Another week has gone by and I have had another disappointment in the House. I wanted to speak on Wednesday on a resolution of Trevelyan's about secret diplomacy. The Speaker promised to put me on if there was time, but there wasn't.

I have little doubt as to what I was going to say on the subject. Of all the agitations of our time that against secret diplomacy was the silliest. All negotiations, whether concerning the sale of a horse or a proposal of marriage, must be carried on confidentially. Secret commitments are another matter and in peacetime should be avoided, but so long as statesmen communicate through headlines in the daily press, which seems to be the meaning of open diplomacy, they are not likely to reach agreement about anything.

On Monday evening I dined in the House and went to a meeting of the 1900 Club, where Macquisten spoke on his political levy bill. The majority were bitter against the action taken by the Prime Minister. I spoke against the majority.

There are no further entries in the diary until April 24th.

I made my second speech in the House. I had a long wait from three till ten before I got in. The subject was the Geneva Protocol. The speech was a success. Several people said it was better than the first one. Winston, who hadn't heard me before, was most enthusiastic.

I took on at this time, in order to earn a little money, the task of supplying the *Saturday Review* with a weekly report on the House of Commons. I called it "The Comedy of Westminster," signed it "First Citizen" and successfully concealed my authorship from my colleagues. It had the salutary effect of compelling my attendance at important debates on subjects in which I had little interest. I kept this job for nearly three years until I was obliged to give it up on becoming a Minister. Reading some of these articles again I am not ashamed of them. Dr. Johnson in his parliamentary reports "took care that the Whig dogs should not have the best of it," and those that I wrote were plainly the work of a Tory, but allowance being made for political prejudice, they are seldom unjust and never ill-natured. It would be difficult to imagine more arid reading material than the thirty-year-old reports of debates that had little interest when they were fresh. I have therefore been pleasantly surprised on glancing through these forgotten articles to find my attention often held and a smile occasionally provoked.

On August 12th I explained my neglect of my diary as follows:

For three months I have written nothing in this book. I was so busy during the summer in London that I had no time to write: what with the House of Commons, my correspondence, visits to the constituency and other places to speak, in addition to writing a weekly article, I had hardly a moment to myself. During that time I read a paper on Egypt to the Institute of International Affairs, took part in a debate against Sir Alfred Mond at the Oxford Union on the subject of the Budget and in another with Rebecca West in London on the rights of women, spoke on the League of Nations at East Ham and at Grantham, addressed a congress of teachers at the Holborn Restaurant, went to a Conservative fête at Walsall, went twice to Oldham and spoke twice in the House, once on Widows' Pensions and once—only a few words—on the Oldham by-election.

It was certainly a full summer. The Oldham election had been rendered necessary by the appointment of my colleague Sir Edward Grigg to the post of Governor of Kenya. The Conservative Party decided not to contest the seat, which was therefore easily won by Mr. Wiggins, a local Liberal, who received Conservative support against Labour. Resentment was not unnaturally felt by the Socialists, who believed that in a three-cornered contest they would have won, but the Liberals would have been equally indignant if the Conservatives had tried to capture the seat of a Liberal on whom the Conservative Government had conferred a position of high responsibility.

The year 1925 was not eventful. Many people believed that the Treaty of Locarno was of importance, and Austen Chamberlain received the Order of the Garter in recognition of his services in concluding it. People believed that it had brought Germany back into the comity of nations and that it would serve as the basis of her future relations with France and England. But the Germans saw it merely as a step towards recovering the strength they needed to wage a war of revenge, and they broke its terms as soon as it suited them to do so. Their true intentions were made perfectly plain to the ex-Crown Prince of Germany at the time by Stresemann, who had signed the treaty on behalf of Germany.

Later, when I came to know Grandi while he was Italian

Ambassador in London and before we had driven Italy into the arms of Germany, he told me that during the Hague Conference he had seen a great deal of Stresemann and would often go back with him to his hotel after the day's work was over. Stresemann would always drink a bottle of champagne before going to bed, and in the course of one of their late conversations he said to Grandi with unusual solemnity: "I am an old man, and I am dying, but you are young and you will live to see the second Punic War." This was told to me long before the formation of the Axis or the advent of Hitler to power, and should be remembered by those who are inclined to attribute all the crimes of Germany to the Nazis.

In the autumn I suffered one of those disappointments which await all aspirants to political promotion. My former master, Ronald Mc-Neill, had returned to his post at the Foreign Office when the new Government was formed. He was now promoted to the Financial Secretaryship of the Treasury, and the Under-Secretaryship at the Foreign Office was therefore vacant. It was the *Manchester Guardian*, that great Liberal newspaper, that said I was obviously the man for the job, and was responsible for raising my hopes. It would in those days have been considered very swift advancement, but I was the only new member on the Conservative side who had made a mark. My speeches had been mainly concerned with foreign affairs and there was no other obvious candidate. There followed a long and to me very painful delay, before the appointment was made and I learnt through my friend Sidney Herbert that my name was being considered. I learnt also that my supporter was William Tyrrell, the Permanent Under-Secretary of State for Foreign Affairs, who was also a friend of the Prime Minister's and one whom he consulted on matters besides those connected with his department. The decision, however, when it was reached went against me. An elderly member of the party was selected for the post, in which he terminated a career of mediocrity.

Had the decision gone the other way it would have made a great difference to my future. I should have spent three and a half years at the Foreign Office before the next General Election in 1929, and I should presumably have gone back to it when the National Government was formed in 1931. To me in fact would have fallen the opportunity that fell to Anthony Eden. How I should have dealt with it I cannot say.

Readers of fiction prefer happy endings. It may be doubted whether the same is true of readers of history. Events that ended well are soon forgotten, but the great calamities have a mysterious attraction and are studied again and again.

The General Strike was an important event in British history, but when people are talking of the past it is seldom mentioned, and I am not aware that there exists any full historical account of it. Yet it continued for ten days, it divided the people into two camps, it threatened the survival of parliamentary government, and it brought the country nearer to revolution than it has ever been.

It was difficult then, and it is impossible now, to form an accurate estimate of the danger. The misfortunes we escape cannot be measured, nor can the margins by which we escape them.

I have already alluded to the unhappy domestic atmosphere that followed the first World War. Among the many evils that war breeds are contempt for law and readiness to adopt violent methods in order to obtain satisfaction. Genuine and justified discontent with social conditions provides a perilous reception area for a home-coming army of four million men who have been torn away from their peaceful occupations and compelled to accustom themselves to bloodshed and to face death. More than seven years had passed since the end of the war and they had no doubt had a settling and salutary effect on the minds of the population. But the menace remained.

In 1925 the Government had granted a large subsidy to the coal industry in order to enable the rate of wages then being paid to continue, while a Royal Commission enquired into conditions. This had been done to meet the threat of an immediate strike in the coalfields, which would have had the sympathy of the whole Trade Union movement. The Commission had now reported. The miners refused to accept its recommendations and demanded the continuance of the subsidy pending a settlement. Negotiations broke down and the Trades Union Congress called upon all the Trade Unionists in the country to show their solidarity with the miners by coming out on strike.

I had given up keeping a diary at this time but I began it again on the first day of the strike, a Monday morning, and went on with it until the end. Old men forget, and a few pages penned at the time have a higher value for the historian and, I hope, a livelier interest for the general reader than the most careful reconstruction of damaged hieroglyphs carelessly scattered in the recording vaults of the mind. I will therefore print what I wrote as it was written without altering a word.

Monday, May 3rd, 1926. This morning we drove up from Breccles, where we had been spending Saturday and Sunday. It had been a pleasant party—we left soon after nine. It was a very bright morning. We wondered whether we should have any difficulty in getting petrol but at Barton Mills they gave us as much as we wanted. We stopped in Epping Forest to lie in the sun and get warm. We arrived in London about one o'clock and went out to luncheon at the Embassy. It was not very full. After luncheon I drove down to the House of Commons. Questions went quickly and nothing of interest occurred until the Prime Minister came in, when the Conservatives stood up cheering and waving their order-papers. This seemed to irritate the Opposition, who felt obliged to do the same thing, rather aggressively, both for Thomas and Ramsay MacDonald. The latter had already been in once without any reception, so that the cheers were only for his second appearance. He said that he did not propose to vote against the address on the declaration of a state of emergency. But his party took no notice of this and all voted against it, he weakly voting with them.

The Prime Minister spoke for about an hour—an excellent speech which was well received. Thomas followed him and also spoke well and with moderation. He is a better orator than the Prime Minister. Lloyd George then delivered a miserable speech, blaming the Government for withdrawing the subsidy which he had originally blamed them for granting. He also attempted to distinguish between two different kinds of general strike, arguing that a strike to compel Parliament to legislate was obviously wrong and unconstitutional, but that a general strike over a mere wages dispute might be justifiable. As Winston pointed out afterwards, no such distinction exists and the present strike is in fact an attempt to compel Parliament to legislate, i.e. to prolong the subsidy which was the only way of averting the strike. I never heard Lloyd George worse—every fact, every figure, every date was wrong. Sir Robert Horne followed him and spoke well. Then Ramsay MacDonald, who looked ill and made a rather muddled speech but not a bad one. Winston replied for the Government. He spoke with great eloquence and great firmness. His speech sounded at times provocative, but having read it since I can find nothing in it to criticise. This was supposed to conclude the debate. But when he sat down Kenworthy got up. The House could hardly have emptied more rapidly if there had been a fire. Many members had been sitting there, as I had, for five solid hours. The dining-rooms filled up as rapidly as the House emptied and it was impossible for some time to get a table. The Whips wouldn't let us go out because they thought the debate might collapse at any minute, and then in the natural course of business we should have had to proceed with the Budget resolutions. It was not until past nine that Sidney and I found a table in the Strangers' dining-room. I strolled back into the House soon after ten. Saklatvala was speaking. He was less violent than usual. Headlam followed him and made a very sensible speech. My namesake Couper, who was sitting next to me, asked me whether I was going to speak. I said no, having never thought of doing so, but I then began to think of it, and when Headlam sat down I got up. The Speaker put on an incoherent Labour Member. When he had finished I got up again and was called. I spoke for only nine minutes. I tried to distinguish between the issues, i.e. the dispute in the coal trade and the general strike. There was only one other speaker after me, and the House rose at eleven. There was a huge crowd in the square outside—sightseers—but no sight to see. I went to the Café de Paris to pick up Diana, who had been dining with Ivor Wimborne. She was in very good spirits, having had her anxiety about her mother's health removed. We went home—waited for a little for Max to ring us up with the latest news—but as he didn't we went to bed.

Tuesday, May 4th. We received *The Times* newspaper this morning —only slightly smaller than usual. I stayed in until luncheon writing letters. Maurice came to lunch feeling ill and very depressed. Diana also was depressed and anxious. I drove down to the House in a taxi. There were as many as ever of these today and a few buses. Questions were got through quickly as there were hardly any order-papers, so that nobody except the asker of each question knew what was being asked. On the Budget resolutions Snowden explained that the Labour Party must vote against them but would not debate. Lloyd George said the same, so we then spent the afternoon trooping through the division lobbies. There were nine divisions. At half-past five there was a meeting of Conservative members in a committee room. The Prime Minister took the chair and Steel-Maitland made a speech on the facts of the situation and corrected various misstatements which Thomas and Ramsay MacDonald had made yesterday. The Prime Minister said that some members for industrial constituencies might be well advised to visit them but asked them not to do so without consulting the Whips, as it was important to keep a large majority in the House.

Subsequently we had a meeting of Lancashire and Cheshire members where everybody talked about themselves and no useful purpose was served. I walked home about seven o'clock. In Trafalgar Square I met Winston walking with Morrison-Bell. He looked young and carefree. I showed him the evening paper I had just bought—a single leaf, the size of a half-sheet of writing paper. Except that there were more motor-cars than usual about with more people in them, there was nothing unusual in the appearance of the streets.

Maurice came to dinner. He was much more cheerful than in the morning, because he has got a job—A.D.C. to Trenchard—and he had been working all the afternoon. But Diana was as unhappy as ever. She insisted on ringing up Clemmie Churchill after dinner in search of news. She learnt that the Government were issuing a newspaper from the offices of the *Morning Post*—and that Winston was at work at it then. Hilary [Belloc] came round later, in the highest possible spirits and cheered us all up.

Wednesday, May 5th. A wet morning and so dark that at midday it was impossible to see to read without electric light. The electric light was faint and yellow. I went to White's, where there were a lot of people discussing absurd rumours—one was that Winston had been assassinated. There were some half-dozen in full policemen's uniform. Buffles Milbanke very smart as a sergeant. I went on to Buck's, where everybody was asking what they could do. Tommy Bouch had been sent off yesterday to feed starving horses—but when he got to them couldn't persuade them to eat. Diana asked me this morning how soon we could with honour leave the country. I said not till the massacres begin. We lunched in Avenue Road with John and Kakoo [Diana's brother and sister-in-law]. John is a special constable and works every night from six to nine. Diana drove me down to the House and I got her a seat in the Speaker's Gallery. There were a lot of questions about the new newspaper, the *British Gazette*, which contained an attack on the Trade Unions. The debate was on the regulations which the Government is bringing into force. Joynson Hicks made a good quite moderate speech. Henderson followed. Later Hugh Cecil spoke and then Thomas, who said that the Government and the T.U.C. had reached an agreement on Sunday night and the latter were still trying to persuade the miners to accept it when the Government broke off negotiations on account of the strike in the *Daily Mail* offices. It seemed to me and to many in our Party that this statement was rather damaging to the Government's position. We had some heated arguments in the lobbies. I talked to Winston, who said that Thomas's statement, to which the Prime Minister had agreed, was untrue. Maurice, Hutchy, Diana and I all dined in the House and went back to the debate after dinner. On the adjournment the Prime Minister made a further statement which put rather a different light on the matter, but I still think the Government were over-hasty in breaking off negotiations. Thomas replied and made a poor show. He can't speak the truth. The House rose at 11.30. Hutchy drove back with us and sat talking for some time.

Thursday, May 6th. The weather still very cold. I went to Buck's before luncheon. The streets are much emptier today owing to the taxis having come out. We lunched at home. Alan and Viola came. We went down to the House afterwards. Diana went to the Ladies' Gallery. It was a dull and trying afternoon. The more violent of the Labour Members spoke and made such ridiculous and tiresome speeches that it made me feel physically ill to listen to them. At 8.30 I went to a meeting of the Westminster branch of the Primrose League in the Caxton Hall. I had thought there would be nobody there so had hardly bothered to prepare a speech. I found a very enthusiastic audience of about two hundred people—and I spoke for about half an hour quite well. I then went to the Eiffel Tower to get some dinner —joining there Diana, Maurice, Tommy [Bouch] and Ivor Churchill. Then I returned to the House. At eleven o'clock Simon made a most important and impressive speech, in which he condemned the strike uncompromisingly and laid especial stress upon its illegality. The Labour Party left the Chamber before he began, but all the Liberal Party were there with the exception of Lloyd George, and they were solidly behind him. That speech may prove the way to his supplanting Lloyd George as their leader. The latter has missed another chance.

Afterwards about a dozen or more of us went to Printing House Square, as last night they had great difficulty in sending *The Times* off; those who were engaged in doing so had a severe fight with the picket. We found drinks and sandwiches prepared for us in the board room, where we had a long wait. When the moment came and we sallied forth to fight we found there was practically no opposition at all. It was really a waste of time, but rather amusing. I walked all the way home and arrived at about three o'clock.

Friday, May 7th. The House met at eleven o'clock. Diana drove me down there, and we arrived shortly after eleven. A few little bills of minor importance were dealt with. I left shortly before one, seeing that there was going to be no division. I was sorry afterwards, as there was a heated discussion on the adjournment. I lunched with Diana at the Ambassador and spent the afternoon at a cinema. Diana and I went to a play called *The Ringer* in the evening which we enjoyed. Afterwards we drove people home to Dalston and Hackney—and other foot-passengers back to the Tottenham Court Road. We finally had a little supper at the Eiffel Tower —Clifford Sharp was there and proudly presented us with a copy of the *New Statesman* almost up to pre-strike strength. It was full of lies but had an article by Hilary which made up for them. The news with regard to the strike is on the whole reassuring.

Saturday, May 8th. I have nothing to do. I passed the morning pleasantly enough in reading a French book called *La Mort et la Résurrection de M. de la Piverdière*—one of a series of famous crimes. I finished it in time for luncheon. Alan came to lunch. Afterwards we went to a cinema. I went to Buck's before dinner and played a game of bridge with Tommy, Eddie [Grant] and others. Eddie is a special constable. Everybody at Buck's is doing something. I only am idle. Tommy, Hilary and Maurice came to dinner. It was not a very successful evening. Hilary hates talking about the strike and nobody can talk of anything else. He holds such peculiar and impossible views about politics that to argue with him on that subject is like talking to a brilliant Hottentot. We made him read some of his own poetry to us before he left—and he read it most beautifully.

Sunday, May 9th. An uneventful day. Diana drove down to Binfield in the morning to see Iris [Tree] and distributed copies of the *Sunday Express* on her way. I lunched at White's. Lionel Tennyson was there, dressed as a ful' police inspector. Afterwards I joined Hilary, who was lunching at Buck's, where he and Maurice and I sat round the table till nearly five o'clock. Then I played some bridge at White's. We dined with Christabel McLaren—the Jowitts, the Holdens and Maurice were there. It was quite pleasant. We played bridge afterwards and I won £17. There was really no news today.

Monday, May 10th. I went to Buck's in the morning. Nobody had any news. They are all becoming special constables. Tom Trower was in the highest spirits, having become a whole-time constable and thus escaped from his office. John, Kakoo and the Duchess came to luncheon.

The Home Office vote was down for discussion in the House—and the debate beginning on the *British Gazette* and Special Constables wandered far and wide. I got up to speak once but I was glad afterwards that I hadn't. There were some violent and some mild speeches. It all fizzled out about eight o'clock.

Maurice, Hilary and Diana dined with me in the House. Afterwards we joined Venetia and went with her to the Eiffel Tower. She had been in a railway accident on her way from Breccles at Bishop's Stortford—one man was killed. She is staying with us.

Tuesday, May 11th. Venetia, Diana and I lunched at home. Ivor Wimborne came in afterwards in a high state of excitement. He had been with J. H. Thomas all the morning and with Lord Reading and he asserted that they were coming to terms with the Government. I don't know whether there can be anything in it. The House opened calmly. I went to the Library to write an article for the *Saturday Review* and strolling back into the Chamber about six o'clock found Simon delivering a very important speech. In the course of it he produced a formula for agreement. Opinion differed as to its value. Both sides are so suspicious. The House was adjourned at seven. I went to Buck's and then had to return to the House as I had promised to dine with Lady Astor, who has just discovered Will Rogers. We were a party of about twelve—all men, except her, in a private room, and Will Rogers was, I must say, most amusing. But he went on too long. Thence I went to pick up Diana at the Holdens' and she later drove me down to *The Times*, where I worked, counting papers, till nearly four. David Margesson was very optimistic. He had seen Ramsay MacDonald, who was angry at Simon's attempt to butt in—but otherwise hopeful. Diana came and worked at *The Times* office too—against my instructions. A very wet night.

Wednesday, May 12th. Ivor Wimborne telephoned early this morning and said that the T.U.C. had decided last night to call off the strike, and that they were going to Downing Street this morning to settle it. I confess that I didn't believe him. I went to the offices of the *Saturday Review* about twelve to give them my article and then strolled to Buck's. There

I saw on the tape that the T.U.C. leaders really were at Downing Street, and then while I was having a drink with Tom Trower the news came through that the strike was definitely off. The relief was tremendous. I never hoped for so sudden and so entirely satisfactory an end. I came home to lunch. Tommy Bouch, Venetia and Diana Westmorland were there. We were all in the highest spirits. Tommy drove me down to the House. The Prime Minister had a tremendous reception. He only said a few words—and Ramsay MacDonald said equally few. The rest of the afternoon was devoted to the Merchandise Marks Act, and the House rose at half-past eight. I came home and dined with Diana and Maurice and went early to bed.

Thursday, May 13th. This morning, thinking that all was over, Diana and Venetia left for Paris. When I went to Buck's, however, I found everybody in consternation. The triumph of yesterday had given way to panic. All the strikers were said to be still out and there were rumours of worse riots last night than on any previous one. The same feeling prevailed in the House of Commons. It was rumoured that employers were refusing to take people back except at reduced wages. More moderate Labour Members who were supposed to have been against the strike before were said to think that it was justified now. We were promised a statement by the Prime Minister at 6.30. The House at that hour was more crowded than ever. Ramsay MacDonald spoke first and was rather feeble but very moderate. The Prime Minister then delivered an admirable speech. He took the firmest possible stand against any attempt to reduce wages or to lengthen hours. Ever since the strike began until yesterday morning I have had a sensation of sick anxiety. This afternoon it returned, but the Prime Minister's speech dispelled it for good. Thomas followed with a few misrepresentations. He contrasted the Prime Minister's statement of yesterday about no victimisation with certain notices issued by the Admiralty and War Office, concealing the fact, until forced by a question to reveal it, that the notices had been issued several days before, while the strike was still on. Lloyd George made a short speech which for once was not mischievous, and the House broke up feeling that everything was once more well. I came home and dressed for dinner for the first time since the trouble began. I dined at Buck's with Sidney, who had to go off afterwards, as the Prime Minister was meeting the miners.

Friday, May 14th. I went to the House of Commons at eleven, when we discussed the financial resolution to the Electricity Bill. At four o'clock the Prime Minister made a statement to the effect that the railways had just arrived at an agreement, that negotiations with the dockers were going on satisfactorily, and that he had prepared proposals for settling the mines dispute which he was going to submit to both parties. Ramsay MacDonald and Lloyd George had nothing to say except to express the hope that Baldwin himself would take part in the negotiations between the mineowners and the miners. It was the final culminating scene in the greatest personal and public triumph that any Prime Minister has ever had.

When I came to write my weekly article I insisted that the dispute in the coal industry was no more the real issue during the General Strike than was the levy of ship-money the real issue during the Civil War. On each occasion the issue had been whether the country was to be governed by Parliament or not. I believed that many members of the Labour Party had understood this, and while I strongly condemned their conduct in leaving the House in a body rather than listen to the important speech of Sir John Simon, I was able to praise the rest of their behaviour.

Their trial [I wrote] has been a stern one. The size of the majority against them in the House of Commons has never been so evident as during these days when Conservatives have come down in full force. The knowledge that they are fighting a losing cause must have been constantly present to the wiser minds among them. The conduct of their opponents has not always been calculated to calm their passions. Their own leaders have to a large extent ceased to lead. In these circumstances they have shown forbearance, moderation and good temper. When official reports once more become available they will be found to contain little that anybody need regret. The more violent members of the Labour Party have taken refuge in silence; it is even reported that one of them, anxious not to be provocative but doubtful of his own powers of self-control, migrated to Glasgow in order to run no risk. However wrong their opinions may be, however heavy may be their responsibility for the great disaster, they have at any rate become during the crisis Parliament men and have behaved in a manner worthy of the traditions of Parliament.

There may be gleaned from this account some impression of what the effect of the General Strike might have been and of what it was. My own feelings during it were apprehension and distress. I could not regard a large section of my fellow-countrymen as enemies, however much I disagreed with their politics and disapproved of their actions. However certain I felt of the justice of my cause, I could not wish that those who supported the other should suffer for their opinions. The thought of revolution or civil war is so appalling as to render that of international war easily acceptable.

Events seemed to belie the graver fears that some had felt, but different events might have confirmed them. If, as has been asserted by Sir Osbert Sitwell, the Government had resolved, on the eve of the settlement, to arrest the Trade Union leaders, an explosion might easily have followed, which would have firmly united those whose support for the General Strike had been flaccid and failing, with the more violent section who may well have been under Communist influence. Happily no grave errors of judgment were made by either side, and the remarkable result was achieved of complete victory without vindictiveness on the one side or rancour on the other. The air was cleared, and from that day to this relations between capital and labour have been happier in Great Britain.

CHAPTER TEN

IN OFFICE

1926–1929

THE diary stops. Henceforward I shall have for many years no sure guide to steer me on my journey into the past. Engagement books which fix dates, letters which happen to have been kept, and the doubtful torch of memory which flames and flickers, are like the half-obliterated names on old signposts which greet the late traveller's anxious gaze when night is falling.

During the years 1926 and 1927 I was a very busy Member of Parliament. I was in demand as a public speaker, and I did not shirk the demands that were made upon me. During the year 1926 I spoke at seventeen political meetings outside my own constituency and in the following year at twenty-seven. These included by-elections and those melancholy occasions, party fêtes, which are held annually in the summer in order to arouse enthusiasm and to collect funds. If they are well organised, if the weather is fine and the fête a success, those who take part in it enjoy themselves and are most reluctant to leave the fun in order to listen to a political speech by the gentleman who has come down from London and whose name they have probably never heard. If on the other hand the whole thing has been ruined by rain, as not infrequently happens, the field has turned into a marsh, the side-shows are closed down for want of custom and the tea tent has run short of provisions, the welcome that awaits the un-known orator from a damp, disgruntled audience is apt to be chilly.

At the same time I was visiting Oldham regularly and speaking in the House of Commons, six times in 1926 and eleven times in 1927. I was continuing to write my weekly parliamentary article for the *Saturday Review* and, in the summer of 1927, I took on the task of writing a much longer weekly article for the *Graphic*. I was given a free hand in this article, which included comments on current events and on books that had recently appeared.

In addition to all these labours, a new and a self-imposed one began to occupy a great deal of my time. My attitude towards the League of Nations so long as I was a member of the Foreign Office, holding strongly Conservative views, had been one of sceptical benevolence, an attitude which I do not think I am unjust in saying was shared by the majority of the Civil Service. Nobody wished any ill to the League, but few believed it could do any good. Here was a new piece of nonsense, created by the politicians for their own purposes, primarily to placate the all-powerful but singularly impractical President Wilson, and secondarily to serve as a smoke-screen behind which the diplomatists, and especially the British Foreign Office, could conceal from the public the fact that they had no foreign policy at all. When pressed on the subject by inconvenient people who wanted to know, they could always make their retreat into a mist of platitudes about their firm belief in this great human experiment entirely devoted to the improvement of international relations and to the promotion of the peace, progress and welfare of mankind. I had shared the disdain with which the colder-blooded Civil Servants looked down upon this claptrap of the hustings.

The profession of politics, if it serves no other purpose, should at least teach an honest man to define his opinions. When I found that the League of Nations was a live issue my first instinct was to denounce it for the sham I believed it to be. Before doing so I felt bound to give some attention to the subject, and the result of my enquiries convinced me that either the League of Nations must triumph or there must be another war. So that, as in the case of St. Paul, the converted persecutor, only a potential persecutor in my case, became the apostle. I served on the executive committee of the League of Nations Union. I travelled all over the country on its behalf. In the years 1926 and 1927 I spoke at twenty-eight League of Nations Union meetings, including one in the United States.

Often people would say to me, people who were surprised that I should take the subject seriously, "Do you really believe in the League?" I would retort, "Do you believe in the fire brigade? I disapprove of houses on fire and I know of no organisation for putting them out other than the fire brigade. It may be badly managed, it may be inefficient, but none the less if I could help it I would certainly do so. I disapprove also of war. I know of no mechanism that exists for preventing it other than the League of Nations. The League may fail. If so God help us all. But so long as there is the faintest chance of its succeeding I believe that we should give it all the help we can."

I have often thought that if the League had had some openly declared enemies it might have had a better chance of success, but when all pay lip-service and few have faith the cause is doomed. The Church would have greater influence in England if there were, or had ever been, an anti-clerical party in the country, committed to the uprooting of religion. The opponents of the League never appeared on the platform.

I remember after one successful meeting the Mayor of the town where it took place saying that he wished that old Dr. So-and-so had been there that night, and then explained that the gentleman in question was one of the most popular citizens in the borough, a great character, witty, brilliant and universally admired, and that he was accustomed to say that the League was nonsense, that there always had been wars, that there always would be, and that no League was going to stop them. "Since your friend is a doctor," I said, "tell him with my compliments that he is wasting his time. There always has been disease and it looks as though there always will be. The one thing that is perfectly certain is that all his patients are going to die. So that if he follows his principles he should abandon his practice, which at best can only postpone the inevitable."

I tried to persuade my audiences that the League was not the invention of starry-eyed idealists, enjoying the blessing of the Churches and the patronage of the Crown, and therefore to be spoken of respectfully but not to be taken seriously. I would explain that there were only three forms of foreign policy that the country could possibly adopt. The first was one of isolation, which was then being advocated by the newspapers under Lord Beaverbrook's control. The plan was to cut ourselves off from Europe and devote our energies to the development of the Empire overseas. I considered this a delightful, idealistic dream which was unfortunately quite impracticable. How could we cut ourselves off from Europe so long as we occupied Gibraltar and Suez, the two gateways to the most important

European sea, and the island of Malta, in the middle of it? How could we remain indifferent to the fate of a continent from whose shores our own could be bombarded? If the United States, separated from that continent by the Atlantic Ocean, had been forced to take part in the last European War, how could we hope to keep out of the next one?

If then the policy of isolation were abandoned, the policy of alliances naturally suggested itself as an alternative. There was much to be said in favour of it, despite the fact that it was the policy which had often been followed in the past and had usually resulted in war. At that time, however, we had no allies and no party in the State was in favour of getting any. Therefore support of the League imposed itself as the only policy that could in practice be adopted, the simple principle upon which it was based being to set up in international affairs a supreme authority which should be able in the fullness of time to maintain law and order among the nations, just as they were maintained within the confines of each State by the police and the courts of justice.

It was not such folly as it may now appear, to have believed at that period that the League of Nations might succeed in the purpose for which it was created. The first World War had profoundly shocked the conscience of mankind. There had grown up in the comparative calm of the nineteenth century a self-satisfied belief in progress and a confident hope that the more civilised nations were becoming capable of settling their disputes without recourse to violence. Neither the Crimean War nor the Franco-German War of 1870 had seriously disturbed the minds or the lives of Europeans, although some of the more discerning had detected in the latter a new spirit of ruthlessness which seemed to differentiate it from wars of the same and even of the previous century. This, however, was ascribed to the influence of the Prussians, who, people were asked to believe, were different from the other inhabitants of the German Empire founded in 1871. There existed therefore in 1919 a sentiment, which it would hardly be an exaggeration to call universal, that such a thing must never be allowed to happen again.

If President Wilson had been able to steer his country into the peace as skilfully as he had steered her into the war, if he had sent to

Europe a powerful, all-party delegation and had stayed at home himself, if he had concentrated his energies on persuading Congress to accept the League and on persuading his people that the time had come for them to assume world-leadership, all would undoubtedly have been very different and great disaster might have been averted. But, none the less, there existed behind the League an enormous force of goodwill and faith, such as the United Nations Organisation has never enjoyed for a moment. Had there been present a realistic states-man capable of appreciating the vast potentialities of that goodwill and that faith, and of directing them towards the construction of a new international society, miracles might have happened. But those who believed in the League were not trusted by their own people, and those who were trusted by their own people were not willing to risk losing that trust by demonstrating faith in the League. So the League gradually sank in public repute, and long after it was dead and ought to have been decently buried its lip-servants continued to pay homage to the corpse that was beginning to stink.

The winter of 1927–28 was a severe one, and at the New Year some friends of ours invited us to accompany them on a visit to North Africa in search of sunshine. We gladly accepted, only to learn that in the month of January the rain can be as heavy and the wind as cold in North Africa as in any part of Europe. Having had to change our route owing to floods in the Sahara, we arrived at Biskra, where I received a letter from the Prime Minister, which must have been written on the day that I left London, offering me the post of Finan-cial Secretary to the War Office.

Telegraphing my acceptance I left my companions in the desert and travelled home by the first train. Mr. Baldwin had wisely taken my agreement for granted and I read the announcement of my appointment in the newspaper when I reached Algiers. I was very happy. Office is the ambition of every Member of Parliament, com-petition for it is eager and its attainment is affected by chance as well as by merit. It is the first rung on the ladder but not the easiest to mount.

The Secretary of State for War was Sir Laming Worthington-Evans, whom I hardly knew. He proved the most considerate of chiefs. He was a lawyer by profession and concealed beneath a cheerful, rubicund exterior an acute brain, which had been concerned more with finance and commerce—he was an authority on Company Law—than with military affairs. He was pleasant to work with, both in the House of Commons and in the department. He was equally prepared to accept responsibility or to delegate it. He would sometimes hand me a formidable file and say, "This seems to be a complicated question. I haven't looked into it and don't propose to do so. You can settle it as you think right."

It is not generally known that when payment of Members of Parliament was introduced, emoluments of Ministers were automatically reduced, since a Minister does not receive his ministerial salary in addition to what he receives as a Member. The latter is deducted from the former. The Minister is also obliged to give up any other money-earning occupation in which he may be engaged. In those days Members received only £400 a year. It is now £1,000. The salary of the Financial Secretary was £1,500, but when £400 had been deducted little more was left than what I had been earning by journalism.

The work of a junior Minister, so far as I have had experience of it, is not, or was not, heavy. If his chief is in the House of Commons the volume of it is much lighter. In those days the Service departments had each two junior Ministers, a privilege not enjoyed by other departments. The War Office had an Under-Secretary of State as well as a Financial Secretary. The former was usually a member of the House of Lords and was charged particularly with questions concerning the Territorial Army and the ownership of land. This lightened still further the burden on the shoulders of the Financial Secretary.

The life of a junior Minister—I was to have about six years of it in all—is not a disagreeable one, but it provides little in the way of training for the higher responsibilities to which it should lead. At the same time it deprives the young politician of opportunities of distinguishing himself or of improving his technique in the House of Commons. He sees no Cabinet papers and remains therefore hardly better informed on matters of high policy than his contemporary back-benchers. An incident illustrative of this disadvantage occurred when I returned to the position of Financial Secretary three years later, at which time Lord Hailsham was Secretary of State. I had been invited to address the Egyptian students of the University of Birmingham on Anglo-Egyptian relations, and in the course of my remarks I had adumbrated a scheme of settlement on the basis of moving British troops out of Cairo and Alexandria in return for being granted a free hand in the Sudan. I was summoned by Lord Hailsham, who was a much more remote chief than Worthington-Evans had been. He told me that the terms of a treaty with Egypt were then under discussion in the Cabinet, that he with the support of his military advisers had been strenuously opposing the evacuation of Cairo and Alexandria, and that his position was therefore rendered extremely difficult when the policy that he was opposing in the Cabinet was advocated by his own junior Minister before an audience of Egyptian students. I could only plead in defence my entire ignorance of what questions the Cabinet might be discussing.

Nor is it open to a junior Minister to enlighten his ignorance by asking questions in the House of Commons. He can no more ask a question than he can make a speech except when the affairs of his own department are under discussion. So far as the War Office was concerned this occurred only twice a year, at the presentation of the estimates and the passing of the Army Annual Act. Junior Ministers are in fact put into cold storage, and if they remain there too long their faculties may suffer from lack of employment and even become atrophied. Too often it happens that a promising back-bencher, who has been a capable Under-Secretary, proves a great disappointment upon higher promotion.

My first experience of office, however, was to be too short rather than too long. I kept myself fully employed during the course of it. During the year 1928 and the first four months of 1929 I spoke, outside my own constituency, at forty-eight political meetings and at nineteen on behalf of the League of Nations Union. I also supported my chief in the House of Commons, where within the same period he had twice to present the estimates and twice to supervise the passing of the Army Annual Act.

In the autumn of 1928 I was one of the team of British delegates appointed to attend the General Assembly of the League of Nations at Geneva. This was my first and only experience of the League at first hand. It was not disillusioning, for I flatter myself that I had no illusions, but it was discouraging, and those who were maintaining the cause of the League needed encouragement.

The head of our mission was my old master, Ronald McNeill, who had become Lord Cushendun and Chancellor of the Duchy of Lancaster. He was for the time being Acting Secretary of State for Foreign Affairs, for this was the period when Governments still sent representatives of the highest importance to Geneva. Briand represented France. I was present when he spoke in the Assembly, and I still think he was the greatest orator I ever heard.

But the numbers of committees which talked interminably and accomplished nothing, which indeed never hoped to accomplish anything, the gossip of the cosmopolitan politicians, the huge dreary dinner-parties given by different nations in turn, the depressing cocktail parties and receptions, created an impression of confusion and gloom. The contrast with the Congress of Vienna struck me. That Congress was accused of dancing, and dance it did, but behind that genuinely gay façade it also worked, and to the sound of music made a Europe that lasted for a hundred years.

Among the committees upon which I was assigned to serve was one charged with the duty of dealing on an international basis with the evils of alcoholism. Our first meeting was in the evening, and before proceedings started we were served with port and other apéritifs. After the danger of alcohol had been roundly denounced by all, our chairman, a Frenchman, explained that wine of course was not alcohol nor, for that matter, were the products of the Cognac district, which were all derived from the grape. His views were warmly supported by the representatives of Italy, Portugal and Spain. I then felt bound to remind the meeting that, while I entirely shared the views of the previous speakers, my country did not enjoy the same quantity of sunshine as blessed their happier lands, and that its inhabitants had even greater need than had their fellow creatures of that internal warmth and stimulus which the fermented juice of the grape bestows. Unfortunately the vine did not flourish in Great Britain, but we had made an effort, especially in the northern and coldest part of the kingdom, to produce a substitute, which had been found so satisfactory that we were now able to export it in considerable quantities to foreign countries, and I felt confident that this agreeable and beneficent beverage, which many doctors recommended in preference to wine, would not come within the purview of our enquiries.

I think that this committee met two or three times. I cannot remember reading its report, if it presented one, but it accomplished as much as many of the other League committees, which was precisely nothing, and it must have left in the minds of most of its members, as it left in mine, an impression of futility and farce.

While I was at Geneva I delivered a lecture over the preparation of which I took some trouble and the text of which I retain. The subject of it was "The Barbarians," and it set out to show how all the civilisations of which there remain traces in the short recorded history of man had been destroyed by the action of man himself. Those who were responsible for such destruction I designated the barbarians, and I suggested that there existed many of them still who might yet destroy the civilisation that we in Geneva in 1928 were anxious to defend and develop.

A few years later I could have given the names and addresses of those barbarians and of the countries they controlled, but my thesis at that date was that the barbarians had become themselves international and could be detected only by the causes they espoused and the opinions they expressed. I considered extremists, whether of the right or the left, most theorists and all fanatics, to belong to the ranks of barbarism, and I estimated their numbers to be larger than those of civilised men. Our hope was based, at that time, on their lack of leadership and cohesion. I concluded by saying:

There are grounds for hope. The barbarians are many but they are unaware of their own numbers. They have in common a subconscious hatred of civilisation, but they have no definite objective towards which they aim. Their forces are scattered and they have not learnt to co-operate. To hate one another is their guiding principle and they practise it within their own ranks. At present they are still suffering from recent self-inflicted wounds. Full advantage must be taken of this interval in order to prepare for the next assault. We cannot hope to see the completion of the building, but let us endeavour so to lay the foundations and to construct the framework that the barbarians shall not prevail against it, and that our own descendants may behold the finished temple in the fullness of time.

Reading that lecture again after a quarter of a century I can find no word in it that I would change. Even then I denounced the folly of attempting to lay down which weapons it was legitimate to use in warfare and which should be forbidden. Never in the height of my enthusiasm for the League of Nations did I advocate disarmament. I used to say that I would no more recommend disarmament in the cause of peace than I would suggest the dissolution of the police force in the cause of law and order.

The Conservative Government, although they might have remained in office until the autumn, decided to go to the country in the spring of 1929. Shortly before the General Election the Liberals of Oldham made what for me was the fatal decision to present two candidates. My Liberal colleague, Mr. Wiggins, wiser than his supporters, refused to be one of them, and the two young men who presented themselves in his place succeeded only in splitting the anti-Socialist vote and found themselves at the bottom of the poll.

The result of the General Election of the spring of 1929 was a grave disappointment to the Conservative Party. The five-and-a-half years' record of the Government was good. In foreign affairs they had concluded the Treaty of Locarno, which was considered a great achievement, and there were no storm-clouds on the European horizon. At home they had broken the General Strike and dispelled the dread of revolution. The problem of unemployment was unsolved but the number of the unemployed was smaller than it had been in the past or was to be for some time in the future. The financial blizzard from the west had hardly begun to blow. There seemed to exist neither abroad nor at home any cause for alarm.

This was possibly the reason why the slogan of "Safety First," with which the Conservative Party went to the country, proved disastrous. There can be no better appeal than to the instinct of self-preservation when people are frightened, there can be no worse appeal when people are convinced that no danger exists. Ten years had passed since the war. There seemed little likelihood of another one. Social unrest had calmed down, and while there was sufficient cause for complaint, there was no apparent reason for fear. Conditions were improving, but the improvement was so gradual as to be almost imperceptible. Security breeds boredom, and the truth of the matter was that the country was bored to death with the Government. No greater psychological mistake could have been made than to promise safety to a people pining for excitement.

It was a hard fight at Oldham. I needed the help of all my friends. Even Hilaire Belloc lent a hand. He hired a hall himself and issued an announcement that he would hold a meeting which all of his faith were invited to attend. He was alone on the platform and explained to the audience his own attitude towards politics, how he cared nothing for either party and that the only thing that mattered was the future of the Catholic schools, that my undertaking with regard to them was more satisfactory than those of my opponents, and that I, having held office, would have some influence in the Government, whereas my opponents would have none. I fear he won few votes. The Roman Catholic vote was as solidly Labour on this occasion as it had been solidly Conservative at the previous General Election.

He was sitting in the club next morning over a glass of beer when an enthusiastic young man was shown in who wanted the honour of a word with him. The young man explained that he was a fervent supporter of the principle of distributism, the political theory for which Chesterton and Belloc were supposed to stand and which advocated the small ownership of the national wealth. Belloc said he was glad to be assured of the young man's support, and added that so far as he could see there was only one difficulty in the way of his policy being adopted.

"What is that?" eagerly asked the young man, anxious to learn.

"It is," answered Belloc, "like trying to force the water at Niagara to go *up* instead of coming *down*." The young man went away sorrowful.

I had good meetings throughout the election, and enthusiasm for the Conservative cause seemed to be growing in the constituency. On this occasion the votes were not counted on the night of the poll but on the following morning. When, therefore, the polling-booths were closed and there was no more to be done, I returned to Manchester and a quiet dinner at the Midland Hotel. We were interrupted in the middle of it by some of my supporters who said we should really come back to Oldham to see the scenes of enthusiasm which were taking place there. It was indeed worth the half-hour's drive. The whole of the main street in which the Conservative Club stood was crowded with people waving the Conservative colours and cheering for the cause and the candidate. There was no rowdyism because there was no opposition. It seemed that night that there was not a Liberal or a Labour man in the town.

The next morning the atmosphere had changed. News was coming from all quarters of Conservative defeats. Confidence gave place to doubt and doubt to despair. The result. when it was announced, was what might have been foreseen, although the figures, compared with those of the previous election, were far from unsatisfactory. In 1924 I received 37,419 votes in all, which was only 600 more than those given to Edward Grigg. That half his votes were Conservative and half mine Liberal was a fair assumption, there being no other Liberal or Conservative candidate standing. In 1929 I polled 29,424 votes, which was only 3,303 less than one of the two successful Labour candidates. If, then, my Conservative support at the previous election was roughly 18,000, I had succeeded in increasing it by 11,000, and there can be no doubt that if there had been one Liberal instead of two standing—they scored respectively 20,810 and 13,528 —I should have held the seat. At a time when Conservative seats were being lost all over the country, here was nothing of which to be ashamed.

I was sad to leave Oldham. I had learnt a great deal there. The strong attachment to the Conservative cause that exists among the working class had surprised me. No appeal was made for funds, but at each election several hundred pounds were contributed in shillings, half-crowns and larger denominations from the electorate. When I left, after being their Member for little more than four years, they made me a splendid present and after its presentation found that they had collected more than its cost, so that another present was forthcoming for Diana, which necessitated another presentation. I have often thought that in the mist and drizzle of that dreary town there live the kindest-hearted people in the world.

CHAPTER ELEVEN

LITERATURE AND POLITICS

1929–1935

I HAD read at school among the stories of Rudyard Kipling two which dealt with the personality of Talleyrand, and they had made a deep impression upon me. I think it was these stories that first interested me in Talleyrand. I certainly told Kipling so when I came to know him, and he was pleased. When I was enjoying my Paris leave in 1918 I read Albert Vandal's *L'Avènement de Bonaparte*, and it was after reading that absorbing book that I made the resolution to write something about Talleyrand before I died. There was no adequate biography of him in existence at the time. The first of Lacour-Gayet's four volumes appeared in 1928. Meanwhile I read everything upon which I could lay my hands that dealt with the man or the period. I had thus devoted ten years to the task when after my defeat in the election of 1929 I sat down to write the first lines of my first book.

We were living in a little house by the sea near Bognor which Diana's mother had acquired many years before and which we had gradually appropriated. It was a happy summer. I kept no diary, but I cannot remember that I was unduly depressed by having lost my seat in the House of Commons, although I was determined to get another as soon as possible. I used to play golf regularly either at Goodwood or at Littlehampton, and although I acquired little proficiency at the game I found the golf course an admirable place for literary preparation. Those who have never tried to write a book, and perhaps some of those who have, may think it a simple matter. To me it has always been a painful process, and the first paragraph is the most difficult of all. I was in my fortieth year. Apart from journalism I had published nothing, and when I contemplated the great historical epoch covered by Talleyrand's eighty-four years of life I was appalled at my ignorance and my temerity.

I had the good sense not to hurry, although money cannot have been plentiful at the time and additional liabilities were occurring. I think that the *Graphic* had ceased to appear, and being no longer a Member of Parliament I could not return to my weekly articles in the *Saturday Review*. I had therefore no regular employment, and it was not until more than two years later that my book was published.

But events of importance occurred long before the date of publication, and the most important was the crown of happiness that was set upon that hot, happy, leisured summer by the birth of our son in September, ten years after our marriage.

My political life continued, although I was no longer in Parliament. I still served on the executive committee of the League of Nations Union and attended their weekly meetings, which I thought were too frequent and too large for the efficient conduct of business. I spoke both for the League and for the Conservative Party, when I was asked to, and I busied myself in seeking another and a safer seat.

Constituency-hunting is not an agreeable occupation, and I sometimes thought that the members of the small executive committees, "drest in a little brief authority," took a certain pleasure in humiliating the candidates who presented themselves for approval. There had been many Conservative casualties at the General Election, so that the stock of candidates was large and the competition keen. After one or two failures I was offered the constituency of Winchester, provided I was prepared to wait for it until the next General Election, which might well not be for three or four years. The sitting member, Sir George Hennessy, afterwards Lord Windlesham, did not intend to stand again. He was one of the party Whips, and it was due to his good offices that I was offered the seat, which I accepted.

It was early in 1930 that I made this decision and I nursed the constituency of Winchester for a year. There is a world of difference between a county constituency in the south of England and a borough constituency in the north. The main advantages of the former are aesthetic. To visit the city of Winchester and to drive about the country that surrounds it must give and continue to give pleasure, even when it becomes a duty. County seats are also more likely to remain firm in their allegiance. But I soon discovered that Winchester was no longer the Conservative stronghold that it had been in the past. Eastleigh, which formed part of it, was becoming a great railway centre and an industrial town of importance, and the ever-spreading tentacles of Southampton were stretching out into what had hitherto been rural districts.

The demands made on a Member by a county seat are more numerous than those made by a borough. Each village feels itself entitled to as much attention as its neighbours. Big halls where large audiences can be collected are rare, and the rarer they are the greater the number of meetings that must be held. Large distances have to be covered not by the constituents but by the candidate. In a borough there may be two or three important annual events—a dance, a reception, a flower show, a dinner. In the country such events must be multiplied by the number of villages. A borough is for convenience divided into wards, but the inhabitants are not "ward-conscious" and there is no inter-ward jealousy. But strong local jealousy exists between villages, and what the candidate does for one he must do for the other. I was not, however, dismayed by the prospect. We took a small house in the town and I looked forward to the prospect of making Winchester and the country round it my permanent home.

Meanwhile events were taking place in the political arena which were to have an important effect upon my future and to sever that connection with Winchester upon which I was beginning to count. Stanley Baldwin was proving an unsatisfactory leader of Opposition. He had none of the qualities that the task demands. Bolingbroke wrote of the House of Commons more than two hundred years ago: "You know the nature of that assembly, they grow, like hounds, fond of the man who shows them game, and by whose halloo they are used to be encouraged." The nature of the assembly has changed little in the centuries. Mr. Baldwin never showed game, and when he saw hounds hunting, his first instinct was to call them off. His love of peace could easily be mistaken for indolence, and his desire to be fair to his political opponents could be represented as secret sympathy with their views. The back-benchers were growing impatient. They were awaiting a trumpet-call which never sounded, and their discontent was assiduously fed and fostered by an important section of the Conservative press under the control of Lords Rothermere and Beaverbrook, who had long been bitterly opposed to the Conservative leader.

These divisions and discontents found a focus in the Indian question, which was then passing through a delicate phase. All parties in Great Britain were vaguely committed to a policy which should gradually increase self-government. The differences were matters of temperament rather than of principle, but they were none the less important for that. The question was not one of direction, but rather of degree and of speed. Something had to be given away. Was it to be given soon and with good grace or slowly and grudgingly?

Baldwin had appointed Lord Irwin Viceroy, who had shown from the first a tendency towards propitiation and appeasement which had doubtless the full approval of the Government. He had consistently followed the same line under the new administration, and many Conservatives, who had been growing restive while their own party was in office, broke out into violent criticism both of the Viceroy and of the India Office. While not denying that self-government remained the ultimate objective of British policy in India, they believed that in their conduct of that policy the Government were going too fast and too far. Most important of those who took this view was Winston Churchill, who when he was unable to persuade his colleagues, the leaders of the Conservative Party, to share his opinions, severed his connection with the Shadow Cabinet.

I have always thought that this was the most unfortunate event that occurred between the two wars. It reduced Winston Churchill to impotence for ten years and deprived the Government of the services of a man who plainly saw the growing German menace and who, with his great gifts and dynamic personality, might have averted and certainly would have prepared to meet the disaster.

Nor can I think that he was justified in his decision. Such knowledge as he possessed of India he had acquired as a young cavalry officer in the reign of Queen Victoria. His opinions on the subject were probably identical with those of Rudyard Kipling, opinions with which I was and remain in sympathy. I have not the slightest doubt that the vast population of India were happier under British rule than they had ever been before, happier than they have been since, happier than they are likely to be again. I hated the decision to abandon India, but I believe that that decision was wise and could not have been long postponed. It was not the Indian people nor Indian sentiment that made it impossible for the British to remain in India. It was the British people and British sentiment, strongly supported by the sentiment, based largely upon ignorance, of their American cousins. The idea of the inhabitants of an island in Europe governing against their will an Asiatic population ten times more numerous than themselves is not acceptable to the modern mind. Whether the idea is wrong in itself, or the modern mind wrong in rejecting it, I will not explore. Europe was probably happier under Roman rule during the first centuries of our era than it has ever been since. But the Romans could not continue to rule Europe, any more than the British could continue to rule India. The art of politics is to make the best of the inevitable.

The graver consequences that were to follow the withdrawal of Winston Churchill from the high position he occupied in the councils of the Conservative Party were not then apparent, although it seemed at the time to threaten a serious cleavage in the ranks of the Opposition. For four years he had occupied the post of Chancellor of the Exchequer, which often carries with it the reversion of the premiership. Discontent with Baldwin's leadership was not confined to those who doubted the wisdom of his Indian policy, and the most vociferous section of the Conservative press was in full cry to bring him down. It was in these circumstances that in the middle of February 1931 there occurred the death of my former master, Sir Laming Worthington-Evans, who sat for the St. George's division of Westminster, the safest Conservative seat in the country.

It so happened that Diana and I were about to pay a visit to Sweden, where I had accepted an invitation to deliver a short series of lectures on the British Empire. It was to conclude with a lecture in Berlin. We left London the day after the sad event, and while we were in Sweden we were surprised to learn from a friend who telephoned from London that no candidate had been adopted for the St. George's division, as the one who had been expected to come forward and who had already held a minor office in the previous Government had declared himself unable to support the present leader of the party. When we returned to London a fortnight later the situation had further developed. Sir Ernest Petter, an engine manufacturer from the West Country, had presented himself as an independent, anti-

Baldwin Conservative. He had the enthusiastic support of the Rothermere and Beaverbrook press, and the official Conservative Party organisation were still without a candidate. It was strange that at a time when so many Conservatives were looking for seats none should have come forward.

I soon discovered that there existed at headquarters an atmosphere of perplexity and defeat. The belief that there must be a change in leadership was by no means confined to the two press Lords, nor to Winston Churchill and the India Defence League, as his followers styled themselves. It spread to many moderate and sensible Conservatives, who would have witnessed Baldwin's departure with regret as an unpleasant necessity. The Central Office had been criticised for the last defeat, and the unusual step had been taken of appointing a prominent politician to reorganise it. Neville Chamberlain had therefore been appointed chairman of the party, and as he was also Baldwin's obvious successor, he could hardly be blamed for not wishing to defer too long the date of his succession. The central organisation of the party was therefore not robust in its support of the leader, and in the Whips' office the opinion was openly expressed that no pro-Baldwin candidate could hold a seat in London.

I will not pretend that I shared this view or thought that I was taking a serious risk when I decided to abandon Winchester and offer myself as the official Conservative candidate for St. George's. Before I could meet the executive committee or be formally adopted I had to attend a meeting at one of the villages near Winchester that had been arranged previously. It was well attended and enthusiastic. I could not say publicly that I was leaving Winchester, because I had not been adopted by St. George's, but I never felt more like a traitor than while listening to the laudatory speeches from the platform expressing confidence in their candidate. I stayed that night at Hursley Park, once the home of Richard Cromwell, where lived Sir George Cooper, the president of the Winchester Conservative association. I told him what I meant to do. He took it very well, but I felt badly, and I felt worse the next morning when, travelling to London by the early train, I met many of my supporters who were reading in their morning paper the first announcement, unconfirmed and inaccurate, of my decision.

One of the people whom I had already told was Lord Beaverbrook. If we were in for a fight, I thought we had better begin, as I hoped we should end it, on good terms. He sought in the friendliest way to dissuade me. He felt sure I should lose, that my support of Baldwin, who would have to retire, would do me no good in the party, and that I should forfeit Winchester, where they would certainly not re-adopt me after my desertion. To avoid argument I told him that I was too far committed to withdraw, which was the case.

I had no difficulty in securing nomination as the official candidate. There was only one competitor, who had already expressed opinions unfavourable to Baldwin, and who, after being rejected, gave his full support to Sir Ernest Petter.

The fight was short and fierce. It lasted hardly a fortnight. There was no third candidate, so that the issue was clear. If the Liberals had harmed me at Oldham they helped me here, for any Liberal or Labour candidate must have taken votes from me rather than from my opponent, who represented the most uncompromising brand of Toryism. Petter made an initial error when, asked for a statement by the local branch of the League of Nations Union, he said that he was too busy to attend to such matters as the League of Nations. Here my record must have helped me.

The constituency, which no longer exists, covered Mayfair and Belgravia, extending in the south-west to include Victoria, Pimlico and the confines of Chelsea. The wealthiest residential district of London, it contained no suitable place for a large public meeting, and the only one that we held during the election took place in the Queen's Hall, which was outside the constituency. Here Stanley Baldwin spoke with more fire and vehemence than he had ever been known to display.

Although the St. George's division was overwhelmingly Conservative it did not easily adapt itself to a political campaign. It is difficult to lure rich people to political meetings, especially in the centre of London, where there are so many more agreeable ways of spending an evening. Domestic servants, more numerous than their masters in those days, had little leisure to devote to politics, and it was hard for a canvasser to know the best hour to approach them. Their opinions were usually Conservative, but there was no saying how they would choose between the two candidates. A stately butler informed one of my supporters that he was voting for Petter, explaining that he had always worked for the aristocracy and that Sir Ernest was a man of title, whereas he was informed that Mr. Cooper had been a clerk in an office, and not even a British office but a foreign one.

Servants have little time to read a newspaper in the morning, but if they do cast an eye on one in the West End of London it will almost certainly be either the *Daily Express* or the *Daily Mail*. In the afternoon, when they have more time at their disposal, they will turn to the *Evening News* or the *Evening Standard*. These four papers were my chief opponents, and every issue of each of them was devoted to damaging my cause. The only other evening paper, the *Star*, was neutral, as was the rest of the press, with the exception of the *Daily Telegraph*, which gave me support.

Beaverbrook fought hard and spoke daily. Rothermere, who disliked public speaking, never appeared on the platform. Petter, an amiable old gentleman with thick white hair, was not impressive and had difficulty in answering the questions which my friends put to him at every meeting. Hard words were said on each side in the course of the contest but they left no bad blood behind.

It was strange to see the windows of stately houses, which in those days were all inhabited, flaunting posters for one side or the other, and to find open-air meetings being held in Bond Street or in Grosvenor Square. Every evening after the tiring labours of the day were ended we had a supper-party at Lady Stanley's in Grosvenor Street, or at Lady Juliet Duff's in Belgrave Square, or at Londonderry House which, standing between the two in the very heart of the constituency, was a fortress of generous hospitality and loyal support.

Although the election had its gay moments and the atmosphere was more congenial than that of Oldham, I was very glad when it was over and I was very pleased with the result. I won by more than five thousand votes. In my short speech of thanks to the returning officer I urged that the breach should now be healed, the quarrel forgotten and the party reunited. This was what happened, and both the party and the country gained by it. If Petter had been elected Baldwin would have had to go, and his going might have led to a serious split in the Conservative Party. The press Lords had by their attack strengthened his position. The moderate element that had been conscious of his shortcomings had rallied to his defence, preferring to accept imperfect leadership rather than hand over the fate of the party to irresponsible owners of newspapers. No important member of the party had given open support to Petter. During the election a large meeting had been held at the Albert Hall, where Winston Churchill had addressed the India Defence League, but the greatest care had been taken by all speakers to avoid any reference to the election that was taking place within half a mile of the hall. Had they not done so they would have incurred serious penalties under the electoral law. If, however, in such a Conservative stronghold as St. George's an adverse verdict had been given on Baldwin's leadership, which was the real issue of the election, he could not have retained his position. Within six months there was to come the complete collapse of the Labour Government. The leaders of it, however, were able to work with Baldwin and to form the National Government. It is probable that such an alliance with Neville Chamberlain would have proved as impossible then as it was to prove nine years later, when, in the midst of war, the Labour Party, under new leaders, made it a condition of their entry into coalition that Chamberlain should no longer be Prime Minister.

When a newly-elected Member takes his seat in the House of Commons he walks up the centre gangway accompanied by a sponsor on either side, and three bows are made before they reach the Speaker's chair. When I took my seat on this occasion Mr. Baldwin walked on my right—a rare honour to be accorded by the leader of the party. He knew how important the result of the election had been to him.

I was not very well during the months that followed, and can remember speaking only once before the House rose at the end of the summer. We had been invited to go for a cruise on a yacht to the Greek islands but had got no further than Le Touquet when we received a telegram to say that the yacht had broken down and the cruise was off.

That evening in the casino I met Lord Rothermere, whom I knew very slightly and whom I had not seen since the election. He bore no malice and we had a friendly conversation. He congratulated me on having, as he said, cleverly changed the issue in the election from Baldwin's leadership to the dictatorship of the press. He told me the Government were in a desperate position and that he believed they would fall before meeting Parliament in the autumn. I thought he was exaggerating, but he was right.

Our holiday plans having been disorganised by the collapse of the yacht, we proceeded by easy stages through France to northern Italy, Venice being as usual our objective. When we were staying at Talloires on the Lake of Annecy, we learnt that Mr. and Mrs. Baldwin were at Aix-les-Bains and invited them to luncheon. They accepted. He had already, since leaving England, been recalled for an interview with the Prime Minister. We had hardly sat down before Diana said gaily:

"Come on now, tell us every word that Ramsay MacDonald said."

He only grunted but Mrs. Baldwin looked horrified and exclaimed:

"I would never dare ask him such a question."

This, combined with the fact that Diana, despite my protest, was wearing trousers, which were less conventional then than now, made me feel that my political future was at the bottom of the lake.

A few days later we were lunching at a small hotel on the shores of Lake Garda, when we were surprised by the sudden appearance of Leo Amery. He had been climbing in the mountains north of the lake and had spoken to Neville Chamberlain on the telephone that morning. He had learnt that the situation was more critical than ever, so that he was on his way to Verona to catch the Simplon express and return to London. He might have finished his holiday, for he was not to get office again for nine years. It seemed a cruel irony that he, who had been the most consistent supporter of protective tariffs and the ablest exponent of the cause, should have found no place in the first Government that adopted a wholeheartedly protectionist policy.

We went on to Venice the same day, but on the morrow there came a telegram from the Speaker to say that the House of Commons was reassembling. I left that evening by train and a few days later I was once more Financial Secretary to the War Office.

I was very pleased with my appointment. In a Conservative

Government I might have expected promotion, but room had to be found in this administration not only for a fair representation of the Liberal Party, but also for those of his own party who had followed the Prime Minister, Ramsay MacDonald, and to whom the name of National Labour was now attached. I therefore considered myself fortunate to be included.

In one way also I could consider that the post was a kind of promotion, for the new Secretary of State was Lord Crewe, which meant that I was the only representative of the department in the House of Commons, and it would fall to me to present the estimates each year. As a gesture to economy I combined for the time being the post of Financial Secretary with that of Under-Secretary of State, but after the General Election, which took place in October, when Lord Crewe was succeeded by Lord Hailsham, an Under-Secretary was also appointed.

I never liked an election so much as that one. No challenger appeared in the St. George's division, so that I was returned unopposed. I was able therefore to devote myself to others, and the Central Office made out for me an itinerary which covered a good deal of the country. In our small motor-car we travelled as far north as Edinburgh, across to Glasgow and back through Lancashire, where I visited Oldham again. It was beautiful autumn weather and we enjoyed the daily drives and the nightly meetings.

We had a party at Gower Street on polling night, at which some of the newly elected London Members arrived fresh from their victories. Belloc was there, and when among the first returns there came, as usual, the two Salford divisions with, not as usual, substantial Conservative majorities, he said, "That means it's a landslide" and it was. He had himself been Liberal member for South Salford from 1906 to 1910.

The Labour Party in the House of Commons was almost wiped out, and the only member of the former Cabinet to survive was George Lansbury, upon whose shoulders fell the too heavy burden of leading the Opposition. When his extreme pacifism compelled him to give it up, Mr. Attlee, who had held no higher post than that of Postmaster-General, succeeded because he also was one of the few survivors of the storm.

The four years that followed the General Election of 1931 were pleasant but unimportant ones in my life. I remained a junior Minister. In 1932 Diana appeared in *The Miracle* at the Lyceum Theatre in London, where it ran successfully for a few months, and later in the year and in 1933 it was produced in all the largest towns in Great Britain. Sometimes I would travel to spend Saturday to Monday where she happened to be acting; more often she would come to London after the last performance on Saturday.

At the beginning of 1933 I began to keep a diary again. It lasted less than five months. I wrote on the 1st of January:

> The year 1932 has been for me an uneventful one, in contrast to 1931 which was crowded with events. I have continued quietly to function at the War Office and have made only two speeches in the House of Commons, one introducing estimates and the other on the subject of Waterloo Bridge.
>
> For me the chief event of the year has been the publication of my *Talleyrand*, which I had been contemplating for fourteen years and actually writing for three. It came out on October 3rd and has had a greater success than I dared to expect. The publisher tells me that over five thousand copies have been sold already, which, in the present state of the trade, is remarkable for a 12s. 6d. book.

The reviews that appeared in the press were unanimously favourable and some of them gave me higher praise than I felt I deserved. Seldom can an author's first book have had a kinder reception.

While I was seriously thinking of writing another on an entirely different subject, which had long been occupying my mind and which remains unwritten to this day, an event occurred which altered the direction of my literary efforts.

On Thursday morning, March 23rd, I was told that General Fisher, Director of Recruiting, wished to speak to me. I imagined it was some small matter of routine. He seemed nervous and began by telling me he was one of Lord Haig's executors. I thought it had to do with the long dispute that has been going on about his equestrian statue. He then told me that he wanted me to write Haig's life. I was astonished and immediately thought of all my disqualifications—not being a soldier, not being interested really in military matters, having read very little on such subjects and comparatively little about the war—and, above all, not having known the man. I mentioned them. He said that he and his co-executor had thought of them all. They had offered the job first to John Buchan, who had accepted but Lady Haig had taken strong exception and had written him an insulting letter. The matter was dropped for the time and later George Trevelyan was approached. He had at first liked the idea but had finally refused on the ground that he had done nothing of the kind before and that it would interfere with his other work. Then, having over-persuaded Lady Haig, they had gone back to Buchan but he refused to reconsider it.

I was and have been in great perplexity. It is a great opportunity. The material is wonderful—many volumes of Haig's diary, most carefully kept, which have never seen the light. The book, whoever wrote it, would be of the greatest importance. It would take me a long time, but Fisher assures me there is no hurry—he mentioned three or even four years. I might and probably should be criticised for undertaking such heavy work while a Minister. I don't mind that, but supposing I were promoted to higher office, I might really have no time at all except during the summer holidays.

On the whole I have practically decided to accept, but I shall insist on being given a completely free hand to put in or leave out what I like and to make the book whatever length I please.

I did accept and set myself forthwith to the task, which I completed in two years and a half. I was correcting the final proofs of the second volume when I was promoted to the Cabinet after the General Election of 1935.

In the summer of 1933 we set forth on a motoring tour through Germany to stay with friends who had taken a house in Austria. We had thought to stay the first night after leaving Belgium at Aix-la-Chapelle, but were discouraged by the appearance of the town and of the large empty hotel, where we were advised by the hall porter to go to a small place not far away called Montjoie. Here we found everything we wanted in delightful, rural surroundings, but several times in the course of the night I was awakened by the sound of men marching and of words of command given in raucous voices. It was my first contact with the Nazis.

A few days later we stopped at Beyreuth, expecting on the strength of its musical reputation that it would prove an agreeable stopping-place. Again we were disappointed at finding a very commonplace, noisy, provincial town without charm or character. Diana boldly plunged into a shop and explained the kind of place we were seeking —a small country inn by a stream. The information was at once forthcoming. At Berneck, we were told, less than thirty kilometres away, there was just such a place as she described. By now we had

grown accustomed to finding every man fit to bear arms in uniform,
as they had been in England fifteen years before, and so the fact that
the small hotel seemed to be in military occupation did not deter us,
for in other respects it had much to recommend it. As we were
finishing dinner the proprietor came to our table and said that he
hoped we had been satisfied. He added that if the service had not
been all it should have been, the reason was that the Führer with his
staff had come to spend the night there at very short notice. We had
been asked to hand over our passports on arrival, and he said that he
had learnt from mine that I was a Member of Parliament and held
some official position. Perhaps I would like to meet the Führer. I
said I would. He withdrew and when he returned asked me to follow him. I did so, expecting that I was going to be ushered into the
presence of the dictator. But it was only Alfred Rosenberg whom I
saw. He explained that Hitler was busily preparing a speech, but that
if I would wait he would probably be glad to see me later. I said I
would wait downstairs with my wife, where after a while he came
to tell me that Hitler excused himself on the ground of fatigue but
hoped that we would come to the meeting at Nuremberg where he
was speaking next day and for which he presented us with tickets.

I have been glad since that the interview did not take place and
that I never shook hands with the vilest criminal whose name sullies
the pages of history and brands with lasting infamy the people who
acclaimed him. We went to the meeting at Nuremberg. The speech
was not one of those tub-thumping ranting orations which used to
move the Germans to hysteria. It was supposed to explain the relation of Nazism to art. He read every word of it and I feared that I
had lost my knowledge of German completely, for I was quite unable to understand what he was talking about, but when I read in
The Times a few days later what was, I have no doubt, an accurate
translation I found it equally unintelligible, and I felt that it must
have been the work of one of the numerous learned German meta-
physicians who accepted with such slavish docility the poisonous
puerilities which constituted the Nazi philosophy. The tedium of it
was such that we insisted, to the shocked horror of the audience, on
leaving before the end of the speech.

On returning to London I had to address a small meeting of the

Junior Imperial League in my constituency. I told them something of what I had seen on my recent travels and informed them, as I thought it my duty to do, that Germany was preparing for war on a scale and with an enthusiasm unmatched in history.

The graver section of the press ignored this speech but my friends Rothermere and Beaverbrook pounced upon it. In scathing language I was denounced in their morning and evening papers as a warmonger. Not only was what I said untrue, but even had it been true I had no right to say it. Indiscretions of this kind disturbed the peaceful international situation. The Cabinet, so the *Daily Express* insinuated, were much distressed and I should probably be dismissed from my employment.

It so happened that on the day when this outburst appeared in the morning newspapers we were due to have luncheon at the German Embassy. Hoesch, the Ambassador, was an old friend whom we had both known before 1914, when he had been a popular figure in London ballrooms and one of Diana's frequent valsing partners. We had met him again on our honeymoon in Paris, where he had been appointed Chargé d'Affaires during the Armistice. He had been touched to find that we bore him no malice and were glad to see him again. Few French people would speak to him in those days.

We telephoned to him that morning, and asked whether he had seen the papers and still wanted us to come to luncheon. He treated the matter as a joke and said he was looking forward to seeing us. I talked to him on that occasion and others about the new régime in Germany, which he wholeheartedly accepted, and I gave him my views frankly but, I hope, politely. I am glad that we remained friends until he died suddenly in London two and a half years later.

The prophet of war is never popular. Cassandra ended her days, after all her true prophecies had been disregarded, as the slave of Agamemnon and the victim of his wife. I ought not therefore to have been surprised, although I was, by the great hostility that I aroused by saying that Germany was preparing for war. The forces of the Left in Great Britain were still preaching disarmament and circulating the idiotic peace ballot with the alleged object of discovering whether people preferred war or peace, an enquiry which hardly justified the time and stationery devoted to it. To them naturally the news that the most powerful people on the Continent were arming was unwelcome. It was a fact that they preferred to ignore.

But the Right was almost as unwilling as the Left to listen to rumours of war. By some curious mental aberration people came to believe that those who saw the danger actually wanted that to happen against which they gave warning. Not only was "warmonger" a term of abuse in the cheaper press, but even such a highly respectable figure as Dean Inge declared that he did not see why the world should be plunged into war in order to please Mr. Duff Cooper.

These were the days before the Axis, as the alliance between Hitler and Mussolini was termed. At Easter 1934 we paid a visit to Rome, where I had an interview with the Duce. I was favourably impressed. There were no histrionics, nor was I obliged, as I had been told would happen, to walk the length of a long room from the door to his desk. He met me at the door and accompanied me to it when I left. We agreed on the importance of rearmament and he laughed when I said that the idea that armaments produced war was as foolish as to think that umbrellas produced rain. Because he laughed at my joke I thought he had a sense of humour and was quite prepared to imagine he had other good qualities. It is too early to pronounce a final verdict upon Mussolini. The more I read about him, especially in the pages of Ciano, the less I like him, but no trustworthy biography has yet been written, so that it is wiser to withhold judgment. He is not, like Hitler, condemned out of his own mouth, nor by the notoriety and magnitude of his evil deeds. It may be that he began well and meant well, like so many of the Caesars before him, but that he ended ill as they did owing to the corruption of power.

For three years in succession my parliamentary activities had been practically confined to the introduction of the estimates, for there was usually little to be said about the Army Annual Act and few questions to be answered. I naturally took much trouble over the preparation of these estimates speeches and always delivered them without the aid of notes. I never attempted to learn by heart.

At the end of June 1934, my yearly parliamentary labours completed, I accompanied the Chief of the Imperial General Staff, General Montgomery-Massingberd, and some twenty or thirty senior officers, on a visit to France to study the battlefield of the Aisne. Hardly had we arrived at Soissons, which was to be our headquarters, when I was told that the Prime Minister wished to speak to me on the telephone from London. It was Ramsay MacDonald offering me the post of Financial Secretary to the Treasury. It seemed fated that I should receive news of promotion in strange places. I was very glad to accept. I had had enough of the War Office, and the occupant of the Financial Secretaryship to the Treasury was considered designated for the next place in the Cabinet.

The room in the Treasury assigned to the Financial Secretary in those days was the pleasantest of all ministerial apartments. Looking out on to the quietest corner of the Horse Guards Parade, its peace was disturbed only during the short period when rehearsals for the Trooping of the Colour took place. The work had the great merit of variety. One day I would find myself fighting against the demand for equal pay for men and women, a demand put forward by every Opposition and resisted by every Government. On the next I would be justifying the purchase of the *Codex Sinaiticus*, or presiding over a committee appointed to study the abuses of industrial assurance. I had feared that my limited acquaintance with political economy and my ignorance of finance would prove serious handicaps, but within a week of my appointment I had to wind up a debate on currency in the House of Commons and, speaking without the slightest knowledge of the subject, I was able, by drawing attention to the discrepancies in the remedies proposed by the previous speakers, all of them experts, to create a favourable impression and to earn many congratulations.

Neville Chamberlain was Chancellor of the Exchequer. He had none of the geniality of Worthington-Evans. At our first interview he reminded me that I had a reputation for indiscretion and warned me that while the unguarded words of most junior Ministers mattered little, an indiscretion by the Financial Secretary to the Treasury might bring down the Government.

I had been told that my new post involved more work than any other, and I had feared that I should have to give up writing the life of Haig, with which I had already made some progress. I soon found that I had been misinformed. The month was July and the final stages of the Budget had just been concluded. During the first four working days of the week the Financial Secretary is fully occupied, but when the House rises on Friday afternoon, or very often on Friday morning, he is at liberty. I have never considered a man hard-worked who is employed only in office hours, and who is not obliged to take work home with him. Still less can he complain if he has Saturday as well as Sunday free. My constituency required very little attention, and during the year and a half that I was at the Treasury I usually contrived to devote the greater part of Friday, Saturday and Sunday to my literary work.

This was my second book. The contrast between the two men who formed the subjects of these biographies could not have been greater, and while there could be no question as to which of the two characters was the nobler, it was the less noble that formed the more fascinating study for writer and reader alike. But the writing of the life of Haig was a simpler task than I had expected. A vast library might be collected of Napoleonic literature, and there would be hardly a volume in it with no mention of Talleyrand. Books about the 1914–1918 war in the west which are worth reading are not numerous, and in no others does the name of Haig occur, except, in footnotes perhaps, in the history of the war in South Africa. I had access to all the diaries he had kept at various periods and to the most important of all which he kept daily from the begin-ning to the end of the first World War, which he began as a Corps Commander and ended as Commander-in-Chief. When I accepted the task I knew no more of him than did the ordinary newspaper-reader. Before I finished it I felt that I knew him well and I admired him deeply.

The first volume appeared in the autumn of 1935 and the second early in the following year. On the day of publication a violent at-tack on the book appeared in the most prominent position in *The Times*. It was the work of the newspaper's military correspondent, a brilliant writer who had devoted his life to the study of military matters and who was the ablest exponent of the view that British strategy had been wrong throughout the war, which could have been more easily won by a flanking movement in the east than by the series of costly hammer-blows delivered on the western front. His article was a polemic rather than a review of a biography. He set out to prove that Haig had always been wrong and it therefore followed that anyone who sought to defend him must have written a book that was misleading and worthless.

The other newspapers followed suit. They all gave it to their military rather than their literary correspondents, and while it provoked some argument in military circles it was treated by nobody on its merits as the biography of a human being or as a work of letters.

The subject was one that no longer made a great appeal to the larger public. The first World War was beginning to be forgotten, and the second World War was soon to obliterate such memories of it as still lingered. People felt no obligation to read the life of Haig and many were doubtless glad of the excuse that adverse criticism gave them for not doing so. I feel sure that most of my friends never opened it. Literary critics have not been unkind to me. They have indeed, as I have already said, been generous, but I think that this particular book, which was never reviewed by literary critics, had less than justice done to it, and for this reason I make bold to brave the charge of vanity and to quote from letters received from people whose opinions are more important than those of all the military correspondents in the world.

Maurice Baring, who had paid me no compliments on *Talleyrand*, wrote:

You have by your *Haig* entered calmly and firmly into that permanent hall of English literature where only the *best*, the chosen, picked best, abide, and among them there are very few biographers, Boswell, Lockhart, etc. You are with those; with the best. You have done two things equally difficult and you have done them equally well. To make a living portrait of a translucent character whose very simplicity would baffle most biographers and to set it against an epic background, and while allowing the reader to take part in the epic to maintain a sense of proportion. The book is riveting, poignantly moving at times, beautifully disciplined and admirably written. You rise to the "height of your great argument" when the occasion demands it. Your comments are shrewd, sensible and acute. Your outlook large, comprehensive and understanding. It is a *great* achievement and you have my warmest, deepest and truest congratulations.

Rudyard Kipling wrote:

Ever so many thanks for the first volume of your *Haig*. I was reading it most of yesterday afternoon. It's, naturally, guarded—guarded up to the hilt, as you might say, but it gives one a truthful notion of the tug-of-war between politicians, "public opinion" and the general mess of unpreparedness and jangling commands. Also it reveals, as with "artlessness," the soul of L.G. I think, as a layman, that you're right about the Somme being a pivot of later victory. I'd like to talk that, and many other matters, over with you when next we meet at the Beefsteak. Then I can tell you how greatly I admire the "form" of the work and the clarity of your expositions.

Maurice Baring was an old and intimate friend and Kipling was a recent one, so their testimony may be thought prejudiced, although I know that neither of them would ever have allowed friendship to influence a literary verdict. Dr. G. M. Trevelyan, I am sorry to say, I have never met, yet he was kind enough to write to me about both the first and the second volume. His second letter runs:

I have been reading your second volume of *Haig* on the voyage out to America. . . . I can't resist writing to tell you how very good I think it is. I liked the first but this second is much better, indeed it would be difficult for it to be better. You seem to me to have wiped the floor with "the adversary" and sundry minor adversaries in a way the plain man can understand. . . . Better still, in the affirmative sense you have made us feel how and why Haig was a great man—and made us love him.

John Buchan, who, as has been shown, might, like Trevelyan, have written the book himself, and who was now Lord Tweedsmuir and Governor General of Canada, wrote from Ottawa:

My warmest thanks for the second volume of *Haig*. I have just finished it. I must send you at once my very warmest congratulations. Good as the first volume was, this is far better, for the story has become more dramatic, and you have managed the drama perfectly. I like especially your "falling close." You have handled the controversial parts brilliantly and with the most perfect good manners. Your answer to Lloyd George is shattering— more shattering because of its quietness, for you never raise your voice. As for your estimate of Haig's achievement and of his character, I do not think that could be praised too highly. I agree with every word; and it is done with a sober dignity which Haig would have loved. I really think you have achieved one of the two or three first-class military biographies in our history, and I cannot tell you how rejoiced I am to feel that a man who was not easy to understand has been perfectly comprehended and made wholly intelligible to the world. I finished the book not only with admiration, but with a strong feeling of personal gratitude to you.

I must quote one more tribute, that from Margot Oxford:

Dearest Duffy, I would not *turn a hair* were I you over the spiteful criticisms of your *Haig*. My autobiography was cursed and abused by everyone at the time, but on reading it again the other day (for the first time!) I think it very good.

So far as I remember, I incurred no criticism for having produced a work in two volumes at the end of four years' service as a junior Minister. I fear that similar tolerance would not be shown today, and indignant questions would be asked as to why a full salary should be paid for what must be a half-time job. I should have defended myself by saying that so long as I gave satisfaction to the head of my department and to the House of Commons, the employment of my leisure was my own affair.

My relations with Neville Chamberlain were friendly but never intimate. He was not a man whom it was easy to know well. Ungregarious by nature, he never frequented the Smoking Room of the House of Commons, where Stanley Baldwin and Winston Churchill were familiar figures, often in the centre of groups which included political opponents. In 1935 I assisted the Chancellor to steer the Budget through the House and he was generous in praise of the help I gave him.

In November of that year came the General Election. I was not unopposed on this occasion. A gifted young lady represented the Labour Party, but I felt sufficiently secure to spend the greater part of the election touring the country and only a few days in my own constituency. I spoke in Glasgow, Liverpool, Birmingham and Manchester, and of course at Oldham, returning to London on the eve of the poll, when I was returned by a handsome majority.

A week later I was shooting in Lincolnshire when I received a message during luncheon saying that if I was returning to London that evening the Prime Minister would like to see me before dinner. I fear that my mind was not on the pheasants during the remainder of the afternoon, and it was full of speculation as I travelled from Grantham to King's Cross and from Gower Street to Downing Street, where Mr. Baldwin informed me that he wished me to enter the Cabinet as Secretary of State for War.

CHAPTER TWELVE

SECRETARY OF STATE FOR WAR

1935–1937

ENTRY into the Cabinet is a great event in the life of a politician. For most it is the summit of their ambition: few aspire to be Prime Minister. It brings with it membership of the Privy Council and a nominal salary of £5,000 a year. In my day this amount, although already reduced by taxation, still represented more than £3,000, a larger income than I had ever had, and it was supplemented by the money that I received at the same time from the publishers of *Haig* and by an additional sum paid by a Sunday newspaper for the rights of serialisation. Half the money earned by the book went to the Haig estate, but what remained was for me a great deal and made me feel for the first time rich as well as happy.

The question that was occupying people's minds when I joined the Cabinet at the end of 1935 was the situation in Abyssinia. For a long time the Abyssinians had proved difficult neighbours to the Italian colonists in that part of Africa. There was no question but that Abyssinia was what is termed a "backward" country, in that it permitted slavery and other practices which Western Europe and the United States had long abandoned. Nevertheless it was Italy who had proposed that Abyssinia should become a member of the League of Nations, for she had not been an original member, and the other states, including Great Britain, had weakly assented.

In the spring of 1935 the British Prime Minister and Foreign Secretary had met the Italian Dictator at Stresa, and although the Foreign Office must have been aware, for the public was, of what the Italian Government were intending to do in Abyssinia, the subject had not been mentioned. The besetting sin of British foreign policy is refusal to let other nations know beforehand what Great Britain will do in certain circumstances. This reticence is often taken for compliance, and it is only when they are too far committed to a line of policy to withdraw from it that the foreign nation is given to understand that its continuance may involve war with Great Britain.

In the early summer of this same year those of us who were already aware of the ever-growing German menace were deeply concerned lest disagreement with Italy over Abyssinia might weaken or destroy what was then termed "the Stresa Front," meaning the solidarity of Great Britain, France and Italy. At a mixed dinner-party in a private room in the House of Commons, at which Winston Churchill and Lord Tyrrell were present, we discussed whether it might not be possible to send somebody to Rome who would warn the Italians of the risk they were running. Neither Churchill nor Tyrrell then held any official position, and it was not the business of the Financial Secretary to the Treasury to intervene in foreign affairs. So Diana was our emissary. It happened that she had been invited by a friend who had a house in Rome to attend the canonisation of the two English saints, Sir Thomas More and Bishop Fisher. She saw nobody of political importance, and when she told her Italian friends that Great Britain would resent Italian aggression against Abyssinia, nobody believed her. It was just the kind of war that the British had so often waged themselves against barbarous tribes, she was told, and surely if we had had any objection we would have mentioned it at Stresa? The gentle words she said aroused only bitter resentment.

Later in the same year I had to speak at a political meeting at Strachur on the shores of Loch Fyne. I there elaborated a thesis that had occurred to me only a few hours before, and which was prompted by my eager desire not to forfeit the friendship of Italy. I argued that it was useless to pretend any longer that the League of Nations represented what those who had been its creators had hoped it would become. Of the seven Great Powers which then existed, three had defied it—Germany, Italy and Japan; the United States had never joined it, and the adherence of Russia was recent and unreliable. It therefore no longer bore any relation to that original conception of an international body, including all nations, the overwhelming strength of which could impose law and order on the world. It was now merely a group of Powers, not including a majority of the great ones, with no very definite commitments towards one another. If therefore the worst should happen and all our efforts to prevent war between Italy and Abyssinia should fail, it might be our wisest course to abstain from interference, to hold the ring for a fair fight and to offer our services as mediators at the first opportunity.

I have no record of the words I used and am not sure that I went so far as the last paragraph suggests, but I feared afterwards that I had gone too far, and I spent a sleepless night in the hotel at Glasgow, wondering whether I had not made the indiscretion against which Neville Chamberlain had warned me, the one that might bring down the Government.

Whether the speech was reported in the local press of Argyll I never knew. It was certainly reported nowhere else, and neither the Government nor I was compromised by the advocacy of a policy which I still believe would have been a wise one. The opportunity of finally dissolving the ties that bound us to the decaying corpse of the League of Nations was unique. Now that three out of the seven Great Powers had flaunted the League with impunity, while the United States remained obstinately aloof, it could no longer inspire either reverence or respect. Italy had good grounds for complaint against Abyssinia and, had the latter not been encouraged to fight, she might have capitulated. In any case we should have retained the friendship of Italy; and the Axis, which was to prove the pivot of Hitler's assault upon Europe, and without which he could hardly have launched the second World War, would never have been formed.

There was, however, one other policy which I myself would sooner have seen adopted but which had little likelihood of recommending itself either to my colleagues or to the House of Commons. Sir Samuel Hoare had recently become Foreign Secretary and he had initiated his tenure of that office by a bold speech in which he gave uncompromising adherence to all the principles of the League. Those who still had faith in it had been encouraged. If we had then followed up these words by action, if we had unhesitatingly imposed every economic sanction ourselves, by a blockade prevented others from assisting Italy, closed the Suez Canal to Italian shipping, and at the same time mobilised the fleet, we should have rendered it quite impossible for Italy to continue the war unless she had been prepared to use force against Great Britain. Rumours were rife of the terrible

strength of the Italian navy and of the "mad-dog act" to which any
further irritation might drive the Duce. How little truth there was
in such rumours we learnt later, but at the time they caused alarm.
Yet we had little to fear. Italy had no allies. Germany would not and
could not then have raised a finger to assist her. All the smaller
Powers that were members of the League were pledged to aid us,
and between them they controlled the whole of the Mediterranean
seaboard that was not actually in Italian hands. Can we believe that
the mad dog would have been mad enough to go to war against such
odds? Can we doubt that had he done so he would have been
muzzled for life? It would have been the end of Mussolini and the
end of Fascism, a triumph for the League of Nations and a warning
to the Nazis.

If there had been a great leader in a high position at that time he
might have rallied the country to the support of such a policy, and if
Great Britain had led, the smaller nations would have followed. It is,
however, a curious fact that the British, who fight with the most
glorious courage and the toughest tenacity, have such a horror of war
that they will never support a policy which entails the slightest risk
of it. Nor have they yet learnt that reluctance to take risks is not the
way to acquire security.

The British people were very angry with Mussolini and very sorry
for the Emperor of Abyssinia, but they were not prepared to give
grounds for war to the former or effective help to the latter. Sir
Samuel Hoare and Monsieur Laval sought to give shape to these
sentiments by an agreement which, while handing over the substance
of Abyssinia to Italy, would have left a shadowy remnant to the Emperor. We do not even know whether Mussolini would have accepted this compromise. He would have been wise to do so, as Hitler
was wise to accept three years later what he was given at Munich. In
the one case as in the other the man who had grasped the substance
could add the shadow to it whenever he chose.

But before the Duce had had time to declare himself there arose a
howl of indignation from the people of Great Britain. During my
experience of politics I have never witnessed so devastating a wave of
public opinion. Even the easy-going constituents of the St. George's
division were profoundly moved. My post-bag was full and the let-

ters I received were not written by ignorant or emotional people but by responsible citizens who had given sober thought to the matter.

That outburst swept Sir Samuel Hoare from office. He was forced to resign. When he spoke in the House of Commons, explaining his resignation, I thought he made the same mistake that Edwin Montagu had made. Instead of defending his policy he excused his conduct. It would have been more effective if he had carried the war into the enemy's camp. He had been driven from power because he had suggested a solution of the problem which did very little for the Emperor of Abyssinia. Who, he might have asked, among his critics was prepared to do more? Was there a party in the House, or a single Member, who was willing to go to war, or even to risk becoming involved in war, in order to help the Emperor of Abyssinia? The proposals for which he was responsible would have left the Emperor with something. If within a few months he were to be left with nothing at all, and driven a homeless exile from his country, was there anybody in the length and breadth of Great Britain prepared to make an effective protest or strike a blow on his behalf?

For that was precisely what happened. The half-hearted sanctions that we imposed served only to infuriate Mussolini and drive him into the arms of Hitler. Doing the minimum of harm we incurred the maximum of ill-will, and at a time when the wind of fear was rising and the nations were anxiously watching for indications of weakness or strength, Great Britain appeared before them as a friend not to be relied upon and a foe not to be feared.

I will not pretend that I took a strong line in Cabinet when the question of Abyssinia was discussed. I was a newcomer, and as such it behoved me to voice my views with becoming modesty. I remember once saying that I had of course little experience, but those of my colleagues who had sat longer in Cabinet must surely have had occasion in the past to envisage the possibility of resort to force. One of them said to me afterwards that he had been struck by what I had said, but that, looking round the table, he had thought that Sir John Simon was the only one there who had ever been obliged, as a Cabinet Minister, to face the spectre of war. Yet it was only sixteen years since the Peace Treaty. Perhaps one of the reasons why so little is learnt from experience is that the men who conduct the affairs of nations are always changing, and that too few of them read history. This is particularly true of democracies.

I remember also that, in reply to something I had said, one of my colleagues turned on me, almost savagely, and asked: "Are all your preparations for war completed? Is your expeditionary force ready to sail?" Having taken charge of the department only a few weeks previously, I was quite unable to answer such questions. So far as I knew, the War Office might still be preparing for war against Russia in Afghanistan, as they had been when I was Financial Secretary.

The war in North-east Africa continued, and interest in it diminished when it became plain that the Abyssinians could not long maintain with their inadequate supply of nineteenth-century weapons the combat against modern aeroplanes and poison gas.

Early in the new year of 1936 King George V died. I had never known him, but I must have been one of the last Ministers to receive the seals of office from his hands. He told me on that occasion that he had liked my biography of Haig, which pleased me. I was attending a dinner given in honour of some German Generals when our chairman, Sir Frederick Maurice, read out the message "The King's life is drawing peacefully to its close." I was deeply affected. I was not enjoying the evening between two Germans whose conversation I found wearisome in the extreme. When tears came into my eyes I feared that my neighbours were noting them and would make a report to their Führer. I felt, without any logical justification, that we were passing another milestone on the road to disaster.

During the war in which I had fought I had felt no hatred for Germans, and had been inclined to despise the old ladies and gentlemen at home, whom such hatred obsessed, who discovered spies everywhere and swore that they would never speak to a German again. During that time a report appeared one morning that Count Mensdorff, for many years the popular Austrian ambassador at the Court of St. James's, had said something particularly insulting about the British. I dined that evening at Crewe House, where everybody was denouncing the former ambassador and vying with one another in devising the form of punishment he should suffer. Somebody turned to our host and said, "What would you do if you were ever to meet Mensdorff?" "First," said Lord Crewe, "I would shake hands with him, because he is an old friend. Then I might ask him about an unpleasant report which had appeared in the newspapers, and about which he could no doubt offer some satisfactory explanation." I felt, as I often did in the presence of Lord Crewe, that I had been taken back into a more civilised century.

After the war I found that those who had been the keenest of spy-hunters and the most determined in their oaths never to speak to a German again were precisely the people who forgot the real crimes of Germany most quickly, and many who had demanded that the Kaiser should be hanged were in favour of making friends with Hitler. I have always been anti-Nationalist and anti-Socialist, and therefore the combination of Nationalism and Socialism with a ruthless criminal at the head and a vast population of brave, competent, cruel people behind seemed to me the most fearful menace that civilisation had ever faced.

International law has never existed in the full meaning of the words because there has never been a sanction to enforce it. Christendom imposed a certain code of behaviour on princes, and those who, like Caesar Borgia, defied it, incurred universal odium. When the Reformation split the Church and religion began to lose authority, ruling families, closely connected with one another, and populations believing in the progress of humanity and all subscribing to the Christian ethic, continued to uphold a certain standard of conduct between Governments. But in the age of the dictators jungle law among the nations has revived, and in the jungle the first sign of weakness provokes attack.

Hitler was not slow to act upon the evidence of weakness which Great Britain's handling of the Abyssinian question seemed to have betrayed. In March 1936 he marched German troops into the Rhineland. Hitherto, in the rantings with which he delighted the German people, he had referred only to the hardships inflicted on Germany by what he described as the "dictated" Treaty of Versailles, a treaty that had been so much criticised both in Great Britain and America that to this day there are many people in both countries who are unaware that the terms of it were generous to Germany, that no effort was ever made to enforce the harsher financial clauses, that it sought to carry out President Wilson's idealistic theories of self-determination, and that it had already permitted defeated Germany in the course of sixteen years to become the most powerful nation on the continent of Europe. It was true to say that it was a treaty agreed to by a conquered country, but it was signed by the accredited representatives of that country, and if it was to be considered invalid because one party to it was weaker than the other, few if any treaties would ever be valid again.

But the occupation of the Rhineland went further than the already familiar denunciations of the Treaty of Versailles. It was a flagrant, unprovoked and indefensible violation of the Treaty of Locarno, which had been supposed to take the place of the former peace treaty, and which had been freely negotiated and agreed upon with the full and openly expressed approval of the German people.

In the light of after-events, a light that is always denied to us, this was undoubtedly the moment when Great Britain and France should have taken a firm line and insisted upon the withdrawal of the German troops as a preliminary to any discussion. Germany was not ready for war and had no allies. Hitler would have been forced to capitulate and the corner-stone of the great prestige that he built up in the minds of his fellow-countrymen would not have been laid. But even if we had been more determined, and even if we had received greater encouragement from a stronger French Government, there would have been one almost insuperable obstacle to firm action. It was not the strength of our armed forces but the mind of the British people that was unprepared for war.

The sea, which has proved so sure a protection of our shores for nine hundred years, has lulled our people into a sense of security that even two world wars, in both of which we narrowly escaped defeat, have failed to disturb. And from this sense of security there has developed a lack of interest in foreign affairs that constitutes a grave danger in a democracy. The average Englishman was quite unable to appreciate the significance of Hitler's military occupation of the Rhineland. "Why shouldn't the Germans move soldiers about in their own country?" was the not unnatural reaction of the ignorant. They could not understand that by this act a ruthless dictator had torn into shreds a treaty upon which the peace of Europe depended.

Nor was this lack of understanding confined to the less educated classes. A suggestion was put forward by His Majesty's Government that, pending settlement of the affair, the territory in question should be occupied by an international force. This innocent proposal so outraged the feelings of a Canon of Liverpool that he gave orders that there should be no more prayers offered up for the Government in the cathedral.

I was vexed by this pronouncement made by so distinguished a member of the Established Church. It seemed to me to display not only political ignorance but faulty theology. Surely if the Government were as wicked as the Canon believed, they were in greater need than ever of the prayers of the clergy? If the clergy were only to pray for the good and to preach to the converted their duties would become as light as many scoffers wrongly believe them to be.

To continue an enforcement of the spirit of inequality upon Germany [thundered the Canon] is a proposal unworthy of our creed and of our country. To renew an occupation of their homeland is a proposal monstrous and unjustifiable; it is an unnecessary degradation of the soul of a great people. To add to it that we shall do it again at the dictation of France is to lend aid to malice and to surrender right to vengeance. We cannot pray a blessing upon such proposals.

It should be remembered that when the Canon expressed these violently pro-German and anti-French views, it was of Nazi Germany that he was speaking, that Hitler had been in power for over two years, and that anybody who read the newspapers was aware not only of the hideous persecution of the Jews which he had initiated, but also of the blood-bath of June 1934 in which he had slaughtered without trial so many of his own closest associates.

But this opinion, held by a well-educated man holding a position of responsibility, was shared by a great number of his fellow-countrymen, and in a democracy such as ours the Government was bound, in forming policy, to take public opinion into account. It has been claimed that the Government should have educated and guided public opinion. This is an inadmissible claim, and one fraught with danger. So long as the press is free and competent the public can obtain from it all the information they require and, if they wish, can be guided in their interpretation of the news and the forming of their opinions by the editorials the press supplies. The British newspapers had never sought to conceal the crimes of Hitler, although some had gone far towards condoning them.

I denounced the views expressed by the Canon of Liverpool, and about the same time I strongly criticised a sermon delivered by a Bishop in which he seemed to advocate the dissolution of the British Empire. I also in the course of a speech in Manchester urged that in view of the widespread pacifism in the Church of England the leaders of the Church should tell the public plainly where the Church stood in this important matter, and say whether it was right or wrong for a Christian to take up arms in defence of his country.

I thereby incurred an undesired and undeserved reputation as a baiter of Bishops and an enemy of the Church. This doubtless harmed me and I regretted it. I have been all my life a supporter of the Church of England and a practising member of it. Without claiming to be deeply religious I believe that religion helps humanity and that the world is suffering today from the lack of it. I believe that most men are wise to remain in the faith to which they are born and bred. I admire the broad-mindedness and adaptability of our Church; I venerate its splendid liturgy, and I find even in its lack of discipline and uncertainty of doctrine something that is peculiarly English and lovable. I am also proud that my cousin, Cecil Cooper, Bishop in Korea, should have spent his life as a missionary of our Church and should have suffered for his faith at the hands of the Communists.

But at that time my mind was ever occupied with the war that I believed to be coming, the possibility of which so many people refused to recognise. It was my responsibility to see that the British Army was ready for that war, and the problem of recruitment seemed almost insoluble. While I was grappling with it I felt that it was wrong that good men, whose merits had been rewarded by official recognition, should be doing all in their power to persuade the youth of the country not only that it was unnecessary but even that it was wrong to join the armed forces of the Crown.

There was a popular and well-known clergyman, a Chaplain to the King, who had formed a society that was known as the Peace Pledge Union, members of which solemnly undertook that in no circumstances would they fight for their King and Country, and their numbers, I believe, amounted to over a hundred thousand. There was another cleric, also a Chaplain to the King, who publicly announced that nine out of ten of the best young men in Cambridge University would be less ashamed of going to prison than of joining the army. Men can conscientiously hold such views and have the right to express them, but such men should not, in my opinion, find shelter in the Established Church, which forms part of the constitution of the country.

It was not only, however, preachers and pacifists who increased the difficulties of my task. The reluctance of Englishmen to pay for armaments in peacetime is notorious, and ever since the war the Treasury had insisted that service estimates should show an annual reduction. In the General Election of 1935 "re-equipment" had been mentioned, not very often or very loud. But it is one thing to get a principle accepted, and another to put it into force.

If we were to obtain more recruits for the regular army and for the territorial army we could only do so by rendering life in both forces more attractive, which could not be done without spending more money on them. I devoted a great deal of time and effort during the holiday period of 1936 to preparing a paper in which I included every method of improving recruitment which had occurred to me or to my advisers. I had this document ready for circulation to my colleagues, so that it could be discussed at the first Cabinet meeting in the autumn. It was therefore with bitter disappointment that I received a message from the Chancellor of the Exchequer to the effect that no paper could be circulated to the Cabinet until it had received the approval of the Treasury, who would have to consult the other departments concerned. As I had suggested, among many other things, giving preferential treatment to old soldiers in the police, the postal service and indeed in all branches of the administration, I saw that the Chancellor's suggestion would mean consultation with nearly every government department. I said that this meant delaying consideration of my memorandum until Christmas. He replied that this was nonsense. The work could be done in two or three weeks. I forget how long it was before it came before the Cabinet, but I know that, after it had been referred to a committee of the Ministers principally concerned, as I had expected it was not discussed until early in the following year.

This and similar incidents which followed created unhappy relations between Neville Chamberlain and myself. One of my many failings is that I am apt to become heated in argument. If I lose my temper it is only for a moment but during that moment I often say more than I mean. I am sorry afterwards and willing to apologise. I forget quickly but others remember, and not forgetting cannot always forgive.

I had sympathy with Chamberlain's attitude. He had become Chancellor of the Exchequer in 1931 when the country, we were told, was on the verge of bankruptcy. He had brought about a great financial recovery. He was about to welcome the return of prosperity and he hoped to use the money in beneficial measures of social reform. Suddenly he saw his dream dissolving. The plenty that he had laboured so hard to collect was going to be thrown away upon rearmament, the least remunerative form of expenditure. But all was not yet lost. There was no certainty of war. He himself hated the idea of it. So, he believed, did all sensible men. Mussolini and Hitler must surely be sensible men too or they would never have risen to the great positions they occupied. Therefore they could not want war. There were certain things that they did want, and there were certain things that we could give them. If he were in control of foreign policy he could meet these men round a table and come to terms with them. The danger of war would be removed and we could all get on with social reform.

Chamberlain had many good qualities but he lacked experience of the world, and he lacked also the imagination which can fill the gaps of inexperience. He had never moved in the great world of politics or of finance, and the continent of Europe was for him a closed book. He had been a successful Lord Mayor of Birmingham, and for him the Dictators of Germany and of Italy were like the Lord Mayors of Liverpool and Manchester, who might belong to different political parties and have different interests, but who must desire the welfare of humanity, and be fundamentally reasonable, decent men like himself. This profound misconception lay at the root of his policy and explains his mistakes.

In this winter occurred the abdication of King Edward VIII. I had known His Majesty for some years and he had always shown me the greatest kindness, which he has never ceased to do since. I was aware of his affection for his present wife but had not guessed that he was contemplating matrimony. I learnt this from the Prime Minister, whom I happened to meet one afternoon in one of the corridors of the House of Commons. "Just the person I was looking for," he exclaimed. "Come to my room for a minute." When we reached it he told me that the King meant to abdicate and to marry, and had asked him, for the King behaved with punctilious constitutional rectitude throughout the crisis, whether he might see one or two Cabinet Ministers with whom he was on friendly terms. I was one of them and I had an audience on the following day.

I began by asking the King whether it was any use my trying to dissuade him from his intention or whether I should be merely wasting my time and his. He said that it would be quite useless, and I believed him. I then suggested postponement, which seemed to me the only alternative to abdication. It was a solution that I had known to work in the affairs of humbler folk and I had accepted it in my own case. I thought that if they would agree not to meet for a year, during which he would be crowned and perhaps attend a Durbar, of which there seemed some possibility at the time, he would at the end of that period have grown more accustomed to his position and more loth to leave it. I also secretly thought that he might in the interval meet somebody whom he would love more. He never has. He refused to consider the suggestion for a reason which did him credit. He felt it would be wrong to go through so solemn a religious ceremony as the Coronation without letting his subjects know what it was his intention to do. I could not argue against such scruples, but could only respect them. When we parted he said that we would have further conversations on the subject, but I did not see him alone again for many years, for soon afterwards the matter was given full publicity and there followed the rapid events that led to the abdication.

I was sad at his going. No such event had ever happened in English history. I felt that we were losing a personality of value to the State and I feared lest the prestige of the monarchy should suffer, a fear which happily proved groundless. He had many qualities that fitted him for his great position—charm of manner, sympathy with suffering, courage and sincerity, keen interest in politics and in the services.

One morning shortly after his accession, Field-Marshal Sir Cyril Deverell, Chief of the Imperial General Staff, was granted an audience. He came to my room in the War Office when he returned from it. He was a Yorkshireman of few words, not prone to enthusiasm, but on this occasion his tongue was loosened and his eyes were dancing. He told me all that the King had said to him and how deeply he had been impressed by His Majesty's obvious love of the Army and his interest in it. "The interview," he said, "was really inspiring."

When I say that King Edward VIII was interested in politics I cannot add that we were always in agreement on the subject. He hoped, as so many people did at the time, that we should be able to come to terms with the new régime in Germany, and he regretted my attitude towards it.

In the summer of 1936 I was invited to attend the annual dinner in Paris of the Great Britain–France Society, the object of which was to promote friendly relations between the two countries. I had to make the principal speech on that occasion. I took a great deal of trouble about this speech and wrote it out in English and French, which it is not my habit to do. I then sent it to the Foreign Office for approval. It was returned with certain changes suggested. I made the changes and sent it back again. I heard no more from the Foreign Office.

In the course of the speech I insisted that Great Britain and France were bound to stand together, that their interests were identical and that they were threatened by the same danger. I made no mention of Germany but my meaning was perfectly plain. The speech created something of an uproar in the British press. It was said that the Secretary of State for War had proposed a military alliance with France and had openly threatened Germany. The day after my return from Paris I met the King at dinner. As he approached me I saw that his face was heavy with displeasure. I expected a rebuke and I think he was preparing one, but suddenly the frown fled, giving way to his delightful smile as he laughed and said: "Well, Duff, you certainly have done it this time."

The King's sentiments on the subject were shared by the Labour Party. The speech was delivered on Wednesday, but it was not until Monday that they raised the matter in the House of Commons. They had doubtless been reading the Sunday newspapers and were anxious not to miss an opportunity of annoying the Government. They demanded the adjournment of the House "on a definite matter of urgent public importance." The Speaker granted their request, and that evening my speech formed the subject of a debate which was opened by Attlee, the leader of the Opposition, and in which, among others, Winston Churchill, Lloyd George, Archibald Sinclair, Harold Nicolson, Herbert Morrison, John Simon and my old friend Sidney Herbert took part.

It was a poor debate. The Opposition case was feeble. They sought to show that what I had said differed in some way from the declared policy of the Government. Sinclair quoted with disapproval my words "Your frontier is our frontier," but Baldwin had already said "Our frontier is on the Rhine." Attlee said that "to stress overmuch friendship with one country may lead possibly to other countries wondering why some stress was not laid on the need for friendship with all countries," and he insisted on the sacredness of the Treaty of Locarno which Hitler had already torn to shreds. Winston Churchill, the first speaker on our side, warmly defended me. "I cannot for the life of me see," he said, "that any difference exists between the Secretary of State and the Government and the Prime Minister," and he trusted that "His Majesty's Government are not going to apologise and whittle away the speech of the Secretary of State."

Sidney Herbert said: "I do not recollect a motion being moved on such a frivolous occasion as that of tonight. Not a single quotation has been made from the speech . . . which has for one second borne out the contention that it advocated any policy contrary to that of His Majesty's Government."

Sir John Simon, then deputy leader of the House, wound up for the Government. The great advocate never had a better brief and he made the best of it.

The Opposition were beaten in argument as soundly as they were beaten in the lobbies, for they took the matter to a division, but on

reading the debate again after many years I can understand the reasons
for their objections to my speech, as I can understand the lack of enthusiasm that it aroused in my own party. It was not accurate to say
that I had advocated a policy that differed in any way from the policy
of the Government. I had said nothing with which the Foreign Secretary, Anthony Eden, disagreed, but I fear that I had said a good deal
which he would not have said himself. I had shown him the draft
and he had suggested changes. I had changed all the passages to
which he objected, but in its final form the speech was much more
definite and unequivocal than anything that had hitherto been said
with authority. I defined beyond a shadow of a doubt a policy that
had previously been little more than adumbrated.

John Bull is represented as a blunt, bluff fellow who is fond of
speaking his mind. But in point of fact the ordinary Englishman dislikes plain speaking, just as he dislikes cold logic or facing hard facts.
The English love postponement and have a genius for compromise.
Both postponement and compromise can often be employed in
politics most usefully, but when war is approaching they should be
abandoned.

In the summer of 1936 I was sure that war *was* approaching. I believed that there was only one way of preventing it, and that was to
convince the Germans that if they fought they would be beaten. I
did not then know that the German Generals were convinced at that
time that they would be beaten, and remained so for two more years.
When I spoke in Paris I wished to show them, and the world at large,
that Great Britain and France stood firmly together and were not
afraid.

But the people of Great Britain did not feel as I did. They believed,
as they always do, that war is a fearful catastrophe that must be
avoided at almost any cost. Their minds had not been prepared
either by the Government or by the press to accept the idea that any
immediate danger existed. To talk as if it did seemed to them unwise, rash and almost indecent—just as in cases of serious illness there
are certain dread words which men hesitate to use, as though the
mere use of them may evoke what is dreaded. So at this time men
preferred to go on muttering vague generalisations about the League
of Nations and the Treaty of Locarno, as if they still meant real living

things and were not mere dead, empty words. The speeches of the Labour and Liberal Parties in that debate gave a not unfair representation of the mind of the people.

It was typical of Stanley Baldwin, who was Prime Minister at the time, that he never spoke to me on the subject of this speech or of the debate that followed it. The topic of foreign affairs was so uncongenial to his mind that he preferred to ignore it. I incurred, however, his disapproval on another count. I said in a public speech, which was duly reported, that I did not consider that members of the Communist Party ought to be employed in positions of trust under the Government. A question was addressed to the Prime Minister in the House of Commons as to whether the opinion of the Secretary of State for War reflected the policy of the Government. Baldwin replied emphatically that it did not, so that the Secretary of State for War was humiliated and for years the British Government continued to tell their secrets to their enemies with results that might have been expected.

I acquired little credit during my tenure of the War Office. With the means at my disposal there was not much to be done. Chamberlain knew that he could not save money on the Navy or the Air Force, therefore the Army offered the only hope of economising. A distinguished General, whom he had met fishing, had implanted in his mind the pernicious doctrine that if we contributed to the cause the greatest Navy in the world and a first-rate Air Force, our allies could hardly expect more. His aim, as his biographer Mr. Keith Feiling has told us, was an army of four divisions and one mechanised division, and he held that the duties of the Territorial Army should be confined to anti-aircraft defence. He also believed firmly "that war was neither imminent nor inevitable, that we could build on some civilian elements, such as the instability of German finance, which made it less likely."

It was generally known at the beginning of 1937 that after the Coronation, which was to take place in May, Baldwin would hand over the premiership to Chamberlain. So slight were my chances of survival in the new régime considered that the editor of a London newspaper called on me and made me a handsome offer of employment after I should have left the Government. When I expressed some surprise he assured me that his sources of information were better than mine and that I was sure to be dropped.

When I rose to introduce the Army estimates in the spring of that year I noticed that the Chancellor of the Exchequer remained in his place. It is not usual for busy Ministers to listen to the introduction of Service estimates, and there is no period when the Chancellor is so busy as in the spring. I felt sure that he was waiting to form an opinion as to whether my parliamentary abilities atoned for my other shortcomings. My estimate speeches were always well received, and this one was no exception, but when, a fortnight after the Coronation, while Chamberlain was known to be forming his Government, I received an invitation to call upon him in his room in the House, I felt great uncertainty as to my future. I thought that I should either be dropped or left where I was, and I was astonished when I was offered the Admiralty, which is generally considered a more desirable post than the War Office. The First Lord has one of the finest houses in London, and a yacht in which to sail the sea. He knows also that in any encounter he may have with his colleagues he has the country on his side.

Yet I had many regrets when I came to cross the road. I felt that I had been a true friend to the Army, and that the Army needed friends, that I had been working with a loyal and competent staff, and that after eighteen months I was beginning to learn my job.

CHAPTER THIRTEEN

FIRST LORD OF THE ADMIRALTY

1937–1938

OF the various posts that I have occupied in the Government—six in all—the one in which I was happiest was the Admiralty. It was also the one in which I found most work to do. But the work was comparatively simple. I had spent much time at the War Office writing memoranda for the Cabinet entitled "The rôle of the Army," in which I sought to persuade my colleagues to share my views as to the purposes for which the British Army existed. No similar problem awaited me at the Admiralty. Everybody knows what the Navy is for.

It is also far easier to form in the mind a clear picture of the ships and men of which the Royal Navy is composed than of the scattered units of Regular and Territorial Forces which form part of the British Army, distributed, as they were at that time, all over the world. I had not been long at the Admiralty before I knew the age and tonnage of every capital ship in the fleet and could have repeated from memory the various classes of cruisers and destroyers. I kept closely in touch with the construction programme and remembered the appropriate dates at which the principal new vessels would be in commission. It was a subject which, with a little application, any man could master.

To visit ships was also for me a great pleasure, although my dislike of inspecting factories extended to dockyards and shore stations in general. But the greatest pleasure of all was to have a ship at my own disposal, and I made the fullest use of the Admiralty yacht, H.M.S. *Enchantress*, during my tenure of office. Questions were sometimes asked in the House of Commons about my cruises and the expense that they entailed. Members failed to understand, and I never had an opportunity of explaining to them fully, that every ship in the Navy is continually being sent on cruises, without which it would be impossible to give the necessary training to the crews. The

Enchantress was a man-of-war, a sloop, and immediately on the out-break of war she was re-converted, at very slight expense, to her original purpose. She served with the fleet throughout hostilities. The cruises on which she sailed with the First Lord aboard would have taken place, or similar ones, if she had not borne the temporary appellation of "yacht"; and the increased charge to the taxpayer, if it existed, was negligible.

Such visits, I was assured, were welcomed by the Fleet. Sailors, like other men, are glad to think that interest is taken in their activities by those who are set in authority over them, and it is better for the prestige of the Board of Admiralty that the First Lord should pay visits under his own steam rather than as a passenger in some travelling battleship or cruiser.

That summer of 1937 we sailed from Holyhead round the north of Scotland and down the other side, visiting Scapa Flow, Invergordon and Rosyth. At the beginning of October we met the yacht at Venice and did a tour of the eastern Mediterranean—Skyros, Rhodes, Cyprus, Alexandria and Malta. At all these posts I was able not only to visit ships of all categories but also to make the acquaintance of naval officers, including the Commanders-in-Chief of the Home and Mediterranean Fleets, Admiral Backhouse at Invergordon and Admiral Dudley Pound at Alexandria, whose rival claims to succeed Admiral Chatfield as First Sea Lord I had to consider.

The cruise ended at Naples, where we were treated with the greatest courtesy by the Italian officials. A complete carriage with a suite of compartments, which included a kitchen, was put at our disposal, in which there was room for our whole party—we had three friends travelling with us, Lord and Lady Gage and Diana's niece, Lady Elizabeth Paget. It remained on the train, as we did, from Naples to Calais. Unfortunately there was set into the wall of the principal compartment an engraved tablet containing the names of those countries which had applied sanctions against Italy during the Abyssinian war, and an intimation that Italy would never forget. High on the list stood the name of Great Britain.

At the beginning of 1938 I started to keep a diary again, and as it was to prove an important year in my life I am glad that I did so. Referring to events of the past year I wrote:

Looking back on it now I believe I was much nearer being dropped [when the new Cabinet was formed] than I thought at the time. I was quite astonished when the Prime Minister offered me the Admiralty. I had rather then have remained where I was, but now I am very glad that I was moved. However, to be moved from an office after having held it for only eighteen months must imply some measure of failure, an impression which I have got somehow to wipe out in my new position.

I don't think that at present I have succeeded in doing so. I cannot adopt spectacular methods. I know myself that I did not do badly at the War Office and that that was also the opinion of the Army. But it takes some time for the opinion of a service to reach the public, and many of those who were my advisers and supporters have been dismissed.

Whether I shall do well at the Admiralty remains to be seen. I doubt whether I have any particular gift for administration, and during recent weeks I have been suffering from a certain lack of self-confidence which is new to me and depressing. I ought not really to mind because I think I should be happier out of office. My political ambitions have dwindled. I have always wanted to be Prime Minister. I want to be so no longer. I have got near enough to see the position without the glamour. I see more plainly the endless, thankless work, the worry and responsibility and the abuse. F. S. Oliver says that the great statesman must have a passion for power. I don't think that I have any desire for it. I have a growing dislike for public speaking and for publicity. I love leisure but I should never relapse into idleness, for there are books that I want to write, and I enjoy writing.

On the other hand I like my present job better than any that I could be offered. I came to it comparatively ignorant, but I am learning rapidly and I feel that it is one I can grasp. I am determined to make a success of it if I can, and then if I care to retire from politics I shall be hardly over fifty and shall still have time for other activities.

The subject that occupied much of my working time at this period and fills many pages of my diary was the future of the Fleet Air Arm, the control of which had recently been transferred from the Air Ministry to the Admiralty. This decision had been taken in the face of violent opposition from the Air Ministry, where it had left such bitterness and rancour that it sometimes seemed as though members of that department were determined that the new arrangement should work as badly as possible. It would be tedious now to revive the details of this old controversy, which seemed at the time, and which indeed was, of the first importance.

I profited a great deal from my friendship with Louis Mountbatten, whom I had known for many years. He had just been promoted and was the youngest Captain in the Navy. Temporarily on half-pay, his last post had been in the Fleet Air Arm division, and he was therefore able to supply me with precious information and advice. Nothing can be more valuable for a Minister than the opinions, confidentially given, of a junior officer upon whose integrity and intelligence he can rely.

The most important event that occurred in the early days of 1938 was the offer received from President Roosevelt to call a conference of minor European Powers in Washington in order that agreement might be reached upon certain political principles, the agreement to be subsequently submitted to the great Powers for their adherence. The scheme itself was open to criticism, but the offer by the President of the United States of direct intervention in European affairs presented an immense opportunity which, if it had been seized upon, might have proved one of the turning-points in European history and would probably have averted the coming war.

Anthony Eden, the Foreign Secretary, was taking a short holiday in the south of France when the message arrived. Neville Chamberlain, without consulting him or any other of his colleagues, rejected the President's proposal within twenty-four hours. In his reply he stated that he himself was contemplating conversations with Mussolini, which would of course necessitate the recognition of the Italian conquest of Abyssinia, and he feared lest the President's plan should interfere with these negotiations. The President in reply deeply regretted the decision to give *de jure* recognition to the Abyssinian situation, which he knew would have a deplorable effect on public opinion in America and would strengthen the hands of those who were opposed to any intervention in European affairs. When Eden returned he was horrified at what the Prime Minister had done in his absence. He tried to set it right by sending further messages to the President, expressing qualified approval of his plan. But it was too late. The great opportunity had been missed.

These matters of high policy were at that time discussed and decided by the Foreign Policy Committee of the Cabinet, of which the Defence Ministers were not members. The Cabinet as a whole learnt of the President's message only when the whole matter was past history, nor were we told that there had been any divergence of opinion between the Prime Minister and the Foreign Secretary. I wrote in my diary on February 13th:

The press this week have got hold of a quite untrue story that there is a profound disagreement between Anthony and the Prime Minister over friendship with Italy. There is no foundation for it.

In this case the press was better informed than the Cabinet Minister, and when a special meeting of the Cabinet was announced for Saturday afternoon, February 19th, I had no idea of the reason for such an unusual procedure.

I had been glad when Eden had become Foreign Secretary and I had always given him my support in Cabinet when he needed it. I believed that he was fundamentally right on all the main problems of foreign policy, that he fully understood how serious was the German menace and how hopeless the policy of appeasement. Not being, however, a member of the Foreign Policy Committee, I was ignorant of how deep the cleavage of opinion between him and the Prime Minister had become. It is much to his credit that he abstained from all lobbying of opinion and sought to gain no adherents either in the Cabinet or the House of Commons.

Had he made an effort to win my support at the time he would probably have succeeded, but with regard to Italy I held strong opinions of my own. I felt, as I have written earlier, that the Abyssinian business had been badly bungled, that we should never have driven Mussolini into the arms of Hitler, and that it might not be too late to regain him. The Italo-German alliance was an anomaly. The Germans and Austrians were the traditional enemies of the Italians; the English and the French, who had contributed so much to their liberation, were their historic friends, and Garibaldi had laid a curse upon any Italian Government that fought against them. The size and strength of the Third Reich made her too formidable a friend for the smallest of the Great Powers, who would soon find that from an ally she had sunk to a satellite. These were the thoughts that were in my mind during the long Cabinet meeting that took place that Saturday afternoon.

The Cabinet then learned for the first time of the rift which had opened between the Prime Minister and the Foreign Secretary. The

Prime Minister was anxious to open conversations at once with the Italians and to announce publicly that we were doing so. The Foreign Secretary thought that Mussolini must carry out some of the engagements he had already made, especially with regard to Spain, before conversations were started. He believed that there was some secret agreement between Hitler and Mussolini and that the latter had received some *quid pro quo* for his acquiescence in the assault on Austria. Grandi had denied that this was so. The Prime Minister believed him: the Foreign Secretary did not. This did not seem to me to be of very great importance. What was it that Mussolini might have received? Assurance that Hitler would come to his help if we attacked him? Such an assurance was of little importance, as we had no intention of attacking anyone. The Foreign Secretary wanted to defer the open-ing of conversations until the Italians were behaving better. But it seemed to me that, if the conversations were not opened now, the Italians, far from behaving better, would behave worse. If it were a question of timing—whether to hold conversations now or in a month's time or even in three or four months' time—the Foreign Secretary would doubtless be the best judge; but if it were a question of now or never, it seemed to me to be better that the conversations should be opened without delay.

At the end of our long discussion Eden made it plain that he meant to resign. This was a surprise to many of us. We all realised what a tremendous blow it would be for the Government. It might even bring about the Government's fall. The Cabinet's discussion was adjourned until three o'clock on the following day.

On the Sunday morning the story of Eden's resignation appeared fairly accurately in most of the papers.

My Parliamentary Private Secretary, Hamilton Kerr, rang me up in alarm, and then came round to see me. He said the situation in the House would be hopeless, that more than a hundred of our supporters would vote against us. I gathered that he would be inclined to do so himself. I argued with him on the merits of the case.

I went out to luncheon at Buck's, where I found the dining-room quite empty. Soon after I had started David Margesson came in. He had been with the Prime Minister in the morning and told me that the position seemed hopeless. He was inclined to favour Malcolm MacDonald as a successor to Eden and I was inclined to agree with him.

When the Cabinet met in the afternoon it appeared that all efforts to find a solution had failed. Indeed, it was now clear that the difficulty between the Prime Minister and the Foreign Secretary was not confined to the means of handling the immediate issue; there was a deeper difference of outlook between them that made it difficult for them to work together. There was, for instance, the letter which the Prime Minister had addressed to Mussolini, and the manner in which he had rejected President Roosevelt's proposals, both actions taken without consulting his Foreign Secretary. All attempts to find a compromise were unavailing, for the two protagonists saw that their divergence was fundamental and that there were no means by which they could compose their differences. Ultimately it was left to a smaller group of Ministers to see whether any formula could be found to avert Eden's resignation. He undertook to meet that group later in the evening and give them his decision. The rest of us would then be told the outcome.

This is what I wrote in my diary at the time:

We know not what will happen. My own belief is that he means to go because he doesn't want to make terms with Italy, and he feels that he will never be allowed to pursue his own policy with the P.M. at his shoulder. If he goes it will certainly be a body-blow for the National Government. There were crowds in Downing Street last night and tonight, and when he drove off there were loud cheers. This I am afraid will stiffen his attitude, because he will feel that he has popular opinion behind him, which indeed he has.

This was written immediately after the meeting on the Sunday afternoon. It is followed by a later entry which records the outcome.

I dined with Maureen Dufferin. There were a great many men there and only two other women, Anne O'Neil and Maureen Stanley. I was sitting next to the latter, but dinner had hardly begun when she got a call from Oliver on the telephone and went off to join him. She told me that he had been very ill all day and had had a high temperature this morning. Esmond Harmsworth was on my other side. He of course welcomed the prospect of Anthony leaving the Cabinet. Towards the end of dinner he went out to see if he could collect any news on the telephone, and came back to tell me that he had heard there was a Cabinet meeting at 10.30. Then Maureen reappeared with the news that the meeting was at ten. It was already a quarter past and it was twenty-five past by the time I got there. A letter from Anthony had been read, announcing his inability to accept any of the compromises suggested and his determination to resign. Anthony was not there. The Prime Minister looked very exhausted.

That was the end of the crisis, which was followed by a debate in the House of Commons. Of the large number of Conservatives who were going to vote against the Government only one did so. It was Vyvyan Adams. Let it be recorded to his credit.

During the two days' debate one could feel opinion veering steadily towards the Government. Anthony's statement was very dignified; Bobbety's [Lord Cranborne], rather unexpectedly, was more violent. To talk about "surrender to blackmail" seemed to me to exaggerate. Nor do I think it was true to say, as Anthony said, that there was anything in the nature of a threat. He could justify it to some extent by the fact that Grandi had said that unless Italy came to terms with us soon she would be obliged to make what terms she could with Germany. He could also quote a message sent via Lady Chamberlain from Ciano, to the effect that terrible things were happening in Europe, and that if we did not come to terms now it might in a few days be too late.

I was unhappy about Anthony Eden's departure. I wrote to tell him so and to say that I had always found myself in agreement with him, except on this one question of Italy. He knew more than I did, but neither he nor I knew that behind his back our own Prime Minister was in secret communication with the Italian Ambassador. The three of them (Chamberlain, Eden and Grandi) had met together on February 18th, and on the very day we were discussing whether Eden should remain in the Cabinet, Grandi was reporting to his Foreign Minister, Count Ciano:

Chamberlain, in fact, in addressing his questions directly to me, expected from me—this was obvious—nothing more nor less than those details and definite answers which were useful to him as ammunition against Eden. This I at once realised and naturally tried to supply Chamberlain with all the ammunition which I considered might be useful to him to this end. There is no doubt that in this connection the contacts previously established between myself and Chamberlain through his confidential agent proved to be very valuable. Purely as a matter of historical interest, I inform Your Excellency that yesterday evening, after the Downing Street meeting, Chamberlain secretly sent his agent to me (we made an appointment in an ordinary public taxi) to say that "he sent me cordial greetings, that he had appreciated my statements, which had been very useful to him, and that he was confident that everything would go very well next day."

The Prime Minister was, in fact, deliberately playing a part throughout the Cabinet discussions. While allowing his colleagues to suppose that he was as anxious as any of them to dissuade the Foreign Secretary from resigning, he had, in reality, determined to get rid of him, and had secretly informed the Italian Ambassador that he hoped to succeed in doing so. Had I known this at the time, not only would I have resigned with Eden, but I should have found it difficult to sit in Cabinet with Neville Chamberlain again.

Throughout my tenure of the Admiralty I had to maintain a perpetual struggle with the Treasury, who never ceased, as they never have ceased, to maintain that the finances of the country were in a desperate condition. It should be remembered, in reading selections that I shall give from my diary, that the year was 1938, that no sensible, well-informed person could doubt that there was imminent danger of war, that war almost broke out in September of that year, and would have done so had not the Government by abject surrender postponed the outbreak by less than twelve months.

January 23rd. I had a discouraging letter from the Chancellor of the Exchequer [Sir John Simon] last week. He wants us to reduce our proposed estimates by £6,000,000 and I don't see how it can be done. Meanwhile the Chiefs of Staff are preparing a report for the Committee of Imperial Defence to the effect that our rearmament programme is quite inadequate to meet the dangers with which we are faced, and that we must either increase the scale of it, or reduce our liabilities by making friends with one of our potential enemies. The same thing was mentioned at the C.I.D. on Thursday, à propos of the increased Italian garrison in Libya. . . . I urged that we should endeavour to come to terms with Mussolini and there was general agreement with my view.

The following week I mention:

a letter from the Chancellor saying he cannot possibly accept our building programme and we must produce a smaller one. This at a time when the Chiefs of Staff fear that our preparations for war are inadequate, and when the C.I.D. are seriously discussing, as they were last week, whether the time has not arrived when we should take stronger measures to hasten the production of munitions, even going so far perhaps as to interfere with industry and compel some of the big firms to release their men for government work.

I have written to the Chancellor saying that I cannot produce what he asks for—"a very much smaller programme"—without a Cabinet decision. To reduce and slow down our preparations at this time seems to me to be indefensible.

February 13th. I have agreed with the Chancellor a figure for my estimates, leaving for the time being the construction programme out of the
question. We both gave away more than we wanted to and I had some
difficulty in persuading Chatfield to accept the final settlement, because it
did mean the delay of certain preparations for war which are necessary.
Inskip has produced a memorandum which, so far as I can understand it,
means fixing a global sum for all rearmament and leaving the three services to squabble over its distribution. Both that and my construction programme will come before the Cabinet on Wednesday. The prospect of
the battle has revived my interest and sharpened my appetite for politics.

During this year I wrote my diary once a week, on Sunday, and
on February 20th I had a good deal to recount, including the resignation of Anthony Eden.

The past week has been a busy one, full of events. The full significance
of Hitler's summons to Schuschnigg appeared gradually. It was nothing
less than the end of Austria's independence: a portentous event in European history about which nobody here seems to think or care.

At the Cabinet on Wednesday full information was not yet to hand and
comparatively little time was spent on foreign affairs. The main subject
of discussion was a report which Inskip has produced on the future of rearmament. The demands of the three services over the next four years
amount to something in the nature of £2,000,000,000 and the Treasury
say that £1,650,000,000 is all the money that can be made available. Inskip's simple solution is to divide that sum in certain proportions to be decided upon between the three services. My advisers tell me that according
to their calculations the Admiralty would be reduced to construction programmes, the annual cost of each of which would be about £12,000,000.
The one that we had already put forward for this year was £70,000,000
and last year's was very little less. It would mean that we could not possibly complete even the modest plan to which we are committed, let alone
the New Standard, which has not yet been approved, but which all the
experts consider is the minimum consistent with security.

I told the Cabinet this, and pointed out that if we were at war, which I
thought we soon might be, we shouldn't dream of accepting an arbitrary
figure given us by the Treasury, and I reminded them that at the beginning
of the last war the Treasury view was that it must end in 1916 owing to
lack of money.

However, the Cabinet eventually adopted the Inskip report and postponed consideration of my reconstruction programme as being affected by
the report. I protested that consideration of the report would take months,
that the programme must be settled before the defence debate at the beginning of March, and that it was unfair to make the report apply to the
1938 programme of one of the services and not to those of the others. It
was however eventually settled that I should discuss the matter with the

Chancellor and the Minister for Co-ordination. The Cabinet sat for three hours in the morning and three and a half hours in the afternoon.

February 27th. At the Cabinet on Wednesday we discussed my construction programme. I put forward three, my original one (70 million), a 36-million one and a halfway-house to the tune of 48 million. I spoke strongly in favour of the first, but I knew I shouldn't get it. . . . It was decided that Simon, Inskip and I must discuss it further and come back to the Cabinet if we couldn't agree. We discussed it on Thursday and have communicated since but have not yet reached agreement.

On Wednesday I went down to Cambridge to propose "The immortal memory of Samuel Pepys" at the annual Pepys dinner at Magdalene. I stayed with the Master, Ramsay, who was my tutor at Eton, and I enjoyed the evening. I hadn't given as much time as I intended to my address, as I had meant to write it during the last week-end, that was so fully occupied with other things. However I think it was adequate, and they seemed pleased.

In the following week I was struck down with the worst attack of influenza from which I have ever suffered. I was laid up for more than a fortnight. The next entry in my diary is dated March 17th.

I am still in bed. I have missed four Cabinet meetings and today I should have introduced the Navy estimates, which were introduced instead by Geoffrey Shakespeare. It has been a long and tedious illness and isn't over yet. I have never felt very bad but don't get any better. I have enjoyed reading *Is he Popenjoy?* and re-reading *La Cousine Bette* and *Tom Jones*.

Last Saturday there was an emergency Cabinet in the morning over the Austrian *coup d'état*. I sent the Prime Minister a letter beforehand, suggesting that a suitable reaction on our part would be an increase in our already published naval construction programme. He read my letter to the Cabinet but said that he would prefer an increase in the Air Force. Hore-Belisha wrote and told me this and so did Oliver, to whom I spoke on the telephone.

I got up that afternoon and worked at my estimate speech. The result was that my temperature went up and I am supposed to have had a definite relapse.

There was another Cabinet on Monday, and before it I wrote the P.M. another letter, pointing out that more air construction wasn't going to impress anybody, that we probably shouldn't get delivery even if we gave the orders, and that if we did we shouldn't have the pilots. Also that our action would be interpreted as yielding to internal criticism. The increased naval construction on the other hand was easily practicable, and had in fact been contemplated, and it would be a direct reply to the aggressive policies of both Germany and Japan. He read it to the Cabinet but said that it didn't alter his views. . . .

On Monday [March 21st] the doctor said he wouldn't come again unless I sent for him, and that morning I went out for a drive with Diana in
the park. It was a most beautiful warm spring morning and I felt all the
keen enjoyment of coming to life "again with the revolving year."

I learnt there was to be a special Cabinet meeting the following morning
and I determined to go to it. The agenda arrived after I had gone back to
bed. There were two documents—a note to the French Government and
a parliamentary statement. The note was a cold refusal to give any support to France if she went to war on account of Czecho-Slovakia, and the
parliamentary statement read like a declaration of isolation. When the
night nurse came she found that my temperature had gone up again. I told
her that it was due to the documents I had been reading, and that I meant
in any case to go to the Cabinet next day. I had a bad night and the doctor
came again the next morning, but my temperature was down, I wasn't
coughing and they had to let me go.

I fought hard at the Cabinet, not quite in favour of giving the guarantee
to Czecho-Slovakia, but for making a more friendly gesture to France. I
insisted that when France fought Germany we should have to fight too,
whether we liked it or not, so that we might as well say so. . . . It was
decided that the two statements should be redrafted but that the policy
should remain.

I felt ill and depressed. After lunching with Diana I went back to bed.
I got up for tea with Liz, who was very sad about the fate of Austria. After
she had gone Dicky Mountbatten came to see me to talk about the Fleet
Air Arm.

The next day we went down to Lavington, the house of our dear
friends the Euan Wallaces, where I spent four days of convalescence.
Belloc came to lunch one day. He said that the Prime Minister had
written a poem which went

> Dear Czecho-Slovakia,
> I don't think they'll attack yer
> But I'm not going to back yer.

The Prime Minister's speech in the House on Thursday was a great success. It was very different in tone and emphasis from the draft the Cabinet
were asked to consider last Tuesday. Without saying so definitely, he
quite clearly implied that if France went to war we should go too. This
was all that I wanted. It was perhaps wiser in the long run to imply than
to state it. Our own public opinion is reluctant to accept the unpleasant
necessity. In this way public opinion is allowed two stages in which to
approach it instead of being obliged to swallow it in one.

During the Easter recess we paid a visit to Paris, where we had
luncheon at the Ministry of Marine with Campinchi, a valiant Corsi-
can, who was then Minister.

It was a small party, Daladier [who had recently become Prime Minister], La Chambre, the Minister for Air, our Ambassador and Lady Phipps, and half a dozen others. I sat next to Madame Campinchi with the Chief of the Naval Staff on my other side [this was Admiral Darlan, who seems to have made little impression upon me]. Campinchi made the whole thing go. He talked incessantly and lightly, ragged Daladier and was extremely amusing. I found that all the French Ministers with whom I talked—and the only other one was Mandel—were very sceptical about the value of our agreement with Italy. Daladier went so far as to say that it had saved Mussolini from disaster. They all take the view that Italy's word is not worth having, and that she will always betray her allies, as she did in the last war. I argued that Italy will certainly pursue her own interests—who doesn't?—but that her interests lie with ours. The absorption of Austria by Germany is a greater blow to her than it is to France or England, and a German victory in a great war would reduce Italy to the rank of a third-rate power, existing at Germany's mercy, whereas an Anglo-French victory would leave her as she is. Germany, now that she includes Austria, will soon be demanding a port on the Adriatic. Mussolini is an intelligent man and knows this. Daladier suggested that Mussolini's intelligence is not what it was, that he had become a visionary, hardly sane.

We lunched with the Phippses the first day, and there we found Hilary who was staying with them. It was odd to see the old boy against the background of an embassy. He looked much smartened up and was wearing the button of the Legion of Honour. We saw a good deal of him afterwards and spent Easter day with him, driving out to Les Loges in the Forêt de St. Germain, where we had an excellent luncheon and returned through the valley of Chevreuse. It was a beautiful, sunny afternoon and he was in wonderful spirits, singing half the time.

The bickering about naval expenditure continued all that summer. In May I wrote:

I have had a busy week preparing a paper for the Cabinet on the future of the Navy. In it I suggest that we should abandon the absurd new system of rationing the defence departments. I suggest that the sensible plan must be to ascertain your needs for defence first, and then enquire as to your means of meeting them. If it is really the case that they cannot be met, then there must be some fundamental change of policy, either foreign, imperial or domestic. I sent advance copies of my paper to the P.M., the Chancellor and Inskip on Thursday. Markham, my private secretary, writes to me [I was on board the *Enchantress* at the time, on my way to the Scilly Isles] "Your memorandum has, I think, satisfactorily fluttered the dove-cotes. . . . Woods [the Chancellor's private secretary] rang me up to say that the Chancellor was regarding the memo askance, but was unwilling to take the view that it should be withheld from the Cabinet." There is however a danger that he and the P.M. may decide to withhold

it. But I don't see how they can indefinitely postpone further consideration of the naval situation.

The P.M. and Halifax [who had succeeded Eden at the Foreign Office]
have slightly altered their views about military conversations with the
French, and asked to be given a free hand to agree to them if necessary.
Kingsley Wood, who clings to the idea of friendship with Germany and
hates the thought of getting too closely tied up with the French, is
alarmed at the prospect, and so are others, but of course the P.M. will get
his way.

The following week I wrote:

As I feared, Simon prevented my memorandum from being circulated
to the Cabinet. I had a talk with him about it on Thursday, which was, as
I knew it would be, pure waste of time. The only result was that we are to
have a further talk with Inskip and the Prime Minister tomorrow. Simon
had no suggestion to make except that I should at least put forward some
proposal, as Hore-Belisha had done, whereby the money could be saved.
My answer was that before the Admiralty can be asked to sketch an
imaginary fleet they must be told for what purpose it is to be used. If we
are told that it is to fight Germany and Japan and that the Treasury figure
is the limit, we can only answer "It can't be done for the money." Either
their demands must be lower or their figure must be higher.

In their conversations with Daladier and Bonnet the P.M. and Halifax,
disregarding the views of many of their colleagues, agreed to naval staff
conversations. The naval staff have always strongly opposed this, for fear
that it would give Germany a good excuse for breaking the naval treaty.
Personally I don't mind at all, because I believe that the Germans will break
that and any other treaty as soon as it suits them to do so.

My meeting with the P.M., Simon and Inskip on Monday resulted in a
long and profitless argument which at moments became, on the Prime
Minister's side, rather acrimonious. I cannot help irritating him. The up-
shot of it was that the Chancellor wrote me a letter asking for certain
definite figures, which we are preparing for him. . . . I am inclined to believe now that the best plan may be to avoid taking any decision on policy
as a whole and to rely upon the Treasury being obliged to agree to what
we want from time to time as we want it.

There is no doubt that in the month of May 1938 Hitler intended
and wanted to go to war on the question of Czecho-Slovakia, and it
has been widely believed that he was prevented from doing so by the
firm attitude adopted by the British Government. I believe that, on
the other hand, it was a faint flicker of protest from Paris, an ominous
rumble from Moscow, but above all the very firm opposition of his
own General Staff, that forced him to abandon his plan. His military

advisers knew then, and they had not changed their minds four months later, at the time of the surrender of Munich, that Germany was in no condition to embark upon a great war.

Here at least is how it struck a contemporary Cabinet Minister. The crisis occurred, as it is the inconvenient custom of crises to do, between Saturday and Monday and found us at Cranborne, where among a large party the Winston Churchills were staying.

With the evening papers [on Saturday] came the news that two Sudeten Deutsch farmers had been shot in Czecho-Slovakia, and then a message from the Resident Clerk at the Admiralty to say that there was to be a meeting of Ministers at five o'clock the following day. This was all most annoying. Diana and I had arranged to drive down to Plymouth this afternoon and stay the night with the Commander-in-Chief. I wanted to inspect the Fleet Air Arm recruits in the *Hermes*.

It was a very beautiful evening. The place was looking as like an earthly paradise as it is possible to conceive. Betty has given all her time to the garden of recent years and made it more beautiful than ever. In such surroundings the folly and horror of war seemed ten times more foolish and horrible. And I feel that war is very near. I couldn't help remembering another beautiful Sunday twenty-four years ago when I was staying at Stanway and was recalled to the Foreign Office.

May 22nd. After a very pleasant luncheon we motored up to London through the country, looking its loveliest in perfect weather. Ministers met at five. We sat only for an hour, as there was very little to say. The general feeling seemed to be that great, brutal Czecho-Slovakia was bullying poor, peaceful little Germany. . . . It was decided to send off a telegram to tell the French to go carefully and not to rely too much on us, and another to urge the Czechs to make large concessions.

The result was better than anybody could have foreseen, and quite different. The crisis passed over. The Germans decided to do nothing, and everybody believes it was entirely due to the firmness of the British Government. I consider this a complete misapprehension—but so is history written. Even well-informed people, like Winston, with no desire to give credit to the Government, believe that it is so. And Belloc, who came to dinner here the other night, was under the impression that we had said to the Germans that if they crossed the Czecho-Slovak frontier we should go to war. Of course we never said anything of the kind. There exists also a belief spread by the *Evening Standard* that Poland adopted a very firm anti-German attitude. There is no word of truth in it. On the contrary, the Poles refused to give the French any assurance or support whatever. One cannot be surprised that Hitler is annoyed to read over and over again in the French and English press that his bluff was called and that he was humiliated by the western democracies.

There came before the Cabinet in the course of this summer a proposal that we should lend twenty million pounds to the Chinese, which it was said would enable them to carry on their war against Japan for another year. I was opposed to this.

My continual obsession was the possibility of having to fight a war simultaneously against Germany, Italy and Japan. I was not sure that we should win that war. The suggested loan to China would be direct intervention in the Far Eastern war. Was this the moment to do it, when the Czecho-Slovak question was still unsettled, when our relations with Italy were passing through a period of deterioration and when the new Government in Japan was definitely more moderate than its predecessor and was endeavouring to improve Anglo-Japanese relations? It had been said that our prestige would suffer if the Japs won. But it would suffer much more if we had definitely backed the Chinese and yet the Japs won. Could anybody believe that £20,000,000 was going to make the difference between victory or defeat?

The proposal was eventually abandoned.

In the end I was not dissatisfied with the result of my long struggle with the Treasury over finance.

My interview with the Chancellor on Monday (July 25th) was satis-actory. I expected he would try to beat me down to accepting a round sum of £400 million for the next three years. My people thought they could just do with £405 million, but I succeeded in getting 410. The Controller and the others were very pleased.

When I came to review the past months I wrote:

The main public events have been the resignation of Anthony Eden and the absorption of Austria. Both are to be deplored. The former has materially weakened the Government and the latter has weakened Europe. The former has diminished both our popularity and our efficiency. Anthony, although I disagreed with him about Italy, was a good Foreign Secretary. His whole heart and mind were in his work and he knew Europe.

Writing about the Cabinet as a whole, I expressed the opinion that if one compared the six new members since Chamberlain became Prime Minister with the six who had left, the result was not encouraging. The departed were Stanley Baldwin, Ramsay MacDonald, Runciman, Eden, Swinton and Ormsby-Gore. The new arrivals were Lords Winterton, De La Warr, Maugham and Stanley, Leslie Burgin and John Colville. There could be little doubt as to which half-dozen possessed the superior mental equipment and the greater political experience.

In the first days of August we set forth in the *Enchantress* on a cruise in the Baltic. We took with us Brendan Bracken, as well as the same party who had accompanied us to the Eastern Mediterranean in the previous year.

We visited Kiel, Gdynia, Danzig, Helsingfors, Stockholm and Copenhagen. It was a very happy voyage, although at Kiel we had to drink the health of the Führer, at Gdynia we had to make the acquaintance of Colonel Beck, and at Danzig that of the execrable Greiser, who was to end his days on the scaffold. Such minor annoyances were amply atoned for by the arrival on board at Kiel of our Naval Attaché to Germany and the Scandinavian countries, Captain Tom Troubridge, who remained with us for the rest of the cruise. A brilliant naval career awaited him before his too early death. The presence of Greiser at Danzig was made up for by that of the League of Nations High Commissioner, Carl Burckhardt, with whom and his wife we then laid the foundation of a lasting friendship. I was glad also to meet again at Helsingfors the veteran Marshal Mannerheim, whom I had entertained in England when I was Secretary of State for War.

On Sunday, August 28th, we were lying off Langeland when a wireless message arrived to say that a meeting of Ministers was to take place at Downing Street on Tuesday morning. Hasty calculations showed that we could just get back in time if we went through the Kiel Canal, which we had not intended to do, and if there were no delays due to fog or other causes.

Two days later I woke in the early morning. I found that we were at anchor in the Thames, nine miles below Gravesend, and that we were enveloped in an autumn mist. Anxiously I went on deck, where I found that the Captain took an optimistic view and believed that the mist would soon rise. He was right. We arrived in good time. I was glad to go ashore. I should not have been so glad had I known that I was leaving the *Enchantress* for ever and that within a month I should be leaving the Admiralty.

CHAPTER FOURTEEN

RESIGNATION

1938

FIFTEEN years have passed since the crisis that culminated at Munich, but the British people have not forgotten the anxieties and the humiliations of that fateful month of September. There was a curious lull in the normal work of the Admiralty, so that I had plenty of time to record what happened and I wrote in my diary regularly. While it would not be in accord with constitutional precedent nor with a Privy Councillor's oath to set down here the opinions expressed by Ministers in the confidence that Cabinet confers, the following account is based upon the record that I kept from day to day, sometimes from hour to hour, and its accuracy can be attested.

The meeting for which I returned from the Baltic took place on the morning of August 30th. At that time there were two alternative suppositions. Either Hitler was determined on war, in which case there was nothing to be done except to prepare for it, or else he had not yet made up his mind. If the latter were the case we could either tell him now that if he invaded Czecho-Slovakia we should declare war, or else we could continue to keep him guessing. The great danger, as it seemed to me, was that Hitler might think he could get away with a lightning attack which would give him the Sudeten territories before France or England had had time to move. He would then stop, declare for peace and give good terms to the Czechs. If such a policy were to come off it would be disastrous for the future of Europe. All the smaller Powers would give up hope and would immediately make the best terms they could with Germany. England would be humiliated and the Government would be very hard hit. However, I did not believe that this policy would succeed, because I thought the French would come in as soon as the Germans crossed the Czech frontier. That would mean a European war. At that time much confusion of thought was caused by people asking whether we should or should not fight for Czecho-Slovakia. But that was not the issue. Nobody wanted to fight for Czecho-Slovakia. The question was—could we or could we not keep out of a European war in which France was engaged? I was convinced that we could not.

If Hitler was at that time still in some uncertainty as to what action Great Britain would take (and our conduct over the last five years certainly gave him good ground for such uncertainty), I thought that we should do everything in our power to indicate by action the line we meant to adopt. A suitable warning would be to bring the crews of our ships up to full complement, which would amount to semi-mobilisation. No such decisions were, however, taken at that time, and after this first Cabinet meeting I began to feel that my views were not in agreement with those of the majority and the most important of my colleagues.

On August 31st we had a meeting of Service Ministers with their principal advisers under the chairmanship of Tom Inskip. It took place in my room at the Admiralty, as we thought that if we all turned up at the C.I.D. it would attract too much attention. We discussed our preparations for war and whether there was anything more that we could do. So far as the Navy was concerned we decided to hurry up the return of the *Repulse*, and send the *Hood* to Gibraltar instead of to the Eastern Mediterranean, as had previously been arranged. There was nothing much more that we could do, short of bringing the crews up to full complement.

The question that has been principally occupying Backhouse and me is the potential threat to our Fleet caused by the German naval manœuvres in the North Sea, and as a result of them we have determined to send the Fleet up to the north by the westerly rather than the easterly route.

I completed today a paper depicting the present naval situation, which is complicated by the fact that five of our fifteen capital ships are temporarily out of action. I go on to describe the steps we have already taken to increase our preparedness, steps which were limited by the Cabinet's decision that we were to do nothing which would attract public attention, and I conclude by saying what further steps could be taken.

1. Equipping Seventh Destroyer Flotilla.
2. Bringing crews of minesweepers up to full strength.
3. Ditto minelayers.
4. Ditto the whole Fleet.
5. General mobilisation.

This paper has gone off to Inskip and the Prime Minister.

On Sunday night, September 4th, I travelled up to Drumlanrig with Euan Wallace, and there I stayed for three days, grouse-driving every day.

I enjoyed it enormously. I am nowhere quite so happy as on the hill. I shot badly but not too badly. It was a pleasant party and I love the place.

I hoped to stay until Thursday evening, but when I got in from shooting on Wednesday I was told that my Private Secretary wanted to speak to me from the Admiralty. It was to say that Inskip was having another meeting of Service Ministers on the following day and that the Prime Minister was returning and might possibly call a meeting in the afternoon. So I caught the night train to London.

September 8th. The meeting of Service Ministers accomplished very little. The other Ministers had produced papers similar to mine on what they had done and what remained to do. We did little more than read and take note of them.

In the afternoon Buck De La Warr came to see me. He is very distressed about the situation and feels strongly that we are not taking a sufficiently decided line. He told me that Halifax is not going to Geneva and that he himself would therefore be head of the mission. He thought we ought to have a Cabinet meeting before he left. I agreed with him. A great deal has happened since our last meeting, which was ten days ago. The latest development is a very mischievous leading article in *The Times*, in which the handing over of the Sudeten territories lock stock and barrel to Germany is almost advocated.

September 9th. Backhouse came into my room just before luncheon to tell me that the latest Secret Service reports indicated that the Germans were definitely moving troops in the direction of Czecho-Slovakia. This was serious news but there seemed to be no action that we could take about it. It was indeed to have been expected that such a move would have been made earlier.

I went into the country at the end of the week and returned on Monday morning.

September 12th. There were a lot of Foreign Office telegrams to read, including one admirable one instructing Henderson to make it quite plain to the German Government where we should stand in the event of war. In reply to this there was a series of messages from Henderson which seemed to me almost hysterical, imploring the Government not to insist upon his carrying out these instructions, which he was sure would have the opposite effect to that desired. And the Government had given way. By the Government now is meant the P.M., Simon, Halifax and Sam Hoare. Henderson had already left Nuremberg, therefore it seemed to me that the Cabinet was called at the worst possible moment—too late to take any action before Hitler's speech, too soon to consider the new situation which that speech might create.

When the Cabinet met on September 12th, I said that we were being advised on all sides to do the same thing—to make plain to

Germany that we would fight. This advice came from the press, almost unanimous on Sunday, from the Opposition, from Winston
Churchill, from the French Government, from the United States
Government, and even from the Vatican: this advice supported by
such an overwhelming weight of opinion we were rejecting on the
counter-advice of one man, the hysterical Henderson.

The P.M., who hates any opposition, replied rather tartly that it wasn't
one man, but the result of that one man's contacts with many others. He
was on the spot and must know more about it than the Vatican. Besides,
it was not a question of never taking the action suggested, but only of not
taking it now, when Hitler's speech was still in the making, and when it
might produce the opposite effect to that desired and drive him to making
a violent speech instead of a conciliatory one.

I said that I expected he would make a conciliatory speech, as according
to all our information his plans for war would not be ripe for at least ten
days, but that I did hope that after the conciliatory speech, if he made it,
we should reconsider the desirability of taking some action on the lines
suggested.

September 12th. At 6.30 Winston came to see me and I got Backhouse
in to meet him. We had an interesting talk on naval preparations. Winston was in excellent form but very critical of the Government for not
pursuing the policy which I had been urging.

I dined with Oliver [Stanley] at Buck's. He is much concerned about
the situation and shares my views. Anthony Winn came in after we had
finished dinner. He is working on The Times. He told us that The Times
are starting tomorrow morning a correspondence on the desirability of the
Czechs handing over the whole of the Sudeten territories to Germany.
Nothing more mischievous at the moment could be imagined. The German press will quote only that part of the correspondence that suits them,
and the opinion will prevail that the whole correspondence is a kite sent up
with the approval of the Government. Oliver and I took so serious a view
of it that we rang up Downing Street, where we heard that the Big Four
were in conclave and we told the Private Secretary what we had heard.
He rang me back about twenty minutes later and told me that Edward
Halifax had taken the same view of it as we had, that he had immediately
got on to Geoffrey Dawson and spoken to him very strongly. It was too
late to stop the edition, but Dawson had promised to do his best to "bottle
up" the correspondence, whatever that may mean. I suppose only not to
continue it. I walked home with Oliver.

September 13th. Hitler's speech last night committed him to nothing.
It was violent in tone and calculated to give trouble. I came to the conclusion today that it would be a wise move to mobilise the Fleet. The
time, I felt, was past for messages or words. The sands were running out.
Facts were needed to convince both Hitler and the German people of our

intention to fight if war was inevitable. From Secret Service sources we learnt this morning that all German Embassies and Legations had been informed that Hitler intended to invade Czecho-Slovakia on September 25th.

At six o'clock on September 13th there was a meeting of Service Ministers and Chiefs of Staff at 10 Downing Street. We had each prepared statements on the further steps that could be taken to increase our war-readiness. For my part I said that, while I realised that the meeting was not qualified to give authority for such action, I felt bound to propose that the Fleet should be mobilised. While this step could be justified on grounds of national security, it was not on those grounds primarily that I put it forward, but because I believed that it would have an effect, which nothing else could now produce, upon the mind and imagination of Hitler and of Germany.

I thought at the time that my colleagues were rather impressed. The Prime Minister said he would discuss it at the Cabinet on the following day. I asked whether we could afford to wait so long, whether the situation was not so critical as to justify calling the Cabinet together the same night. All the afternoon news had been of incidents, shooting and martial law in the Sudeten territory. Bonnet had approached Phipps in a state bordering on panic. It was finally agreed that we should wait. We then discussed the various items of our different programmes and decided on very little. The Prime Minister was most reluctant to sanction anything that involved publicity.

September 14th. This morning the news seemed less sinister than it had appeared last night, and the papers were on the whole calm in tone, although the *Daily Mail* announced the mobilisation of the Fleet.

At the Cabinet meeting that morning the Prime Minister revealed his intention of paying a personal visit to Hitler. We were being told, not consulted, for the telegram had already gone out. Approval was unanimous and enthusiastic. But I foresaw the danger that we might strengthen the case of the Germans, if they accepted the plan that we proposed, and the Czechs didn't, and we might be represented as having betrayed and deserted the cause.

No reply had yet been received from Germany to the suggestion of a visit by the Prime Minister, so that secrecy was imposed upon us and I was unable to tell the news to Winston Churchill, Venetia and

Walford Selby, who lunched with me at Admiralty House. My diary records that at about 7.30 Edward Bridges rang me up and told me that the answer was yes, and that the announcement might be made at 9 p.m. I had a dinner-party at Admiralty House. Maureen and Oliver Stanley, Walter Elliot, W. S. Morrison, Edward Stanley [of Alderley], Gerry Koch and Bridget [Paget]. At nine I told them the news, and those who didn't know it already were very much impressed.

Diana telephoned from Geneva. She had been sitting next to de Valera when Euan, who had been host at the dinner, a British Empire dinner, had made the announcement. De Valera had been the first to break the silence that followed and he had said "This is the greatest thing that has ever been done."

Oliver came round to see me before dinner. He and I think alike on the situation and are equally afraid of being accused of having betrayed the Czechs or of having encouraged the French to do so. But he is most anxious, and I agree with him, not to form any sort of group of those who share our opinion.

Friday, September 16th. At three o'clock Eddie Winterton came to see me at the Admiralty. He fears the Government will show weakness and thinks that those who differ from them must press their views to the point of resignation.

When he left me Oliver came round. He was even more dejected than usual. He was much occupied as to what was the minimum that we could stand upon. He thought we could accept a future plebiscite in Czecho-Slovakia but not an immediate one. The Prime Minister was due back about six o'clock and Oliver thought we ought not to leave London. I had arranged to go to Lavington and I eventually went, catching the 6.50. There was a nice party there and I spent a pleasant evening and forgot my worries.

At the Cabinet meeting on September 17th, Runciman was present and described his experiences in Czecho-Slovakia. It was interesting, of course, but quite unhelpful, as he was unable to suggest any plan or policy.

The Prime Minister then told us the story of his visit to Berchtesgaden. Looking back upon what he said, the curious thing seems to me now to have been that he recounted his experiences with some satisfaction. Although he said that at first sight Hitler struck him as "the commonest little dog" he had ever seen, without one sign of distinction, nevertheless he was obviously pleased at the reports he had subsequently received of the good impression that he himself had made. He told us with obvious satisfaction how Hitler had said to someone that he had felt that he, Chamberlain, was "a man."

But the bare facts of the interview were frightful. None of the elaborate schemes which had been so carefully worked out, and which the Prime Minister had intended to put forward, had ever been mentioned. He had felt that the atmosphere did not allow of them. After ranting and raving at him, Hitler had talked about self-determination and asked the Prime Minister whether he accepted the principle. The Prime Minister had replied that he must consult his colleagues. From beginning to end Hitler had not shown the slightest sign of yielding on a single point. The Prime Minister seemed to expect us all to accept that principle without further discussion because the time was getting on. The French, we heard, were getting restive. Not a word had been said to them since the Prime Minister left England, and one of the dangers which I had feared seemed to be materialising, namely trouble with the French. I thought we must have further time for discussion and that it would be better to take no decision until discussions with the French had taken place, lest they should be in a position to say that we had sold the pass without ever consulting them

We met again that afternoon. I then argued that the main interest of this country had always been to prevent any one Power from obtaining undue predominance in Europe; but we were now faced with probably the most formidable Power that had ever dominated Europe, and resistance to that Power was quite obviously a British interest. If I thought surrender would bring lasting peace I should be in favour of surrender, but I did not believe there would ever be peace in Europe so long as Nazism ruled in Germany. The next act of aggression might be one that it would be far harder for us to resist. Supposing it was an attack on one of our Colonies. We shouldn't have a friend in Europe to assist us, nor even the sympathy of the United States which we had today. We certainly shouldn't catch up the Germans in rearmament. On the contrary, they would increase their lead. However, despite all the arguments in favour of taking a strong stand now, which would almost certainly lead to war, I was so impressed by the fearful responsibility of incurring a war that might possibly be avoided, that I thought it worth while to postpone it in the very faint hope that some internal event might bring about the fall of the Nazi régime. But there were limits to the humiliation I was prepared to accept. If Hitler were willing to agree to a plebiscite being carried out under fair conditions with international control, I thought we could agree to it and insist upon the Czechs accepting it. At present we had no indication that Hitler was prepared to go so far.

We reached no conclusion and separated at about 5.30. David Margesson motored me back to Lavington, where we had a pleasant evening, but I felt very depressed on waking the next morning. It was pouring with rain. I read the Lessons in church, a special Intercession Service by the order of the Archbishop. I drove back to London after dinner.

September 19th. Some of the papers this morning contained statements as to the terms which the French and British Ministers in consultation yesterday decided should be offered to the Czechs. They amount in substance to the cession of the Sudeten territories in return for a guarantee by

England and France of the remainder. Such comment as appears is mainly favourable, including rather surprisingly that of the *Daily Herald.*

When the Cabinet met that morning we learnt that the reports which had reached the press from the French were substantially correct.

September 20th. Every morning one wakes with a feeling of sickening anxiety, which gradually gives way to the excitements of the day. This morning I had to receive the call of the Egyptian Minister of Finance, Sabri Pasha, and later gave a luncheon party of some twenty for him at Admiralty House. I sat between him and an Egyptian colonel. It is apparently no part of good manners in Egypt to make conversation at meals. Whatever I said to either of them they answered briefly and left it at that, so that there were many and long silences.

Later in the afternoon I went round to the Stanleys', where the usual people collected. Oliver and I feel strongly that there ought to be another Cabinet meeting before the Prime Minister goes back to Germany. He must insist when he sees Hitler on some minimum concessions, such as an international commission or demobilisation.

At about seven Diana and John Julius returned [from Geneva] looking very well and cheerful. I was even more than usually delighted to see them. We dined at the Fitzgeralds'.

At the Cabinet meeting on the following day we discussed the question of the Polish and Hungarian minorities. The Prime Minister reminded us that Hitler had said at their first interview that he was not interested in them; that his sole concern was with Germans. If at their next interview Hitler took a different line, the P.M. intended to refuse to discuss the question and to say that he must return to consult his colleagues. There was a good deal of talk about the guarantee, who should be parties to it, and whether it should be joint or several. Then came the question of *modus operandi.* The P.M. thought that Hitler would want to march his troops in at once, in order to occupy the districts where there was an over-whelming German majority. Others felt that there must be a decent inter-val, in order to enable those who wanted to leave to do so. We couldn't abandon the Czechs and still more the German Social Democrats etc. to the tender mercies of the Nazis. I had no doubt that if once we agreed to German troops marching in before the frontier had been fixed, they would not stop until they had overrun the whole of Czecho-Slovakia. They would very easily find an excuse to do so, as they would always be having trouble on the outskirts of the occupied territories. I felt that we had reached the limit. Not a shadow of a concession, not a word of goodwill, had we received in return. Since the Prime Minister's visit the German press had grown steadily more violent. Hitler could have restrained it had he wished. Equally easily could he have prevented the formation of Hen-lein's Frei Korps. I hoped that when the Prime Minister saw Hitler he

would say to him that he had done all and more than all that he had undertaken, that he was bringing him Czecho-Slovakia's head on a charger, and
that in order to do this he had incurred charges of surrender, betrayal and
cowardice. Further he could not go. He would prefer, if it were necessary,
to go to war. He would do so with the country solid behind him, and with
all the sympathy, and probably later with the assistance, of the United
States. And much as we should suffer at the beginning of such a war, we
should undoubtedly win it in the end, and Hitler, instead of giving all the
benefits which he so much desired to give to his country, would have
brought about his country's ruin.

September 22nd. This morning I was rather later than usual in getting
to my office and was reminded when I got there that there was a meeting
of the C.I.D. at eleven. I went straight off there without having had time
to read my telegrams. The matter under discussion was one of little importance to the Admiralty.

When I got back to the Admiralty and read the Foreign Office telegrams I found one which had been sent off after yesterday's Cabinet meeting, and which seemed to envisage our agreeing to the early occupation of
Czecho-Slovakia by German troops. As this was just the point that I had
most strongly objected to in Cabinet, I immediately wrote to Edward
Halifax saying that I thought I ought to make it plain that I could never
consent to such procedure. I rang up Oliver, who had read the telegram
but had thought that it must have been sent off before the Cabinet meeting.
When I convinced him that this was not so he came round to see me.
I showed him my letter to Halifax, with which he quite agreed and said
that he would write to him in the same sense.

I lunched at home with Diana, Conrad Russell and George Gage. We
had hardly sat down before Markham came along with Halifax's reply to
my letter. He said that he entirely agreed with me. That he had no intention of allowing German troops to enter Czecho-Slovakia except with
the consent of the Czecho-Slovak Government, and that Henlein's invasion, to which I had referred in my letter and which I had said that I
thought we should insist on being recalled, had created a new situation.
This so far as it went was satisfactory.

Winston came to see me in the afternoon. He was in a state of great
excitement and was violent in his denunciation of the Prime Minister. I
explained the situation to him as I saw it.

We went to a cinema after dinner, but before going I rang up the Resident Clerk to know if there was any news. He told me that they had sent
a telegram to Prague to the effect that we could no longer be responsible
for advising the Czechs not to mobilise. I couldn't stay at the cinema for
more than a quarter of an hour as the inanity of it got on my nerves. I
walked home and sent for the latest telegrams. A vast procession was
marching down Whitehall crying "Stand by the Czechs" and "Chamberlain must go." I rang up the Private Secretaries at Downing Street; nobody was there. I rang up the Foreign Office and learnt that Halifax,

Simon, Hoare, MacDonald and Inskip were in conference, and that there had been a message from Horace Wilson from Godesberg which was "not too good." I sent in a message to the effect that we Service Ministers were being put in a very difficult position. The country might be within twenty-four hours of war and we were not being given the latest information which was available to some of our colleagues.

After half an hour, having received no reply, I rang up again and learnt that the Ministers had dispersed. With some difficulty I got on to the Cabinet Offices and spoke to Ismay. He told me that he himself had given my message to Tom Inskip, who had immediately got up and gone home to bed.

I told Ismay that among other things I was worried about the merchant ships now in the Baltic or on their way there. Ten days ago I had proposed warning them to come back, but since the Prime Minister's first visit to Germany was announced, all action of this nature had been held up. Ismay said that the same thing had occurred to him and that he was seeing Oliver later that night to get his authorisation to go ahead.

It was then 11.30. Diana rang up from the Savoy Grill to ask the news and I went round there to join her and Conrad and Bridget. Oliver was still there with a party and I had a few words with him, telling him what had happened. He had spoken to Ismay and was going home then to meet him.

September 23rd. I had a letter from Edward Halifax this morning explaining away last night's meeting. I wrote him a reply but didn't send it as I have no wish to worry him or cause trouble at the present time.

It appears now that the breach has occurred, as was to be expected, over the question of the immediate occupation of Czecho-Slovakia by German troops. This is one point, the other is the delimitation of the frontier. Hitler has shown the Prime Minister the line that he proposes, which is, of course, in advance of what we had considered would be fair. He has offered after a certain period of months to hold a plebiscite in the more advanced doubtful districts. The Prime Minister has said that he is prepared to put the question of the frontier-line to the Czech Government, but that he is not prepared to consent to the German troops marching in forthwith.

At four I went to see John Simon at his request. Walter Elliot and Kingsley Wood were there and we were joined later by Oliver, John Colville and Hailsham. Simon seemed to me to be in a robust mood, quite prepared for the fray. He and Halifax had removed the ban on Czech mobilisation in spite of a rather feeble protest from the Prime Minister at Godesberg.

"But," Simon said, "how is the Prime Minister going to react to this? If the worst comes to the worst, will he be ready to go to war?" He asked Kingsley, who knows the P.M. better than most of us. Kingsley said that it was his impression that before the P.M. left for Germany he thought that it was all "U.P." Before we left we heard that Hitler's reply to the

P.M.'s note of this morning had been received, that Hitler was sticking to his point, but that as there was some obscurity he had been asked to furnish a memorandum in order to clear it up.

During the afternoon Simon and Halifax sent a telegram to the P.M. asking for his authority to get on with all preparations, including mobilisation. Before dinner I took it upon myself to authorise the recalling of men from leave, the bringing of all crews up to full complement, the despatch of 1,900 men to the Mediterranean to bring that Fleet up to establishment and to man the Suez Canal defences, and also one or two minor measures.

24th September. There was little news this morning. Backhouse tells me that the *Deutschland* is at Vigo and that the Germans have two submarines in those waters. The Prime Minister left Godesberg early and is due in London about noon.

The text of the German ultimatum to Czecho-Slovakia has arrived. It is couched in the most violent terms and the conditions are such as could only be imposed on a people defeated after a long war.

The Cabinet met that evening. The Prime Minister looked none the worse for his experiences. He spoke for over an hour. He told us that Hitler had adopted a certain position from the start and had refused to budge an inch from it. Many of the most important points seemed hardly to have arisen during their discussion, notably the international guarantee. Having said that he had informed Hitler that he was creating an impossible situation, having admitted that he had "snorted" with indignation when he read the German terms, the Prime Minister concluded, to my astonishment, by saying that he considered that we should accept those terms and that we should advise the Czechs to do so.

It was then suggested that the Cabinet should adjourn, in order to give members time to read the terms and sleep on them, and that we should meet again the following morning. I protested against this. I said that from what the Prime Minister had told us it appeared to me that the Germans were still convinced that under no circumstances would we fight, that there still existed one method, and one method only, of persuading them to the contrary, and that was by instantly declaring full mobilisation. I said that I was sure popular opinion would eventually compel us to go to the assistance of the Czechs; that hitherto we had been faced with the unpleasant alternatives of peace with dishonour or war. I now saw a third possibility, namely war with dishonour, by which I meant being kicked into the war by the boot of public opinion when those for whom we were fighting had already been defeated. I pointed out that the Chiefs of Staff had reported on the previous day that immediate mobilisation was of urgent and vital importance, and I suggested that we might one day have to explain why we had disregarded their advice. This angered the Prime Minister. He said that I had omitted to say that this advice was given only on the assumption that there was a danger of war with Germany within the next few days. I said I thought it would be difficult to deny that such a danger existed.

Finally I suggested that we should approach the Egyptian Government about putting into force the precautionary period of the protection of the Suez Canal. I did not think anybody could have any objection to the preliminary steps being taken to protect one of the most vital and vulnerable points in the Empire. The Prime Minister, however, said that he did object very strongly, and that he saw no reason why we should take such a step at present.

It was pouring with rain when we came out from the Cabinet and Hailsham gave me a lift as far as the Admiralty. I said that I didn't think we could ever get the Prime Minister's policy through the House of Commons. To my surprise he said at once, "Of course you can't," and went on to tell me of the strength of feeling at Oxford, where his son is standing as a parliamentary candidate, among all parties against surrender.

Personally I believe that Hitler has cast a spell over Neville. After all, Hitler's achievement is not due to his intellectual attainments nor to his oratorical powers, but to the extraordinary influence which he seems able to exercise over his fellow-creatures. I believe that Neville is under that influence at the present time. "It all depends," he said, "on whether we can trust Hitler."

"Trust him for what?" I asked. "He has got everything he wants for the present and he has given no promises for the future."

Neville also said that he had been told, and he believed, that he himself had made a very favourable impression on Hitler, and that he believed he might be able to exercise a useful influence over him. I couldn't help saying that that influence could not be very valuable if Neville ceased to be Prime Minister—a not improbable contingency.

Shakespeare Morrison came to dinner, and the Rothschilds, and we had a very pleasant meal at which the political situation was not once alluded to. I had a talk with Shakes after dinner. Oliver came round later. He feels just as I do, and will act, I think, as I shall. A bad night.

On Sunday, September 25th, the Cabinet met at 10.30. One of the first points that I raised was that of the guarantee, but we didn't get very far with it. The discussion turned mainly on the question whether we should go to the help of France. A message was brought in that Masaryk wished to see the Prime Minister. There was one question that obviously he would ask—"If we reject Hitler's ulti-matum, will England support us?" I thought we ought to make up our minds at once what the answer was to be to that question. I had consented to the Berchtesgaden terms because I thought they might postpone war, but that argument no longer influenced me in face of the Godesberg claims, because I thought that if we accepted them we should be swept out of office and the country would go to war under worse leaders. The other reason why I thought we could not advise the Czechs to accept these terms was that I myself, if I had been Minister in Prague, would have been ashamed to offer such advice. The issue now was not self-determination, nor the manner in which it would be carried out, but so far as we were concerned it was the honour and the soul of England which were at stake.

When we resumed our meeting in the afternoon the Prime Minis-ter asked that the differences of opinion between us should not be exaggerated, that it would be a great mistake to show weakness at the centre at the present time. He was going to see the Czech Minister that afternoon, and the French Prime Minister and Foreign Secretary would be received by him and some of his colleagues later. This arrangement was very unsatisfactory to me, as I could not feel that the views which I held would be fairly represented at these meetings. We had talked for five hours and had reached no conclusion as to what was to be said to the French. The Prime Minister had said that we must not show weakness at the centre, but it was better to show it than to be paralysed by it, which was what was now happening. I therefore felt that it was better I should go, because my continued presence in the Cabinet was only a source of delay and annoyance to those who thought differently from me.

The Prime Minister said he had been expecting me to suggest doing so, but he asked me not to take any precipitate action. I agreed not to do so.

I went to see Sidney Herbert before dinner. He is in bed with bron-chitis. He feels so strongly about these events that when the Berchtesgaden terms were published he telegraphed to the Prime Minister that he would not be able to support him on that question.

Oliver and Maureen came to dinner and Walter Elliot, Shakes Morrison and Hore-Belisha. At 11.30 we were sent for to go back to Downing Street. We were told that the French had been very evasive but according to Neville's own account they hadn't been nearly so evasive as he had. I practically said as much and made myself pretty offensive. The French had at least said that if Czecho-Slovakia were attacked they would "fulfil their obligations," but they had not apparently said in so many words that they would go to war, nor could I discover that they had been pressed to do so.

However, at the end, the Prime Minister said that he proposed to make a final effort. He was sending Horace Wilson to Hitler tomorrow with a personal letter appealing to him to allow the details of the transfer of territory to be settled by an international body of Germans, Czechs and English. If he refused this appeal, Horace Wilson was to tell him that France would fight for Czecho-Slovakia and that we should fight on the same side.

The Prime Minister made this announcement almost casually and I could hardly believe my ears. It was after all a complete reversal of what he himself had advised us to do the day before. I had to ask him to repeat it, for I thought I had misunderstood him. None of those who had supported his policy all day said a word of criticism on its reversal. Oliver observed rather acidly that apparently we were to tell the Germans that the French would fight, although we had just heard that the French themselves refused to say as much. However, there it was. The Prime Minister looked, for the first time, absolutely worn out, and I felt very sorry for him.

September 26th. We had a Cabinet meeting at twelve this morning. The French Ministers were just leaving and I had a word with Daladier. I asked him if he was satisfied and he said yes, that everything was very satisfactory. Earlier in the morning Leslie [Hore-Belisha] had rung me up and said that the French Military Attaché had told him that the French Ministers were furious at their reception, that they had been browbeaten and cross-examined on technical military matters of which they knew nothing, etc.

Oliver had been to see me and had said that we must insist on the French being told definitely before they left London that we should support them, and that otherwise we should resign. I entirely agree, but Daladier's *"Tout est très bien"* seemed to change the situation. So indeed it had. The Prime Minister told us that the French had been quite definite this morning that they would fight, and that we had quite definitely assured them that we would support them. It was odd to notice that not a murmur of protest came from any of those who had yesterday advocated a different policy.

I felt it incumbent upon me, in view of what I had said yesterday about resigning, to state that I was in entire agreement with the policy now adopted. I added that if in our recent meetings I had expressed my opinions too frequently and too forcibly and had thereby added to the Prime Minister's heavy burden, I was very sorry. The Prime Minister had said that he was going to see the leader of the Opposition. If as a result of such conversations he thought it wise to broaden the basis of his Government, I, for one, should be very glad to serve him in any subordinate position or to continue to support him as a private Member of Parliament.

At three we had a kind of glorified C.I.D. meeting with nearly all the Cabinet there except the P.M. We took dozens of decisions which would have taken months or years to get through in peacetime.

September 27th. We had a meeting at Richmond Terrace at 10 a.m. to deal with censorship, which was soon disposed of. I find my colleagues a prey to unreasoning optimism. Hore-Belisha bet me yesterday £2 to £1 that there would be no war. Brendan bet me an even fiver. This was after Hitler's speech, which both he and Winston thought was a retreat. "He is on the run," they cried. I could see no sign of it. This morning Tom Inskip said "I have got a kind of a hunch that this war won't take place."

When I got back from luncheon there was a telegram from Henderson saying that he had seen Goering the previous evening. Goering had been "absolutely confident." It had been quite obvious from this conversation and from one that he had had with General Bodenschatz, "that the die is now cast, that British mediation is at an end, and that if delegates do not arrive in Berlin with full authority to make the best terms they can on their own with the Germans before 2 p.m. tomorrow, general mobilisation will be ordered at that hour and occupation of the Sudeten territories will begin immediately."

Henderson's own incredible comment on this is "If His Majesty's Government do not at this eleventh hour advise Czechs in the name of humanity and of Czechs themselves . . . to make the best terms they can with Berlin, we shall be exposing Czecho-Slovakia to the same fate as Abyssinia."

Having read this telegram I sent a message to the Prime Minister saying that in my opinion we should mobilise immediately and that I could see no justification for delay. Later I heard that Inskip and the Chiefs of Staff were with the Prime Minister, and later still I learnt from Backhouse on his return that it had at last been decided to mobilise the Fleet. The Prime Minister will announce it this evening in his broadcast speech; meanwhile he wished no action to be taken which would give it publicity. We are to have a meeting of the Privy Council tomorrow morning. This at last is satisfactory.

At 8 p.m. we listened to the Prime Minister's broadcast. George Gage, Venetia, Diana and I, in Diana's bedroom. It was a most depressing utterance. There was no mention of France in it or a word of sympathy for Czecho-Slovakia. The only sympathy expressed was for Hitler, whose feeling about the Sudetens the Prime Minister said that he could well understand, and he never said a word about the mobilisation of the Fleet.

I was furious. Winston rang me up. He also was most indignant and said that the tone of the speech showed plainly that we're preparing to scuttle.

The Cabinet met at 9.30 that evening. A series of gloomy reports were presented to us. Our Military Attaché in Berlin had reported that the morale of the Czech army was very bad. Lyons had sent a discouraging telegram from Australia. Te Water had said that South Africa would hesitate to come in, and Herzog was reported to have said that after Hitler's speech it was plain that responsibility did not lie on the shoulders of Germany. The Government had sent a telegram to Prague informing them of everything that was calculated to discourage and depress them, but not giving them any advice.

Then Horace Wilson told us of his mission to Germany. He had not delivered the important part of his message, namely that England and France would fight, at his first interview with Hitler, so that Hitler had not heard it before his speech. When he had delivered it on the following day it was so tied up with additional clauses that it had lost half its force. It was significant that even after he had told Hitler this, the latter remarked that he couldn't believe that we should fall out. In Horace Wilson's opinion the only thing to do now was to advise the Czechs to evacuate the territory. He had drawn up a draft telegram containing this advice.

I spoke at once. I said that we had listened to a recital by the Prime Minister of all the gloomiest facts he could collect. Not a word had been said about the brighter side, about President Roosevelt's telegram and one from the President of Brazil; not a word about the much better reports that were now coming from France about the hardening of opinion and the temper of the people; not a word about the similar tendencies of world opinion regarding Hitler's ultimatum and his last speech. Our Military Attaché in Berlin was no doubt much under the influence of his Ambassador, who had shown himself a defeatist from the first. As for the Dominions, could we expect that they would ever all be united on the prospect of coming into a European war? They were not necessary to us for the conduct of the war. We began the last one with South Africa in a state of revolution. If we were now to desert the Czechs or even advise them to surrender, we should be guilty of one of the basest betrayals in history. I was bound to say I had been disappointed that the Prime

Minister in his broadcast had been unable to give them a word of praise
or encouragement and had reserved all his sympathy for Hitler. If we
gave way now, I was going to say that it would be the end of England and of democracy, but I didn't really believe that; what I did
believe was that it might be the end of this Government, and that it
would certainly be the end of my connection with it.

After the meeting was over, I apologised to the Prime Minister for
having criticised his speech, but said that I had to speak out what I
thought. I added that I had understood he was going to announce
the mobilisation of the Fleet. He said he had meant to originally, but
that later he had decided not to. I said casually that there was, I supposed, no point in keeping it secret. He agreed. I felt that if I had
asked whether I could make a press announcement he might have
hesitated. As it was I ran home across the Horse Guards Parade, telephoned to the Press Section of the Admiralty and told them to give
it without delay to all the morning papers. It was then past eleven.

September 28th. Privy Council at 10.30 for the Order in Council
authorising mobilisation. The King kept me behind after the others had
gone and we had half an hour's talk. He was very nice and very cheerful,
envisaging the war with great equanimity.

When I got back Oliver came round, gloomier than ever. He talks of
resigning after the P.M.'s speech this afternoon if it doesn't suit him.
He says the plot now is to frighten the French into ratting and then
to get out on their shoulders. The depressing telegram from Lyons
which the P.M. had read out yesterday had been followed by one from
our High Commissioner in Australia, saying that the Lyons telegram by
no means represented public opinion and that it would be universally condemned if it were known. Also the message from the Military Attaché in
Berlin was corrected by one from the Military Attaché in Prague, who
took a very different view of the morale of the Czech troops.

I lunched at Buck's with Diana and the Cranbornes. They are of course
boiling with anti-Government indignation. I drove with them to the
House. Then there came the Prime Minister's speech. I listened to it in
considerable gloom until he came to the end when he announced his latest
démarche and its unexpected success. The telegram announcing Hitler's
agreement [to the Munich meeting] was only handed to him while he was
speaking. The scene was remarkable, all Government supporters rising
and cheering while the Opposition sat glum and silent. And then when
Attlee gave the plan his blessing our side all rose again and cheered him,
cheers in which the Opposition had to join, though looking a little foolish.

Now I believe for the first time that there will not be a war. It seems hardly credible that four men meeting together cannot agree upon the method of handing over certain territories, the cession of which has already been decided. I believe also that the mobilisation of the Fleet has had something to do with it, because by that action we eventually succeeded in persuading Hitler that we were prepared to fight. He had previously been assured that the opposite was the case and we had never said or done anything to convince him.

We were nine to dinner this evening and a lot of people came in afterwards. At dinner were Winston, Walter Elliot, the Cranbornes, Barbie [Wallace] and Hutchy. It was the first really cheerful evening we have had since the night of Neville's first flight to Germany.

September 29th. I thought I should sleep well last night but I didn't. I got up at 6.30. We drove down to Heston to see the P.M. off. It was John Simon's idea that the whole Cabinet should turn up as a pleasant surprise for him. It was certainly a surprise. We and the Elliots and Anthony Winn had breakfast in the restaurant there after he had gone.

There is a slight sense of anticlimax. We are going on with all our war preparations. We had a meeting of Ministers at the C.I.D. this morning.

That evening I was present at a dinner-party of men only. They were most of them Members of Parliament, proprietors of newspapers or prominent journalists. As we dined news of the terms that had been accepted at Munich arrived in instalments. The more voluble members of the company condemned them and I listened with increasing gloom. Argument grew fierce and heated. A very distinguished elderly publicist declared that he had been insulted and left the building. I was still a member of the Government and felt myself in loyalty bound to defend their policy. I did so for the last time.

September 30th. The full terms of the Munich agreement are in the papers this morning. At first sight I felt that I couldn't agree to them. The principle of invasion remains. The German troops are to march in tomorrow and the Czechs are to leave all their installations intact. This means that they will have to hand over all their fortifications, guns, etc. upon which they have spent millions, and that they will receive no compensation for them. The international commission will enjoy increased powers but our representative on it is to be Nevile Henderson, who in my opinion has played a sorry part in the whole business and who is violently anti-Czech and pro-German. While I was dressing this morning I decided that I must resign.

There was a meeting of Ministers and advisers at the C.I.D. at 11.30 to discuss the slowing down of war preparations.

I went to see Oliver at the Board of Trade. Walter Elliot was there.

They are both of opinion that we should accept these terms. Walter said he felt that if I went he ought to go too. I said that was not my view. It would be easier for me to go alone, as I had no wish to injure the Government, which I should not do if my resignation were the only one. We talked at some length and reached no conclusion.

When I got back to the Admiralty I learnt that there was to be a Cabinet at seven. The Prime Minister arrived at about twenty past seven amid scenes of indescribable enthusiasm. He spoke to the mob from the window. I felt very lonely in the midst of so much happiness that I could not share.

The Cabinet meeting lasted little more than half an hour. The Prime Minister explained the differences between the Munich and the Godesberg terms, and they are really considerably greater than I had understood. Nevertheless after a few questions had been asked and many congratulations had been offered, I felt it my duty to offer my resignation.

I said that not only were the terms not good enough but also that I was alarmed about the future. We must all admit that we should not have gone so far to meet Germany's demands if our defences had been stronger. It had more than once been said in Cabinet that after having turned the corner we must get on more rapidly with rearmament. But how could we do so when the Prime Minister had just informed the crowd that we had peace "for our time" and that we had entered into an agreement never to go to war with Germany.

The Prime Minister smiled at me in a quite friendly way and said that it was a matter to be settled between him and me. And so it was left. Leslie drove me back to Admiralty House and came in. He urged me strongly not to go. I dined alone with Diana and went early to bed, but slept badly.

Here the diary stops and it was a long time before I started to write one again.

CHAPTER FIFTEEN

THE RESPITE

1938-1939

ON the following morning I went to see the Prime Minister. Our interview was as friendly as it was brief. I found it a relief to be in complete agreement with him for once. I think he was as glad to be rid of me as I was determined to go. I saw the King the same afternoon. He was frank and charming. He said that he could not agree with me, but he respected those who had the courage of their convictions.

I had thought that this would be the feeling of most people, but it was not. Great bitterness arose within the ranks of the Conservative Party and among their supporters. Political acquaintances cut me, and one old friend, a member of the executive committee of my constituency, on learning that I was to speak at a ward meeting which had been arranged to take place in his house, cancelled the meeting rather than allow me to cross the threshold.

That people who were ignorant of foreign affairs, as most English people are, should have felt as they did, was not surprising. For many days they had been preparing for war with all the anguish that such preparation inflicts upon the human mind. They had foreseen financial ruin and sudden death. Those who had survived the first war felt that it was all to be borne again, with the lives of their children, instead of their own, at stake. Suddenly, in the twinkling of an eye, the clouds dispersed, the sky was blue, the sun shone. There was to be no war, neither now nor at any future date. And this miracle had been performed by one man, and one man only. No ounce of credit for it was given to anyone else. The aged Prime Minister of England had saved the world. Even in France a subscription was raised to present him with a country house and a trout stream, for the French had learned that fishing was his favourite sport. At this great and glorious moment one of the hero's least considered colleagues had come forward and proclaimed his dissent, had resigned his office, and had disfigured the smiling landscape with a hideous blot.

I spent the end of that week with the Euan Wallaces at Lavington. Oliver Stanley was there. It might be thought from the previous chapter that I resented his not offering his resignation when I offered mine. I had no such feeling. Neither then nor ever was there the slightest cloud over our happy relationship, which only ended with his death, when I lost a dear friend and the country one who might have proved a great servant. We had all changed our views during that agitated month. At the beginning of it I was outraged by the suggestion that the Sudeten territory should be handed over to Germany. At the end of it I had been willing to accept that outrage, on condition that it was carried out with some respect for common decency. When he returned from Munich the Prime Minister was able to persuade me, as well as my colleagues, that he had accomplished a great deal there, and that the Munich terms differed substantially from those of Godesberg. We were, in fact, mistaken, for even *The Times* newspaper admitted a few days later that the Germans had already got more than Godesberg would have given them. But I could not blame those whose views were closest to mine for being able to accept a little more than I could.

Oliver was also suffering at the time from a great personal anxiety. His elder brother Edward, who had only recently joined the Cabinet, was dying, and his father, Lord Derby, was an enthusiastic supporter of the Prime Minister, and would have been deeply grieved by his resignation.

Unhappy as I was at the time to leave the Admiralty, I have never regretted doing so. I have no intention here of re-examining the controversy. I thought that I was right then; I know it now. Every fact of which we were ignorant at the time and that has come to light since, such as the inadequacy of German preparations and the deep discontent and even conspiracy of the German Generals against Hitler, has confirmed the view that I took. But even had that view been wrong, had Hitler proved as good as his word or had his régime collapsed owing to internal causes, I hope I should not have regretted what I did, for I believed it to be my duty.

I had thought that one of the compensations for leaving office would be a period of rest and tranquillity. I was soon undeceived. Over four thousand communications reached me by post and telegraph. I had to engage a special staff of secretaries to deal with them, since I have always made a rule of replying to any civil letter that I receive. A very few were abusive, and these were mainly anonymous. I have often wondered what satisfaction there can be in writing a rude letter and not signing it. If the writers could see with what contempt their work is thrown into the waste-paper basket it might cure them. Ninety per cent, however, were congratulatory, and many of them came from people whose support I was proud to receive.

Lord Chatfield, who made his maiden speech in the House of Lords to affirm his belief in the Munich policy, was good enough to write that my resignation was

a great misfortune to the Admiralty, whose interests and problems you have made your own. I am sure all the Board will be grieved, especially my successor to whom you would have been so great a support. This is a moment when I should like to reiterate how much I owe to your complete support of the Navy on so many important occasions. No Board could have wished for more than you so willingly gave.

Lord Cork, who was then Commander-in-Chief at Portsmouth, wrote:

May I say how sorry I am that you have found it necessary to resign, and how much I admire you for having done so. I find myself in complete agreement with your views and regret that I am not in a position to say so publicly.

Louis Mountbatten felt strongly on the subject.

I expect it is highly irregular of me, a serving naval officer, writing to you on relinquishing your position as First Lord, but I cannot stand by and see someone whom I admire behave in exactly the way I hope I should have the courage to behave if I had been in his shoes, without saying "Well done." . . . Your going at this time is a cruel blow to the Navy; none knows this better than I, who enjoyed to a certain measure your confidence. A great friend of mine has just written to me from Paris, "Until yesterday I did not think that one solitary statesman of the four powers who sold Czecho-Slovakia could possibly emerge with honour from the crisis, but yesterday your First Lord emerged with great honour."

I must quote one more naval tribute which touched me deeply at the time. It came from Commander Frend, the Captain of the *Enchantress*.

I am writing on behalf of the Officers and Ship's Company to say how very sorry we all are that you are no longer our First Lord. . . . It has been a genuine pleasure to serve under you; and if you had been on board yesterday evening when the news came through you would have appreciated how much you are respected and liked by all on board by the gloom that descended on the "little ship."

The House of Commons met on Monday. Conservatives rose and cheered when the Prime Minister entered the Chamber. Some members of the Labour Party, such as George Lansbury, had given him their outspoken approval, more were tacitly in favour of what he had done, and the Independent Labour Party was unitedly and openly behind him. Everybody was anxious to hear what he had to say, and as I had to speak first, I had an unsympathetic and impatient audience.

I said that I could well understand the reluctance of people in this country to go to war on account of Czecho-Slovakia, and it was for that reason that I had sought to persuade my former colleagues from the first not to see the problem only in terms of Czecho-Slovakia. Had we gone to war, as we so nearly did, it would not have been for Czecho-Slovakia that we should have been fighting, any more than it was for Serbia or for Belgium that we fought in 1914. (Had I been given the power of prophecy I might have added that it would not be for Poland that we should be fighting within less than a year.) We should have been fighting, I said, in accordance with the sound, traditional foreign policy of England, in order to prevent one Great Power, in defiance of treaty obligations, of the laws of nations and the decrees of morality, dominating by brute force the continent of Europe.

I had felt from the first that if we could convince Hitler that we were, in certain circumstances, prepared to fight, he might moderate his demands. He had never been convinced, and therefore he had never moderated his demands, until he came to Munich. But why had he accepted the Prime Minister's invitation, and why had he come to Munich? I reminded the House that on the morning that

Hitler had accepted that invitation the first news that he had received was that the British Fleet was mobilised, and I suggested that it was this fact rather than the Prime Minister's invitation that had weakened the resistance with which he had repulsed so many previous appeals.

I explained with what difficulty I had come to consent to the policy of advising the Czechs to cede the Sudeten territory to Germany. It had been very hard to urge them to give up everything for which they had been prepared to fight. But I had thought that when they had agreed to do so they would at least be spared the ignominy and horror of invasion, and would have been given time to remove their own property from the territory they were being forced to abandon. "When Naboth had agreed to give up his vineyard he should have been allowed to pack up his goods and depart in peace."

In addition to this, having agreed to the destruction of the only defensible frontier of Czecho-Slovakia, we had guaranteed that frontier. We had guaranteed the maintenance of what we had just destroyed. It was as though we had dealt a man a mortal blow and then insured his life. If we meant to uphold this commitment we must rapidly create and equip an army upon a continental scale. But how could we expect the people of Great Britain to accept the sacrifices that such an effort would entail when they had just been informed by the Prime Minister that he had brought back from Munich not only peace with honour but peace "for our time"?

I went on to refer to that miserable scrap of paper which the Prime Minister had so proudly waved in the face of the public, signed by Hitler and himself, and recording their agreement never to go to war. I said there was perhaps little harm in such a document, but I suggested "that for the Prime Minister of England to sign, without consulting his colleagues, without any reference to his allies, without any communication with the Dominions and without the assistance of any expert diplomatic advisers, such a declaration with the dictator of a great state is not the way in which the foreign affairs of the British Empire ought to be conducted."

And to what did this famous declaration amount? So far as we were concerned, nothing, for we had never had any intention or desire to go to war with Germany. So far as Hitler was concerned, it was a pledge. The Prime Minister had confidence in the good faith of Hitler,

although when Herr Hitler broke the Treaty of Versailles he undertook to keep the Treaty of Locarno, and when he broke the Treaty of Locarno, he undertook not to interfere further or to have any territorial aims in Europe. When he entered Austria by force he authorised his henchmen to give an authoritative assurance that he would not interfere with Czecho-Slovakia. That was less than six months ago. Still the Prime Minister believes that he can rely upon "the good faith of Hitler."

I concluded as follows:

The Prime Minister may be right. I can assure you, Mr. Speaker, with the deepest sincerity, that I hope and pray that he is right, but I cannot believe what he believes. I wish I could. Therefore, I can be of no assistance to him in his Government. I should only be a hindrance, and it is much better that I should go. I remember when we were discussing the Godesberg ultimatum that I said that if I were a party to persuading, or even to suggesting to, the Czecho-Slovak Government that they should accept that ultimatum, I should never be able to hold up my head again. I have forfeited a great deal. I have given up an office that I loved, work in which I was deeply interested and a staff of which any man might be proud. I have given up association in that work with my colleagues with whom I have maintained for many years the most harmonious relations, not only as colleagues but as friends. I have given up the privilege of serving as lieutenant to a leader whom I still regard with the deepest admiration and affection. I have ruined, perhaps, my political career. But that is a little matter; I have retained something which is to me of greater value—I can still walk about the world with my head erect.

The Prime Minister, who spoke next, referred to my speech with sympathy and said that he had not listened to it without emotion. He paid tribute to my sincerity and went on: "I am sure my right honourable friend will not think me discourteous if this afternoon I make no attempt to answer him or to defend myself against the strictures which he has made upon the policy which the Government has been pursuing." He suggested that there would be opportunities later for replying to what I had said. There were. The debate went on for four days. Five other members of the Government took part in it. The Prime Minister himself spoke again on the last day, but neither he nor any one of his colleagues referred to my speech nor made the slightest attempt to answer it.

I had hardly sat down before I received a note from Winston Churchill.

Your speech was one of the finest Parliamentary performances I have ever heard. It was admirable in form, massive in argument and shone with courage and public spirit.

Harold Macmillan wrote the same day:

It was the finest thing I've heard since I've been in the House; the deep sincerity gripped even those members who most disagreed with your argument. I can assure you that it has heartened a great many of us more than you know.

I will quote only two more of those four thousand letters, two which did not come from close personal friends or from political supporters. That grand old veteran of the Left, Josiah Wedgwood, wrote:

Love and admiration more than you have dreamt of will I hope compensate for loss of office and salary. Anyhow this old colleague from better days is proud of you. Also I think it is a good spot on a bad page of English history. I do dislike belonging to a race of clucking old hens and damned cowards.

Of my former Cabinet colleagues the only one who wrote to me was Malcolm MacDonald. I was particularly pleased to receive his letter because he was one who had consistently taken the opposite view to mine.

I have frankly disagreed with you during the crisis, and since the Cabinet as a whole also took a different line from yours, I am certain that you did the right and honourable thing in resigning. Nevertheless, on personal grounds I am very sorry that we are no longer colleagues. I have always admired the conviction with which you held your views, the brilliance with which you expressed them, and the courage with which you were ready to make any sacrifice in defence of them. I remember the way in which, when you were at the War Office, you fought an almost ceaseless duel with the then Chancellor of the Exchequer, regardless of the fact that he was to become Prime Minister within a few months and that his displeasure might result in your exclusion from the new Government. Some people would have done anything rather than quarrel with Neville Chamberlain then!

One further consequence of that speech should be recorded. I had, during the crisis, seen a lot of Anthony Winn, a hard-working journalist, many years younger than myself, who, having served his apprenticeship in the provinces, had recently acquired the post, an enviable one for a man of his age, of lobby correspondent to *The Times.* He duly reported the speech and what had been thought of it. I never saw what he wrote, but it did not accord with the policy of the paper. Not only did the editor suppress it but he inserted a concoction of his own in which the speech was described as "a damp squib" and headed it "from our lobby correspondent." Anthony Winn resigned his position. It was an heroic action, the more so because very few people were ever likely to hear of it. It might well have ruined his career in journalism, for editors of newspapers no more appreciate independence in their staff than do leaders of political parties. Two years later he was killed in action.

That long debate was part of the special session caused by the crisis. When it was over the House adjourned until the date previously fixed for the opening of the autumn session, November 8th. I successfully mastered my swollen correspondence, and that done, we left for France, where we spent a peaceful week at Versailles.

I was distressed to find that my French friends were even more enthusiastic in their support of the Munich policy than were the majority of my friends in England, and that there were fewer exceptions. Only one non-Communist deputy had had the courage to vote against it in the Chamber. When the Comte de Paris, recognised by all Royalists as King of France, ventured to criticise the terms of the agreement, he was denounced by *L'Action Française*, the organ of the Royalists, for sympathising with Communism.

In England, on the other hand, where party discipline is stronger, the issue was one which to a large extent cut across parties. There were at least a score of Conservative members of the House of Commons who were opposed to the settlement, and it was perhaps from them, led by Winston Churchill and Anthony Eden, that the strongest opposition came. The Labour Party were handicapped in presenting the case by the fact that they had consistently opposed any increase in armaments. Condemnation of the Government for weakness came ill from those who had resisted all that Government's endeavours to make itself stronger.

Nor did the Labour Party try to make much political capital out of the Munich settlement, for the very good reason that they knew it was popular in the country. As the ingenious authors of the fatuous Peace Ballot had discovered, most sane people prefer peace to war, and when they have been threatened with war and are presented, at the last moment, with peace, they are too pleased to enquire closely what the blessing may have cost or who has paid for it. There was indeed a suggestion amongst supporters of the Government that it would be well to precipitate a General Election so as to cash in on our triumph. That suggestion was squashed by one furious speech that Sidney Herbert made in the House of Commons. It was his last. He died not long afterwards.

There was at that time a large body of moderate public opinion that was profoundly disturbed. They had lost faith in the Government without gaining any in the Opposition, and they sought vainly in the public press for any expression of their views. A significant sympton of this distrust of the press was the appearance of a number of privately circulated newsletters. Some of them had short lives but some continued throughout the war. They thrived on the suspicion that truth was being concealed, and they satisfied the demand for it that was felt by men and women of all parties. I say "men and women" because I could count at that time, among my own acquaintance, twelve happily married couples who were divided upon the issue of Munich, and in every case it was the husband who supported and the wife who opposed Chamberlain. Many would have expected that women would have been more ready than men to accept the spurious peace at its face value. But it was not so.

I have always had a great respect for the political judgment of women, although I have never thought that the House of Commons was the right arena in which they should display it. That House was fashioned by men in the course of seven hundred years, and men of all parties and all classes adapt themselves to its usages with astonishing rapidity. But there is no place in it for women, and women cannot excel there any more than they can on the football field. This does not mean that women's brains are not capable of comprehending and solving political problems. Politics are not an abstruse science. Common sense, clear vision, knowledge of human nature, courage and patience are the qualities that they demand, and with all these qualities women are endowed at least as richly as men.

Immediately after my resignation I accepted an offer from the *Evening Standard* to write a weekly article in their columns. The political views of the proprietor were very different from mine, but the editor undertook to alter nothing that I wrote, reserving only the right not to publish it, in which case he would pay for the article none the less.

This weekly obligation combined with attendance at the House of Commons, where I spoke occasionally, kept me sufficiently employed during the months that followed, months during which, because nothing in particular happened except increased persecution of the Jews in Germany, those who had been responsible for the Munich surrender began to congratulate themselves on the success of their policy. Members of the Cabinet vied with one another in optimistic assurances to the country, and one of them coined for those of us who like myself still sounded notes of warning the appellation "Jitter-bugs."

Early in March the press received authoritative assurances from the Government that the international outlook was more than usually serene, and *Punch* was so far misled as to publish a cartoon in which John Bull was represented as awakening from a bad dream which, bearing the name "Danger of War," was seen flying out of the window. The cartoon appeared on the Ides of March. On the same day German troops marched into Prague, the sham of Czecho-Slovakia's independence was disclosed and the Prime Minister declared in the House of Commons that the guarantee that Great Britain had given to protect her frontiers no longer existed.

All this time the small band of dissident Conservatives continued to suffer persecution in their constituencies, which may or may not have been fomented by the party's Central Office. I have often noticed that the narrower the division between different schools of thought the more intense is the bitterness. When I was in the House of Commons the most reactionary of the Tories, to whom I was an abomination, used to sit on the same bench with the small Independent Labour Party, and I am sure that a harsh word never passed between them, whereas the different brands of the Liberal Party, and there were three at the time, were hardly on speaking terms with one another.

Owing to the exceptional character of my constituency we seldom held public meetings, and one of the very few important annual occasions was a luncheon at the Café Royal, which was arranged for the convenience of the Conduit Ward, containing all the more influential constituents engaged in business. Of recent years I had always secured a Cabinet Minister to speak at this luncheon, and I anticipated no difficulty in 1939, for most of my former colleagues had remained my friends.

The first to whom I applied answered that he would have been delighted to accept but that there was "a general ruling that he should not speak at functions representative of only one constituency but only at area or county meetings." The second wrote more frankly: "I am afraid I must ask you to let me off the luncheon, until the dust over Munich settles down a little. I feel that my appearance might be misconstrued. . . . I am frightfully sorry to say this but I will not just put off an old friend with an excuse." I was genuinely surprised. I thought the party had forgiven us by then. I sometimes wonder whether they ever have.

My third application was accompanied by a warning. I recounted whom I had already invited, explained why they had refused, added that it was plain how strong the feeling still was, and warned my friend that if he accepted my invitation he would probably do himself harm both with the Government and with the party. Mr. R. S. Hudson, who was then Minister of Transport, accepted without a moment's hesitation, and made an excellent speech. Storms produce lightning, and by those flashes in the dark we can see men, if only for a moment, as they really are.

How strongly this hostile feeling towards us persisted even up to the eve of the war is illustrated by a letter which one of my constituents, who was also a Member of Parliament, addressed to the editor of the paper in which my articles were appearing. It is dated the 9th of August.

As Chairman of one of the Ward Committees in Mr. Duff Cooper's constituency, I cannot conceive why you should think it worth while to publish the vaporous effusions which flow at more or less regular intervals from his pen. Not content with having resigned from the Government at a very critical juncture in foreign affairs and having subsequently employed language in Parliament about the head of a foreign State which I submit is consistent neither with the dignity of the House of Commons nor with that restrained and responsible attitude which we have a right to expect from an ex-Cabinet Minister, he apparently thinks he is serving the best interests of humanity at large by keeping his fellow-countrymen in a constant state of jittery anticipation, and endlessly fanning the flames of prejudice and hatred against the wicked Nazis on account of their supposed acts of aggression.

There may be those who think these articles increase the standing and prestige of your paper. I am not among them.

I spoke twice in Paris during those months. On the first occasion my visit coincided with the arrival of Ribbentrop, who came to sign with the French Foreign Minister an agreement which of course proved as worthless as that which Chamberlain had signed with Hitler. Our ambassador, Sir Eric Phipps, thought it unfortunate that our visits should clash and was nervous about what I might say. I gave him the script of my *conférence* and accepted certain alterations that he suggested.

I thought it unlikely that a British politician, not even holding office, would be able, talking about foreign affairs in Paris, to fill a theatre. I was therefore surprised not only to find the theatre crowded but to be asked to repeat the lecture on the following day, which I did before an equally large audience, and to be assured that if I would do it again the third day, which I refused to do, there would be no falling off in the attendance. I wondered how many people would turn up in London to hear a French deputy talk on the same subject.

In April I spoke again at the annual meeting of the Royal Society of St. George, a branch of which had recently been founded in Paris. The annexation of Czecho-Slovakia had already taken place and it had been followed soon afterwards by the Italian occupation of Albania. Our Government's reaction to the former had been to double the Territorial Army, a foolish gesture, since that army was not even then up to establishment, there was little hope of the necessary recruits coming forward, and if they did it would be a further penalty imposed upon patriotism for the benefit of the lazier and more selfish section of the population. All this time the Prime Minister and the little circle who surrounded him were resisting the demand for conscription which was being pressed on them from many quarters, and by nobody more persistently than by Hore-Belisha, the Secretary of State for War. After the Albanian affair I thought the Prime Minister would be bound to yield to this demand and I surmised in my Paris speech that it would come shortly. The next morning it was announced that he had yielded. Conscription was to be introduced forthwith. Nobody in Paris credited me with intelligent foresight. Everybody was convinced that I had had prior information, which was not the case.

Yet even this final and enforced manifestation of energy was followed by a reaction towards appeasement among an important group of the Government's supporters. "Danzig is not worth a war," was a new slogan of *The Times*, in whose columns aged politicians crept out of obscurity in order to sign letters urging further negotiations with the dictators, who, on their side, had never shown the slightest desire to negotiate.

At the beginning of August the House was to rise for two months and the Prime Minister was going to Scotland to fish. The debate on the adjournment, usually a formal and friendly affair, became heated. Winston Churchill, Leo Amery and others opposed the adjournment, whereupon the Prime Minister made of it a vote of confidence against which no loyal member of the party should vote. I left for the country before the division took place. The following day I wrote to Stanley Baldwin.

I see it is your birthday so I am writing to wish you many happy returns. I wish that you could return to your old office for I foresee great dangers arising from the present conduct of it. I often wish I could discuss the present situation with you.

The Prime Minister's main mistakes seem to me to be two. He believes public opinion is what *The Times* tells him it is—and he believes Conservative opinion is what the Chief Whip says it is. . . . The result is that the P.M. has come to make that fatal error of relying on his right wing and believing that they represent the party. This was the very error that you always so bravely and brilliantly avoided—thereby incurring at times the violent animosity of the right wing. But you knew that they would always come home in the end because they have no other home to go to.

Last night (August 2nd) was the worst example yet of his failure—and wilful failure—to conciliate any opposition. The House was in a mood to discuss the question on an entirely non-party, patriotic basis, but the P.M. took advantage of some unguarded words of Greenwood's in order to turn the debate into a vote of confidence. There was a great deal of feeling about it—amongst many who eventually voted for the Government.

If the international situation deteriorates, which I believe it will, we shall be compelled to have a Coalition Government. I don't believe that Neville could ever lead such a Government, especially after a performance like that of last night. What are the alternatives?—Halifax or Winston. I don't really believe the former is up to it, and the latter has so many and such violent enemies—not only in the House, but there are large numbers of people in the country who admire but don't trust him.

It is for these reasons that I am wondering whether after two years' rest you feel you could come back. Men are only as old as they feel, and I can't tell how you feel. Mr. G. was in his prime at seventy-two and so was my friend Talleyrand. But you may feel, as I'm sure I shall much sooner, that "there remaineth a rest for the people of God and I have had troubles enough for one."

I am sure you will forgive this letter and understand the feeling in which it is written, which is not a passing mood of irritation but a growing sense of anxiety and disquiet.

I kept no copy of this letter, but the original was found by his biographer among the very few papers that he left. It was no doubt a foolish appeal, but it reveals how I was feeling. Baldwin replied a few weeks later, thanking me for my good wishes, saying he had had an enjoyable visit to America and, typically, making no allusion whatever to the matter about which I had written.

I did another foolish thing during that month of August. An old friend was commanding the Third Battalion of the Grenadiers and he suggested that I should do ten days' training with them at Aldershot as a member of the Special Reserve. I consented and bought new uniform and boots for the occasion, discovering when it was all over that, according to regulations, I should have worn plain clothes. They were strenuous days, sleeping out of doors, fording rivers and taking part in most energetic operations. I enjoyed it, but suffered from shyness with officers of my own rank, subalterns, who were young enough to be my sons, and with senior officers whom I had met when I was Secretary of State for War, and whose instinct was to salute me when I should have saluted them. The Commander-in-Chief at Aldershot, with whom I dined one night, was Sir John Dill, who had been Vice Chief of the Imperial General Staff when I was at the War Office.

We were living then in our little house by the sea, at Aldwick near Bognor, and at the end of August I began to keep a diary again.

On the morning of September 1st I played golf at Goodwood. I never played worse. I couldn't concentrate on the game because I was thinking of what had happened the night before. We had listened to the eleven o'clock news and had heard the German sixteen points to Poland given out without commentary. I was horrified. And I was the more horrified because Diana hearing them said that they did not seem to her unreasonable. I tried to explain to her how they meant the end of Poland, but I felt that the reactions of millions of people might be the same as hers.

I rang up Winston, who said he felt exactly as I did, but that he had already spoken to the *Daily Mail*, who were inclined to take a favourable view of the German proposals. I then got on to Camrose, who also agreed with me. He was awaiting some guidance from the Foreign Office as to what the press was to say, but had received none hitherto. I urged that the *Daily Telegraph* should come out with a strong leading article condemning the terms.

When we had finished our round of golf we went into the club house for a drink. Two men sitting at the bar were discussing future race-meetings. One of the two, the secretary, I knew slightly. As we left he said to me, "Hitler started on Poland this morning." I asked him what he meant. He said that the Germans had invaded Poland and bombed several cities. He then turned back to his friend and went on talking about the St. Leger. That was how I heard that the second World War had begun. As we drove back to Bognor my heart felt lighter than it had felt for a year.

CHAPTER SIXTEEN

THE BEGINNING OF THE WAR

1939–1940

THE beginning of the second war was very different from that of the first. There were no cheering crowds this time. There was no enthusiasm. If any had existed it would have been dimmed by the black-out which descended upon us even before the declaration of war. People acquired later the habit of coping with it. They grew accustomed to darkness and the electric torch lightened their ways.

When we returned from our game of golf there was a telegram to say that the House of Commons was meeting at six o'clock that evening. Little occurred. I described at the time the Prime Minister's speech as "unimpressive and hardly worthy of the occasion."

We dined that evening at the Savoy Grill with Winston Churchill, George Lloyd, Duncan Sandys and his wife. Winston had to leave before the end of dinner to see the Prime Minister, who had already invited him to join the Government, although there had been no announcement to that effect. When we emerged from the restaurant we found ourselves in the unfamiliar darkness without any conveyance. A rich friend in a car took pity on us and gave us a lift. He began immediately to abuse the Jews, saying that the Savoy was full of them. I have always been a friend and admirer of that great race, and since the hideous persecution which they had suffered in a Christian country I felt strongly that it was not for Christians to despise Jews, who had far better grounds for despising Christians. However, I reflected that we were guests in the car and that it was not incumbent upon me to defend the Jews in the presence of the good Samaritan. I therefore restrained myself, but when our friend went further, rejoiced that we were not yet at war and added that Hitler knew, after all, that we were his best friends, I could hold back no longer and said that I hoped he would soon find out that we were his most implacable and remorseless enemies. The remainder of that journey passed in silence. The next morning somebody asked me at the club whether our benefactor of the night before was a friend of mine. I said that I knew him only slightly. "Then why," I was asked, "did he ring up so-and-so this morning to say that if there was a war it would be entirely due to the Jews and Duff Cooper?"

The Prime Minister's statement in the House of Commons the following evening gave the impression to the whole House that even at this late hour Great Britain was going to repeat the surrender of Munich. When Arthur Greenwood, acting leader of the Opposition, rose to reply, Amery shouted to him across the floor of the House, "Speak for England," inferring that the Prime Minister had failed to do so. Greenwood made a robust speech and was cheered by the Tories, who had listened to their own leader in embarrassed silence.

The feeling was astonishing. Anthony was sitting between Amery and me. Many of those sitting in front of us urged him to speak. Indignation was by no means confined to our group. Old Wardlaw Milne, who was sitting on the other side of me, was feeling as strongly as anybody. He is a very loyal supporter of the Government. I thought it would be much better if he spoke than if any of us did, and I urged him to do so. He did and it carried great weight. The whole thing was over in half an hour. I never felt so moved.

I went back to pick up Diana at Chapel Street and we went to the Savoy Grill. I felt that I could eat nothing—but dealt very successfully with a cold grouse. Ronnie Tree and Jim Thomas joined us. They were of course feeling as I did. Harold Balfour [Under-Secretary of State for Air] walked past our table. I asked him if he was still a member of the Government. He made a gesture of shame and despair. Later Euan [Wallace, who had recently become Minister of Transport], Oliver [Stanley], Walter [Elliot] and Shakes [W. S. Morrison] came in and sat at another table. I heard afterwards that they thought I would cut them if they came near me. They were there a very short time and hurried away again. Euan left a message for me with Harold Balfour to say that I must keep my hair on—that the announcement had taken the whole Cabinet by surprise and that they had insisted on holding another Cabinet meeting that night.

At about 10.30 I went round to Winston's flat, which he had asked me to do. . . . He considered that he had been very ill-treated, as he had agreed the night before to join the War Cabinet but throughout the day he had not heard a word from the Prime Minister. He had wished to speak that night in the House but feeling himself already almost a member of the Government had refrained from doing so.

There were present at his flat Anthony, Bob Boothby, Brendan Bracken and Duncan Sandys. We were all in a state of bewildered rage. Bob was convinced that Chamberlain had lost the Conservative Party forever and that it was in Winston's power to go to the House of Commons tomorrow and break him and take his place. He felt very strongly that in no circumstances now should Winston consent to serve under him. On the other hand, if Winston now backed Chamberlain he could save him. Was it better to split the country at such a moment or bolster up Chamberlain? That seemed at one time the decision that Winston had to take.

To the accompaniment of a tremendous thunderstorm we talked and argued far into the night. At last we received information that when the House met at noon the following Sunday morning it would be announced that the country would be at war in the afternoon.

This altered the whole situation. Our heated discussion cooled down. Winston said that he would send in his letter (which he had just drafted) to the Prime Minister none the less, and so in the small hours we wandered home through the dark streets.

The next morning I attended a meeting of our small parliamentary group in Ronald Tree's house in Queen Anne's Gate. There at eleven o'clock we listened to the Prime Minister's broadcast statement that we were already at war with Germany. I recorded in my diary that "we all thought he did it very well." Our meeting broke up soon after he had finished as the House was meeting at noon.

As we left the house we heard strange sounds and said, laughing, that it sounded like an air-raid warning, which indeed it proved to be. We walked on towards the House of Commons—Anthony, Derek Gunston and I. Derek said, "We're walking pretty fast, aren't we?" which we were. When we arrived there we were directed to a room opposite the downstair smoking-room, which was full of an odd mixture of people—servants, typists and the Speaker. We didn't stay there long but wandered out on the terrace, where we watched the balloons go up, which they did with great speed. It was a beautiful morning. The House met at twelve as arranged and the All Clear signal went during Prayers. I did not think the Prime Minister so good as he had been on the radio, nor did I think any of the speeches reached a very high level. Greenwood's was about the best.

I took Terence O'Connor out to luncheon at Buck's. We both envied the people we saw there in uniform. He at least has something to do—and plenty to do. I have nothing.

This was the chief problem with which the war in its early stages presented me. At the beginning of the first war I had too much to do, now I had too little. My contract to write articles for the *Evening Standard* was coming to an end. The editor did not offer and I had no wish to renew it. And what useful part could a back-bencher play in the House of Commons? Independence is a blessed thing in time of peace, but it becomes a curse in war. Criticism is a useful function until the State is in danger; then it must take second place to service. To desire to serve and to find no means of doing so is an unhappy experience. To have held high office, far from making it easier to find employment, as some might suppose, makes it on the contrary more difficult. Many people who would be glad to offer some subordinate post to an educated man of forty-nine with the necessary qualifications, would be most reluctant to give it to an ex-Cabinet Minister.

I sought to give some expression to my feelings at this time in the following verses:

As autumn fades and winter comes
    With menace deep and dire,
We sit and twiddle useless thumbs
    And chatter round the fire.

When young we fought with might and main,
    Our comrades by our side.
They were the noblest of our strain—
    Those friends of ours who died.

We mourned them, but we still believed
    They had not died in vain.
And there was glory while we grieved—
    The noblest of our strain.

But doubts begin to rise today
    Like ghosts beside the grave.
Have we in weakness thrown away
    All that they died to save?

We ask. We hear the answer bold
    And know again the tone
Of voices that have not grown old
    With years, as ours have grown.

"Though much be lost which we had won,
    Not yours, old friends, the blame.
The battle is but re-begun,
    The quarrel is the same.

"We fought that men might still be free,
    As men have fought before,
Nor hoped for final victory
    In any single war.

"Man's life, at best, is sad and brief,
    What matters loss or gain?
Whoever dies for his belief
    Will never die in vain."

We hear their words; we know their truth,
    And feel through ageing blood
The impulse of eternal youth
    Surge like a rising flood.

Oh England, use us once again,
    Mean tasks will match the old;
Our twiddling thumbs can hold the skein
    From which the wool is roll'd.

More gladly though would we give all
    That yet we have to give.
Oh, let the old men man the wall,
    And let the young men live.

It may not be. Not ours to fight,
    Not unto us, O Lord,
Shall twice in life be given the right
    To serve thee with the sword.

Yet our deep love and fierce desire
    Must aid our country still—
The steadfast faith, the quenchless fire,
    Th' unconquerable will.

Because I thought there must be many people feeling as I did, I sent these verses to *The Times* with a letter to the editor, whom I had known well in the past. He had been the most fervent advocate of the Munich policy and we had become completely estranged. I wrote that if the war did nothing else it should at least bring such quarrels to an end, as we all had now only one policy and one purpose. He neither published the verses nor answered the letter.

A year before, at the time of my resignation, I had received from an American organisation an invitation to undertake a lecture tour in the United States. I had answered that it was impossible for me to do such a thing at that time but that I should be glad to do so in the following year if conditions were favourable. I believe that I signed some agreement but I had little doubt that the outbreak of war would absolve me from any liability.

September 11th. I received this morning a telegram from the agent who was arranging my lecture tour in America, hoping that I was still coming and suggesting that I should come earlier.

I was faced by a problem. There are obvious objections to a man's leaving his own country when it is at war and expecting bombardment. Those objections are increased when he is travelling to a safe, neutral country where he expects to make money. At the same time I felt that I might be of some use in America and that I was being of little or none in England. I consulted my friends but found no unanimity among them.

On the evening of the day when I received the telegram I dined at a small dining club founded by Winston Churchill and F. E. Smith in the first decade of the century. Our chairman that evening was Lord Gort, who was leaving the next day as Commander-in-Chief of the expeditionary force.

I consulted Terence [O'Connor] about my projected visit to America. He was very much against it. He takes a flattering view of my abilities and says that I shall certainly be wanted here very soon. Discontent with the Government, he says, is growing rapidly. The atmosphere of the House of Commons is impregnated with gloom and criticism. Shakes Morrison, on the other hand, was all in favour of my going. He said it was the most useful thing I could possibly do. Winston was not very helpful. He said that if I went I must go not as the emissary of the Government but as an ordinary lecturer on a commercial basis. There seemed to be a good deal of pessimism prevalent. The sinkings last week were as bad as in the worst week of the last war. Winston told me that Chamberlain doesn't take him into his confidence. That they meet only across the table. There is obviously no love lost between them.

Two days later I happened to meet Lord Salisbury. " I asked his advice about going to America. He was uncertain, but inclined to be against my going." The same afternoon

Winston came up to me in the smoking-room [of the House of Commons] and said that he was afraid he had not given his mind sufficiently to the question of my going to America when I had asked him about it the other night. He was still against it, owing to the uncertainty of the future and the impermanence of the Government. He wished there was some job he could give me under the Admiralty, but he simply couldn't think of one—nor could I. I told him I had nothing whatever to do at present, as my contract with the Evening Standard came to an end in three weeks and they didn't want to renew it. He suggested that I should take over the contract he had been obliged to break with the *Daily Mirror* and promised he would communicate with them about it. I told him that I had no wish to get into the present Government or to serve under Chamberlain again, but that I looked forward to the time when he would become Prime Minister.

That evening I met some of the leading American press correspondents in the rooms of a friend. They were complaining of their treatment by the censor.

I consulted them with regard to my private problem. Gunther and Knickerbocker were strongly in favour of my going to America. Duranty was inclined to be against it—but he did not feel strongly.

I also record a long talk with Lord Cranborne. He was on the whole in favour of my going to America.

So far the main argument that had been put to me against going was that I might do better for myself by staying at home in the hope that something would turn up. This carried little weight with me. In time of war activity appeals to the most lethargic. The rôle of a back-bench supporter of the Government in the House of Commons is not a very active one at the best of times, but when that Government is conducting a war, and when the back-bencher if he indulges in criticism is apt, on account of his past history, to be suspected of spite and malignity, the effect is paralysing.

Gradually therefore I came to the decision to go. But there were two more people whom I had to consult before acting upon it. One was the Lieutenant-Colonel of my regiment. He happened to be the same officer who, as Acting Commanding Officer of the Fifth Battalion, had bidden me good-bye on the platform of Waterloo Station when I left for France twenty-one years before. Colonel Mark Maitland received me with the greatest courtesy and kindness. When I told him that I was proposing to leave the country for five or six months but would not do so if he had or foresaw any possibility of having any need of my services, he was obliged to say that he had none and foresaw none. There were plenty of former officers, younger and with more military experience than I, who were waiting to fill any post that might become vacant.

The only other person whose approval I felt I should obtain, and who certainly had more places of employment at his disposal than the Lieutenant-Colonel, was the Prime Minister.

September 21st. In the afternoon I had an interview with the Prime Minister. . . . I had thought that he would have said one word of regret at not having been able to offer me a post in the Government and perhaps would have suggested that he might be able to do so later. It would not have meant anything but would have been civil. He said nothing of the kind but merely suggested that in six weeks' time, "when things would be getting pretty hot here," a man of my age might be criticised for leaving the country. I said that that was my own responsibility and was a question that I could settle for myself. I had come to ask him whether on public grounds he saw any objection to my going. After some humming and hawing he said that it would be a good thing for me to go—and so I left him.

There existed in the country at that time a certain amount of feeling that can best be described as unhealthy. It was not disloyal or defeatist, but it was liable to be too easily affected by the disloyal and defeatist elements that crouched beneath the surface. Among the latter were both the Fascists and the Communists. The former had long advertised their admiration for Hitler and could give no sincere support to a war against him. Communists were in a more difficult position, and their leader committed at the outbreak of war the greatest blunder of his life by pledging his party to support it. Having been taught to denounce the Nazis ever since they had come into being, knowing that to be a Communist in Germany was a crime, and learning that his country had declared war against the Nazis, he innocently believed that his Russian master must be in favour of such a war and that he could not be wrong in giving it his blessing. He forgot that Stalin had made a pact with Hitler, that Molotov and Ribbentrop had shaken hands, and he could not know that so little did Communism count for Stalin that the German Communists who had taken refuge in Russia had, by his orders, been handed over to the tender mercies of the Nazis.

The mistake of their leader was soon rectified. The British Communists, like patient oxen, proceeded to shamble in the opposite direction under the goad of the Muscovite, and were regaled as they did so by the spectacle of their trusted leader eating his words. Henceforth the Communists continued to do everything in their power to undermine the war effort and to aid the cause of Hitler until, to Stalin's astonishment, Hitler attacked Russia, when contrary orders came over the wires and the British Communists had to turn right about face again and became, within an hour, the most blatant of patriots. They still, however, were under orders to steal any information they could lay their hands on and convey it secretly to the Russian Embassy.

But between these two extremities of political thought there was a considerable body of opinion whose attitude towards the war was not satisfactory. It was a vague body, almost nebulous; it had little form and fortunately no leader. It was composed of disparate entities. The left wing of the Labour Party included not only a few sincere pacifists but also larger numbers whose detestation of war was so intense that they doubted whether anything could be worth fighting for, and they felt that something ought to be done to stop it. In the right wing of Conservatism, on the other hand, there were to be found some who, without having any sympathy for the Nazis, believed that Communism was the greater danger, and felt that Hitler had rendered his country a service by suppressing the Communists and might render Europe one by protecting it from the red peril.

There existed also an attitude even less definite and harder to define, originating probably in the fact that the public mind was ill-prepared for war. People had been told recently by Ministers, and some sections of the press had never ceased to tell them, that there was no longer any danger of war, so that when it happened they could hardly believe it; they felt that there must be some mistake and clung obstinately to the hope that the whole thing could somehow be patched up. When it became apparent, as it soon did, that Poland was doomed, these people began to say that they were very sorry for the Poles, but that there was nothing more to be done about it, and why should we go on fighting?

I was very conscious that this feeling was present, during these distressful days of comparative idleness, lounging and gossip. I watched for it and stalked it because I wanted to strangle it, but it was most elusive and would vanish suddenly into thin air. One afternoon in the House of Commons I heard plainly the sound of the evil thing I was hunting. It had borrowed the finest instrument in the House, the mellow, persuasive voice of David Lloyd George. "I urge," it was saying, "that the Government should take into consideration any proposals for peace which are specific, detailed, broad . . . which review all the subjects that have been the cause of all the troubles of the last few years." He suggested that we should hold a secret session to discuss peace terms.

When he sat down I sprang to my feet. A newspaper reported next day that I was white with anger. I accused him of preaching surrender. I said that his speech would be received with delight in Germany, where it would be said that the man who claimed to have won the last war was already admitting defeat in this one. What sort of terms would the Germans offer? "They have destroyed," I declared, "a great country, they have wiped it off the face of the map. A country that came into existence as the result of the last war and has been there for twenty years exists no more. Is it suggested that they will offer terms that will do anything less than register that victory and stamp it on the face of Europe? Are they going now to suggest setting up again a real independent Poland? And if they did who would be fool enough to believe in their sincerity or to trust their word?"

Lloyd George was stung to interruption. Rising, he said in his most solemn and prophetic manner, "The right honourable gentleman will live to regret what he has said." I have not done so yet.

The next speaker was a Labour Member and a Welshman, David Grenfell from Glamorgan. He expressed the sincere admiration he had always felt for Lloyd George, and then proceeded to denounce his speech in language not less vigorous than mine. So the great man heard himself condemned in the accents of his own country.

It was shortly after this debate that we sailed for America. On the evening before we left the Prime Minister sent his Parliamentary Private Secretary to see me with the request, almost the order, that in the course of my lecture tour in the United States I should abstain from anything that might be considered British propaganda. Surveyed at this distance of time the demand seems almost incredible. A former Cabinet Minister arrives from England, when his country has just entered on a great war, and he is advertised to lecture all over the

United States on topics of current interest. What will his audiences expect of him except information about this war, the causes and the prospects of it? How can an Englishman give such information without presenting and defending the cause of his country? And what better form of propaganda could there be?

I cannot remember with what assurances I sent away the Parliamentary Private Secretary. If they satisfied him they must have been disingenuous. I was not going to America to talk about history or literature. I should not have felt justified in doing so at such a time. I was going there to support our cause and in the hope of so rendering it some service, for I had heard already that it was suffering from lack of advocacy.

The United States are perhaps more subject than are other countries to inundation by great waves of conviction. Certain opinions take on temporarily the guise of articles of faith. What elsewhere might be called a craze becomes there a creed. At this fateful moment of history the majority of American citizens were possessed by two firm convictions. One was that they had been enticed into the first World War by the craftiness of British propaganda; and the other was that the second World War was due to the harsh conditions imposed by the French and the British upon the defeated Germans in the Treaty of Versailles. These opinions were due to faulty representations of recent history which had appeared in publications that have mercifully been forgotten. In them no mention was made of unrestricted submarine warfare decreed by Germany, which must have brought about the death of innumerable American citizens or else have driven American shipping off the seas. Nor did they tell how the idealistic President Wilson was the principal author of the Treaty of Versailles. These were among the misapprehensions which I wanted to correct in the course of my lectures.

The British Government, having been informed of the exaggerated ideas entertained in the United States as to the power and the danger of propaganda, decided to abstain from it altogether. This was, to say the least of it, an extraordinary decision. True, it was taken on the advice tendered by the British Ambassador in Washington. Lord Lothian was a man of singular charm, of considerable intelligence and with a wide and intimate knowledge of America. But his judgment was easily influenced and his opinions underwent great and frequent changes. Born and brought up in the Roman Catholic religion, he had abandoned it for that of Mrs. Eddy, a conversion that shook the faith of many in his intellectual discernment. A fine athlete with a splendid constitution, a total abstainer and a non-smoker, he died at the height of his powers and at the moment of his greatest usefulness of a malady which, owing to his refusal to see a doctor, was never diagnosed.

The importance of influencing public opinion both in neutral and in enemy countries had been amply demonstrated in the former war. That attempts to exercise such influence should not be crude or tact-less was evident, but to abandon all such attempts through fear of fall-ing into crudity and losing tact was plainly foolish. The main reason for its folly in this instance was that not a single American citizen throughout the country was going to give us credit for such absten-tion. When they saw no sign of our propaganda they naturally as-sumed that we were doing it very badly, and hence concluded that if we were conducting the war in Europe as inefficiently as we were conducting our propaganda in America, we were likely to lose it.

In the ship in which I crossed the Atlantic there were two English writers who had made a regular practice of delivering lectures during the winter in the United States. Neither of them was concerned with politics. They spoke on literary and artistic subjects. On landing they were classed with me as the three British propagandists whom the latest ship had brought to New York. When an agitated official from the British Library of Information, a very useful peacetime in-stitution, called on me to implore me not to indulge in propaganda, I drew his attention to this fact, and told him that any British subject who spoke in America at that time would and must be dubbed a pro-pagandist, and that as we could not clear ourselves of the accusation the best that we could do was to accept it and to make our propa-ganda as effective as possible.

On one point, however, I could assure him, and I had no doubt given the Prime Minister's Private Secretary the same assurance: I would not urge nor even suggest that the United States should come into the war. It was the easier for me to give this assurance because it coincided entirely with my own convictions. I could see no reason whatever why America should come into the war at that date, and I considered that the repeal of the Neutrality Act was all that we had the right to expect. If we had fought a year before, we could have said with truth that we were fighting for a great principle, the observance of international law, and for the existence of a small country which had come into being in accordance with President Wilson's doctrine of self-determination. We had not been willing to fight then, and after that we had accepted the kick in the back of Prague and the slap in the face of Albania. We were fighting now neither for a principle nor for others. We were fighting for our lives. It might become an American interest to save our lives, but until it plainly was so I could see no reason for their intervention. I had some heated arguments before leaving London on this question with friends who found me too pro-American. I could not tell them, for it was still a secret, how, when the President, at the risk of his political life, had suggested intervention in Europe, he had been snubbed by the Prime Minister.

On my arrival in the United States a friend, who knew me well, said that he had only one fear in connection with my visit, which was that I should lose my temper. I made a bet with him that I would not do so until I sailed again. I won that bet and I was proud of having done so, for self-restraint is not among my natural advantages.

I had indeed very little provocation, and never any on the public platform. I gave, during the five months that I was there, sixty-one set lectures, not to mention a number of after-luncheon and after-dinner speeches. I travelled across the whole country from Oregon to Florida, from Texas and California to the State of Maine. I also crossed the border into Canada. Nowhere did I have a bad reception and nowhere did the press give me an unfavourable report. One Labour Member said in the House of Commons that I should be recalled and interned because I was doing immeasurable harm. Some American papers quoted him with surprise, but none supported him.

My principal object in these lectures was to give information and to correct misunderstanding. Not one per cent in any audience had heard of the Statute of Westminster or believed that the Dominions were really self-governing. Equally few were aware of the Mahommedan problem in India or had any idea of the bloodshed that was bound to follow British withdrawal. I told them how the war had come about and what Hitler had done in Germany. "The Survival of Liberty" was the title of many of the lectures, but I sometimes felt like Mark Twain who, giving his lecture-agent a list of titles from which his audiences could choose, said "They'll get the same lecture anyway."

The cause of Great Britain was not popular in the United States at that time. It was more popular than the cause of Germany, and most Americans hoped that we would win. That Germany could ever become a menace to America would have seemed fantastic had anybody suggested it. The policy of appeasement had gone far to discredit Great Britain. I remember some publication that appeared that winter containing an account of the horrors perpetrated on the Jews by Hitler. I suggested to a prominent columnist and radio speaker, who wished us well, that he should give some publicity to it. "But we have known all that for a long time," he objected. "We withdrew our Ambassador from Berlin in protest. What did you do?" I admitted that we had done nothing. "Yes, you did," he said; "your Prime Minister signed an agreement with Hitler."

The general feeling was that Europe was at war again, that Hitler was an abomination, but that so was Stalin. It was to be hoped that the British would win, but it was to be hoped still more that no American boy's life would be thrown away fighting for the British Empire. The United States had won the last war, and had hardly been thanked for it. They had not even been repaid the money they had lent. The United States had been caught once; they were not going to be caught a second time.

I think that is not an unfair sketch of moderate American feeling at the time. There was of course, from the first, a solid body of thought that favoured intervention, but it was a minority, the size of which it would have been difficult then, and would now be impossible, to estimate. I shall never forget a large luncheon party that I attended at Mr. Tom Lamont's upon Election Day, November 7th, 1939. I think we were the only English people there. At the end of the meal Mrs. Lamont rose and said, "I'm going to give you a toast which nobody need drink if they don't want to. Here's to the victory of the Allies and to hell with neutrality." I have never been able to express the gratitude I felt at that moment, but looking round the table I saw

there were many who drank reluctantly and deplored the imprudence of their hostess. It was all the braver of Mrs. Lamont to propose the toast because her husband was a partner in the firm of Mor-
gan, who were accused by the pro-German propagandists at that
time of having played some sinister part in getting America into the
other war for their own financial advantage.

It is because the American people were feeling as they were at that
moment that I have never ceased to wonder at the warmth of our
reception wherever we went throughout that great country. Lightly
to make generalisations about a whole people is usually foolish. To
say that the French are clever, the Spanish proud, the Italians light-
hearted, or the English morose, is to assume more knowledge and
experience than any individual can possess. Yet from my limited
opportunities of observation I would assert that the Americans have
the best manners in the world, and I would add that the reason why
they have the best manners is that they have the kindest hearts.

Although I visited only twenty-one out of the forty-eight States I
can claim to have seen a good deal of the country and of most sections
of society during my journey. Twice in the course of those sixty-one
lectures I met with a little organised opposition, once in Brooklyn
and once in Boston. On both occasions it owed its origin to the
embers of the ancient Irish feud. At Brooklyn a few pathetic pickets
marched round the hall in heavy rain warning the public not to go
in lest the wicked English speaker should lure the United States into
the European war. At one of several meetings that I addressed in
Boston there were a few interruptions which were instantly quelled.

Often after these lectures, especially ones that were given in smaller
places, people would come to me to apologise for the tone of some
of the questions that had been asked. Such questions, dealing, for
instance, with our failure to pay the American debt or our treatment
of the Indian people, I considered perfectly legitimate and, indeed,
natural. I never resented them, but my courteous hosts would express
regret that such questions had been put and would assure me that
those who had put them were not inhabitants of that city but strangers
who had come in from distant, unknown places.

I had been warned that American hospitality was overpowering
and that the endless social functions which the lecturer had to attend

were more fatiguing than the lectures. Such was not my experience. I was on the contrary surprised by the thoughtful tact with which we were treated. Often we arrived in the early morning. There would always be somebody at the station to receive us and take us to the hotel. Then, more often than not, they would say, "You must be tired and would like a quiet day to yourselves. We have arranged for a car to be at your disposal, and if you would care to come around for a cocktail this evening before the lecture we should be delighted to see you."

There would usually be photographers waiting at the hotel, whose behaviour I found was always considerate. They would ask for ten minutes or a quarter of an hour and would undertake, having had it, to make no further demands. I have never had trouble with representatives of the American press, and when people do have such trouble I believe it to be their own fault. The American press respond to civility. They are also quite capable of responding to incivility. During all the time I have spent in that country, and this was neither my first visit nor my last, I have never been misreported or misrepresented in the press of the United States. I cannot say as much for the press of any other country in which I have lived.

In the course of my travels I had the honour of being received by President Roosevelt and having luncheon alone with him. He sat behind his massive writing-table in the room where he worked. An admirable contrivance was rolled in bearing the luncheon and keeping it hot. "I usually drink tea," he said, "but there is always coffee there too because most people prefer it. I know that you, being an Englishman, will prefer tea, so you shall have it today and I will drink coffee." I forbore to say that neither was among my favourite luncheon beverages, and I reflected on how ignorant even the greatest men can be of the customs of other countries.

He was then evolving his theory of the four freedoms, about which he talked to me, and also about the problem of unemployment, which he suggested might be solved by the development of central South America. I was much impressed by him but I felt that he was disappointed in me. I am not at my best in duologue and even the excellent tea failed to loosen my tongue.

Those were very full months and I was more exhausted at the end of them than I have ever been. I cannot say if I did any good but I am certain that I did no harm. I have kept many of the kind and indeed enthusiastic letters that I received at the time, and I have maintained many of the friendships that I made. One of the most reassuring letters, because it is carefully weighed and as unaffected by enthusiasm as one would expect from a Civil Servant, came from our Consul General in Chicago, where I spoke several times and where nobody can allege that there is any pro-British bias. He began his letter by repeating all the then familiar arguments against attempts to spread propaganda in America, and then went on:

Having given expression to the only possible criticism of your lecturing here, I say with the greatest assurance that you do nothing but good in so far as your listeners are concerned. Such talks as that of last Monday cannot fail to further sentiments of good will, and I think you are doing a fine job. If I were you I would not permit either the criticisms which occasionally appear in the press or the whispering propaganda which German-Americans undoubtedly conduct to influence me from my course. You should be able to go home at the expiration of your sojourn here with the feeling that you have done something to clarify our position in this war.

But what can one lone voice achieve in attempting to carry conviction to a population of a hundred and fifty millions? The night before we left America at the beginning of March we found ourselves in company with half a dozen of the most staunch and stalwart American supporters of our cause. They were all men in walks of life that enabled them to gauge the trend of public opinion. They were unanimous in the view that during the first six months of the war the Allies had lost popularity. Whether the Germans had gained what the Allies had lost was another question, and one on which they were divided, but the unanimity on the former point was as impressive as it was depressing. Many reasons were given, but to my mind they all amounted to one, which was that our publicity was being badly organised. I resolved that on my return I would do what I could to set this matter right.

CHAPTER SEVENTEEN

MINISTER OF INFORMATION

1940–1941

WE sailed from New York on March 9th in an American ship which called at Gibraltar, Naples and Genoa, where we landed. Genoa, usually one of the busiest and noisiest towns in Europe, was like a city of the dead. Never before or since have I found it so attractive. Lack of petrol was the chief reason for the silence that had fallen upon it. Had Italy been at war the condition of Genoa would have been comprehensible, but that Italy would within two months voluntarily go to war seemed hardly probable. Nor do I believe that she would ever have done so had it not been for the sudden and unexpected fall of France. Mussolini, like many better-informed people, believed that the war was over, and his natural instinct impelled him to dash to the assistance of the victor, in order to share the spoil.

We travelled to Paris with comfort and punctuality. We found there many old friends. It was Easter time and the weather was fine. Belloc was there, still gay and confident. I saw Mandel, who was gay and brave. He was Minister for the Colonies. I called on him in his office. His table was littered as usual with documents which appeared to be in complete confusion, but he could without hesitation lay his hand on the one he wanted. I asked him about the French air force, of which I had heard disquieting reports. He laughed and said that every time he asked about it he was told there were fewer machines than when he last enquired. He seemed so cheerful I thought I had misheard him, but he had meant what he said.

I saw also Henri de Kerillis, the only non-Communist deputy who had voted against Munich. He was not cheerful at all. The menace of the Fifth Column obsessed him. He assured me that it was they who had advocated sending help to Finland, which would have brought Russia into the war on the side of Germany. The strength of the enemy would then have been so great that France would have been forced to surrender, which was what they wanted to do.

The French Government fell while we were in Paris. Daladier was succeeded by Reynaud. We hoped that it might be an improvement, but it was not.

On our return to England we found a very different atmosphere from that which we had left. Discontent with the Government had grown more open and more violent, and the Prime Minister's method of dealing with it was not to strengthen his team by the introduction of new men, but to shuffle the pack and put down the same cards in different places. He had dropped Hore-Belisha, and he was unjustly suspected of having done so because he was opposed to the democratisation of the Army. He had recalled from retirement Sir John Gilmour, who had always been a popular member of the House of Commons, but who had never been suspected of powerful intellectual or dynamic qualities, and who had been dropped from the Cabinet by Baldwin four years earlier. He died in the same year.

Our own small group had been scattered. Those of them who were of military age had gone to fight, two of them to die. Our leaders, Anthony Eden and Winston Churchill, were members of the Government. The remnant had, however, been gathered under the powerful and respectable wing of Lord Salisbury, in whose house we held weekly meetings, where criticism of the Government and suggestions for improving it were not forbidden.

One night when I was already in bed and asleep at Bognor the telephone rang. It was Winston Churchill speaking. He had been called to France for a ministerial conference at short notice and he was due to make the principal speech at the annual luncheon of the Royal Society of St. George two days later. He wanted me to take his place. The notice was short and the responsibility great, but I accepted. The attendance was large. I was distressed, just before the luncheon, to hear an old gentleman in the club say that he had come all the way from Yorkshire for the pleasure of hearing Winston, and when it was announced that he would not be present something like a groan of disappointment rose from the audience. When the chairman went on to say that they had been fortunate to get me to take his place, the applause was feeble and perfunctory. Yet it so happened that this was the most successful speech I ever made. At the end of it the whole audience rose spontaneously to their feet, clapping and cheering. I was much encouraged by such a reception.

The end of April and the two months that followed were to witness an accumulation of disasters for the Allied cause; and already there was developing in parliamentary circles in London a feeling, which was shared and strengthened by members of the forces returning on leave, that there was something grievously wrong with the conduct of the war. The dismal failure of the Norwegian campaign brought matters to a head, and on the 7th of May there began in the House of Commons the two days' debate which sealed the fate of Chamberlain's Government. I think that most people were surprised by the result. I know that I was. But on re-reading the account of the debate in Hansard it is still more surprising to find how feeble was the support of the Government except numerically. Fortunately Chamberlain himself recognised that this was so, for in spite of all the damaging speeches that had been made, in spite of over thirty members of his own party voting against him and twice as many abstaining, he still retained the substantial majority of eighty-one. He might have clung to office had he been unwise enough to do so.

Feeling ran very high in the House during those two days. The dead columns of Hansard cannot reproduce it. They can only provide those who were present with the necessary aids to memory. Five members of the Conservative Party spoke against the Government, and only six, apart from Ministers, spoke for them. Nor was there a single parliamentary figure of note in the latter half-dozen. They seemed rather to have been detailed for the job by the Whips, who felt that out of so large an army there must be a few private soldiers to man the trenches.

The two sensations of the first day's debate were the speeches of Roger Keyes and Leo Amery, both of whom spoke, of course, from the Conservative benches. Keyes came to the House wearing the uniform of an Admiral of the Fleet. He had consulted me on the subject and I had strongly advised him to do so. The great effect that his speech produced was certainly enhanced by this gesture. It showed that for him at least this was no ordinary debate about the conduct of the war but a solemn occasion which might decide the fate of the country.

The Admiral was not a good speaker, and personally, perhaps because I was so anxious that he should succeed, I feared that he had failed. But I was wrong. The effect that he produced was tremendous. The sincerity that lay behind his words gave them life. Those who listened knew that here was no scheming politician, no seeker after office, no captious critic and, although all his principles were Conservative, no party hack. The loyalest of men, he could no longer offer his loyalty to the Prime Minister. He knew that it was no little thing that he was doing, and in order that others might understand what it meant to him he put on for the occasion the uniform that he had so nobly earned the right to wear—the livery of glory.

Amery spoke later in the evening. His speech was not only a criticism of the Norwegian campaign but an indictment of the Government's whole record. "We cannot go on as we are," he said; "there must be a change," and he concluded by quoting the fierce words that Oliver Cromwell addressed to the Rump of the Long Parliament. "You have sat here too long," he said, addressing his words to the Government's front bench, "for any good you have been doing. Depart, I say, and let us have done with you. In the name of God, go."

So the battle was joined, and it was fought to a finish on the following day. Herbert Morrison opened for the Opposition and made the important announcement that the Labour Party intended to put the matter to the vote. The motion before the House was the purely formal one "that this House do now adjourn." No vote was necessary and many had hoped it would be possible to avoid one. Morrison's statement was therefore a challenge. When he had sat down the Prime Minister rose to his feet. He was obviously angry. He accepted the challenge and appealed to his "friends in the House—and I have friends in the House" to support him. The words were unfortunate; the issue was one upon which the outcome of the war depended, and it was no time for a personal appeal to friendship. I said as much when it came to my turn to speak, and I added that it was my intention to vote against the Government for the first time during the eighteen months that had elapsed since I left it. I urged that it was high time for a coalition Government, and I reminded the House that Anthony Eden had advocated one at the time of the Munich debate, when his suggestion had hardly been taken seriously by the Government, secure in its huge majority. I also referred to the fact that the debate was to be closed that evening by Winston Churchill on behalf of the Government. I warned members against being too much affected by his brilliant oratory. "He will be defending," I said, "with his eloquence those who have so long refused to listen to his counsel, who treated his warnings with contempt and refused to take him into their confidence. Those who so often trembled before his sword will be only too glad to shrink behind his buckler."

The division was dramatic. I saw a young officer in uniform, who had been for long a fervent admirer of Chamberlain, walking through the Opposition lobby with the tears streaming down his face. When the figures were announced which disclosed the number of dissentient Conservatives, one of the Tory opposition began to sing Rule Britannia. The Government had a majority of eighty-one, but more than thirty of their usual supporters had voted against them and many had abstained.

The next two days were full of rumour and gossip. Chamberlain's first idea was to form a coalition Government under his own leadership, but on the first of the two days the attitude of the Labour Party convinced him that this was impossible.

On the second day—Saturday, May 10th—the Germans invaded Holland and Belgium. It is curious that Chamberlain's first reaction should have been that this terrible event gave him an excuse for remaining at his post. It is a proof of how men in very high office can acquire the sincere conviction that their services are indispensable and that in moments of crisis they cannot be replaced. Kingsley Wood, upon whose advice he relied, convinced him that these events only added urgency to his departure. His choice then lay between Halifax and Churchill, the same two that I had mentioned a year before in my letter to Baldwin as the only possible coalition Prime Ministers. Churchill's stock had risen since that date. He had shown himself a highly competent First Lord of the Admiralty, his speeches in the House of Commons had been better than those of any of his colleagues, and everything that he had prophesied in the past had come disastrously true. Halifax had merely remained the Foreign Minister of Munich. So, on the very day when Hitler launched the real war upon Europe, Winston Churchill became Prime Minister of England. It was high time.

The next day was Whit Sunday. The weather was beautiful, as it seems so often to be at critical moments in English history. I was summoned during the course of the morning to call upon the new Prime Minister at the Admiralty, which he still occupied. I was shown into the room which had been mine two years before.

The Prime Minister explained to me that his hands had not been free in the construction of his Cabinet, and that he had been obliged to proceed on strictly party lines, giving so many places to the Labour and so many to the Liberal Parties. He said this by way of prelude and almost of apology for offering me the Ministry of Information. He added that the status of the Minister was to be raised, and that he was to attend meetings of the War Cabinet in order that he should, for his guidance, be fully informed upon everything that was taking place.

There was no need of apology so far as I was concerned. I was delighted. It seemed to me that here was a job I could do. During my visit to America I had formed strong views on the need for propaganda and on the manner in which it should be done. I was given Harold Nicolson as my Parliamentary Under-Secretary and I persuaded Ronald Tree, who had already been working in the Ministry, to remain as my Parliamentary Private Secretary. They were both old friends and I felt confident of success.

The early days of my service in the Ministry were full of incident. One disaster after another befell our forces on the battlefield and it was my duty to announce them, or to allow them to be announced to the public with suitable comment. I sought never to distort or minimise the truth but to keep it in proper proportion to the whole. In the state of mind that war produces people are too apt to exaggerate the importance of events and to believe that after one victory the war is won and that after one defeat all hope is lost.

On the 2nd of June I flew over to Paris in order to meet the new French Minister of Information, Frossard. I dined at the Embassy with our Ambassador, Ronald Campbell. It was a melancholy evening. In the garden was smouldering a huge fire in which our confidential archives were being burnt. There were only men present, and the only one that I remember besides the Ambassador was Julien Cain, head of the Bibliothèque Nationale. He said that he wished it were possible to go to sleep and not to awake until the war was over. I believe that he suffered terribly at the hands of the Germans, but he survived and occupied again the position he was then holding.

I remember that on the following morning, one of the loveliest June days imaginable, Jean Giraudoux published an article in which he said that even to think that defeat was possible was an act of treason. Had that been true, there must have been many traitors in Paris that day.

We held our conference in the Hôtel Continental, which the French Ministry of Information had requisitioned. We gravely discussed such matters as the best hours for releasing news, transmissions from London in French and from France in English, and the various small methods by which the two Ministries could give assistance to one another. An atmosphere of unreality hung over our proceedings. We felt like a party of the condemned playing at cards while awaiting the summons to the scaffold.

We went on to attend an official luncheon at the Ritz, but as we arrived an air-raid warning sent all the waiters underground, where they were bound by law to remain until the raid was over. So we were confronted by a long table, sumptuously laid, a grapefruit and a roll in every place, and not a soul to serve. We sat about in this curiously dream-like situation, talking in a desultory manner, since none of us were well acquainted, until I suggested that we might as well fall upon the grapefruit, and having consumed it, those who were really hungry, as I was, could stave off the pangs by eating bread and butter. The suggestion was accepted and presently another siren sounded and as by magic the room was full of waiters.

That evening I dined with my friends Mr. and Mrs. Reginald Fellowes, who had a beautiful house with a large garden at Neuilly. I thought it brave of them to be there still, for he had been caught in August 1914 in Berlin, where he was accompanying his father, who was nearly blind and receiving treatment from a German oculist. He had spent the whole of that war as a prisoner in Ruhleben and was determined never to be caught by the Germans again. It was a very pleasant dinner-party. Georges Mandel was there, whom I saw for the last time. I returned the next morning to London.

I kept no diary during those days. They were too fully occupied. I seldom left my office before eight and sometimes returned afterwards, and I worked seven days a week. Many of the staff worked as long hours as I did, some longer. Few left the Ministry before seven. When the heavy nightly bombing started in the autumn these hours could not be maintained. Most of the workers lived in the suburbs and had to get home while travel was possible. So permission was given to leave at five, and the Ministry was almost empty at six. Yet I am quite sure that as much necessary work was done as before and that efficiency in no way suffered. Ever since I have been sceptical of the value of long hours of work, and I am convinced that many people waste a great deal of time in their offices which might be more profitably spent elsewhere.

As I kept no diary I have no first-hand evidence of the events of this period, but concerning the one active adventure in which I took part I have a letter that I wrote to a friend which tells what happened almost from hour to hour.

26.vi.40.

It seems a very long time since I wrote to you, and how many terrible things have happened in the interval. I have had no time—really no time. Never have I worked so hard. Today I am writing under peculiar circumstances. Last night we (the Government) learned that the last remnants of Paul Reynaud's Government—the men who were against surrendering—were on their way to Morocco, and at close on midnight it was decided that I should fly out this morning to meet them in the hope of persuading them to form a new French Government in North Africa to carry on the resistance. Hardly had we made this decision when an air-raid warning went—and there we all were cooped up at Downing Street with no means of getting away. It was a funny party in the cellar, from Mary Churchill, Winston's very pretty youngest daughter, to old Mr. N. C. in a very mouldy dressing-gown. I didn't stay there long but walked in the garden with Brendan and eventually walked home where I had to pack my grip. I didn't get to bed till four and had to get up at six. It was a lovely morning and I have enjoyed the journey so far. My travelling companions are my secretary Sammy Hood, and Lord Gort. We left London at 7.45, changed into a flying boat at Calshot which we left at nine, and now at four o'clock are cruising down the coast of Portugal and hoping to be at Rabat before seven. It is not a very comfortable machine. Two long couches each side of a square table, and conversation is almost impossible on account of the noise. I am lucky to have *Fanny by Gaslight* with me which I advise you to read.

Two days later.

We arrived at Rabat soon after seven as expected. A beautiful white city standing in the desert. We made a wonderful landing in a very narrow waterway where no flying boat had ever landed before. Large apathetic crowds principally of Arabs watched our arrival. All the flags were flying at half-mast. Nobody was there to welcome us. When eventually we got ashore we found a British General called Lord Dillon who is liaison officer to General Noguès, the Governor of French Morocco. He told us our reception would not be good, that they had telegraphed—too late—to stop us coming, and that the authorities were determined that I should see none of the people I had come to see. The people in question were not at Rabat but at Casablanca—about an hour and a quarter by car. I went to the British Consul General and got him to telephone to the Consul at Casablanca to send a message to my friend. The telephone was obviously tapped, for a few minutes later the Deputy Governor, called Morisce, rang up to say he had instructions to prevent me from getting into touch with any of the French ex-Ministers, and that he hoped I would comply, as otherwise he would be compelled to take steps that he would much regret. I asked if he would see me and he agreed. I found him a tall, thin, rather attractive man in a very nervous and emotional state. He had tears in his eyes most of the time. He said that he was only an official and that he must carry out any orders he was given. "If General Noguès tells me to shoot myself I will gladly obey. Unfortunately the orders he has given me are more cruel." By which he meant that he had to treat the former Ministers of France practically as prisoners.

There was nothing to be done. I had to say that I would make no further effort to see them. But I sent Mandel—the best of the Ministers—a message through our Consul, in cypher, saying I would do everything I could to get him out and would send a ship if necessary the next day, from Gibraltar.

I went back to the Consul General, and we dined with some friends of his. It was a beautiful, romantic, African night and the scenery was lovely. The house was like a villa at Eastbourne and the food was filthy. There was plenty of inferior wine.

Gort and Dillon, old friends, had been dining together at the hotel. When they were leaving to join us, Gort had been told by a French private soldier that he was not permitted to leave. This was a bit too much. The Commander-in-Chief of the B.E.F., wearing the Grand Cross of the Legion of Honour, practically put under arrest by a French private soldier. Dillon rang up Morisce who said he knew nothing about it, but within five minutes the soldier came back and said he was sorry he had made a mistake. So they came along and joined us. While we were discussing what to do the telephone rang. It was to say that Morisce was waiting for us at the Consulate General to offer his apologies. When we got there he did his best to explain away what had happened, and apologised. It was not a pleasant scene. However, I said the incident was closed and we would say no more about it. We decided to return to the flying boat and sleep on board, which we did, very uncomfortably, not undressing and with very little means of washing. We flew at dawn. Apparently the take-off was very difficult and dangerous, but I knew nothing about that until later. We got to Gibraltar soon after eight. It was pleasant to feel we were under the British flag again and to be welcomed by A.D.C.s, by butlers and footmen, by hot baths and eggs and bacon. All this was in Government House, very English in its dowdy dignity and Victorian comfort. We spent a pleasant day there—a real holiday—reading and sleeping in a beautiful garden. I finished *Fanny by Gaslight* and enjoyed it to the end. The Governor and his wife are nice people, their food and wine are excellent. Do you know a poem by Shelley which begins

> "Many a green isle needs must be
> In the deep wide sea of misery."

This day was such a green isle and I enjoyed it. We slept there, were called at four this morning and rose from the water over the Pillars of Hercules at 5.30 by the light of a blood-red dawn. It is now 2.30 and we hope to see the coast of Cornwall in three quarters of an hour.

Oh, I have just seen it. Apparently we have had a favourable wind these last few hours, so that we are three quarters of an hour ahead of time. From this cabin you can't see much ahead. It is like looking out of the window of a railway carriage, and as I looked down on the sea there suddenly was England under my eyes—Cornish fields, little white cottages, the coast-guard station, small roads running down into coves by the sea. I was so foolishly moved, perhaps just because it was unexpected. This passionate patriotism is I suppose rather nonsense, but so too I suppose is passionate love. I think that I should die if we had to surrender.

The last sentence of this letter shows what apprehensions then occupied men's minds. We were very near to defeat that summer. There were many who never knew it, there are as many, perhaps more, who prefer not to remember it. In both the great wars of this century the margin between victory and defeat has been very narrow, and it is much to be feared that the majority of our people, having ignored or forgotten how narrow it was, have developed a mood of complacency that is fraught with mortal danger.

I had now served in four government departments—Foreign Office, War Office, Treasury and Admiralty—so that I had some knowledge of the Civil Service, and some idea as to how a department should be run. The former Government was often blamed for not having foreseen what would be necessary in time of war and not having taken steps to prepare for it. In this respect, however, so far as the Ministry of Information was concerned, they were guiltless. On the day of the outbreak the vast machine came into existence and 999 officials sprang to their office chairs. The result was formidable. A monster had been created, so large, so voluminous, so amorphous, that no single man could cope with it. Within the mind of the monster there lurked as much talent, as much experience, as much imagination and brilliance, and as much devotion to duty, as could ever have been collected in any one department of state. Ex-ambassadors and retired Indian Civil Servants abounded, the brightest ornaments of the Bar were employed on minor duties, distinguished men of letters held their pens at the monster's service, and all were prepared to work at any hour and without holiday in their enthusiasm for the cause. It was tragic to see so much ability, so much goodwill so nearly wasted.

A government department is an organism, not a machine. Man can make a machine but he cannot make an organism, because an organism has life, and the creation of life remains a mystery which baffles science. If I were ever called upon to create a Ministry, I should select a man, give him an office and a cheque-book and tell him to hire others as the need for them arose.

It would be profitless and wearisome to enlarge upon all that was wrong with the Ministry. The main defect was that there were too few ordinary Civil Servants in it, and too many brilliant amateurs. The word I got most used to hearing and most to dislike was "frustration." Day after day admirable, although temporary, officials would come to me offering their resignation. And in every case they wanted to leave because their work was being frustrated. They had conceived some brilliant idea and put it forward to their official superior, who had either turned it down flat or else had altered it in such a way as to destroy its usefulness. Had they been regular Civil Servants they would have been neither surprised nor aggrieved, but not being accustomed to such treatment they were astonished and indignant.

The presence of so many able, undisciplined men in one Ministry was bound to lead to a great deal of internal friction, and we were at the same time subjected to a continual bombardment of criticism from without. Since the beginning of the war the Ministry of Information had filled the rôle of Aunt Sally among government departments. Even if the Ministry had been more efficient than it was this would probably have happened. The press must have a target, and in wartime patriotism and censorship reduce the field of fire. Nor is the average man likely to feel convinced in his heart that he himself could better conduct the foreign affairs of the country, the fighting services, the supply of munitions or such matters as seem to demand some technical knowledge or experience. But everybody knows that he would make a first-rate Minister of Information. All that is required is common sense and tact, sympathy with the feeling of others and a sense of humour, qualities which even the most modest men usually concede to themselves.

During the summer of 1940 these attacks reached a peak of virulence and became centred on me personally. This may have been due to the private spite of powerful individuals or to an honest but mistaken belief that I intended to tighten up the censorship to the disadvantage of the press. When I came to the Ministry I found that such a scheme was under contemplation, in accordance with instructions received from the Cabinet, who had been alarmed by one or two unfortunate leaks. I consulted the press, which I found unanimously opposed to any alteration of the existing system, and I consulted Cyril Radcliffe, who had been charged with the arduous task of preparing the new scheme. He told me that he doubted whether any great benefits would accrue from it, and as I knew with what hostility it would meet, I decided to report to the Cabinet against making any change. It was a sub-committee of the Cabinet to whom I reported, and who had in turn to report to the War Cabinet itself. My recommendation was eventually accepted, but all this took many weeks, during which the attacks increased in intensity.

It was discovered that a number of carefully selected people had been charged by the Ministry of Information with the duty of studying the state of public opinion and reporting on the kind of criticism that was being made of the authorities. It was their business to find out what regulations were causing unnecessary distress, what shortages were being most felt and where, in fact, the shoe was pinching. At a time when censorship forbade the airing of certain grievances in the press these investigators could and did render valuable service. I could claim no credit in the matter, as it had been set going before I became Minister, but now I had to bear the whole brunt of its misrepresentation. It was alleged that I had instituted a system of espionage which gave certain people the right to pry into the affairs of their neighbours, and "Down with Cooper's Snoopers" became a slogan of the popular press.

That was a melancholy autumn. Every evening, or so it seemed, the warning siren sounded simultaneously with the coming of the black-out. We lived at the Dorchester Hotel, which was never hit. The Ministry of Information was hit, I think, nine times, but it was a robust modern building and remained upright. My morning drive from the one to the other was depressing. Bloomsbury suffered severely, and nearly every morning there was fresh damage to note, and often I met cars—you could read it on the faces of the drivers— containing the bodies of the victims.

But with the turn of the year things began to improve. In North Africa we scored our first victories, the nights grew shorter, and although the heaviest bombardments were yet to come, they were far less frequent than they had been.

My relations with the press improved. In the previous August a larger dinner-party had been arranged at the Garrick Club, where I met all my critics. I have forgotten who was responsible, but I know that J. B. Priestley kindly took the chair, and so far as I remember the result was very satisfactory. Subsequently I gave small luncheonparties for journalists, for editors, lobby correspondents, neutral observers, the provincial press, etc. The United States had an exceptionally fine team of correspondents in London at that time. They were, almost without exception, anti-German and they rendered great service to the common cause.

Although my last six months at the Ministry passed more peacefully, I was never happy there. I believe the truth of the matter to be that there is no place in the British scheme of government for a Ministry of Information. Publicity has assumed in our days an increased importance owing to the rapidity and diverse methods of communication. We have not yet learnt how to deal with it, but let us hope that the lessons of the last war have been taken to heart. All foreign propaganda should be under the direct control of the Foreign Office. A small branch should exist to deal with it in peacetime, capable of swift and wide expansion on the outbreak of war. The other departments should conduct their own publicity through public relations officers, all of whom should meet regularly together to ensure the necessary co-ordination. In the last war the Ministry of Food insisted on conducting all their own publicity. This had been settled before I came to the Ministry of Information and I resented it. But I must admit that the Ministry of Food's publicity was better than that of any other department.

With them I had no relations, but with other departments I was continually squabbling, especially with the Foreign Office and the three Service departments. When I appealed for support to the Prime Minister I seldom got it. He was not interested in the subject. He knew that propaganda was not going to win the war. Looking back, I think he was right, but I could not think so at the time. One cannot do even propaganda well unless one believes it to be of the very highest importance. I told him that I thought nobody had the right to resign in wartime or I would offer him my resignation, but that I would be grateful if he could find me another job. He very soon did so. Brendan Bracken took over the Ministry of Information and was a great success there.

I had been sorry to leave the War Office, and very sad to leave the Admiralty, but I left the Ministry of Information with a sigh of relief.

CHAPTER EIGHTEEN

SINGAPORE

1941-1942

WITH what enthusiasm I welcomed the prospect of leaving the monotonous life of wartime London and the thankless toil of the Ministry of Information may be imagined. The editors of the London daily papers gave me a dinner at the Savoy before I left. They were all represented except *The Times*, which from beginning to end of my tenure of the Ministry had refused to give me any help, collaboration or goodwill. We had a cheerful evening, not as Minister and editors but as friends, and I could feel that in all their most savage attacks upon me there had never been any personal spite.

It was good to leave the Ministry, but it was far better to set forth on a mission to the Far East. The Prime Minister, with unerring prescience, felt that trouble was brewing in the Pacific and he was not satisfied that all necessary steps were being taken to meet it. He decided to send a representative to Singapore to report on the situation. He has given in *The Second World War* his reasons for selecting me for the appointment. I was made Chancellor of the Duchy of Lancaster, so that I should carry Cabinet rank, and on the 6th of August 1941 we set forth upon this new adventure.

The prospect of it was pleasanter to me than to Diana. She had always been opposed to all forms of air travel. It makes little appeal to most people of our generation. With difficulty she had been persuaded to go up once in Texas. It was a private plane with every convenience and luxury, a cloudless and windless day, and the countryside was as flat as a billiard table, without hedges or fences, so that it would have been easy to land anywhere at a moment's notice. The experience, however, had only intensified her dislike of the air and strengthened her determination never to fly again. Now she had to face flying across the Atlantic and Pacific Oceans in wartime conditions and, as it turned out, she had within the next six months to make the complete circuit of the earth by air. She hated every minute of it. But she did it.

One pleasure that our journey to Singapore brought us was a meeting with our son. He had been due to go to a preparatory school in Switzerland the month the war broke out. I had always thought it good for boys to see something of the outside world before being launched into the narrow channel of public school and university, and I myself had gained very little from the preparatory schools I had been to in England. It would, however, have been obviously imprudent to send an English boy to school in Switzerland when Europe was at war, so in 1940 we had sent him to the preparatory school of Upper Canada College, which had been strongly recommended to me by Vincent Massey, who was then Canadian High Commissioner in London. He was happy there and well taught. Our American friends Mr. and Mrs. William Paley generously undertook to look after him during the holidays and he was therefore with them on Long Island in August and they brought him to meet us when we arrived at La Guardia airport.

We spent three days at Lisbon owing to engine trouble in the flying boat, and nearly a fortnight in the United States, where I had a number of things to do and people to see. I spent some of that time in Washington, where I attended a large press luncheon with the Ambassador and was the principal speaker. I also acquired in Washington the services of Tony Keswick, a director of Jardine Matheson & Co. and a specialist in Far Eastern affairs, who accompanied me to Singapore as my chief adviser, and whose services proved invaluable. I had an interview with the President and one with Mr. Cordell Hull.

During the short time that I was there I did not gather the impression that the majority of the American people regarded entry into the war any more favourably than they had from the beginning. The British were more popular than they had been. The twelve months during which we had fought alone and the manner in which we had borne the bombardment of London had produced a strong reaction in our favour. Now, however, that Hitler had been so foolish as to drag Russia into the war, it was thought that with Russia's huge army and American equipment we should be able to win. The Americans sincerely hoped that we would win but they were less inclined than ever to take action themselves which would lead to an alliance with Communist Russia.

The American attitude to Japanese intervention was curiously optimistic. I remember that in the speech I made to the press at Washington I said that I had been assured on excellent authority that it would be suicidal for the Japanese to enter the war, but I would remind my audience that the Japanese were, as a people, addicted to suicide. At Honolulu, our first stopping-place in the Pacific, I found this confidence even more widely spread. The Americans there were accustomed to Japanese servants and I am told there are no better servants in the world. People are slow to imagine that their humble obedient servants can suddenly be transformed into an aggressive nation of warriors.

At Pearl Harbour they seemed to be less conscious of the threat of war than on the east coast of America. I was shown over the military and naval establishments and could not help suggesting that there was a risk in allowing several hundred aeroplanes to lie wing-to-wing in a single park. Of course they would not be allowed to remain like that in wartime, I was rather angrily assured. They could not tell how swiftly and how suddenly wartime would come to them.

Owing to those unexpected and unexplained delays which seem inseparable from air travel, we were held up at Honolulu for a week. At any other time I should have been happy to spend those days at what is certainly one of the most beautiful places on the face of the earth. But I felt I had no right to be there, to be lounging on bathing-beaches and dining with millionaires. I felt restless and ill at ease. There was a drop of poison in every draught of delight, and I was glad when we flew again to Midway, thence to Wake and thence to Guam, spending a night on each island in turn.

We arrived at Guam on September 6th and left the next morning, September 8th, having lost a day. At Manila, which was our last port of call, we met General MacArthur at dinner with the British Consul. I have no gift for forming opinions of people at first sight. All that I remember about the General was that he assured me that he had read and highly appreciated my life of Haig. This sent him up in my estimation.

On the following day we arrived at Singapore. We were most

hospitably received by the Governor, Sir Shenton Thomas, and stayed for a week at Government House. My mission grew in numbers. Besides Tony Keswick and myself we had a military member, Major Robertson, who left us after the Japanese war began, to command his regiment, the Argyll and Sutherland Highlanders, which was fighting in Malaya. He was never seen again. The Colonial Office lent me the services of Alec Newboult, a member of the Malayan Civil Service, and the Foreign Office sent me W. D. Allen from Chungking. I had brought my private secretary, Martin Russell, from England.

We installed ourselves in two houses, divided from one another only by their small adjoining gardens. In these we were able to house the whole mission and have sufficient space for our offices. We had all our meals together and we were a happy party. Our cook was a Chinese and a great artist. He would never repeat himself. When we asked him to give us some particularly delicious dish a second time, he would laugh immoderately and pay no attention. We sometimes wondered whether he understood a word we said.

Diana loved Singapore. Its baroque beauty and bright colours appealed to her. She got on well with the Chinese and the Malays. She began to learn the language and made some progress. She enjoyed the streets and the shops and the people. I suffered for the first time from grandeur. I like, as she does, to wander at will in new cities, explore narrow streets, gaze into shop-windows and sit down in little cafés. But I was too important now to be natural. Such behaviour would have been severely criticised. I should have lost "face" and so would my mission. Indian soldiers stood as sentries at our doors and I could scarcely leave the house except in a motor-car. So I missed much of the fun of Singapore and have often thought that I should like to go back there as a private citizen.

My terms of reference were vague. One thing, however, was certain. I was not concerned with the military situation. Air Chief Marshal Sir Robert Brooke-Popham had been sent out the year before to co-ordinate the activities of the three services. He had the rank of Commander-in-Chief Far East and was still functioning as such. My duty was to enquire into the various forms of civil administration in the vast territories with which Great Britain was concerned, stretching from the eastern confines of India to New Zealand, and their relations with one another.

I found in Singapore the same optimistic atmosphere with regard to the possibility of Japan entering the war as existed in America. It would be idle now to recall the very strong arguments upon which this opinion was based, or the perfectly logical reasoning that led to its conclusion. So far as I remember, Sir George Sansom was the only person who took the other view, and that he did so I discovered only when I pressed him to tell me. He was a scholar and it is no exaggeration to say that he knew more about Japan than most Japanese. Besides having written a Japanese grammar, he was the greatest living authority on Japanese art. He was working at this time for the Ministry of Economic Warfare. When I asked him whether he thought Japan would come into the war, he explained to me gently and very sadly that he was quite sure she would. I have forgotten the reasons he gave but I remember the conviction that his words carried. I wasted no more time collecting the views of soldiers and Civil Servants, but I decided that if my report was to be of any value it must be completed as quickly as possible.

During my stay in Singapore I daily dictated a diary of my official activities, upon which I can rely for facts and dates. A great deal of my time was at first spent in interviews with officials, so that I might discover how the wartime activities of the colony were working. I was distressed to learn that the representative of my former department, the Ministry of Information, was engaged on precisely similar work to that of a representative of the Ministry of Economic Warfare (not Sir George Sansom). Two officials in fact engaged on the same task were reporting to two different departments in London. What was yet more surprising was that this absurd system was working perfectly smoothly, as the two men concerned were on good terms, lived in the same house and showed one another everything they were doing. What they both objected to, however, was that neither of them had access to any naval or military information whatever, as this had been handed over by the naval authorities to an ex-naval officer, who had rejoined the service for the war, having spent the last twenty years as a magistrate in the Fiji Islands, and whose conception of his duties was to prevent anybody, especially the Americans, from obtaining any information whatever.

Our nearest native neighbour was the Sultan of Johore, who had a pretty European wife. I had met him a few years before in London. The officer commanding the Australian troops in Malaya had his headquarters in the State of Johore, which is divided only by the narrow straits from the island of Singapore. I had luncheon one day with the General and was surprised that his nearest troops were distant eighty miles from his headquarters, so that I had not time to visit them.

I had plenty to do during those days. My old friend Archie Kerr, then Ambassador in China, came all the way from Chungking on purpose to talk to me, and Sir Josiah Crosby, our Minister in Bangkok, and the greatest European authority on all things Siamese, arrived about the same time. I learned a great deal from both of them. Crosby wanted me to visit Bangkok, which I was most anxious to do, but the Foreign Office was for some reason against my doing so.

We had, however, plenty of travel during our mission. The first visit was to Batavia. We had been invited by the Governor-General of the Netherlands East Indies. He was living in a summer residence, not that there is any summer or winter in the tropics, high up in the hills of Java, where the climate is perfect and the vegetation, especially the great trees, memorable. The Governor-General was a highly competent Dutchman. He was later to be my colleague in Paris. Our relations were always excellent. His wife was American. They both behaved with great heroism during the years they were prisoners of the Japanese.

Our next visit was to Burma. Travelling as ever by air, we refuelled on the way at Penang and Bangkok. I was sorry not to be able to stop at either of these beautiful places. We did at least see Penang from the air, but the city of Bangkok lay far from the port, where we were received by a number of distinguished Siamese and regaled with tropical fruits and champagne in a bower of orchids.

We arrived at Rangoon in the afternoon and had to spend some hours there before going on by night in the Governor's special train to the north. Here Diana committed her first act of insubordination and this is how she described it in a letter that she wrote at the time:

In Rangoon there is a very famous pagoda called the Shwe Dagôn. It rises gold to the sky. At tea conversation was about it. To my surprise no one had ever been inside. "Footwear," was the explanation; "you have to enter barefoot—an Englishman can't do that—people do everything there—full of lepers—the stink of the place"—out rolled the excuses. I said one's feet were washable, one did much worse with one's hands, leprosy isn't caught that way, a temple *vaut bien* a whiff . . . they looked exaggeratedly shocked. When the conversation was over we drove in closed cars to have a look round. When we came to the temple door I said, "I'm going in." The Governor's A.D.C. looked revolted and Pilatish, Duff shook his cheeks at me, but I am "blind and deaf when I list," and in a flash I had my shoes and stockings off and was following the votaries into the great dark doorway. It was one of the most repaying sights I have ever seen. I was quite breathless with excitement. In this high dark corridor that is always ascending are congregated sleepers, vendors, priests, water-carriers, every caste, every age, every race. Everything sold is beautiful . . . fantastically-made miniature white pagoda-umbrellas to offer to Buddha, bunches of ginger-flowers, lotus and jasmine, cocks and hens like Chinese ornaments, shining gold Buddhaettes and jewels, on and on you mount, the stairs are very steep, faint with the smell of exotic flowers, Burma girls smoking always their "whacking white cheroot, and (actually) wasting Christian kisses on an 'eathen idol's foot," their hair agate-smooth, though, like the White Queen, they carry a comb in it . . . so handy, they wear a flower in it too, and a clean muslin shirt (always clean) above their bright, tight sarong. At last you come out on to an open circular court, in the centre of which rises the cloud-high gold-leaf pagoda, surrounded by hundreds of Buddha shrines. The devotees vary from nakedish men who walk round and round falling whistling-bomb flat between every two steps (progress is slow) and the pretty little maidens, smoking and playing with their babies under Buddha's nose. Orange and saffron priests lounge around, and little oil-saucers, with floating wicks, were everywhere being lit. I wished I could have stayed till dark to see the flickering, but Duff and the Captain were weighing a ton on my conscience, so I hurried round. Even without pausing it took me over an hour. When I came out the atmosphere had improved a bit, my excited radiant expression I think subdued Duff's irritation, but the Captain still looked nauseated and sulked.

We had a dreadful dinner-party of ten white men and one Burman, the acting Prime Minister, complete in sarong, black buttoned boots, native black jacket, bright pink headkerchief, and white European shirt with gold collar-stud, but no collar (*de rigueur*). My going into the pagoda was talked about with bated horror. It may, apparently, lose us Burma, because, so they say, it is a purely anti-British racket. However, Mr. Baxter, Financial Adviser to the Governor, in whose house we had bathed and dressed for dinner, came to my support and said he repeatedly went into the temple, and took all English visitors, Peter Fleming included, and that it was now considered the thing to do. Can you imagine! My reasoning was that if they had put on the "no footwear" order to keep the British out, and the British stayed out, then the Burmese won. I'm glad I did not know all this political significance at the Pagoda gate, for I might have then hesitated to go in. I hope I would not have faltered as I'm sure it's all part of the Raj "tone" here, which is most shocking.

We spent the night in the train and arrived early the following afternoon at Mandalay, which is as attractive as Rangoon is the reverse. The way we allowed British soldiers to treat King Thebaw's fantastic palace there is a sad story. What was left of it seemed then to be falling into further decay. I fear that our relations with Burma do not form one of the proudest chapters in British imperial history.

I was surprised to find that my views were shared by the Governor, an old House of Commons friend of mine, Reggie Dorman-Smith, who had formerly been Minister of Agriculture. He surprised the company at dinner that evening by saying that he could see nothing that we had done to benefit Burma since we took over, no roads, no schools, no health plans, no drains, no agricultural development. He himself, however, was determined to do a great deal, and he had already infused new life and activity into the administration. But alas, it was too late; the days of British rule were numbered.

From Burma we went on to India and visited the Viceroy, Lord Linlithgow, at Simla. We were there only three days, but I saw a number of officials and yet found time for a night in camp with the Viceroy, followed by a delightful day's shooting in a small native state called Darmi. I never knew Linlithgow intimately, but I was always impressed by his wisdom, a quality rarer and more precious than cleverness. I have sometimes wondered whether his gigantic stature had anything to do with the impression of wisdom that he conveyed. We are accustomed to associate largeness with wisdom, which is perhaps why we believe that elephants are very wise. Maybe they are as foolish as kittens and as gay at heart, but are precluded by their shape from giving sign of their folly.

However that may be, I am convinced that Linlithgow was a good Viceroy at the most difficult of all times. He was also a great worker. That night in camp we sat long talking of many things and he gave no sign of wishing us to leave him, but when we went to bed a private secretary appeared with a huge bundle of papers and we left him alone with his files, the stars and the Himalayas.

On our way back to Singapore we stopped again at Rangoon in order to travel inland to where that remarkable American, Colonel Chenault, was training American airmen to fight for the Allies. He had cleared a space in the jungle, where he provided all his own services, including runways, hospitals and a cinema hall. I never rightly understood the status in international law of that formation, where on British territory, with all the assistance Great Britain could give, neutral officers were being trained to fight against a country that still maintained friendly relations with their Government. Perhaps the Germans never knew the facts, or perhaps they felt that protests would be useless.

As soon as I returned from this visit I began to write my report, and I finished the first draft of it in a week. I was conscious of the inadequacy of my enquiries and of the ground that still remained for me to cover, but I pointed out that I had spent the greater part of two months in Singapore, where I had had the advantage of consultation not only with the local authorities but also with our Ambassador to China and our Minister at Bangkok, and that I had visited the Netherlands East Indies, Burma and India. I was about to leave for Australia and New Zealand, and I hoped later to visit Hong Kong, but in view of the rapidity with which events were moving in the Far East I did not feel justified in delaying my report until I had completed these visits. "Counsels of perfection," I wrote, "must give way before the imminence of war."

I wrote that I was sure the Far East was destined to play a far greater rôle in the future than it had in the past. I gave two reasons—one geographical, the other human. The vast oceans, deserts and mountain ranges which had hitherto divided these Asiatic peoples from one another and cut them off from the rest of the world could no longer fulfil the same function since the conquest of the air. The huge populations that inhabited these countries had become aware of themselves, and conscious of their potentialities. They would no longer accept any form of subservience to small handfuls of Europeans.

Great Britain was more closely and vitally concerned with the world of the Pacific than any other European power, but we were continuing to handle its problems with the machinery that existed in the reign of Queen Victoria. Four government departments were concerned: the Foreign Office, the Colonial Office, the Dominions Office, and, so far as Burma was concerned, the India Office. To these had been added since the outbreak of war the Ministries of Information and Economic Warfare. The need for some form of coordination was obvious and, should war break out in the Far East, would become imperative.

I was anxious not to impose on all the controlling bodies yet another one which might only lead to duplication of work and increased confusion. Having therefore examined one or two possibilities, such as the creation of a Ministry of Far Eastern Affairs, and having dismissed them as too cumbrous and complicated for introduction in wartime, I finally recommended the appointment of one official to whom I proposed to give the title of Commissioner General for the Far East.

If war came there would have to be set up a Far Eastern War Council, a kind of War Cabinet for that theatre. The Commissioner General would automatically become the head of it, and he should meanwhile prepare himself for the task by constant travel between the so widely separated centres of interest. I thought that the individual should not be a Cabinet Minister or a Member of Parliament, but somebody of such standing that "in his conferences with Ambassadors, Governors and Commanders-in-Chief he can speak on terms of equality, and who, when he visits India, will be received by the Viceroy and in Washington by the President."

The man I had in mind was Mr. Robert Menzies, whom I knew and admired. He was out of office at that time and I felt that good use could be made of his services in the post that I was suggesting. As a former Prime Minister of Australia, and one who had travelled in Europe and America, he would carry the necessary guns, and I believed he would know how to use them. I discussed the matter later with him in Melbourne and I think he liked the idea of the appointment. Events, however, intervened.

On November 1st Keswick set forth for London bearing the completed report. It was felt that he should go, in case there were requests for further information or any questions about the report were asked. None were. It was printed and circulated to the Cabinet but I doubt whether it was ever discussed. It could hardly have been printed before the end of November, and at the beginning of December the war in the Far East broke out.

We spent that interval visiting Australia and New Zealand. On the way out we stopped one too short night at Bali. I cannot imagine why we did not stop there again on our way back. It is one of the few places in the world that I long to revisit.

Our stay in Australia and New Zealand was completed within a month, so that we cannot pretend to have seen very much of either country. We saw more of Australia, for we were only five days in New Zealand. I found at Sydney, John Loder, who had served with me in the Egyptian Department of the Foreign Office. He was now Lord Wakehurst, Governor of New South Wales, where he and his wife made a brilliant success of the job. We stayed a few nights at Canberra, that strangest of capitals where all is make-believe. I attended a meeting of Parliament and heard Bob Menzies make a slashing attack on the Government. I also attended a meeting of the War Advisory Committee, a non-party body of which Menzies was a member, and I afterwards lunched with the Prime Minister. Lord Gowrie was still Governor-General, and I should say that he was the best-loved Governor-General Australia has ever had. I broadcast one evening from Canberra, and I was particularly pleased when the press commented next morning "Mr. Cooper speaks English almost without an accent."

We stayed for a week at Melbourne with Sir Winston Dugan, who was recovering from a riding accident and was in bed all the time, and we spent Saturday to Monday at Ercildowne, a beautiful country station. We stopped a few more days at Sydney on our way back.

I had not been sure that I should like Australia or the Australians. I certainly did like both very much indeed. I found the country far more beautiful than I had expected, and the people warm-hearted, truly hospitable and tremendously alive. If they can solve their irrigation problems the country can support easily ten times its present population, and I look forward to the time when it will.

Our visit to New Zealand was breathless. We arrived at Auckland one day and flew to Christchurch on South Island the next. The Governor-General, Lord Newall, was staying there. Thence back to Wellington, where I attended a Cabinet meeting, and from Wellington we returned to Auckland by road—a long day.

We got back to Singapore, stopping one night at Soerabaya on the way, on the last day of November. Our return was marked by two events, the arrival of the *Prince of Wales* and the *Repulse*, and the collapse of Diana with dengue fever, caught, we believed, from the peculiarly venomous mosquitoes at Darwin, where we had spent our last, as we spent our first, night in Australia.

She was happily able to see the ships arrive before she fell ill. It was a great moment when they came round the bend into the narrow waters of the straits that divide Singapore from the mainland. We were all at the Naval Base to welcome them, and they arrived punctual to the minute with their escort of four destroyers. They conferred a sense of complete security.

The Admiral in command was Tom Phillips, whom I knew well. He had been Director of Plans when I was at the Admiralty and I had a high opinion of him. He lost no time in calling on me, and his conversation was as reassuring as his ships. That evening Admiral Spooner, commanding the Naval Base, gave a party. Everybody felt cheerful and confident. "There was a sound of revelry by night."

The days that followed were not happy ones for me. Diana was ill and I had really nothing to do. My work was ended. My report had gone. When I sent it I suggested that if I had anything to add after my visit to the two Dominions I could convey it by telegraph. But I had nothing to add, and I had nothing to do at Singapore, nor any reason for being there other than that I was awaiting instructions. The atmosphere was full of rumours. Whether the authorities knew anything save such unreliable scraps of information as secret sources can provide, I could not tell. Nor had I any right to ask.

At 3 a.m. on the morning of December 8th we were wakened by Martin Russell, who put his head into our room and said, "The Japs have landed on the north-east coast of Malaya." There was nothing we could do about it, so we composed ourselves to sleep again, only to be aroused once more by the familiar sound of falling bombs, followed by explosions, followed by guns and finally by air-raid warnings. So the Japanese war had begun.

They hit Raffles Place that night, one of the principal squares in the town, and did more damage than they ever did afterwards so long as we were there. During the next two days I had nothing to do except to meet delegates to the economic conference that I had summoned, and to advise them to go home again if they could. Two anxious days followed. I telegraphed to the Prime Minister asking for instructions and saying that my position at Singapore as a tourist was difficult.

On the third morning the telegram for which I was longing arrived. It may have crossed mine. It told me that I was appointed Resident Cabinet Minister at Singapore for Far Eastern Affairs and authorised me to form a War Council. I saw the Governor that morning and suggested that we should hold the first meeting of the War Council the same afternoon at 5.30, to which he agreed. I then drove across the island to the Naval Base to inform Sir Robert Brooke-Popham, Commander-in-Chief Far East. When I told him, he replied, "I have also something to tell you. The *Prince of Wales* and the *Repulse* have been sunk."

That was the worst single piece of news I have ever received. More disastrous things, such as the fall of France, have happened, but the news of them arrived gradually and the mind had time to prepare itself for the catastrophe. Even on this occasion I was buoyed up by the new responsibility that I was carrying. I had so much to do. We agreed that I should broadcast the bad news that evening.

The preliminary meeting of the War Council took place that afternoon, attended only by the Governor, the General Officer Commanding, General Perceval, and the Air Officer Commanding, Air Vice-Marshal Pulford. We agreed to hold the next meeting at 8.45 the following morning, and while I remained at Singapore meetings of the War Council were held every morning either at 8.45 or at 9 a.m.

At the second meeting Admiral Layton was present. He had been succeeded by Admiral Phillips and was actually on board the ship that was to take him home when news of the disaster and of the loss of Admiral Phillips arrived. There was fortunately time for him to disembark. He proved an invaluable colleague on the War Council, and when he subsequently went on to Ceylon he was able to make use there of the lessons he had learnt in Singapore.

We added two other useful members to the War Council, Sir George Sansom, who became Director-General of Publicity, and Mr. Bowden, who represented the Australian Government.

Although some were uncertain at first of the need for a War Council which met so frequently, I believe that at the end everybody was agreed that it had served a useful purpose. It afforded a regular daily opportunity for all those principally concerned in the conduct of the war to meet one another, and thus saved a great deal of correspondence, telephone calls, arrangement of interviews and minor meetings. It also produced, without any undue delay, agreed decisions on matters where some difference of opinion not unnaturally existed, such as the proclamation of martial law, the evacuation of the civilian population, and the enforcement of the "scorched-earth" policy.

We soon found that too much of the War Council's time was spent on discussing questions of civil defence which did not directly concern the service members. I therefore suggested, and the War Council agreed, to the setting up of a small sub-committee to deal with civil defence. I myself became Chairman, and the other members were Major-General Keith Simmons, the fortress commander, Brigadier Dickinson, the Inspector-General of Police, and Mr. Denham, who had spent most of his life in Asia and who represented the civilian population. Alec Newboult acted as our secretary. We met every afternoon and interviewed the local authorities to find out what had been done and what remained to be done about such matters as air-raid shelters, gas-masks, water, gas and food supplies, rationing, identity cards and siege preparations.

Penang had already fallen, so that we had the advantage of the evidence of many of the officials who had escaped, and we tried to take warning by their experience. In the course of our enquiries I made the acquaintance of Brigadier Simson, Chief Engineer Malaya Command, who had made a special study of air-raid precautions and had lectured on the subject in the principal towns of Malaya since his arrival a few months before. I believe it is always better that any important matter should be controlled by a man rather than by a committee. The Brigadier was a sensible and resolute officer, besides being an expert on the subject, and I felt that if he were in complete control of civil defence, with authority to give orders and to make appointments, much precious time might be saved. I therefore proposed, and the War Council approved the proposal, that Brigadier Simson should be appointed Controller General of Civil Defence under the Governor.

Before hostilities began it had been decided to replace Sir Robert Brooke-Popham at the end of the year by General Sir Henry Pownall, who arrived at Singapore on December 23rd. I had known him before and had great confidence in him. He told me that he did not intend to take over until December 27th, as he wished to go up to the front first and form his own opinion as to how the battle was proceeding.

All this time the news was getting worse. The campaign in the north was going badly. I was too busy to worry and I had understood from the first that it was not our intention to make a firm stand until we reached a certain line in Johore. The troops at our disposal would, it was hoped, prove sufficient to hold this line. We had news also that the 18th Division was on its way and that air reinforcements were arriving, which were sorely needed.

It was, however, a hard time for Diana, who was engaged in cyphering and decyphering telegrams, which she had learnt to do. Our staff was not sufficient to deal with the ever-increasing burden of work that fell upon it. We had a cheerful dinner-party on Christmas Day, when we sat down ten, including Sir George and Lady Sansom and the chief members of our own staff. The black-out presented a great problem in these tropical houses, which were designed to let in the maximum of air. Another of Diana's activities was the giving of, and the encouragement of others to give, blood, of which there was a shortage. She broadcast on the subject. We were glad to learn that science can detect no difference between the blood of the white, yellow, brown or black races—a fact that must have distressed the Nazis.

Diana was also much concerned about rumours concerning the compulsory evacuation of women. An order came through from the War Office that all service wives were to be evacuated forthwith. I wrote in my diary: "This is really an impractical suggestion at present. It is as much as we can do to evacuate those who want to go, and both the Services and the civilians are very largely dependent on female assistance, which would be irreplaceable were it withdrawn." I learnt much later that Diana had decided that if she were ordered to leave she would make no protest but at the last moment, when the ship was about to sail, she would go into hiding and rely upon its being obliged to leave without her.

At the end of the year the news arrived that General Wavell had been appointed Generalissimo for the whole of the Far East. I understood at once that this must mean the end of my appointment. If it proved necessary for him to have a civilian adviser the post should obviously fall to an American, the United States having already displayed great magnanimity in confiding the supreme control of the war in the Pacific to a British officer.

On January 7th my expectancy was confirmed by the following telegram:

Following is Personal and Secret message to you from Prime Minister. Begins.

The increasingly large arrangements which have been developing from our discussions here and Wavell's appointment as Supreme Commander-in-Chief South West Pacific Ocean necessarily bring your mission to an end. You should at your convenience by whatever is the safest and most suitable route come home. If possible without undue risk you should confer with Wavell at his headquarters in Java and tell him what you think and know. Pray let me know your plan.

H.M. Government are entirely satisfied with the way in which you have discharged your difficult and at the time dangerous task and I look forward to our future work together in a world situation which with all its trouble has changed decisively for the better. Ends.

On that same day General Wavell arrived in Singapore. He and General Pownall, who had become his Chief of Staff, dined with us that evening. The Generalissimo's headquarters were to be in Java, and both Generals would therefore be leaving Singapore. We discussed the situation at length. After I had gone to bed I was roused by a message from Pownall enclosing a draft telegram which Wavell proposed to send to the Prime Minister. After expressing some anxiety with regard to the situation in Malaya he wrote:

Meanwhile I would ask you to cancel orders to Duff Cooper for return and to leave him for time being in present position in which he has done much to improve defence situation in Singapore from civilian point of view and in which his resolution in present crisis is most valuable.

I replied immediately saying that I hoped the telegram would not be sent. I could not remain in my present position, because I had no position at all. Having no position, I had no authority. I was no longer Resident Cabinet Minister. I hardly knew by what right I continued to preside over the War Council, which could no longer fulfil the function for which it had been created, namely the conduct of the war. So far as civil defence was concerned, which had never really been my job, I had now handed it over to Brigadier Simson, so that not only had I no position but I was also without any specific work.

Both Generals saw my point when I discussed it with them later, and the telegram was not sent. I did not see then, and I do not see now, how I could possibly have remained unless I had been given some new appointment, and I cannot imagine what that appointment could have been. Yet I had an uncomfortable feeling that I was running away, and it grew worse the following evening when some members of the colony, including the editor of the *Straits Times*, the principal newspaper, called on me in order to urge me to remain. I could only say that I was under orders to go and that if I stayed I should be without any power or significance.

January 13th was the day fixed for our departure. Diana was, I think, more sad to leave than I was. She had come to love Singapore and its people, our Chinese servants and the many friends we were leaving behind. As we left the house that morning she said to our head Chinese boy, "Give me a last gin-sling." He never understood what we said and thought she had said a "large," so he returned with a tumbler full. It stood her in good stead when we arrived at the airfield, which happened to be under bombardment at the time. Some Chinese friends who were with us hustled us into an air-raid shelter made entirely of glass. It seemed a suitable end to our mission to Singapore.

CHAPTER NINETEEN

CHANCELLOR OF THE DUCHY OF LANCASTER

1942–1943

OUR return journey was not without incident. We never knew what our movements were going to be on the morrow. We spent the first night at Batavia, somewhat to our surprise, because it did not lie in the direction in which we were travelling. Our second night was spent at a small place called Sibolga on the southern coast of Sumatra. We slept on board a Dutch steamer. The third night took us to the Andaman Islands, the penal settlement of the Indian Government. The Chief Commissioner was not living in his own house, where he lodged us. It was a large, gloomy building from which the electric light had been cut off. By the flicker of candles we could hardly distinguish the faces of the three murderers who had been given charge of us. We had no word of common language with them, and when they appeared early the following morning making ghastly grimaces, rubbing their stomachs and showing every symptom of acute suffering, it took us some time to understand that they were trying to convey the news that our pilot had been taken seriously ill in the night and that we should not be able to go on that morning.

Fortunately one of our fellow-passengers was an Australian hospital nurse. She proved to be a woman of character. The sick pilot was carried on board and laid on the floor of the machine, another one was discovered, and we reached Rangoon by luncheon time. There was however no food to be obtained there, for the place was in confusion. There had been a bad air-raid a few nights before. We were told that over a thousand had been killed and the population was in a state of panic. We went on to Akyab, where we had a good dinner and a comfortable night, except that we were awakened before dawn by strange and terrible noises. Diana thought it was a new form of air-raid warning. We learnt later that it was a pack of hyenas fighting under our window.

Our next stop was at Calcutta, where the Governor of Bengal came to meet us. He was another House of Commons friend. It seemed to be British policy at that time to govern the great provinces of India through former members of the Whips' office. On our previous visit to India we had spent a couple of days with Jack Herbert and his wife Mary, who was also a great friend, at Darjeeling, a beautiful place with a wonderful view of the Himalayas. Mary was ill in bed this time. Jack and I went to the races in the afternoon. Coming from the zone of war, as we had, the contrast provided by the Governor's box on the peaceful race-course was very striking.

The next morning we went on by seaplane and train to Delhi, where we arrived late in the evening. The Viceroy, with whom we stayed, was unfortunately laid up until the last day of our visit. As usual, we were expecting to leave daily, and as usual there were repeated postponements. But we enjoyed our visit. There is so much of interest to see around Delhi. There is an old Indian superstition that any ruler who makes his home there is doomed, and all around it lie vestiges of past greatness to prove the truth of the belief. Yet the English, too sensible to believe in such nonsense, decided at the beginning of this century to transfer their capital to Delhi, and already they have joined their mighty predecessors, those who once held dominion over India and who are now only incidents dimly remembered in her long history.

After six days we went on and spent one night at Karachi, of which I remember nothing but the oysters, and the next at Basra, where there was nothing so good as oysters to remember. We had luncheon next day at Tiberias on the Sea of Galilee, and descended in the evening on to the waters of the Nile.

Cairo seemed like a foretaste of home. Even the climate in January is more like England than the tropics. And there were so many people that we knew there. Miles Lampson, the Ambassador, had been head of the first department in which I served in the Foreign Office in 1913. Walter Monckton had been my Director-General in the Ministry of Information. He was in charge of all propaganda and information services and was working with Oliver Lyttelton, Minister of State, one of my oldest friends.

Owing to a number of unforeseen difficulties we were nearly three weeks in Cairo. In addition to the normal delays of air travel there existed some rule, for which nobody seemed responsible but which nobody dared to break, that forbade women to travel from Egypt by the ordinary routes. We were seriously urged to go back to England via Brazil and Baltimore. Having witnessed two wars, I am convinced that human beings become crueller, stupider and more gullible during war, and less capable of rising above the silly rules that they impose on themselves.

Owing to this delay we were in Cairo when there occurred the crisis which nearly brought to an end the reign of King Farouk. Everything had been prepared. The cars were ready, the road to the canal was cleared, and at the other end of it was waiting the ship that was to bear the King to his ultimate destination. The experienced hand of Walter Monckton had drafted the abdication, the King had inked his pen to sign it, behind him towered the imposing forms of Miles Lampson and Oliver Lyttelton. The King looked up at them. "Will you give me another chance?" he asked. He was only twenty-one. They relented. The orders were cancelled. The crisis was off, and when we returned from dining with Mr. Kirk, the American Minister, we found most of the principal actors in the hall of the Embassy discussing the evening as people discuss the first night of a play when nobody is sure whether it has been a success or a failure. I am quite sure that those who were responsible for the decision were right. The youthful King expelled by the British would have been a national hero, which there is no danger of the middle-aged King thrown out by his own people ever becoming.

Two days later we were due to leave. Our hospitable host and hostess gave us a great send-off, and after a cheerful dinner drove us themselves down to the river, where, having said good-bye, we boarded the flying-boat. We sat there for an hour in darkness and were then told to disembark. The flight had been postponed for twenty-four hours. We were faced with the unpleasant task first of finding our way back to the Embassy and then of rousing the servants and demanding a lodging for another night.

The next day was Saturday. The Lampsons left for a delightful little house that they had in the desert. Once again we said good-bye to the staff and embarked on the flying-boat, which then took off. About the middle of the night I noticed one of the crew, wearing an expression of great anxiety, in earnest conversation with the steward. The latter then roused the passengers, most of whom were slumbering, and told them they must put on their life-jackets at once. He then climbed the emergency ladder, opened the trap-door leading to the roof and calmly took up his position at the foot of the ladder. I gathered that one of the engines had given out, that there was something wrong with the other and that we were flying at about two hundred feet above the sea.

The most extraordinary thing about that night was that Diana, who never leaves the ground without feeling acutely nervous and who always foresees danger where none can exist, was completely unalarmed. She was only slightly annoyed at having been disturbed when she was comfortably asleep. I thought that things looked bad. I had reason to think so. I repeated to myself the great speech from *Measure for Measure*:

> Be absolute for death; either death or life
> Shall thereby be the sweeter.

I learnt it by heart in the trenches during the first war, and keep it for such emergencies, which fortunately have been rare.

Presently the news grew better. We had turned back and were hoping to get to Aboukir, or Alexandria. Then it was better still. We might get to Cairo, which at 3 a.m. we did, and had once again to wake up the luckless servants at the Embassy. We had a disturbed night, but we both woke up feeling particularly well and in the highest spirits on the following morning. I believe it to be the natural reaction, almost physical, which follows upon the escape from mortal danger.

A week intervened before our next departure. People now refused to say good-bye to us. They were sure we should be back next morning; and once more we were. This time it was learnt after we had left that a flying-boat had started from Lisbon at the same time for Malta, where there was space for only one to lie in safety, so we had to come back. But the next night, which was our fourth attempt, all went well. We arrived at Malta at dawn as the air-raid warning sounded and we left at dusk the same evening to the sound of the All Clear. We had thought to arrive at Gibraltar next morning, but things for once went better than expected and we found ourselves very early at Lisbon, where we learnt that we had just time to catch an aeroplane to Bristol. The same evening we were in London.

I had very little to do during the next five months and yet, for some reason, I gave up keeping a diary. I was still Chancellor of the Duchy of Lancaster, but one hour a week is sufficient to carry out the duties of that department. I had an office in the old Treasury Buildings where the Lord Privy Seal was housed. My room, which I shared with my stenographer, looked out on to the Horse Guards Parade. I received a certain distribution of Foreign Office telegrams and such papers as were sent to Ministers who were not members of the War Cabinet. I regularly attended the House of Commons.

In politics it is damaging to be associated, however distantly, with failure. Singapore signified failure, and I had been out on a special mission to Singapore. The surrender which took place there coincided with my return. The most malevolent of critics, knowing the facts, could not with justice have accused me of any responsibility for what had happened. It was primarily a naval and military disaster and I had had no connection whatever with naval or military affairs. Yet I have no doubt that in the public mind my name was linked with that of Singapore and the fact was bound to tell against me.

I thought at first of speaking in the House of Commons on the subject. I told the Prime Minister, who said he would like to see what I was going to say. I drafted something and sent it to him. He advised me not to make that speech. He gave no reason and as he was very busy I did not press him. I kept no copy and have today no recollection whatever of what it contained.

To fill some of the leisure hours that were now mine I began to write a book on a subject that had been in my mind for many years. I had long thought that the account of the career of David given in the Books of Samuel and Kings was the most interesting story ever told. To my mind also it bears the stamp of truth. Nobody inventing a national hero would make him guilty of a mean, cruel crime.

Therefore I am convinced that David is neither a mythical nor a fictional but an historical figure, and that the account we have of him is either contemporary or written very shortly after his death, nearly three thousand years ago, and thus contains the earliest fragment of truthful biography that exists.

The writing of the book came very easily and I enjoyed it. In June I was given duties that filled my week, so that I had only half Saturdays and Sundays to devote to it, but I finished it in October.

My new employment was to preside over a committee which had been set up in 1940 under the chairmanship of Lord Swinton. At that time invasion was expected and problems of internal security loomed large. Those whose political opinions were shared by our enemies were naturally suspected of having sympathy with them and being ready, should the opportunity arise, to give them aid. A number of such people against whom no charge could be proved were imprisoned at that time and were still in gaol when I succeeded Lord Swinton. I certainly did not add to their number but began rather to consider which of them ought to be released. I was glad once more to have a staff, and particularly glad to find at the head of it Sir Herbert Creedy, who had guided my footsteps during my three periods of service at the War Office. Having served as Private Secretary to seven Secretaries of State for War, he became Permanent Under-Secretary, and retained the post for fifteen years. A scholar with an excellent sense of humour and a born diplomatist, he was the ideal Civil Servant.

I was sometimes doubtful whether this small department was not one of those excrescences that break out on the public service in time of war and survive their utility. A sudden need is felt, an enquiry seems necessary, a committee is set up, it demands executive authority, it requires staff, its numbers increase, its task is performed, but the one thing it will not do is to recommend its own dissolution. There will always be something to justify its continued existence.

There was certainly always something to do during the eighteen months that I held this office. The work was interesting and filled my mornings and, when the House of Commons was not sitting, my afternoons too. I was happy there but when I left I did not recommend the appointment of a successor. I think it continued to be controlled by Creedy until it gradually faded away in the dawn of peace.

During the summer of this year John Julius, our son, came back from Canada. The former Captain of the *Enchantress*, Peter Frend, now commanding a cruiser, very kindly brought him. There was another boy of his age on board and they were both put under naval discipline and obliged to keep watches. He went in the autumn to Eton, where he remained for the rest of the war.

In November took place the invasion of North Africa by combined British and American forces. It was a remarkable achievement on the part of the United States, to be able to stage an invasion on such a scale within less than a year after the fearful losses suffered at Pearl Harbour. It marked the turning-point in the war. Henceforth success was assured.

Only once in the year 1943 did I intervene in an affair that did not concern me, save in so far as all Cabinet Ministers, even those who are not members of a War Cabinet, may be held to have some responsibility for matters of high policy.

I read in some official document that there was under consideration the issue of a warning to neutral countries against giving asylum to war criminals after the war. I had felt after the first war that the cry of "Hang the Kaiser" was one of the least edifying that had ever won a General Election, and I had thought we should have been grateful to the Dutch Government for refusing to hand over the fugitive, and thus sparing us great embarrassment. I therefore wrote a paper urging that we should not begin threatening neutrals before we had made up our minds what we were going to do with the criminals when they were caught. The paper was printed and circulated and in due course considered by a Cabinet Committee which I attended.

My paper was concerned with Hitler and Mussolini, not with the smaller fry, and I had little idea at that time of the crimes of which Hitler was guilty—torture, murder and massacre on a scale without precedent. I insisted only on the difficulty of drawing up an indictment against the head of a state who, basing his defence upon "*Salus reipublicae suprema lex*," can always plead that what he did was done in the honest belief that it was the best that he could do for his native country.

I said that every trial is a drama, and the best part in the play is that of the prisoner in the dock. Common criminals often arouse sympathy, and men who have held the highest positions, who possess personality and eloquence and would doubtless conduct themselves with dignity, might emerge as heroes.

Nothing less than capital punishment would satisfy the desire for vengeance after the war, as the cry of "Hang the Kaiser" had shown—the Kaiser who was an angel of light in comparison with his successor, besides being the grandson of Queen Victoria. I cited a few historical examples of what follows on political executions. Charles I was executed, Charles II was back in eleven years. James II was allowed to die in comfortable exile. No more Stuarts. Louis XVI was executed. Louis XVIII was back in twenty-one years. Charles X and Louis Philippe died in comfortable exile. No more Bourbons. Napoleon I was believed to have been cruelly treated, Napoleon III got back thirty years later. He too died in comfortable exile—no more Buonapartes. And since the demise of the Kaiser in Holland there had been no sign of a Hohenzollern revival.

I did not advocate taking a decision at that time. I thought that "wait and see" was often a wise policy. There were, I suggested, three possible ways in which these two men would end. "First they may solve all our difficulties by taking their own lives. Secondly they may be torn in pieces by their own people. . . . Thirdly they may creep into some neutral country and drag out despised and dishonoured existences until their deaths hardly furnish an item of news."

I was pleased afterwards to have correctly foretold in the first two possibilities the manner in which Hitler and Mussolini met death. I added another paragraph:

"There is one further consideration. Could we, as the allies of Marshal Stalin, go into court with clear consciences and clean hands?"

CHAPTER TWENTY

ALGIERS

1944

ONE day in October 1943 Anthony Eden asked me to call on him at the Foreign Office. He invited me to go either to Algiers as British Representative to the French Committee of Liberation with the rank of Ambassador and the prospect of going on, as such, to Paris in due course, or alternatively to go as Ambassador to Italy, when the enemy were driven out of Rome, which was then expected to take place sooner than it did.

I had no hesitation in preferring the former of the two offers, and asked only for time to consult Diana before definitely accepting. She was living at Bognor and devoting her whole time to farming on a small scale. She was enthusiastic about the work and very happy in it. I feared she would be loath to set out on our travels again. She was, but she agreed to do so, because she knew that it was what I wanted.

I had been following French affairs, and I had become convinced that General de Gaulle, who had first raised the standard of French resistance, had become in these three years not only the generally acknowledged but the only possible leader of it, and that it was to him that, after the liberation, the whole people of France would turn. He had of course many enemies and had no gift for acquiring friends. As Minister for Information I had put the B.B.C. at his disposal when he required it, and I had occasionally had luncheon with him and members of his staff at the Connaught Hotel, where he lived. But neither then nor at any future date was I able to establish relations with him which even approached intimacy.

I used, however, to get easily annoyed with people who, genuinely sharing my love of France and my conviction that the re-establishment of a strong France was to the interest of Great Britain, would yet persist in denigrating de Gaulle. The situation was sufficiently confused. It must, I thought, be wrong to increase confusion. Too many tragic divisions already existed between Frenchmen. It seemed to me wicked to increase their number, and to split up the forces that were opposed to the Government of Vichy. After one particularly heated argument on the subject, in the course of which I doubtless expressed myself with unnecessary violence, the other party to the altercation thought it well to warn the Prime Minister against sending as British representative to Algiers a devoted adherent of the General.

He was disturbed and consulted the Foreign Secretary, who was more amused than alarmed, since his views were in agreement with mine rather than with those of the Prime Minister. I had some correspondence with the latter, who not unnaturally felt that it would be unwise to send to such an important post somebody on whom he could not rely to carry out his policy. He laid before me papers which I had not seen and which contained the record of de Gaulle's misdeeds. I admitted that it was a grave indictment, and I did not feel it necessary to argue that if he had sinned he had also been sinned against, as, for instance, when he was brought back from North Africa to London just before the Anglo-American invasion, or which he had been given no previous information. I was, however, able to assure the Prime Minister that I would lend myself to none of the General's evil machinations and that I would faithfully carry out the policy of His Majesty's Government.

After spending more than half a century in the de-humanising profession of politics, Winston Churchill remains as human as a schoolboy. His friends are right and his enemies are wrong. Throughout the difficulties that I was to have in trying to improve relations between the two men, I was never able to convince the Prime Minister that I was not influenced by the great affection and admiration that I felt for the General. "You like the man," he would say to me; "I don't." In vain I sought to persuade him that whether I liked him or not was of no importance. I believed, and time was to give me proof, that after the war he was destined to dominate French politics, that he might continue to do so for a considerable time, and that therefore it was important that Great Britain should remain on good terms with him.

The Prime Minister was as anxious as I was to reconstruct a powerful and friendly France, but in the course of his visits to America he had been much influenced both by the President and by one or two distinguished Frenchmen whom he had met there, and who were as strongly opposed to de Gaulle as they were to Vichy.

The President's view of the French problem was jaundiced by the fact that he had backed two losers in succession. At the time of the invasion of North Africa he had believed that it would be welcomed by Pétain, and he had drafted a message to the Marshal, from which the Prime Minister had fortunately persuaded him to strike out some of the more friendly and almost obsequious passages. Pétain had treated his advances with contempt and his request for collaboration with defiance.

Who was responsible for persuading the Americans that General Giraud would prove a suitable leader of reunited, fighting France, remains something of a mystery. General Giraud had all the charm which General de Gaulle lacked, but he had nothing else. Once again the President had put his money on the wrong horse, one that could not stay the course or indeed even get away from the starting-post.

Most of this—the deal with Admiral Darlan, his murder, the first stages of the rivalry between the Generals and the completion of the conquest of North Africa by Alexander—was past history when I arrived at Algiers in the first days of January 1944. We left Lynham at 1 a.m. on the 3rd and arrived at Algiers at eleven the same morning. The house that was put at our disposal was cold and comfortless. There was no means of cooking or obtaining hot water. We had to share it with a married couple, members of my staff; we had only some Italian prisoners as servants; the most ordinary domestic utensils were quite unobtainable in such shops as were open; the weather was very cold and for the first few weeks of our stay we endured great discomfort and inconvenience.

It had been arranged that we should for the time being have our meals at the villa where Harold Macmillan was living. He held the position of Minister Resident with Allied Headquarters in North-West Africa. In the events of the past year he had played an influential and efficient rôle. He had won the confidence of General Eisenhower, and even, so far as it was possible, that of General de Gaulle.

All the information and advice that he gave me was reliable and wise. Eisenhower had left before my arrival. General Sir Henry Maitland-Wilson was awaited to take his place, and Macmillan himself was to leave shortly.

I found myself plunged at once into one of those crises which were frequently to recur. The Prime Minister, on his way to Teheran, had called at Algiers in a British man-of-war. He had not asked to see de Gaulle or any member of the French Committee of Liberation, who were beginning to consider themselves the Provisional Government of France, but had invited on board General Georges, who held no official position but was staying with General Giraud as his guest. General Georges was, perhaps unjustly, considered one of those who had been responsible for the military defeat of France, and he was certainly critical both of de Gaulle and of the Committee of Liberation. De Gaulle further complained that on his return journey the Prime Minister had treated North Africa as his own country, that he had ignored the Governor-General of Tunisia, where he had been seriously ill, and since his arrival at Marrakesh, where he was convalescing, he had paid no attention to the Governor-General of Morocco.

There was little ground for these grievances. In the midst of a world war the Prime Minister had undertaken a dangerous journey across Europe and Africa into Asia, he was travelling under an assumed name and it was most important that his whereabouts should not be known. This surely was a time when the trivialities of the diplomatic protocol could be waived. The French, however, are always more respectful of forms and ceremonies than the English, and de Gaulle, ever on the look-out for an insult, was hesitating whether to accept the invitation he had just received to visit the Prime Minister at Marrakesh. However, owing no doubt to Macmillan's skilful handling, he overcame his scruples on this occasion and agreed to pay the visit. Diana and I, it was arranged, were to precede him.

January 10th. At the aerodrome this morning Winston's private York was awaiting us. It is a most luxurious machine, and as soon as we went on board the steward offered us champagne cocktails, which were not refused. Captain Brown, one of the P.M.'s private secretaries, and two other young officers travelled with us. It was really a delightful journey. Perfect weather, an excellent lunch on board, and wonderful views of the Mediterranean and the Atlas Mountains. It took us nearly four hours.

Clemmie and Sarah met us and took us straight to the villa where they are all living—a beautiful place belonging to a rich American lady. There we found Winston in his siren suit and his enormous Californian hat. When it got cooler he completed this get-up with a silk dressing-gown embroidered with gold dragons. He was very pleased to see us.

I had a long talk with him before dinner. He was much annoyed at having lost the Skipton by-election to a Commonwealth candidate.

He has a huge staff, including half-a-dozen cypher girls and a map-room with a naval officer permanently on duty. He took me there and showed me how important the Russian advance was. He thought it was far better than Stalin had expected when he was in Teheran.

He is still very sticky about de Gaulle, and I'm afraid their interview on Wednesday is not likely to be successful. He keeps harping on General Georges and wants to get him back into the Committee. He also feels personally responsible for the future of Boisson and Peyrouton, and favourably inclined towards Flandin. He admits that Giraud is no use, but wants him to remain as a kind of figurehead, "a sort of Duke of Cambridge," as he put it, "with a Wolseley in the shape of de Lattre doing the work."

January 11th. Diana went out shopping early with the Consul's wife. I took it easy. We both went round about twelve to the villa, where we were due to pick up others of the party for a picnic. Some of them had gone on in advance to prepare the way. I drove in the car with Winston. It took about an hour and a half.

They had chosen a pleasant place for the picnic. There were large supplies of food and drink—two servants to wait as well as the staff, and a host of American military police standing round to protect. He sat there for more than an hour after lunch, reading the memoirs of Captain Gronow. This was the seventh picnic they had had during the fourteen days they have been there. It seemed to me a curious form of entertainment. I drove back with Clemmie, Diana going with Winston. Clemmie said she had given Winston a Caudle curtain lecture this morning on the importance of not quarrelling with de Gaulle. He had grumbled at the time, but she thought it would bear fruit.

I sat between Winston and Colville at dinner, and all went well until just as we were leaving, when a message came from Algiers to say that General de Lattre de Tassigny, whom Winston had invited for later in the week, had reported that de Gaulle, whose permission to come he had asked, had answered that it would be most inopportune for him to do so at the present time. This produced an explosion. Winston wanted to send a message at once to tell de Gaulle not to come. I did my best to calm him, and he decided to do nothing.

January 12th. I was woken by the telephone ringing at 8.15. Colonel Warden [the code name under which the Prime Minister was travelling] wished to speak to me. He said he had been thinking things over.

The matter was not so simple, would I go over and see him? I got over to him in half an hour. He was in bed, and had apparently worked himself up again about de Gaulle. He suggested sending him a note to the airfield to say he was sorry he had been troubled to come so far but that he would not be able to see him after all. I strongly dissuaded him from this course, pointing out that we knew nothing of the reasons which had caused de Gaulle to prevent de Lattre from coming here. He might have perfectly good reasons for having done so. De Lattre had not yet received an official appointment and de Gaulle might wish to consult the P.M. as to what was to be done with him. Alternatively, he might have thought that Giraud would be annoyed at a junior officer receiving such an invitation when he was not invited.

This worked, but Winston then said he would receive de Gaulle on a purely social basis, would talk about the weather and the beauty of the place and then say good-bye. This was better, but I suggested that Palewski [de Gaulle's Private Secretary] would probably ask me whether there were going to be serious conversations after lunch—what was I to say? He said he didn't mind having a talk if de Gaulle asked for it, but that he would not take the initiative. Nor would he see him alone. If he did, de Gaulle would misrepresent what he had said. I must be present and Max [Beaverbrook] too, and de Gaulle could bring whom he liked.

All passed off well. Winston was in a bad mood when de Gaulle arrived and was not very welcoming. He had just read of the shooting of Ciano, Bono, etc., which had rather shocked him. As lunch proceeded, however, Winston thawed. He had Diana on one side and Palewski on the other. I sat the other side of Palewski and was able to inform him quietly of the delicacy of the situation and of the P.M.'s irritation over the de Lattre episode. De Gaulle sat opposite, next to Clemmie. When the ladies left, Winston invited de Gaulle to sit next to him, but things were still sticky. We then moved out into the garden—Winston, Max, the British Consul and I on the one side—de Gaulle and Palewski on the other. The conversation lasted about two hours. Winston was admirable, I thought, and de Gaulle very difficult and unhelpful. He talked as though he were Stalin and Roosevelt combined. Winston dealt first with the prisoners question—talked about Georges—about Syria—always on the line "Why should we quarrel? Why can't we be friends?" De Gaulle did very little towards meeting him half-way, but they parted friends and the Prime Minister agreed to attend the review on the following day.

January 13th. The review was a great success. We had to get up early, as it took place at nine o'clock. Winston was in the uniform of an Air Commodore. I could see that he was very much moved by the cries of "Vive Churchill," which predominated even over the cries of "Vive de Gaulle." I couldn't help thinking, as I watched them standing together taking the salute, of the incident twenty-four hours earlier when Winston had said that he would not receive de Gaulle at all. After Winston had left, de Gaulle made a short speech in appreciation of the privilege they had enjoyed in having the *Premier Ministre Britannique* at their review, and extolling the alliance.

There followed a picnic which involved a two hours' drive to the foot-hills. It took place at a very beautiful spot and everyone enjoyed it. Winston was in a heavenly mood—very funny and very happy.

The question of the three distinguished prisoners was to remain a problem until after the liberation. Both Peyrouton and Boisson had served Vichy, and the latter was accused of acts of great cruelty towards the Free French when he was Governor of Dakar. The case against Flandin was the weakest of the three. He had served Pétain as Foreign Minister for a few months but I believe that he had always been well-disposed towards Great Britain. When he was tried after the war he was acquitted, Randolph Churchill giving most helpful evidence on his behalf. The Prime Minister, however, was more concerned about the first two, because he had met them at luncheon during his former visit to North Africa in 1943 and had told them, in ignorance of their records, that they could count on him.

The British, and still more the Americans, found it hard to understand or to sympathise with the bitter hatred which the Free French felt for those who they believed were guilty of collaborating with the enemy. The passions aroused by civil war are ever more violent than those caused by war between nations. Your foreign foe is only doing his duty when he kills you, but your compatriot is guilty of murder, fratricide and treason.

A few days later we dined with General de Gaulle and I had a conversation with him after dinner:

He said that he tries, every day, for a short time to imagine himself looking down on events without prejudice, and from the point of view of the future historian. It then seems to him that of all things the most ridiculous is that the British and French should not be on the best of terms. I did not suggest to him, although I thought of doing so, that he himself was as responsible as anybody for misunderstandings, but I did say that he must understand that, for us, the most important of all things was to retain the friendship of the United States, and that they approached these problems from a different angle from ours. Vichy had betrayed France and had betrayed England, but they had not betrayed the United States, who had —rightly or wrongly—remained for a long time on amicable terms with them, and therefore felt quite differently about the various personalities concerned.

I then raised again the question of the three accused, and asked whether they were still in prison. He laughed and said he supposed he would have to take the finest château in North Africa and put them in it surrounded by every luxury, and when asked why, he would have to explain that it was because they were friends of President Roosevelt and Mr. Churchill. He said that the English and Americans could not understand the bitterness felt by the French against those who they considered had betrayed and subsequently persecuted them. I said that I perfectly understood that, but the Prime Minister saw things from a personal angle. He had had lunch with Boisson and Peyrouton and had told them to count on him. Therefore he felt a measure of responsibility. De Gaulle's only reply was that he ought never to have met them, still less have had lunch with them. I saw that it was useless to argue. He spoke well of de Lattre, but in rather a patronising way, said that he had, of course, served Vichy as other soldiers, including General Juin, had done, but that he was a good general and would command the expeditionary force that would invade from the south. I think he was trying to be as agreeable as possible, but it does not come easily to him.

I had further conversations with the General on this tiresome topic of the accused, which he insisted on treating as a matter of no importance. In fact he resented foreign interference in what he considered was a purely French affair. It was not until more messages had been received from the Prime Minister and more pressure had been brought to bear that, towards the end of February, the three men were finally removed to a house which they admitted was satisfactory.

My work at Algiers was not rendered easier by the presence in the Near East of Sir Edward Spears as British Minister in Syria and the Lebanon. He was a Member of Parliament, representing Carlisle, and a close friend of the Prime Minister's, whom he had assisted in the early days of the war by acting as liaison officer between him and the French Government. He knew France well and spoke the language as beautifully as an Academician. He had been the first to bring General de Gaulle to Mr. Churchill's notice, he had assisted the General to leave France and he had been appointed Head of the British Mission to the General when the latter was officially recognised by the British Government.

Then the two Generals, for Spears was a General too, quarrelled. I have no information concerning the cause of the quarrel, and I am quite prepared to give Spears the benefit of the doubt. He was not the first or the last to quarrel with de Gaulle. From that moment, however, his political opinions underwent a fundamental change.

From having been francophil, or generally considered so, he became the most violently francophobe of all British politicians. The failure of the French Army may have contributed to this change of view. He, like many of us, had had faith in the French Army, and perhaps he resented its collapse as a personal affront. Whatever the cause may have been, there was no doubt about the effect, and by the time I reached Algiers his antagonism to France was notorious. It was deplored by many Englishmen in that part of the world as a cause of complication with the Arabs, and he was regarded by all Frenchmen as their bitterest and most mischievous enemy. They no doubt attributed to him many intrigues of which he was innocent.

The conduct of General Spears had spread the conviction that it was his policy to drive the French out of Syria and the Lebanon, with the assistance of the natives, in order that the British should take their place there. This was not the policy of the Foreign Office, nor of the Prime Minister, but to attempt to persuade the French of this was waste of time, so long as Spears remained at Beirut. While it was easy to quarrel with General de Gaulle, it was not so easy to quarrel with General Catroux, who was ever a model of tact and courtesy. But Spears quarrelled with the one as fiercely as the other, and when years later Catroux came to write an account of what happened he disclosed the belief, which he still held, that Spears could not have pursued his policy without the secret connivance and encouragement of the British Government.

I therefore considered the presence of Spears as a fatal impediment to improved Anglo-French relations, and I had this in mind when I wrote to the Prime Minister on another subject. There had been some complaints in the House of Commons of the large number of members who were absent on foreign duty and whose constituents were therefore no longer represented in Parliament. I think my name was mentioned among others. This seemed to me a justifiable grievance, and I was sorry that the Prime Minister should incur criticism on my account. I therefore offered to resign my seat.

I wrote on February 21st, 1944:

My dear Prime Minister,
  I see that there has recently been some discussion in the House of Commons about those Members of Parliament who are engaged in work

which prevents them from attending the House. In case this should later prove a source of embarrassment to the Government, I now put my application for the Chiltern Hundreds in your hands to act upon when you see fit.

General de Gaulle is not at all well at present. He is suffering, I am told, from malaria and kidney trouble. Palewski came to see me on 18th February and said that the General was concerned about the future of the Le Clerc division. This is, of course, primarily a military question, but it has such an important political aspect that the General hoped you would be able to take it into your personal consideration. All the French attach vast importance to the participation of some French force in the invasion of Northern France. Le Clerc's division, now in Morocco, is obviously the most suitable for this purpose. When I mentioned the subject to General Maitland-Wilson recently he seemed a little doubtful as to whether the necessary transport would be available. On that matter, of course, I have no opinion, but I am sure that even from a purely military standpoint the participation of the French would be valuable, owing to the effect that it would have on the reception of our troops by the population.

Lady Spears has paid us an unexpected visit this week, and conversation with her has left me in no doubt that she and her husband believe that the main object of their Mission is to maintain the rights of the native populations of the Levant against the dominant Power, and even to encourage the natives to assert these rights. That is not my view, nor, I believe, the view of His Majesty's Government. We have surely enough native problems of our own to face without stirring up native problems for others. I think we should try to help the French to rebuild both their country and their Empire, and by our encouragement win their friendship. Spears, owing to what I think is a mistaken view of his local objective, seems to have altered the whole of his European policy and to have become definitely, if not violently, francophobe. He is certainly considered so by all the many branches of French opinion. He has always been a good friend of mine, and I like them both, but I do not believe there will be peace in the Levant so long as they remain there.

To return to the subject dealt with in the first paragraph of this letter, if it were thought that those members of the House of Commons who have been longest absent from their parliamentary duties should be the first to return, perhaps consideration could be given to the three years' disfranchisement that has befallen the burghers of Carlisle.

The reply came by telegraph.

Personal and Private. Following from Prime Minister.
Your reports of Feb. 21st just received. No need for Chiltern Hundreds. Please express my concern to de Gaulle about his illness. I am enquiring about Le Clerc division. Nothing doing about burghers of Carlisle. Love to Diana.

The Prime Minister not only enquired about the Le Clerc division but pursued the matter indefatigably, and despite many technical difficulties that arose he was ultimately successful. The division was transferred from Morocco to Yorkshire, where their training for the great invasion of D-Day was completed. They were among the first troops to enter Paris, and the great epic of their march from Lake Tchad in Central Africa was brought to a fitting end at Berchtesgaden.

One of the main problems that occupied the minds of de Gaulle and his supporters at the time was the civil administration that was to be set up in France immediately after the liberation. It was an urgent question. All the authorities in France were the servants of the Vichy Government and would have to be replaced as speedily and discreetly as possible. To leave them in office would be to provoke violence.

The stumbling-block in the way of reaching any agreement on this subject was the President of the United States. On March 13th I wrote in my diary:

In the afternoon there came a long telegram from the Foreign Office about the negotiations that have been going on in Washington on the subject of the civil administration of France after the liberation. Apparently complete agreement was reached by all the authorities concerned on a procedure that would have satisfied the French, but at the last moment it was turned down by the President against the wishes of Cordell Hull, the State Department and ourselves. We are now leaving the Americans to fight it out with their President. It does seem intolerable that one obstinate old man should hold up everything in this way.

In justice to Mr. Roosevelt it should be remembered that into his ears, ever receptive to anti-Gaullist views, were being poured assurances, not by his official advisers only but by French emigrants and by Americans who had made friends in Vichy, that de Gaulle was not the man whom the French wanted. Fortified by such information he adopted the very plausible line that the French people must choose their own Government and that the Allies must not impose a Government upon them that they did not want. The obvious weakness of this attitude lay in the fact that the French people could not make their choice until a General Election could be held, that to superintend elections there must be some form of Government in existence, and that elections would not be fully representative so long as any part of the country was occupied, and had better be postponed until the conclusion of peace. How entirely the President had been misinformed was proved when elections were held twelve months after the liberation of Paris, and the Assembly, freely elected and representing all parties, offered the Presidency of the Council to General de Gaulle by a unanimous vote.

When I arrived in Algiers Mr. Wilson was there as American representative holding, I think, ambassadorial rank. He had, so I gathered, become convinced of the wisdom of giving all possible support to de Gaulle and of recognising the Committee of Liberation as the Provisional Government.

I had no opportunity of discussing affairs with him because he left for Washington while I was paying my visit to the Prime Minister at Marrakesh. His assistant told me that he meant to impress his views upon the President, and unless he could get approval of them he would not return. He did not return, and the President, to emphasise no doubt his contempt for de Gaulle, did not replace him.

During the remainder of my stay in Algiers the United States were represented by a Chargé d'Affaires, Mr. Selden Chapin. I could not have had a more delightful or helpful colleague. Our offices were in the same building and we worked together in the most complete harmony and friendship.

Another reliable source of support in difficult times was René Massigli. He was acting as Minister for Foreign Affairs, so that I saw him continually. When the General became difficult to deal with I knew that I could always get wise advice and sympathy from his Foreign Minister. He was a loyal colleague and I shall always remember with gratitude the services that he rendered me.

As the day fixed for the landings in France approached, the British Government rightly increased the stringency of their security precautions. On the 19th of April "I found Massigli in despair about the new regulations we have imposed forbidding all communications in cypher with England and making exceptions in favour only of the Americans and the Russians."

What drove Massigli to despair drove de Gaulle to fury. His curious reaction was to refuse to receive my newly arrived

Counsellor of Embassy, whom it had already been arranged that I should take to pay him a formal visit.

May 8th. On my way from the office to the villa it occurred to me that it was worth considering the advisability of inviting de Gaulle to go to London now. It seemed to me that it would rob him of all his grievances if he accepted, and put him very much in the wrong if he refused. So I sent off a personal telegram to the Prime Minister and the Secretary of State suggesting it.

May 22nd. I received this morning the long-awaited reply to my telegram of May 8th in which I suggested that de Gaulle should be invited to go to London. It was a long telegram which sent several complimentary messages to de Gaulle about the conduct of the French troops in Italy and the *Richelieu* in the Pacific, and finally said that I could tell him he was going to be invited to London at some unspecified date. I felt that such a message would hardly make a good impression, as he must now be half-expecting the invitation (there had been rumours of it in the press) and this would only be a disappointment. I therefore telegraphed back asking whether I could give some indication of the approximate date of the visit.

May 23rd. I received a telegram saying that they could not give a date for de Gaulle's visit, but that the invitation should be conveyed to him as soon as possible. I therefore arranged to see him at 9.30 and spent an hour with him. I found him (always unpredictable) in an easy, even genial mood, and he accepted the invitation without any hesitation.

Four days later, however, the wind had changed:

May 27th. I went to see Massigli in the morning. He wanted an assurance about de Gaulle having full liberty of communication while he was in London. I drafted a telegram on the subject and then another personal one to Anthony suggesting that it would be an admirable thing if de Gaulle could be treated as the guest of His Majesty's Government while over there. Before I sent it off I received one from London inviting him to be the guest of His Majesty's Government and assuring him that he would have full liberty of communication.

I went to see de Gaulle in the afternoon to convey to him the invitation and assurances I had received in the morning. I had hoped he would be pleased but he gave no indication of being so, and was as grumpy and sulky as usual, complaining bitterly about the intention of the American Government to issue their own francs when they entered France.

This question of the French notes became henceforth bound up with the question of civil administration and formed a major difficulty over which much time and temper were wasted. Now de Gaulle began to say that there was no point in his going to

London unless the Americans were prepared to discuss with him these questions of outstanding importance.

May 28th. It seems that the Prime Minister had himself suggested to the President that an important American representative, such as Stettinius, should be sent to London for the negotiations with de Gaulle, but subsequently he had been very much annoyed by a statement in the American press that de Gaulle would refuse to come unless somebody of the sort were sent. This was reported to me by telegram from London. I replied that de Gaulle had accepted to come without conditions and must not be blamed for the indiscretions of American pressmen.

May 29th. Of course the statement in the press about which the Prime Minister telegraphed yesterday has had the inevitable reaction and produced a semi-official statement in the *New York Times* to the effect that the President would not send anybody to take part in the conversations in London with de Gaulle. This was so worded as to convey the impression that the United States would not be represented. At the same time a most unfortunate message has been transmitted by Reuter's, saying that Eisenhower was ready to carry on the government of France and would work with anyone who was willing to fight for France now.

May 30th. At 3.15 I went to see de Gaulle who, of course, was much distressed by the statement in the American press and by the Reuter message. I said that he was largely to blame for the former, owing to what had appeared the day before to the effect that he had made a condition of somebody being sent from America. He, of course, denied having said so. I have no doubt that the report originated from him, and I got him into a mood almost of apology. I then asked him if he would be satisfied with an assurance that the United States would take part in the conversations—represented by Eisenhower, Winant or anybody else the President chose to nominate. He said he did not ask more. I said I would try to get it, and I think I shall be successful, as I had always understood that this was the original intention.

May 31st. Massigli came to see me before dinner and asked me what was going on. I had not seen him since Saturday morning, and I explained to him why my last two visits had been to de Gaulle rather than to him, first because I had been instructed to deliver a message to de Gaulle personally, and secondly because de Gaulle had sent for me. He quite understood, but said that he thought that he and I understood one another better than the General and I did, and, so far as possible, it would be advisable for me to see him. I quite agreed and explained to him the present situation.

June 1st. This morning I had a telegram from the P.M. telling me to ask de Gaulle to come as soon as he wished, and offering to send out his own York to fetch him, but making no reference to my request for an assurance that the conversations would be tripartite.

I went and told Massigli and suggested to him that I should urge de Gaulle to accept the invitation, as once he arrived in London it would really be impossible for the Americans to refuse to take part in the conversations, but if they did he could return immediately, thus putting the President completely in the wrong.

Massigli said that such a suggestion would be much more forceful if I could say that I was speaking with the Prime Minister's knowledge and approval and very little time would be lost. After some argument I agreed with him, and telegraphed to the Prime Minister accordingly. I have no doubt that he (Massigli) will himself tell de Gaulle what I said and will use his influence in the right direction.

June 2nd. I received a further telegram from the Prime Minister, reproaching me for not having delivered his message the day before, and containing an urgent personal appeal to General de Gaulle to come at the very earliest possible moment. I went round to see him in the morning to deliver this message, and argued with him for nearly an hour. He said it would be useless for him to go if the conversations were not to be tripartite and he was merely being sent for because it now happened to suit the convenience of the Allies to put him up to make a speech which would give the French people the false impression that he was in agreement with the British and the Americans, which was not the case.

I then went to see General Maitland-Wilson, having previously arranged to do so. I told him that I was disturbed to think that the French were being left completely in the dark with regard to projected operations in the Mediterranean and were perhaps being led to believe that what was only a cover plan was a real plan. I felt that they would be most indignant if they found later that they were being deliberately misled. He told me that General Bethouart and General de Lattre were both completely in his confidence and knew absolutely everything. They had undertaken not to convey that information to their junior officers and he was satisfied that they were both keeping their word. He also said that he was getting on much better with General de Lattre now and had changed his opinion about him. This was very satisfactory.

I looked in on Massigli before lunch in order to tell him of my conversation with de Gaulle. He was, as usual, sensible and also very firm. He said that if de Gaulle refused to go to London he would resign.

We lunched with the two Princesses [Princess Marie de Ligne and Princess Galitzin who lived in a very fine old Moorish house on the outskirts of Algiers], who had arranged a wonderful meal in honour of our Silver Wedding. De Tocqueville and another Frenchman were there. It was a curious day—a heavy white mist.

The three sailors, Wharton, Fitzgeorge and Teddy Phillips [members of the Naval Mission], came to dinner—also Elizabeth de Breteuil. Freddy Fane [the controller of our household] had taken great trouble and had found some bottles of real champagne, so we had quite a feast.

The Committee, I knew, were meeting at five o'clock. About nine, I received a message from M. Joxe, asking me to go and see de Gaulle at eleven o'clock, and later I got a note from Massigli asking me to drop in at his villa as soon as possible. I saw him at half past ten and he told me that the question of de Gaulle's going to England had been voted on by the Committee and only five had voted against it. They included Billoux the Communist, Pleven and Capitant. He said they were going to have another meeting the following day and if de Gaulle still refused to go he and some of his colleagues would resign. I then went to see de Gaulle and stayed with him until after twelve. The argument which seemed to have most effect on him was that simply as a soldier it was his duty to help the battle which was about to take place. He said he might consent to go in that capacity only, in which case he would not take any of his Ministers with him. We had a very animated discussion and I spoke to him very frankly and at times rather rudely, but he took it all in very good part and said he would let me have his answer at ten o'clock on the following morning. He asked me to give him my personal word of honour that when he got to London his movements would be free and that he would have complete liberty to make use of his cyphers for telegrams etc. I said that I had already given him this assurance, having been authorised to do so by H.M.G., but he asked me to repeat it on my own responsibility. I said I gladly would, but of course I was not a member of the Government and all I could say was that if the Government went back on their word, which I didn't think possible, I myself would resign. As he came downstairs with me to say good-bye, he asked how many passengers the Prime Minister's York would take and at what time it would be necessary to start. I took this as a good sign. I stopped at Massigli's villa on the way back and told him what had taken place and then sent a telegram off to London informing them of the situation.

June 3rd. I felt extremely anxious this morning and was most relieved when Palewski turned up with a letter from de Gaulle agreeing to go. In the letter he again referred to the fact that I had given him my personal assurance that he would be free to telegraph etc. We then had to make the necessary arrangements as soon as possible.

We arrived at the airfield about three o'clock. The two Yorks were there and most of the party had assembled. De Gaulle himself was the last to arrive and I was relieved when I saw him inside the plane.

We left at half-past four and got to Rabat in two hours. Stonehewer Bird was there to receive us. In view of the need for secrecy de Gaulle decided not to leave the airfield and to have dinner on the plane. I went round to the Birds' for a drink and brought Mrs. Bird and their daughter back to show them the plane, in which they were very interested. I also introduced them to de Gaulle, who was most gracious. Dinner was rather a sticky affair and afterwards I walked up and down the airfield with de Gaulle for about an hour, talking of everything except, I am glad to say, the present situation. We finally left at half-past ten and had an excellent flight. I slept fairly well and we touched down at Northolt at exactly six the next morning.

In view of the great secrecy that had been enjoined on us, I was rather surprised to see a large Air Force band and a Guard of Honour of at least fifty men. The band played the Marseillaise extremely well and I drove off with Oliver Harvey to the Dorchester.

I was told we were both (de Gaulle and I) to go down to lunch with the Prime Minister at his "advance headquarters." I had a bath and the car came for me at a quarter to ten. I stopped for a few moments at White's on the way to Carlton Gardens, where I picked up the General. Generals Bethouart and Koenig, Col. Billotte and the Ambassador Vienot, accompanied us. I did not know where we were going. It proved to be a train standing in a siding at the small station of Droyford. Here the Prime Minister has been living for the last few days. It seemed to me a perfectly absurd scheme, as he had only one telephone and would have been much better situated from every point of view if he had remained in London. His staff were all complaining bitterly of the discomfort and inconvenience. One of them said to me that he intended to lead a reformed life in future because he now knew what hell was like.

Anthony, Ernest Bevin and Field-Marshal Smuts were there. It had not, of course, occurred to the Prime Minister that Smuts was the most unsuitable person to have selected to meet the French, as they will never forgive him for the speech in which he said France would never be a great power again.

We immediately proceeded to have a conference, at which the Prime Minister, whom I had been unable to speak to before, said just what I would have advised him not to—emphasising the fact that he had got de Gaulle over in order that he might make a speech on the radio before the battle, and saying nothing about negotiations. Anthony tried to raise the latter question without much success, and at a quarter past two we had luncheon. Towards the end of the meal Anthony again raised the question of political talks, and de Gaulle said he saw no reason for them if the Americans were not to be represented. This led to an argument with the Prime Minister, which became rather heated and certainly did not advance matters.

In the afternoon we drove off to Eisenhower's headquarters, about an hour away, where de Gaulle and the other Generals were shown all the plans for the invasion and informed of all the details. Eisenhower also gave de Gaulle the text of the radio speech he was going to make and asked for suggestions and corrections. De Gaulle took it away with him.

Whether there was some misunderstanding with regard to this speech I cannot tell, but it was one of many causes which contributed to what was almost a disaster. De Gaulle, under the impression that he had been asked to do so, suggested certain alterations in Eisenhower's broadcast, all of which Eisenhower disregarded completely, for the very good reason that forty million copies of it had already been printed for circulation.

I spent that night calmly and comfortably at Anthony Eden's house near Midhurst and travelled the next morning to London, where I had much to do after so long an absence. I dined that evening with a friend and awoke the next morning, June 6th, to learn that the invasion of France had taken place. Later I learnt that happenings in London had been almost as stormy as events on the beaches and I was glad that, having left no telephone number at which I could be found, I had been spared from taking part in them.

The Prime Minister had most naturally been in a state of high nervous strain during the night. He had always feared that the first landings might be attended by fearful casualties. Now his vivid imagination presented to him the dread spectacle of British and American troops being hurled against the well-prepared defences of the enemy. And while this dire contest, upon which so much depended, was taking place he was informed that General de Gaulle had refused to deliver a broadcast to the French people and had forbidden his liaison officers to accompany the invading forces.

It may be imagined that his reactions on receiving this information were not mild. He said some harsh words to Vienot, one of the gentlest and the best of men, who had never fully recovered from his wounds in the first war, and he dictated a letter to de Gaulle, which was fortunately not despatched, ordering him to return to Algiers immediately.

The General had characteristically displayed the minimum of tact, but he had, whether by his own fault or another's, been seriously misrepresented. He had not refused to broadcast but had said only that he would not broadcast immediately after Eisenhower. This was due partly to the affront, as he saw it, that he had received by being asked to revise a text that was already printed for circulation, and partly owing to his chronic obsession that he might be represented as the tool of the British and Americans.

With regard to the liaison officers, the Prime Minister understood that they were interpreters whose services might be of vital importance to the landing forces. De Gaulle, however, contended that they were officers who had been trained to carry on the civil administration, and that since no agreement had been reached on this subject their presence in France was superfluous.

I had a talk with Vienot and Oliver Harvey before luncheon and agreed to see de Gaulle afterwards, Vienot saying that only I could persuade him to go back on his decision with regard to the officers. . . . I saw de Gaulle at three o'clock. I pointed out to him that in his own interest he ought to agree to the officers going, as otherwise it would be said of him that he had refused to help us in the battle itself. He would not accept the logic of this argument but eventually said that to please *me* he would agree to send at least some of the officers, if not all. I went back to the Foreign Office to report what had taken place, and was kept there until after five.

At six I went to see Brendan, who was taking a very sensible view of the situation and claimed that it was he who had persuaded the Prime Minister not to send his letter to de Gaulle. . . . At a quarter to seven I went to see Betty Cranborne and Bobbety, who are both quite sound about France—in fact everybody is except the Prime Minister and the President.

What de Gaulle suspected, not without reason, was that the Americans intended to set up a semi-military administration under their own control, which should govern France until they could find out the will of the French people. The circulation of the American-printed French notes, however, presented a serious difficulty, because unless they were guaranteed by some Government they were in fact what de Gaulle contemptuously called them, "sham money" ("*les faux billets*"). Neither the British nor the French Treasury was prepared to guarantee them, but if they agreed that the French Committee of Liberation should do so, they were going very far towards recognising the Committee as the Government of France. Meanwhile the Americans refused to discuss either the financial or the civil administration question with the French.

June 7th. I dined at the Connaught Hotel with de Gaulle, Anthony, Charles Peake, Vienot and two or three other Frenchmen. We had a discussion after dinner, the main point of which was to persuade de Gaulle to enter into conversations with us although the Americans refused to take part in them. He said it was waste of time and it would be a humiliation to both our countries to be obliged, after coming to an agreement, to go and ask the United States for their kind approval. Anthony was wonderfully patient and argued with him on the line of "she stoops to conquer," which we found some difficulty in translating into French. I thought it went fairly well, although on the following day Vienot said he thought the General had been *odieux*.

June 13th. I went to the Foreign Office at Anthony's request. He had had a long and difficult morning with the Prime Minister and the American Ambassador and General Marshall. The two latter had been quite hopeless. Smuts had been present and had said to Winant, "You have got to make up your mind sooner or later between Pétain and de Gaulle." This had irritated Winant, who declared that the United States had no intention of going back to Vichy. This, however, is what they would really like to do. Anthony said that he had never been so unhappy or so perplexed by anything as he was by the French situation and he could not see what was going to be the result.

As sometimes happens to insoluble problems, this one finally solved itself. That same evening the Foreign Secretary gave a small dinner-party for the General. Five of his Cabinet colleagues attended, including Mr. Attlee, who had been most helpful to him during this trying time and with whom I had had a conversation a few days before. The next morning de Gaulle visited France. He returned much cheered by his reception there, leaving behind him a trusty lieutenant, a civilian, who gradually took over the administration of Normandy.

What happened in Normandy happened elsewhere in France. The men of the Resistance gradually took over the administration of the country as it became cleared of the enemy, and those whom they replaced were thankful if they were allowed to disappear quietly. The men of the Resistance were all followers of de Gaulle, so that when the country was liberated he automatically became its master and no decision of policy was called for either from the British or the American Government.

After his visit to France, General de Gaulle wanted to return to Algiers as soon as possible. It was arranged that we should leave on the night of June 16th. On the 15th I dined at the Dorchester with Lady Cunard. It was the night of the first attack by unpiloted planes. My hostess, who disliked the war, but knew no fear and lived on the seventh floor of the hotel, was most indignant when she was informed of what was happening, declared it was quite impossible and only showed how stupid people became in wartime that they could believe such rubbish. One of the hotel servants, on the other hand, said it was a very good sign, as it proved how short of men the Germans were, that they were obliged to send their aeroplanes over empty.

The Prime Minister did not see the General again before he left. They exchanged letters. The Prime Minister's was not as friendly as

I would have wished. I sat with him while he dictated it. When he had finished he said, "I'm sorry but that's the best I can do." I felt that the whole affair had been a failure and very nearly a fiasco, yet a few days later I wrote in my diary:

June 18th. Massigli came to see me at 5.30. He said that on the whole the General was well pleased with his visit. He had been much impressed by the sympathy on his side amongst the public, press and House of Commons. Massigli thought this a very good thing, as it would cure any anglophobia from which he might have suffered.

I took some secret credit to myself for this, as I had worked hard while I was in London and used such little influence as I had with the press to get the French case, as I saw it, fairly presented. It was difficult indeed to foresee how the General would react to events. It was the Americans rather than the British who had been responsible for all the difficulties that he had met with in London. He now decided to pay a visit to the United States and we dined with him the night before he left.

We sat in the garden afterwards and I had a good talk with the General, who was in a happy and tranquil mood. I ventured to suggest the line he should take in America if he had to make any public speeches. I warned him that he was suspected of wanting to be a dictator, and that he should therefore miss no opportunity of proclaiming his attachment to democracy. He took my advice in the best possible spirit, and thanked me for giving it to him.

Ten days later he gave a cocktail party on his return, after having enjoyed, according to all press accounts, an enthusiastic reception.

July 14th. I had a short talk with him about the success of his visit to Washington. Characteristically, he refused to be enthusiastic about it, but merely said that it had gone quite well, and that the general atmosphere had been favourable. I asked him whether the President had been in a good humour, to which he replied that he had, at any rate, sought to give the impression that he was in a good humour.

July 17th. At five o'clock I went to see de Gaulle at his invitation. He said he wanted to tell me about his conversations with the President. The main subjects had been (1) the present arrangements in France, (2) the future of Germany, (3) the necessity for the United States to retain certain strategic bases after the war. He was in a calm, friendly mood, and talked to me also about Anglo-French relations, which he feared would never improve so long as we pursued our present policy in the Levant.

July 18th. I went to see Massigli in the morning. He wanted to know what de Gaulle had said to me, and apparently this is the only means he has of finding out.

Randolph Churchill was staying with us at this time. Both he and Evelyn Waugh had done so on their way to be dropped in Yugoslavia. Their plane had crashed and they were lucky to escape with their lives, as most of the people in it had perished. Evelyn had been severely burned, and Randolph, when he reached us, had water on both knees. He was, however, in high spirits and he gave Monsieur Vincent Auriol at luncheon one day a short lecture on French political and constitutional problems which the future President of the Republic seemed to enjoy.

Randolph was about to leave when news arrived that his father would be passing through Algiers on the morrow, so he naturally put off his departure. I had recently written in my diary:

August 3rd. The Prime Minister made an excellent speech yesterday, excellent especially from the point of view of France. He included France with Great Britain, the United States and Russia as the four great Powers who would settle European affairs, and he paid an unexpectedly warm tribute to General de Gaulle. Massigli rang me up this morning to express his pleasure at what the Prime Minister had said.

It seemed to me therefore that no more suitable moment could have been chosen for the Prime Minister's arrival, which would provide an excellent opportunity for him and the General to make up their quarrel. But there are men whose instinct is to say "no" whenever ordinary people would say "yes."

August 10th. I went to see de Gaulle at six o'clock and gave him the information. He said that he thought nothing would be gained by an interview with the Prime Minister at the present time. I did my best to persuade him to change his mind, reminding him of the extremely warm terms in which the Prime Minister had referred to him in the House of Commons, and saying that it was only common civility to pay a call on so distinguished a traveller passing through French territory. I spent three-quarters of an hour with him, but did not succeed in convincing him, though I persuaded him to send a polite letter to the P.M. saying that he did not wish to disturb the short period he was to have at Algiers between his two flights, for he was to arrive at 8.30 in the morning, and to leave at mid-day. . . . It occurred to me during dinner that it was worth while making one more appeal to General de Gaulle, so I wrote him a letter, pointing out that he had promised to write a letter which was, after all, only a gesture of politeness, and that, as he was prepared to make such a gesture, why not go a little further and pay a call, which would have a much more useful effect? He replied that he had already written the letter, which Palewski would deliver the next morning. I could do no more. It is incredibly stupid on his part, one of the most foolish things he has yet done.

He was to repeat the error the following year when he refused to go to Algiers to see President Roosevelt on his return from Yalta.

A few days later there was another instance of the General's exaggerated susceptibility.

August 15th. I saw Massigli in the afternoon. It appears that de Gaulle is now in a violent rage because the Prime Minister has gone to Corsica without warning the French authorities. I said I thought it quite absurd to make a fuss about such small matters at a moment like this. [We had heard at mid-day that the landings in the South of France had taken place successfully.] We were now in the middle of a battle and the Prime Minister had a perfect right to visit any part of the battlefield he chose. Massigli really agreed with me, but I gathered that he had found the General in so violent a mood that he had not been able to make any protest.

Shortly after this the General left for France, having to the last made difficulties even about his departure. He was assured by experts that there was no French plane in North Africa in which it would be safe to make the journey.

General Eaker, American Air Commodore-in-Chief, then kindly offered to lend his own private Fortress. De Gaulle replied that he would take it only if it bore French insignia and the crew were doubled by Frenchmen. The first, he was told, would be against United States regulations, and the second would merely mean carrying unnecessary passengers, as there are no French airmen trained to Fortresses.

But de Gaulle insisted. There was a quality in his superb intransigence that compelled my unwilling admiration.

I am uncertain how the matter was settled but he so successfully timed his departure as to enter Paris with the first of the liberating forces. When the news was received that Paris had been liberated people wept in the streets of Algiers and embraced one another.

CHAPTER TWENTY-ONE

PARIS

1944-1945

WE travelled overnight from Algiers to London and stayed there for ten days, reinforcing my staff in order to enable them to cope with the work of a great Embassy. It was on the morning of September 13th that we flew to France, accompanied by an imposing escort of forty-eight Spitfires.

We flew quite slowly over Paris and looked down on all the familiar buildings. The streets seemed very empty but I doubt if they are emptier than the streets of London, and there seem to be more bicycles and horse carriages. We were attended on our way from Le Bourget by police motor-cyclists, and everywhere as we passed people seemed pleased to see us, saluting and waving.

We found our Embassy in very good condition and I was able to work there on the afternoon of our arrival, but nearly a month passed before we could inhabit it. There was no water or electricity, and on the ground floor was the furniture of thirty-two separate households who had stored it there for safety when they had to leave Paris in 1940.

My first call the following morning was on Monsieur Bidault, whom General de Gaulle had appointed Minister for Foreign Affairs. I liked him immediately. Sitting in that vast apartment of the Quai d'Orsay he seemed a slight and pathetic figure and he admitted to me that he felt lost. He had been the head of the central committee of the Resistance, an office he had courageously undertaken after his predecessor had been captured and tortured to death by the Germans. He had therefore of necessity been living underground, sleeping in a different place every night, and he knew little or nothing of what had been going on in the outside world. He had nobody to help him, for most of the Civil Servants who were in France had served Vichy, and the Civil Servants who had followed de Gaulle were still in Algiers.

To encourage him I said that I was sure the famous writing-table of Vergennes, at which he was sitting, must prove a source of inspiration. He answered with a delightful smile that he believed it to be a copy, and he preferred to think so because it made him less shy (*cela m'intimide moins*). It was the first of many interviews that I had with this Minister, who proved as loyal a colleague in Paris as Massigli had been in Algiers, and who, if he was intimidated by the writing-table of Vergennes, was never intimidated by General de Gaulle, any more than he had been by the Gestapo.

The Supreme Headquarters of the Allied Expeditionary Force, known as SHAEF, caused both Monsieur Bidault and the diplomatic corps many difficulties, all of which may or may not have been necessary. Their business was the conduct of the war, which, since it was of greater importance than anything else at that time, gave them a very good reason for doing whatever they pleased. The principal ground for complaint was the difficulty in obtaining from SHAEF permission for members of diplomatic staffs to leave Algiers or facilities for doing so.

The situation in France was confused. Owing to the destruction of bridges by the Resistance, which had paralysed the German armies and had enormously helped the invading forces, communications had broken down and the main form of transport was by air. The air was naturally under the control of SHAEF. The only method of learning what was happening in a distant part of the country was to send somebody to find out. But unless the emissary travelled by air, his journey might be long, and reports by post or telegraph might never arrive. Outside Paris the telephone had almost ceased to function.

Wild rumours reached the Embassy of conditions in the southwest, where it was reported that Communists, assisted by red troops out of Spain, had established a reign of terror. A woman, whom I thought highly imaginative and unreliable, arrived from that district and reported that this was all nonsense and that conditions there were normal. A man, level-headed and of scholastic attainments, confirmed the wild rumours. The woman was right.

The confusion was increased by the delay of the United States in recognising de Gaulle and his Ministers as the French Government. It would be interesting to collect historical instances of harm that has been done by the reluctance of men to accept readily what they know they will have to accept in the end. It was two months after the liberation of Paris that the United States recognised the Government of General de Gaulle, which during the whole of that period was carrying out all the functions of government and plainly had the support of the people. The British and the Russians obediently waited on the whim of the President, who early in October appointed an Ambassador to France without asking for the *agrément* of the French. Mr. T. Jefferson Caffery, the new Ambassador, began his mission therefore in anomalous circumstances, as he could hardly be received by the head of the state whom the head of his own state had not recognised as such.

The General meanwhile refused to receive me also. When Massigli came over for a short visit on October 16th:

> He told me that he had himself protested to de Gaulle, saying that it was foolish of him to refuse to receive me in view of the fact that he (Massigli) had been exceedingly well treated in England, had been to stay with the Prime Minister and had been received by the King, and if it was a question of recognition, why had he received Bogomolov? To this de Gaulle replied that the Russian and English positions were different, owing to the way the Prime Minister had treated him. This of course made no sense.

At last on October 23rd the President's ungracious assent was received, and we Ambassadors repaired together to the Quai d'Orsay to convey the good news to the Minister for Foreign Affairs.

We dined with the General the same night. It should have been a gala evening, but gala is not a word included in the vocabulary of General de Gaulle. We were accompanied by Mrs. Anthony Eden, who was at that time controlling with great efficiency the Grand Hotel, which had been turned into a home for soldiers on leave.

> It was an extremely frigid and dreary party, worse even than his entertainments usually are. He made no reference when I arrived to the fact that his Government had been recognised by the three Great Powers that afternoon, and when I said that I hoped he was glad it was finished, he shrugged his shoulders and said it would never finish.
>
> I sat between Madame de Gaulle, who never took her eyes off the General and hardly spoke, and Madame Bonnet, whose husband has been very seriously ill, and who seemed rather overawed by her surroundings. I had a talk with the General after dinner, which was not very useful. The tone of it improved when Bidault joined us. We left about half-past ten.

Beatrice Eden said that the things one dreaded were usually not as bad as one expected, but this had been even worse.

I went to London on the following day. The Prime Minister told me he was thinking of coming over to France to see General Eisenhower. I implored him not to. It would be the last nail in the coffin of his relations with de Gaulle. He said he was not going to suggest visiting the latter and risk receiving another snub such as he had received at Algiers. I said I was sure he would shortly be invited to Paris. Before I left London, five days later, I had, with the help of Massigli, practically arranged that he should go there on November 10th, so as to be present at the military parade on November 11th and thus make sure that he would be seen by the largest possible number of people without any previous announcement being made.

I spent some anxious hours after this decision was taken. Scotland Yard sent out a representative to confer with the French police. He reported on his return that there were still large numbers of Germans hidden in Paris and that it would be dangerous for the Prime Minister to appear in the streets. Some of his colleagues sought to dissuade him from going, and on November 9th, the day before his departure, I had two conversations with him on the telephone. I knew how much trouble the French had taken over their preparations for the visit and how deplorable the effect of postponement would be. For it was postponement that was suggested. I said that nobody could guarantee the life of a famous man in a large crowd, but that in my opinion the danger would be as great in a month's or in a year's time. Such Germans as were hiding in Paris had no wish to draw attention to themselves. Eventually the Prime Minister said, "All right, we will come," and I felt that all the responsibility was mine.

The visit was a very great success. The whole of the first floor of the Quai d'Orsay was put at the disposal of the visitors, who included Mrs. and Miss Churchill. The Prime Minister was delighted to find that he had a golden bath, which had been prepared by Goering for his own use, and still more delighted that the Foreign Secretary's bath was only of silver. Diana and I dined with him and his party, making twelve in all, and we passed a happy evening.

November 11th. We left the Quai d'Orsay at about 10.25 for the Rue St. Dominique [General de Gaulle's headquarters]. The Prime Minister led in an open car, and I followed with Anthony in another open car which immediately broke down, so that we had to change into another. After a short wait at the Rue St. Dominique, we started out again, the Prime Minister and de Gaulle in the first open car, Anthony and Bidault in the second. I followed with Palewski and Nicholas Lawford in a closed car. The reception had to be seen to be believed. It was greater than anything I have ever known. There were crowds in every window, even in the top floors of the highest houses and on the roofs, and the cheering was the loudest, most spontaneous and most genuine. At the Arc de Triomphe the only blots on the proceedings were the American press photographers, whom nobody seemed able to control.

We walked down from the Arc de Triomphe to the tribune, whence we watched the march-past, which lasted nearly an hour. Whenever there was a pause in the procession there were loud cries of "Churchill" from all over the crowd. We then proceeded to the statue of Clemenceau to lay another wreath, and thence to the tomb of Foch in the Invalides. The weather, which was quite good from the beginning, improved all the time, and by one o'clock there was bright sunlight.

Lunch at the Rue St. Dominique—a party of some sixty. I sat between Monsieur Jeanneney and Monsieur de Menthon. De Gaulle made a very good short speech and Winston replied in English. I rather wish he had tried it in French. Anthony added a few words.

After lunch we went upstairs—de Gaulle, Coulet, Massigli, Chauvel and Palewski on one side of the table, Winston, Anthony, Alec Cadogan and I on the other. We talked for about two hours—Winston talking most of the time in his uninhibited and fairly intelligible French. He speaks remarkably well, but understands very little. Both he and de Gaulle were in the happiest of humours. It was all very different from the interview at Marrakesh. There was not an unpleasant word said, although nearly every subject, including Syria, was covered. I was delighted with the result, and we agreed that it would be unnecessary to hold any further conversations between the Prime Minister and de Gaulle, but that the two Foreign Secretaries should meet again to-morrow morning.

The following day was equally successful. I attended the meeting of Foreign Ministers in the morning, where all went well until we reached the question of the Levant, which defied solution. A heavy luncheon at the Quai d'Orsay followed, and then a reception at the Hôtel de Ville. Here the Prime Minister surpassed himself. Unwarned and unprepared he plunged into a speech in French which entirely delighted his audience. He used to say sometimes when defending Spears that the only reason why the French disliked him was because Spears spoke French better than they did. His own method of dealing with the language is certainly more endearing.

We gave a dinner-party that evening to General and Madame de Gaulle, the Russian, Canadian and American Ambassadors, the first two with their wives (Mrs. Caffery had not yet arrived), Monsieur Bidault, Mr. and Mrs. Churchill, Mr. and Mrs. Eden, Air Chief Marshal and Lady Tedder, and Sir Alexander Cadogan. The P.M. was in better form than ever, and was delighted with Madame Bogomolov whom I made sit next to him just before he left. I had to tell him at about a quarter to eleven that he really must leave, as he had to return to the Quai d'Orsay before catching the train. I went to the station to see him off, feeling that it had all been very successful and that I was relieved of a great weight of responsibility.

On November 18th I formally presented my letters of credence to General de Gaulle, taking all my civilian staff with me. "This morning's ceremony was short and formal but de Gaulle was very genial and smiling. His staff say that they have never known him so nearly happy." This curious ineptitude for happiness has proved an unfortunate quality in the character of a remarkable man and has contributed to the failure of his career.

On the day after this interview he left for Russia. I had no doubt at the time that the idea of a Franco-Russian alliance appealed to him. It would have given France a strong background in Europe. With Russia solidly behind him he would have had some justification for treating the President of the United States and the Prime Minister of Great Britain as his equals, as indeed he had always treated them. He had accepted Communists of the Resistance as members of his Government in Algiers, and on arrival in Paris he had added to their numbers, including Maurice Thorez, who had spent the war in Russia. He knew that he could never expect much genuine support from Roosevelt and he had quarrelled bitterly with Churchill. Perhaps Stalin would prove the friend that he was seeking.

A firm Franco-Soviet alliance might at that time have enormously complicated the future of Europe. Instead of cutting the continent into two it would have split it into fragments. Russia, the strongest Power on that continent, with the aid of France, the second strongest, might have made more mischief for the rest of the world than the Soviets and their satellites subsequently succeeded in making. Amongst other results the French Communist Party, which the next elections were to show was numerically the strongest, might have succeeded in getting control of the country. Fortunately none of these possibilities materialised. What exactly happened during de Gaulle's visit to Moscow I do not know. I have, however, the impression that Stalin, ignorant of European affairs, looked upon France only as a nation that had been defeated in war; that had at that time very little in the way of war potential, no guns, no tanks, no aeroplanes, nor the means of producing them; and that therefore France was of no interest to him. He signed therefore one of those vague treaties which form the brittle basis of European peace and sent the French mission home disillusioned.

I paid a short visit to London at the end of the year and had some difficulty in returning because the only means of transport was by air and for several days in succession all traffic was held up by fog. I was able, however, to get back for Christmas, and I found a minor panic in Paris. I was assured by an able American journalist that the Germans were about to sweep us all back into the Channel and that we should not be able to bring off the landings in France a second time. Nervous Parisians were packing their bags.

This was the last desperate effort of the Germans to retrieve the situation and it led the American High Command to what might have been the disastrous decision that they must abandon the recently liberated city of Strasbourg. Charles Peake, who had worked with me in the Ministry of Information, was then attached to SHAEF and by his wise and tactful diplomacy did much to smooth over difficulties that were bound to arise between the all-powerful military at Versailles and the civilian element, French and foreign, in Paris. It was he who brought me the news of this decision, knowing as well as I did the effect it was likely to produce on the French. It would have been one of those blunders which are so easily made when supreme power is in the hands of the military who lack political experience. Strasbourg formed at the time a salient in the front line of the Allied advance. Strategically there was a strong case for flattening that line, but politically the abandonment of Strasbourg would have been an overwhelming disaster which, apart from the horrors that would have been inflicted on the population by the returning Germans, would have struck rage and despair into the heart of France.

As soon as I heard the news I sent a personal telegram to the Prime Minister in which I strongly emphasised this view. He arrived at

Versailles on the following morning, and after a long conversation with Eisenhower, Bedell Smith and de Gaulle it was agreed that two French divisions should remain at Strasbourg to fight it out. They saved the city.

The following day, January 4th, I recorded:

About 11.45 there came a message to the effect that the Prime Minister had not left, owing to the weather, and that General Eisenhower hoped I would go down to Versailles for luncheon. There was little time as I had promised to attend a farewell cocktail party that Brigadier Carthew Yourston (commanding the Paris garrison) was giving at the Officers' Club next door. I managed to look in there for a few minutes and to get to Versailles before one, despite a heavy snowstorm and frozen roads. Eisenhower and Alan Brooke were there when I arrived, and I went up to see the Prime Minister, who was working in bed. I talked to him while he got up and dressed. He had intended, when he found he couldn't fly today, to come into Paris and lunch with us, but Eisenhower had forbidden it on grounds of security, which seemed nonsense to me. We should certainly have given him a better meal.

He seemed pleased with the result of yesterday's conference and said that de Gaulle was satisfied with the compromise. He had had a quite friendly conversation with him after the *conseil de guerre*. At luncheon there were only six of us, the other two being Tommy Thomson and a Scots Guards officer who is Eisenhower's A.D.C. It was not a very cheerful meal. The main subject of conversation was when and where the Russians would attack. There was great hope that it would be soon. But surely we ought to know?

Palewski came to see me at six about issuing a communiqué concerning the P.M.'s visit. The draft he had prepared wouldn't do at all. It suggested that de Gaulle had summoned a military conference which the P.M. and Eisenhower had been allowed to attend. Charles Peake was here and we got out of the difficulty for the time being by saying that nothing should be published until the P.M. was safely home, or at least out of France. (He left by train this afternoon for Belgium.) I said that in any case SHAEF must be consulted. Palewski said he hadn't the General's authority to consult SHAEF but only to get my approval. We took Palewski into the drawing-room to have a drink with Diana.

January 5th. At four I went to see General de Gaulle. I found him in quite a pleasant mood. He told me of his visit to Moscow and we discussed future Anglo-French relations and the possibility of a pact. He is not keen on one or doesn't wish to appear so. Nor is the Prime Minister.

In my opinion a treaty of alliance between Great Britain and France was a matter of the first importance and I was doing everything in my power to bring it about. During the months that I had spent at Algiers I had produced a very lengthy despatch, in which I had reviewed the world situation that I thought would exist after the war and advocated the foreign policy that I believed Great Britain ought to adopt.

The despatch consisted of twenty-nine paragraphs, which I shall here analyse as briefly as possible, for my opinion having changed very little since I wrote that despatch, it may be taken to a great extent as my political testament.

I wrote that there would probably be a demand after the war for the reconstruction of some international organisation with the merits and without the defects of the League of Nations. I said that we should support such an organisation but that we should not stake our future upon it. We had been right to support the League but we had been wrong to have no alternative policy to fall back on when the League proved a failure.

I dismissed the policy of isolation as being impracticable for a country like Great Britain with liabilities in every corner of the earth. While strongly supporting the maintenance of the closest friendship with the United States, I thought that the interests of the two countries were too divergent to render an alliance between them expedient. The future of Mexico, for instance, which must always be a matter of the first importance to the United States, is of little concern to Great Britain, whereas the United States cannot be expected to devote much thought to developments in the Low Countries, which are of such vital importance to the existence of Great Britain. Nor would an alliance with America enable Great Britain to turn her back upon Europe, for modern inventions have rendered our country, more than ever in the past, a part of the Continent.

So far as the Continent was concerned British policy had always been, and must in my submission always remain, to prevent its domination by any one too powerful nation. In pursuance of that policy, we had fought in the past against Spain, France and Germany. "It is to be hoped," I wrote, "and indeed to be assumed with some confidence, that the mistake will not be repeated of allowing Germany, intact, to rearm under the eyes of her victors, and to repeat within another twenty years the crime for which she was insufficiently punished in 1919."

Proceeding on this assumption, which was to prove false, I argued that Russia, when Germany was eliminated, would present the gravest potential menace to the peace of the Continent, but I did not rule out the possibility of an alliance between the two.

Mortal hatred now divides Russia from Germany, but human emotions, whether of love or hate, of gratitude or revenge, have seldom proved durable in politics and have played but a small part in the affairs of nations. It would indeed be rash to rely upon sentiment alone to prevent a Russo-German alliance. . . . Apart from hatred there is nothing but Poland to divide Russia from Germany, and therefore the stronger and the more prosperous Poland becomes the better for the peace of the world.

I was careful, however, not to suggest an alliance either with Poland or Czecho-Slovakia. Experience had proved how powerless we were to give protection to either of those countries. What all the small countries of Europe would demand after their sufferings in the war would be security, and some of them might ask themselves whether they were more likely to obtain it from Great Britain or from Russia. I included France among those in which such doubts might arise, and recalled that there were many in France who had advocated alliance with Germany before the war and had collaborated with the Germans after the defeat. Such people might easily turn to Russia, in default of Germany, and they would have the support of the powerful French Communist Party. I thought that the smaller western Powers would be inclined to follow the lead of France, and I therefore urged that no time should be lost in deciding upon our future foreign policy and in proclaiming it.

Small as the western democracies appeared on the map of Europe, "the combined empires of Britain, France, Holland, Belgium, Portugal and Italy cover a vast portion of the earth's surface and an enormous population. Their resources in raw materials represent a very important part of the world's supplies of tin, rubber, iron, copper, oils and fats."

I had a vision of such an alliance gradually leading to a federation of the western seaboard of Europe together with the principal Powers of the Mediterranean. Practically the whole continent of Africa was at their disposal, and they might have worked together at its development both for their own benefit and for that of the inhabitants. Of the three great world combines, they would eventually have become the strongest. No conflict of interest would have interfered with the bonds of blood, religion and language that would have bound these countries to the New World. An alliance, based upon equality as well as goodwill, would have bridged the Atlantic Ocean, an alliance so mighty that no power on earth would have dared to challenge it, and so at last the world might have found itself on the road to permanent peace.

But although the Foreign Secretary wrote me a friendly letter thanking me for the trouble I had taken, and although the department congratulated me "on the masterly way in which I had dealt with an issue of profound significance," my views did not recommend themselves to the powers that were. From 1933 until 1939 Great Britain had sat staring like a mesmerised rabbit at Germany's preparation for war. Any suggestion for action on our part was discouraged on the ground that it might irritate the monster and produce the very calamity we desired to avert. Such had been the tenor of the messages received before Munich from our Embassy in Berlin. Now I was once more assured that an alliance of the Western democracies would increase the danger, "if indeed such a danger existed," of the Soviet Union pursuing a policy of expansion in Europe. I was also told that the formation of a Western European group might offend the United States. It was the old, familiar attitude—"rather than risk offending anybody, do nothing."

The first step towards carrying out my policy was the conclusion of a treaty of alliance with France. The two great Powers of north-western Europe must form the corner-stone of the vast edifice. As printed copies of my despatch slowly reached other Embassies I was encouraged by the comments of some of my colleagues. Lord Halifax reported from Washington that there was no reason to suppose that the American Government would object to my proposals; Archie Kerr wrote that he did not think they would affect adversely our relations with the Soviet Union, that on the other hand they might have a good effect; and from Brussels came strong support from Knatchbull-Hugessen, who said that the Belgians were growing anxious about the future policy of France and would be glad to see her firmly bound to Great Britain. I also received letters of congratulation and encouragement from several members of the Government to whom my despatch had been circulated.

Emboldened by such support, in March 1945 I returned to the charge. Referring to my first despatch of the previous May, I pointed out that since that date "the U.S.S.R. have tightened their hold upon Czecho-Slovakia, have gained an important diplomatic success in Poland, have asserted dictatorial rights over Roumania and have signed a treaty with France. Meanwhile the relations of His Majesty's Government have remained as vague and indefinite as they were a year ago." We had, however, publicly committed ourselves to restoring the strength of France, and steps had already been taken to equip French troops and to build up her navy and air force. I drew attention to the dangerous folly of allowing military aid to have precedence of political agreement. Surely before giving a man a gun you must have some assurance of the purpose for which he is going to use it. Basing myself upon Knatchbull-Hugessen's opinions, I wrote:

It is to Great Britain that Belgium looks for leadership and security, and I have little doubt that Holland will soon be looking in the same direction. If we again hesitate to give that leadership, as we hesitated between the two great wars, the Powers concerned will be compelled to look for it elsewhere.

It must not be thought, however, that hesitation to make an Anglo-French alliance came only from the side of Great Britain. If Mr. Churchill was not enthusiastic, General de Gaulle was at first even less so. The General was not in the sunniest of moods during these early months of 1945. His Government had now been recognised by the three Great Powers, and it was not unnatural to expect that he would receive an invitation to attend the next meeting of the three leaders. I did everything in my power to bring this about but the opposition of the President proved invincible. It would be interesting to speculate upon how the presence of de Gaulle might have affected the decisions taken at Yalta. The invitation, however, was not forthcoming, and, as already stated, when the President suggested that he should meet the General somewhere in North Africa on his return journey, the suggestion was rejected. De Gaulle was particularly indignant when he learnt that a similar invitation had been extended to the Negus of Abyssinia.

Whether or no de Gaulle was convinced by his reception in Russia that there was no hope of a Franco-Soviet alliance upon which he could rely, it is certain that after his return to France he regarded more favourably the possibility of an alliance with Great Britain. But he allowed long-term policy to be subjected to passing fits of temper, a weakness fatal to statesmanship, and one from which the Prime Minister was not wholly exempt.

April 5th. General de Gaulle wanted to see me at 10.30 this morning. He was most friendly and most anxious for an Anglo-French treaty, which he said he had always wanted. He still, however, thought there was no hurry. I said it would be much better before San Francisco than afterwards. I felt that he was very much alive to the Russian menace and that he had only recently become so. I dictated two long telegrams to the Foreign Office concerning our conversation, one dealing with things in general and the Ruhr in particular, the other with the Levant.

The same evening I met at dinner Monsieur Chauvel, who was then what we should call the Permanent Head of the French Foreign Office.

Chauvel talked to me after dinner. He said that he and Bidault had seen de Gaulle after I had left him this morning and had found him in such a good humour, so eager to get on with the alliance, that they were all now in favour of trying to conclude a real alliance before San Francisco. He seemed excited for one so cold-blooded, and talked faster than ever and was more difficult than ever to understand.

April 6th. At four I went to see Bidault. He confirmed all that Chauvel said last night. We had half an hour's conversation. Having dawdled so long they are now in a hurry. It is always the way. I sent as the result a "most immediate" telegram to London proposing that Chauvel should go over early next week with drafts of (1) an exchange of letters on the subject of the Levant, (2) ditto on the Rhine, (3) an all-in agreement. I hope that something will come of it.

With the picture in my mind of Monsieur Chauvel setting forth to London upon his important mission, I myself with Diana and John Julius, a private secretary, an assistant and three motor-cars, started on a tour of the centre and the south of France.

Our first objective was Lyons, where, as I said at the time, we were received as though we were the King and Queen themselves, instead of their Majesties' unworthy representatives. Nine times in the course of one day we stood to attention to listen to the familiar strains of the two national anthems. The Cardinal Archbishop Gerlier had even contrived that the chimes of the cathedral should ring out the notes of God Save the King.

Monsieur Edouard Herriot, the veteran Mayor, was still a prisoner of the Germans. His place was taken by Yves Farge, who had played a leading part in the Resistance and was now Commissioner of the Republic for that district. He was one of many who would probably have avoided politics if the Resistance and all that followed on it had not obliged them to play a part. I liked him and Madame Farge and hoped that the part they would play might be an important one, but he moved further and further to the left and finally perished in an accident in Russia, whither he had gone to receive some prize from the Soviet Government. We stayed at Lyons with our Consul General, Sir Robert Parr, who although he had only recently arrived had already become a part of the life of the city and who entertained us royally. He also helped me with the many speeches that I had to deliver, as did my secretary, George Lansdowne, in whom the French blood that he derives from Talleyrand seems to make easy the assimilation of French thought and expression. I am always nervous before speaking, and much more nervous when I have to speak in French, when I prefer to have a written text. Here at Lyons I had to face the ordeal of receiving an honorary degree at the university, which entailed a speech before the Faculty and the students.

From Lyons we went on to Avignon, where our large party was hospitably received by the Prefect. Very few hotels were yet open. It was at Avignon on the morning of April 13th that we learnt of the death of President Roosevelt. This sad event had a chastening effect on the remainder of our tour, for a week's national mourning was decreed, and many functions were dropped from our programme, for which we were not sorry. At Marseilles we stayed with the Commissioner of the Republic who occupied the Prefecture, and at Nice we were lodged in a magnificent villa which the American military authorities put at our disposal. We spent three days there and on the last evening gave a small dinner-party for the Prefect and his wife, Monsieur and Madame Escande, the Bishop and one of our former Algerian acquaintances, a Communist member of the Assembly. It was most successful. The Bishop, who had been a soldier in the first war, engaged the Communist in argument and with the utmost good humour got very much the better of him.

On my return to Paris I wrote on April 20th:

Nothing seems to have happened since I went away. Chauvel never went to London although he was invited. The reason was that de Gaulle couldn't decide upon the text of the drafts he was to take with him, and hasn't decided yet.

Once more the Prime Minister felt he had been snubbed, and on the following day:

A personal telegram arrived from Winston reproaching me for having "indulged in a *démarche*" with regard to the treaty, which is quite unjust. I have a good answer. The same evening I saw Palewski and I told him that Winston thought de Gaulle had deliberately slighted England over the Chauvel business, which he of course said was nonsense and that Bidault and Chauvel had exceeded their instructions.

April 26th. A friendly message came this morning from the Prime Minister for General de Gaulle, congratulating him and General de Lattre on the capture of Ulm. We rang up Palewski suggesting that I should bring the message round myself, as I rather wanted to see the General. Having had no reply at four o'clock, I sent George round with the message. Palewski then confessed that he had forgotten to mention it to the General. We then received a very suitable message in reply, and I am to see the General tomorrow.

April 27th. The General did not seem to be in a very happy mood. I was with him for three quarters of an hour. He still feels that he is being left out of everything. I told him it was his own fault. There is trouble about Stuttgart, which the French took, and they have now been told by the Americans to get out of it.

But now a new source of trouble arose in that old seed-bed of Anglo-French misunderstanding, the Levant. The French were about to increase their garrison in the Lebanon and Syria, and our representatives there—Spears had left at the end of 1944—gave warning that if they did so there would be trouble. I went to see de Gaulle about it on April 30th.

I found him, as I expected, in a most unyielding mood. We wrangled for some time. He said frankly that he was convinced it was our policy to oust the French from the Levant. It is impossible to dissuade him from this view; and there is indeed much evidence in favour of it, such as the large number of troops we keep there and the permanent barracks we have built for them. I left him without, I fear, having made any impression.

But on the 5th of May there was another change:

Telegrams from the Prime Minister this morning and a personal message from him to de Gaulle offering to withdraw all British troops from the Levant as soon as the French have concluded a treaty with the States [Syria and the Lebanon]. I took this to the General this afternoon and found him in a much better mood than on the last occasion. Palewski, whom I saw first, told me that he is now desperately anxious to conclude a treaty with England, which he believes is the only thing that can prevent another war. He is obsessed by the Russian menace, and that is one of the many reasons why he is so anxious to retain a base in the Levant. The General said that Beynet was returning to Syria in a few days and that he would hand over one brigade of the Special Troops to the States. I asked him to make some announcement to this effect as soon as possible. He smiled and said, "*Je ferai cela pour vous, Monsieur l'Ambassadeur.*" It was a friendly interview.

May 6th. Palewski came after dinner with the General's reply to the Prime Minister. I thought it most disappointing and told him so. We argued over it for an hour. He said the General was in a bad mood because he had been told by the Americans he was not to have Cologne. In his reply to the Prime Minister he made no reference to his own suggestion to me of going over to London. I asked Palewski to press him on this point tomorrow morning, because he had definitely told me he was going to mention it in his reply and I had informed the Prime Minister accordingly.

On the following morning there was other news of greater importance.

May 7th. General Redman [who among his other duties acted as my liaison officer with SHAEF] came to see me this morning and told me that the unconditional surrender of Germany had been signed in the early hours of this morning at Rheims. He also said that the news was not to be divulged. This last I said was nonsense. The declaration of war was bungled in 1939 and the announcement of unconditional surrender was being bungled now in 1945. However it is great news. Diana broke down when I told her.

And on the following day, when the war officially ended, when the sirens sounded the last All Clear and the church bells of Paris rang out, I found my own eyes were full of tears. The Duke of Wellington was right when he said that a victory is the greatest tragedy in the world except a defeat.

Meanwhile the less edifying contest between the British Prime Minister and the head of the French Government continued, and the

French position in the Levant deteriorated to such an extent that they were obliged to use force and to bombard Damascus in order to maintain order. These events coincided with the highly successful visit to Paris of Field-Marshal Montgomery, whom de Gaulle received most warmly and decorated with the Grand Cross of the Legion of Honour in the courtyard of the Invalides.

On the day that the Field-Marshal left I had an interview with de Gaulle.

All was going well and he had almost agreed to conversations either here or in London and to making a statement that no more troops would be sent to the Levant meanwhile, when I mentioned that the Americans would take part in such conversations. Thereupon he flew into a rage, said that the Americans were in no way concerned, and that he would not allow France to be put into the dock before the British and the Americans. I argued vainly with him for some time and left him still sulky.

In the afternoon I went to see Bidault. I found him friendly as ever, helpful and wise, but very uncertain as to what effect he could produce on the General. He said he thought he would be able to accomplish something at the next meeting of Ministers on Tuesday. He talked of resigning. I think he is in a stronger position since San Francisco.

On the same day the new short-lived "Caretaker" Government was announced in London, and on the following one we left for a tour of the south-west similar to our previous tour of the south. Bordeaux was the most important city we visited, and here again I received an honorary degree from the university. In the smaller towns of this district the welcome that we were given was everywhere as warm as it had been earlier in other parts of the country. Every speech that was made referred to the fight that Great Britain had continued to carry on alone, and to the debt that was owed to her by France and every freedom-loving country in the world. Never has the name of England been so much respected in France, never have Frenchmen been so ready to stretch out their hands in friendship across the Channel. Much more was this feeling made manifest in the provinces than in Paris, and I was haunted by the fear that an opportunity was being missed that would not come again. Statesmen cannot create national feeling but they can take advantage of it. I felt that if the direction of foreign affairs at that time could only have been left to the two Foreign Ministers, full advantage might have been taken of the sentiment that existed.

When I returned to Paris on the last day of May I wrote:

A good deal had happened in my absence—especially today. Anthony had made a statement in the House of Commons to the effect that our Commander-in-Chief Middle East had been ordered to take charge in the Levant. This had been communicated to de Gaulle in a message from the Prime Minister, which unfortunately had reached him an hour after the statement had been made in the House. It is all most regrettable, but de Gaulle has brought it upon himself by refusing to listen to any warning or to do anything that he is asked. It had been arranged for me to see him at 7.15 but we did not reach the Embassy until nearly eight. I then sent a message to say that I was at his disposal. The reply came that he would not trouble me this evening—there was no urgency.

June 2nd. I found Bidault in a state of great indignation. General Paget (C.-in-C. Middle East) has issued a statement that seems designed to humiliate the French, and which I am sure was quite unnecessary. They say it is worse than Fashoda. The General is naturally furious and the problem which seemed to be solving itself is further complicated.

That evening we went to see a French version of *A Midsummer Night's Dream*:

In an interval the manager came forward and said that we were in the theatre. I stood back in the box in order that Diana might receive the first rotten egg thrown, but there was considerable applause and when we left there was a loudly applauding crowd round our car. This after three days of the Levant crisis!

June 4th. At 3.30 I went to see de Gaulle at his invitation. We had a stormy interview. He could not have been more stiff if he had been declaring war. He told me that French soldiers in the Levant had been ordered to stay where they were and to fire on Syrian or British troops if force were used against them. We got into heated argument. He is genuinely convinced that the whole incident has been arranged by the British so as to carry out their long-planned policy of driving the French out of the Levant in order to take their place. I said that if we wanted these disorders, why had we implored him not to send the ships that had caused the disorders? He replied rather feebly that we should have found some other excuse. We had a very unpleasant half-hour.... At 6.45 I went to see Bidault. He gave me the welcome news that the *Jeanne d'Arc* would not go to Beirut—adding that he had been forbidden to tell me so. He said that if only the Prime Minister in his statement tomorrow could say something conciliatory it would help enormously. I promised to ask him to—and I did so by telegraph when I got back. Anthony is ill with a duodenal ulcer, so that Winston is dealing with the Foreign Office. Bidault asked me whether Anthony's illness was a diplomatic one—and said that he felt like having one himself. I assured him that it was not, nor did I think, as he seemed to, that there was any difference between Anthony and the P.M. on the Levant.

While blaming the French for the misconception of what British policy in the Levant really was, we should in fairness concede that their error was due to our action. The retention of General Spears at his post where he was openly pursuing the policy which His Majesty's Government repudiated admitted of no explanation. This was brought home to me during these days when Mr. Gerald Norman, who had been *Times* correspondent throughout my stay in Algiers, and upon whose complete discretion and wise advice I could always rely, called on me on June 5th:

We had as usual a frank and helpful talk. He himself is now forced to conclude that it must always have been our policy to clear the French out of the Levant. This was the more interesting as just before he came I had sent off a telegram to the effect that while I would never allow de Gaulle or anyone else to assert this without contradiction, I thought we ought nevertheless to bear in mind the very strong evidence that existed to support such a theory.

The last exchanges of hostilities between the Prime Minister and the General were perhaps to be regretted on both sides. De Gaulle was due to confer war decorations on a number of British officers, none below the rank of Lieutenant-General, on a certain date. He cancelled the whole affair and at the same time issued orders that certain French Generals, whom I on behalf of the King was to decorate, should not attend the ceremony. At the review which was held on June 18th orders had been given that only French troops should participate. The ambulance which Lady Spears had given to the French Army had taken part, and she had flown small Union Jacks on her four jeeps, side by side with the tricolour. The eagle eye of the General had spotted the offensive flags, though I, standing close to him, had failed to do so. The result was that the Colonel responsible was summoned and ordered to disband the ambulance immediately and repatriate all British members of it. This ambulance, financed by Lady Spears and her friends, had been serving France on all fronts since the outbreak of war and had taken care of twenty thousand French wounded. When I told Bidault he was most indignant. *"Après tout,"* he exclaimed, *"on ne fait pas la guerre aux femmes."* But he could do nothing.

The Prime Minister had his own means of retaliation. It had been suggested to me by Mr. Nicholls, the South African High Commissioner in London, that it would be useful if General Smuts, on his way back to Africa, were to have a conversation with General de Gaulle. I thought it an excellent suggestion, as the advice of so wise and experienced a statesman as Smuts could only be beneficial, and the meeting might go far to correct the unfortunate impression of the speech Smuts had made during the war. Bidault agreed to persuade de Gaulle to consent, but Smuts dined with the Prime Minister and announced on the following day that he had no intention of visiting de Gaulle.

In the same way the Prime Minister later prevented Lord Louis Mountbatten, who had been one of de Gaulle's earliest friends in London, from visiting him in Paris, which he would naturally have passed through on his return from the East. In order to avoid the possibility he was compelled to make a detour via Potsdam, where the Prime Minister happened to be at the time.

The General Election took place on July 5th but the result was not announced until July 26th. During the interval the Prime Minister, who was much exhausted, took a holiday in the south-west of France, staying in a friend's house near Hendaye. He invited me to visit him there. I made the journey with George Lansdowne. The whole party, including the P.M., bathed before dinner and we sat up late talking and arguing.

There is some indignation among the French that de Gaulle should have made no gesture of recognition of the Prime Minister's presence in France. Winston said to me himself "If he had taken a holiday in Scotland I think I should have sent him a message to say I hoped he was having a good time." The local General, the same who was at Marrakesh, had wanted to go to Paris and tell de Gaulle, who is of the same promotion as himself, that he ought to come down and pay the P.M. a visit. He had been restrained from doing so, but the P.M. wanted to consult me as to the desirability of my approaching de Gaulle with the suggestion that they might have a conversation in Paris on Sunday if the P.M. stopped there on his way to Berlin. I was very strongly in favour of the plan. The French have now handed over the Special Troops to the Syrians, and if we could now come to an agreement for the simultaneous Anglo-French evacuation of the Levant the whole question might be settled without any of the delays or difficulties of an international conference. We argued the subject at great length, before and after dinner, and the P.M. changed his view more than once but when we eventually went to bed at two a.m. I had convinced him and had his authority to take up the matter in Paris. George and I slept at the Nairns' villa at Saint Jean de Luz—a charming villa and I slept like a log until I was called by Nairn at eight the next morning.

July 13th. I felt that we should leave early, as there was no time to lose if I was to succeed in my mission. George and I dashed into the sea soon after eight, left the Parme aerodrome at ten and arrived in Paris at 12.30. I was greeted at the Embassy by a message from the Prime Minister to say that I was to take no action whatever on the subject we had discussed last night. This was a great disappointment to me. Another chance missed!

Some confusion was caused yesterday down in the south by the daily King's Messenger, who brings out a bag for the Prime Minister, being struck down with yellow fever. Great embarrassment was caused to poor Eric Duncannon, who, owing to the difficulty of hearing long-distance calls, received the message, "Prime Minister has got yellow fever. Will you telephone to the Foreign Office to have him replaced?" Eric protested, "Surely that's not my job."

July 16th. The Prime Minister has sent a charming message to de Gaulle on leaving French territory, thanking the French Government for having allowed him to come and expressing the hope of seeing de Gaulle before long. These are coals of fire, because during the whole time he was here de Gaulle made no sign of civility whatever.

But now the long antagonism between these two remarkable men was drawing to a close. On July 26th Winston Churchill ceased to be Prime Minister, and six months later de Gaulle resigned the presidency of the French Government. From the hands of the former the ball was snatched in the moment of victory, and the latter in a similar moment contemptuously kicked it away.

The story would not be complete without the epilogue. In the month of November Winston Churchill came to Paris to take his seat in the Academy of Political and Moral Science to which he had recently been elected. The ceremony passed off very successfully. He had to make two speeches in French. The first had been prepared and translated. After it he was conducted on a tour of the building, and we found the Academy of Science in session. His arrival was doubtless expected, for they broke off the business in hand and made him a set speech of welcome. In an impromptu reply he said he was glad to find that the Academy of Science was so near to that of

Morality, as it was important that morality should keep an eye on science in these days.

On November 13th we lunched with General de Gaulle. He was wearing a dark blue suit, in which he looks much better than in uniform. I never liked him or admired him so much. He was smiling and courteous and treated Winston with much more deference than he ever did when Winston was Prime Minister. And although this was the day and almost the hour at which his whole future was at stake [it was the first meeting of the newly elected Assembly], not only was he perfectly calm but one might have thought he was a country gentleman living far away from Paris. There were no interruptions, no telephone calls or messages, no secretaries hurrying in and out, no sign that anything was happening, although Winston insisted on staying till three-thirty talking about the past, and the Assembly was meeting at three. When he left the General came to the front door with him and bowed as the car drove off.

I went straight on to the Assembly after dropping Winston at the Embassy. Duclos was speaking when I arrived. Teitgen and Auriol had already spoken. Duclos is an amusing speaker, cynically and patently dishonest, like all Communists. He was followed by one other speaker, and then the vote was taken. 550 to 0 in favour of de Gaulle—a great triumph especially when it is remembered that the General had then no political party behind him, and that not a single member of the Assembly had been elected as a Gaullist.

It showed also that I had not been wrong during all the time that I had spent trying to persuade the Prime Minister and the President that after their liberation the French people would recognise General de Gaulle as their leader.

CHAPTER TWENTY-TWO

THE TREATY OF DUNKIRK

1945–1947

THE result of the 1945 election came as a surprise to many. It should not have done so. The votes of men serving in the Forces were decisive. Such votes are never likely to be on the side of the party that is in power. To the private soldier the Government is the War Office, and the War Office is the sergeant-major. The exercise of the franchise gives to the private soldier a brief and blessed opportunity of expressing his opinion of the sergeant-major.

If opinions were static, democracy would be a duller form of government than it is. Its merit is that it permits of changes in opinion and gives effect to them without revolution. Between elections opinion must be expected to change, and the longer the interval the greater the change. In 1945 there had not been a general election for ten years, and for fourteen years the same party had been dominant.

At the time of the 1935 election the people were at last becoming aware that the spectre of war was hovering over them. Both parties had recognised its existence. The cry of "Safety First" had proved fatal to the Conservatives in 1929 because nobody believed there was anything to be afraid of, but in 1935 fear played its part, and the voters believed that while the Labour Party might do better in matters of social reform, it was the old Conservative Party that could best be trusted with the conduct of foreign affairs and the defence of the country. Their trust had been ill repaid by a policy of humiliating appeasement culminating in a war for which we were insufficiently prepared.

That we had been saved from complete disaster was very largely due to the leadership of the Prime Minister, who now led the Conservative Party, but that party had kept him out of office for ten fateful years and could not now claim credit for the merits of the man whose counsel they had treated with contempt. On the day of the election Winston Churchill was the most popular man in the country, but there were many who felt that his popularity gave insufficient cause for voting Conservative, and who remembered that his Government had been a coalition in which his Labour colleagues had worthily played their part.

This last consideration was uppermost in my own mind when I faced the prospect of continuing to serve under a Labour Government. I had before the war thrown myself into the game of party politics with the zest and animosity which it demands. But I had never been able to believe that all wisdom and virtue resided in one party and all folly and wickedness in the other. I disbelieved, as I still do, in Socialism both as an economic theory and as a philosophical ideal, but I had made friends and enemies on both sides of the House, and I have little doubt that after Munich my bitterest enemies were on the Conservative benches.

My maiden speech had been on foreign affairs, which, together with questions of defence, had made up my main interest in politics. Foreign affairs have fortunately seldom figured on party platforms in English history, and I had no reason to suppose that a Labour Government's approach to them would differ from that of their Conservative predecessors. There was therefore nothing to prevent me from serving under them. The question was whether they would care to make use of my services.

I was glad when I heard that Ernest Bevin had been appointed to the Foreign Office. I had known him ever since he came to the War Office, years before, as leader of some Trade Union delegation, when I was Financial Secretary. We had got on well on that occasion, and ever since. He seemed to me to fulfil Pope's description of a man as "a being darkly wise, and rudely great."

I wrote to him at once saying that I should not in any way resent his making a change at the Paris Embassy which, mine being a political appointment, he would be amply justified in doing, but that I should regret it because I believed that we could work well together.

I had no answer to my letter and it was a long time before I knew my fate. It would perhaps be more correct to say that I never knew it until the axe fell. Bevin, although a good talker, and one who enjoyed talking, had difficulty in writing. The mere setting of words on paper was for him a long and arduous process. He had a fluent tongue but not a facile pen. He also read slowly. These disadvantages increased enormously the burden of his work. They also rendered my relations with him more difficult. It is a great help to an Ambassador to be able occasionally to write a private, personal note to his Secretary of State, which he knows will be read as from one man to another and answered accordingly. But I never received a letter from Bevin in his own handwriting, nor one that I felt he had dictated himself, and I never wrote to him without suspecting that my letter would be laid before him together with the comments of the department, or at least with those of his Private Secretary.

I know nothing about what took place behind the scenes. Many rumours reached me as to who was fighting against me and who was on my side. I cannot blame the former. In the old days the Paris Embassy was always considered one of the plums of political patronage, and it was not unusual for the Ambassador to change with the Government. There must have been many supporters of the Labour Party who cast envious eyes upon it, and many, without envy, who felt it wrong that so important a post should be held by a Tory politician. I feel sure, however, that Bevin himself resisted the demand for my withdrawal, and that he was able successfully to resist it for two and a half years reflects credit on the magnanimity of the Government as a whole.

August 10th. After lunch we heard that Japan had capitulated, on condition that there was to be no interference with the Mikado. The atomic bomb has done the trick. At 3.30 I went to see Bidault and told him I was going to London and wanted to know whether his views about the alliance were still the same. He said they were and expounded them. He said also that things were going very badly between him and de Gaulle and he didn't know how much longer he would be in office. He told me to tell Bevin that the most important thing for Anglo-French relations was that I should not be withdrawn. It was the one point upon which he and General de Gaulle were in complete agreement. We had as usual a very friendly conversation.

August 13th. Eleven o'clock at the Foreign Office. A conference presided over by Ernie Bevin. About fourteen present. Bevin's policy and sentiments towards France could not be better. There should now be no difficulty about the Levant and little, I hope, about Germany.

We had some private conversation after the meeting. I suggested to him that one way in which we could help France was to reduce the import duty on wine. France had little to export and most of what she had came under our definition of "luxury goods." The duties on wine brought in little revenue and were a form of "window dressing," the assumption being that wine was the rich man's drink and that he ought to be made to pay for it. Bevin agreed. His reply was typical of his sound sense and broad humanity. "I don't care much for wine myself," he said, "I prefer whisky. But I should like to see our people drinking more wine. I know wine is a good thing. When I see a good thing I don't want to stop the rich getting it, but I want the working man to have it too."

I returned to Paris the same day.

August 14th. I went to see Bidault at three. He said the first thing he wanted to know and the most important was whether I was staying or not. I told him that I didn't know. He asked whether I had told Bevin how much importance he attached to it. I said I could not possibly deliver such a message. He said that in that case he would instruct Massigli to do so. I then told him what had passed in London, and he expressed his satisfaction.

Meanwhile de Gaulle was paying a visit to the United States and I heard that he returned "in a bad mood so far as England is concerned. He has no intention of being hurried into a treaty, and prefers to rely upon American support." When I next saw Bidault,

I asked him whether de Gaulle really wanted a treaty with England. He hesitated. There were two men in de Gaulle, he said, *l'homme d'esprit et l'homme d'humeur*. It was the latter who was responsible for all his follies. He knew that a treaty would be a good thing; he knew that the French people wanted it; he knew that the Quai d'Orsay wanted it; yet it was hard to say that he wanted it himself.

On September 11th the first post-war conference of Foreign Ministers opened at Lancaster House. The five Powers were represented by Bevin, Bidault, Byrnes, Molotov and Wang. Three languages were used, which meant that every speech had to be translated twice. I reflected that at the Congress of Vienna in 1814 one language was enough. A century later at Paris two were necessary, and now in 1945 we had to employ three. Such was the march of progress, which would doubtless continue in the same direction until it brought us back to the Tower of Babel.

I attended every full meeting, sitting beside Bevin, and sometimes being of service to him by suggesting arguments he might put forward or pointing out fallacies in those of others. The translations provided plenty of time for thought. It would be of little interest to recount what passed at these meetings, which took place, morning and afternoon, for over three weeks. The Russians were determined to be obstructive, and succeeded, so that nothing of the slightest importance was achieved. At one of the later meetings Molotov said that a resolution passed at the first meeting was rescinded because when one party withdrew from a resolution it ceased to be a resolution. Bevin told him he was talking like Hitler.

At this Molotov flew into a passion, said the chairman ought not to permit such language, "Have we got a chairman or haven't we?" (He had forgotten who it was because it was a different one at each meeting. This time it was Byrnes), and finally he said he would not stay to be insulted and began to leave the room. Bevin laughed, withdrew and apologised. Molotov returned to his seat. He then made a speech, said this was not the first conference that he had attended and spoke regretfully of Anthony Eden. The sitting was long and animated but we made no progress at all. Molotov said there would be no communiqué and no protocol. He spoke with great bitterness of Bevin. The latter does not speak well. He rambles and repeats himself. This becomes apparent when he is translated into French. The interpreter reduces the length of what he has said by half. Byrnes on the other hand speaks quite well.

In the last stages of the conference Molotov tried to confuse the issue by bringing up a resolution passed at Potsdam which would limit the discussion of certain matters to the Big Three, excluding France and China. Bevin defended the cause of France, and by putting China in the foreground got the support of Byrnes, for the Chinese were at that time more popular in America than the French. But it was the French whom the Russians particularly wished to exclude from discussion of certain matters which concerned Europe. On October 2nd the conference came to an end, without having agreed on anything at all.

The most satisfactory evening during that conference was spent at Chequers. I had a car at my disposal and drove down there.

September 16th. I reached Chequers at 7.30. I found the Prime Minister, Mrs. Attlee, their pretty daughter, the two Bevins, Bob Dixon and a lady secretary, all in evening clothes. I had at the last moment, after some hesitation, decided to bring mine. It was lucky. I retired to put them on, and when I returned found that the Massiglis and Bidault had arrived, all dressed. When Winston was in Paris last year I consulted Bidault as to whether we should wear dinner-jackets in the evening, and he told me that he hadn't got one. He has repaired the omission. I sat between Madame Massigli and Dixon. We had a good and cheerful dinner. After the ladies had left we started a serious discussion of Anglo-French relations, which went extremely well. Both Bidault and Bevin were admirable, and the conclusion was reached that conversations should be opened in Paris with a view to settling the question of the Levant. I feel most hopeful. The Bevins returned to London. I stayed the night, the only night I ever spent at Chequers.

My hopes were fulfilled. After further delays and difficulties an Anglo-French agreement on Syria was signed by Bevin and Massigli in London on December 13th. "I was very glad to be there and I do sincerely hope that this may prove to be the real end of the tiresome question which has been poisoning Anglo-French relations for so long."

Bevin left the next morning for Moscow, where a number of decisions were taken by the three Great Powers concerning the drawing up of peace treaties with the defeated nations and the holding of a Peace Conference at Paris in the spring. Bevin insisted that his agreement to all these decisions was conditional on the approval of France. This did much to sweeten to the French the pill of their exclusion from the Moscow talks, and the selection of Paris as the scene of the Peace Conference did more, so that their agreement was given.

So ends the year 1945, a year of great events, the defeat of Italy, of Germany and of Japan, the deaths of Hitler, Mussolini and Roosevelt, the victory of the Labour Party and the overthrow of Winston, the French general election and the confirmation of de Gaulle's position. What does the coming year hold in store, and shall I be here in Paris at the end of it? I wonder.

The first important event of the new year certainly did not strengthen my position. I was informed that the Secretary of State had learned from certain private sources, which I never identified, "that the Communists were about to make an alliance with Herriot and would overthrow de Gaulle, and also that de Gaulle was riding for a fall and that he wanted to go out now in order to come back later with increased power."

The telegram with this information reached me on a day when I was staying in bed with a mild attack of influenza. I replied that both stories seemed to me improbable. Paris was full of rumours at that time which I did not report unless they were supported by evidence. The most common were that the Communists were about to stage a *coup d'état*, or that orders had been received from Moscow to start a revolution. One of my last official reports, two years later, was to contradict such a rumour, which was so widely believed in England that anxious parents were recalling children who were being educated in France.

Scepticism with regard to rumours is usually wise, but there is one rumour in a hundred which proves true and betrays the sceptic. There seemed to be no reason why de Gaulle, who at the end of the year had won a victory in the Assembly in the matter of army estimates, and whom the members of that Assembly had accepted unanimously a few weeks before, should voluntarily throw away the greatest opportunity ever offered to a Frenchman since Napoleon Buonaparte picked the crown of France out of the gutter on the point of his sword. Yet for once rumour was right and reason was wrong. On January 20th, the eve of the anniversary of Louis XVI's execution, General de Gaulle cut off his own head and passed into the shadow-land of politics.

I feared at first that he might have cut off mine too, for he had shown that the Secretary of State in London was better informed as to what was happening in Paris than his Ambassador on the spot. It had indeed been a well-kept secret. I learnt later that Pleven, who was supposed at that time to be more in the General's confidence than any of his colleagues, learnt only on Saturday afternoon what he intended to do on Sunday morning. Bidault, his Minister for Foreign Affairs, was in London and was not given any warning before nor any explanation afterwards.

The General has never fully revealed the true motives that lay behind his extraordinary conduct. The observer therefore can only guess that in the confused political situation of the time he believed his services to be so valuable that his voluntary retirement would be shortly followed by a demand for his return on his own terms. He was dissatisfied with the constitution and wanted one formed on the American model, in which he would exercise the power of an American President. His prestige was so great that he believed himself to be indispensable, which no politician has ever been.

The withdrawal of General de Gaulle from the French Government and the coming into power of a new Government in Great Britain seemed to me to provide an opportunity to revive the topic of an Anglo-French alliance. I had received no reply to my last despatch on the subject dated March 11th, 1945, nor to another one in which I had advocated closer economic ties between the two countries. This latter had formed the subject of an inter-departmental conference on the eve of the General Election, at which the policy that I recommended received general support, and regret was expressed that no very clear conception existed of the policy which the Government intended to pursue. At the end of the meeting the senior Foreign Office representative said that a long-term directive should be sought from the Cabinet after the elections had taken place.

In the despatch which I now submitted I briefly recapitulated all the arguments I had put forward before, from Algiers and from Paris, in favour of forming a solid group of Western democracies based upon an Anglo-French alliance. I deplored the British lack of initiative and compared it to what had happened before the war. "Germany," I wrote, "had no allies when Hitler came to power, but one by one Poland, Italy, Austria, Hungary, Roumania, Spain, Bulgaria accepted what they were offered and made friends with the power of evil because there seemed to exist no power of good. The names of those states ring ominously today."

I expressed the belief

that it had always been the intention of the late Secretary of State [Mr. Eden], as it has always been the desire of the present French Foreign Minister, to conclude eventually an Anglo-French alliance. Repeated postponements have, however, taken place and no progress has been made. . . . Today the mighty arm of Russia is paramount in the countries that are nearest to her borders, and the muscular fingers of that arm are busy in the lands that lie beyond. In no European country is there a Communist majority, but almost everywhere the Communists are gaining ground because of the support from abroad on which they know they can rely.

Only recently the Hungarian Prime Minister complained of this support to H.M. Chargé d'Affaires at Budapest, adding sadly that he himself received no word of encouragement from either Great Britain or America. The time has come, I submit, to count our friends, to fortify them and to bind them closely to our side. Of purely European countries France remains, despite her failures and perplexities, potentially the strongest and the richest on the continent, provided the mistake of allowing Germany to become powerful again is not repeated. An Anglo-French alliance would form a potent magnet for others who are now looking round rather wildly in search of security and salvation.

Soon after this despatch was received in London Oliver Harvey was sent suddenly to Paris.

April 3rd. I gathered from Oliver who arrived this evening that my recent despatch had borne some fruit, and that Bevin, at any rate, was now all in favour of an alliance. It is typical of the Foreign Office that having delayed for two years they should now want to settle everything in twelve hours. Will anything come of it? I hope so.

Nothing did.

This visit unfortunately coincided with a crisis in the French Cabinet over the question of the Ruhr. Monsieur Gouin, the Socialist Prime Minister, and Monsieur Bidault, with both of whom Oliver Harvey had interviews, were thinking more of their own internal affairs than of international agreements, so the matter was temporarily dropped, and shortly afterwards the opening of the Council of Foreign Ministers relegated it once more to the long list of urgent matters awaiting decision.

The confabulations of the Council of Ministers proved very similar to the meetings that had taken place in London the previous year. The Secretary of State was installed with all his advisers in the George V Hotel, which became as busy as a government department. There every morning was held a meeting of our delegation at which subjects that would come before the Council were discussed. These informal gatherings were much more interesting and lively than the Council itself. At one of the latter's meetings I had closed my eyes for a minute when I heard the Secretary of State say: "Tell Duff I'll call him if anything happens," and he added: "He's the most sensible man in the room. It's all waste of time."

I have a complete account of what took place there from day to day, but if it was dull to those who took part in it, to read about it would be infinitely duller, and we can only pity the professional historian whose duty it will be to do so. The Council of Ministers was followed by the full Peace Conference, at which all the United Nations were represented. As a daily occupation this was drearier even than what had gone before. At the Council there was at least the clash of personalities and the interest of improvised dispute, both of which were lacking at the Conference. I wrote at the time: "It is a lamentable entertainment. Each national spokesman reads out a carefully prepared speech. No speech relates to another. There is no argument, no debate, no eloquence."

The evening entertainments, sumptuous as many of them were, were as lacking in gaiety as the meetings of the Conference were lacking in interest. It was after one of these parties that François Mauriac, who was writing regularly in *Le Figaro*, paid an enchanting tribute to Diana which I quote in the original because the prose of the master is as difficult to translate as poetry: "à une fête de ces derniers jours où les visages fermés des Slavs glissaient, tous feux éteints, à travers les groupes, j'observais l'Ambassadrice d'une nation amie, cette figure de Pallas Athenée qui épandait sur ce troupeau sombre et méfiant l'inutile lumière de ses yeux; statue encore intacte, témoin des époques heureuses, sa beauté adorable se dressait en vain, comme un dernier appel à la joie de vivre au dessus d'une humanité sans regard."

I think it was on this occasion that Diana, in conversation with Molotov, through an interpreter, asked him whether we could send our son to live with a Russian family for a few months to learn the language. Molotov replied that he would study the question. Diana said she had had no idea that so simple a question would require study, and as she knew that his time was fully occupied he had better forget it.

It was a cold, wet summer, which lessened the hardship of being obliged to spend it all in Paris. Not until almost the end of October, when the Conference was at last over, did we succeed in getting away for a week. We went to our beloved Venice, which we had not seen since 1937. The weather can be beautiful there in the late autumn, but this year it was cold and cheerless.

I paid a short visit to London in December.

December 18th. I lunched with the Anglo-French group in the House of Commons and addressed them afterwards. I suppose I spoke at too great length for there was no time for questions when I finished. I got a seat in the Chamber and listened to Questions. I suffered no nostalgia. On the contrary, I felt like an older boy who revisits his preparatory school and despises the folly of it. The same foolish questions, the same silly laughter, the same childish anger and quarrels still going on.

On December 31st I summed up:

This has been a year far less eventful than the last and far less satisfactory. In spite of General de Gaulle's resignation and the liquidation of the Levant problem there has been little, if any, improvement in Anglo-French relations, and the German difficulty is greater than it was, owing to the growth of pro-German feeling in England. U.N.O. has not distinguished itself, and the five peace treaties that have taken so long to conclude are no cause for pride. The Fourth Republic is still without a President.

A year ago I wondered whether I should still be here today. Here to everybody's surprise and to the annoyance of many I still am. It is somewhat to my credit, but still more to that of the Labour Government. They are still criticised by their own left wing for keeping me, and prophecies of my imminent departure still appear in the press. They don't worry me for I shan't mind going when the time comes, although I'm not sure where I shall go or what I shall do.

There was a change of Government in France at the end of 1946. After the elections in November the various political parties failed to form the customary coalition, and Léon Blum became the head of a purely Socialist administration. He retained the direction of Foreign Affairs himself and installed Monsieur Lapie, a good friend of Great Britain, as Under-Secretary at the Quai d'Orsay.

December 26th. At twelve I went to see Blum at the Hôtel Matignon [the official residence of the President of the Council]. I first met him there ten years ago, when he was Prime Minister and I was Secretary of State for War. He seemed to me better in health than at any time since his release, and as charming as ever. We talked for an hour and covered nearly every political subject. Unlike Lapie, who thinks the present Government may stay in power indefinitely, Blum is sure that there will be no difficulty in forming a coalition Government when the time comes next month. He certainly agrees with me about the Anglo-French alliance but seemed astonished when I suggested that he himself should conclude it. He said that he would only be in office a few weeks, and that the German question should be settled first.

Diana arrived at one and we had lunch together with Madame Blum and a private secretary. It was a beautiful day, the house is magnificent and the food excellent. Two years ago the Blums were prisoners expecting daily to be put to death. Diana and I walked home in the sunshine.

The following day I met Couve de Murville at dinner. He was then acting as deputy to the Foreign Minister at the Peace Conference and the Council of Ministers.

He said that Blum had been very much interested by my suggestion yesterday that we might conclude an Anglo-French alliance before settling the German question. I had not been authorised to make such a suggestion.

January 7th. We received from the Foreign Office text of correspondence that has taken place between Blum and Attlee. The former wrote on January 1st insisting on the importance of coal for the salvation of France and, basing himself on his conversation with me, said he was eager to conclude an alliance and would be proud to do so during his short term of office. Attlee replied that there was absolutely nothing doing with regard to coal, but that he was all for an alliance and would be very glad to see Blum if he would come over to England as Blum had suggested in his letter.

January 9th. This has been a day of some excitement. In the morning there arrived from London a draft memorandum for the Cabinet suggesting the opening of negotiations for concluding a Customs Union with France. My views were wanted before the submission of the paper to the Cabinet. In a covering letter Sargent said he had little doubt what my views would be.

A little later came the text of a further letter from the Prime Minister to Blum. This was a warm invitation to visit England. I sent it round to him at once and at 3.30 I went to see him. He said that Massigli was to come over on Saturday and that, if he agreed, Blum himself would go to England on Monday, stay Tuesday and Wednesday and return for the presidential election on Thursday. Is it possible that something will be accomplished at last? I telegraphed to the Foreign Office that the visit would do more harm than good if Blum returned empty-handed.

January 11th. Eric Duncannon went to London yesterday. He telephoned this morning. He had seen several people at the Foreign Office. They were still in favour of Blum's visit but not enthusiastically so. Massigli was pessimistic, saying that if nothing came of the visit it would be playing into the hands of the Communists. He is coming to Paris today. What he will say to Blum and what will be the result of it we cannot tell. . . . I got a message at dinner to say that no decision will be taken about Blum's visit until tomorrow. This is very tiresome.

January 12th (Sunday). I got up this morning and dressed in complete uncertainty as to my fate. Nor for some time was there any means of finding out. At last—about 10.30—Robin Hooper [2nd Secretary], who had been round to the Hôtel Matignon, arrived with the news that Blum had decided this morning that he would go to London. At the same time Massigli, who came over yesterday, telephoned to say that Blum had asked him to inform me accordingly. Massigli had himself discouraged the visit. He was on the train and came to have a talk with me on the boat. He said that I was mainly responsible for the visit and that it was therefore up to me to make a success of it.

January 13th. At 2.45 I left with Eric to meet Blum at Northolt. On the way there I remembered that he is Head of the State and that the King therefore should have sent somebody to greet him. John Addis was representing the Prime Minister and Cheke the Foreign Secretary, so I thought that I had better say I was representing the King, who was at Sandringham. I sent Eric on arrival to telephone to the Foreign Office to get approval of this, but of course nobody there was prepared to take the responsibility. So I took the risk, and when Blum descended I said the King had charged me to bid him welcome. Later I got on to Tommy Lascelles, who said I had done quite right.

Blum drove off with Massigli to Claridge's and I went to the Foreign Office where there was a meeting in the Secretary of State's room. I thought he seemed more tired than usual. A communiqué had been prepared to be issued on Blum's departure. I thought it very poor, and so did Bevin. I found him full of the most excellent sentiments with regard to France, but to every suggestion he made some official raised an objection. After some inconclusive talk four of us went to another room to redraft the communiqué. I got them to put something in it very definite about the alliance.

January 14th. The revised statement looked quite good this morning. I went to the House of Commons, where we lunched, ten only—Bevin, Blum and their principal advisers. Bevin was in remarkable form, and despite the difficulty of the language, for Blum doesn't understand a word of English, he managed to keep the thing going in a wonderful way. He ragged me, telling the Frenchmen that I was more French than English, that I had lost all interest in England and that I never stopped telling him what he ought to do to help France. He said that there was only one point on which he agreed with me, namely that the danger still came from Germany rather than from Russia. This was very satisfactory. He told a number of not very funny vulgar stories, which were difficult to translate but at which Blum laughed valiantly. At 5.30 we had a meeting in the Secretary of State's room. It lasted only an hour and everything went very well. I think we shall be able to produce an agreed statement which will be really useful and will look as though something had been accomplished, which it will have been.

On the following day there was a luncheon-party for Blum at 10 Downing Street and then a final meeting between him and Bevin at the Foreign Office. "There was complete agreement on the text, and I felt that something had indeed been accomplished and that I had myself contributed towards it." Blum flew back to Paris early next morning in order to attend the presidential election, and when I arrived there in the evening Vincent Auriol had been elected, the Palace of the Elysées was illuminated and a floodlit tricolour was flying over it for the first time for seven years.

As Léon Blum had himself foreseen, his Government did not survive the election. In the new one, over which Ramadier presided, Bidault returned to the Ministry of Foreign Affairs. My fear was lest he should resent what had been done in his absence and be reluctant to complete the work that Blum had so gallantly begun. I called on him on the evening of January 25th with this uncertainty in my mind.

He could not have been more friendly. He said he might have conducted matters differently himself, that he might have postponed the treaty of alliance until after Moscow, but that he accepted entirely what had been agreed, and that he was prepared to conclude the treaty forthwith. This was all very satisfactory.

There were further delays, further hitches, further small points raised in government departments, but the goodwill of Bevin and Bidault combined to overcome all obstacles, and on February 28th I wrote:

Soon after lunch Ashley [Clarke, Minister in Paris] came with the definite news that the treaty was concluded, that Bevin and Bidault would announce it this afternoon, and that I was to meet Bevin at Dunkirk on Tuesday, where we would both sign it. I was very pleased. It is just three years since I began working for this at Algiers, and although it would probably have come about somehow sometime I honestly believe that it would not have been done now if I had not said what I did say to Blum in our first conversation. Eric and I went to the Chamber. Pierre Cot was speaking—and spoke very well. When he finished there was an interval which seemed to me endless. Hervé Alphand told Eric there had been a further *accrochement*, that Bidault would make no announcement, nor Bevin either. I was very anxious. After nearly an hour's delay the debate continued. We had been told there would be two speeches before Bidault. But he spoke at once. He never speaks well and this was no exception to the rule. He kept the announcement till the end. The applause was universal and then gradually the whole house rose. The Communists applauded less enthusiastically and rose more slowly than the others, but they all applauded and they all stood. It was an impressive sight. Then Herriot, in the chair, interrupted the speaker and said a few words of congratulation. It was a great moment.

A few days later the treaty was signed at Dunkirk. I believe it was Bevin who selected the place of signature. It was well chosen. The old Flemish seaport had often played a part in the long history of England and France. It had belonged sometimes to one of them, sometimes to the other and sometimes to neither. It had witnessed in the last war a tragic but heroic episode. The devastation that had befallen it was still apparent on that wet March afternoon of 1947, but my spirits rose above the weather, and that evening I wrote in my diary "Nunc dimittis."

CHAPTER TWENTY-THREE

THE END OF MY CAREER

1947

AT the beginning of April we went for a short holiday to Monte Carlo, where friends lent us a villa. I fell seriously ill there and was away from Paris all that month. When we returned Ramadier had reformed his Government and got rid of all the Communists who had been members of it. This greatly strengthened France in the arena of international affairs. During the past three years when I pressed the claims of France to receive more consideration and confidence from Great Britain I was met by the argument, difficult to answer, that the French Government contained Communists, who were presumably the servants of Stalin, and would communicate to him any information they obtained.

Ramadier also had the pleasure in this month of May of presenting the French Military Medal to Winston Churchill. This medal is the nearest French equivalent to our Victoria Cross. It is awarded to private soldiers and non-commissioned officers for courage in the field and also to the very highest and most successful Generals. By an ancient and honourable custom it is always presented by the former class to the latter. A five-star General, or a Marshal of France, is proud to receive it from the hands of an ordinary soldier, who has won it in battle. It so happened that Ramadier, besides being Prime Minister, had won the Military Medal in the 1914 war as a non-commissioned officer, and it was he who pinned it on to the breast of the war Prime Minister of Great Britain in the courtyard of the Invalides.

It was in June that the first efforts were made towards the formation of what later became known as the Marshall Plan, and great credit is due to Bevin for the initiative he took.

June 10th. Last night a "most immediate, top secret" telegram arrived on the subject of Marshall's speech at Harvard, instructing me to see·

Bidault at once with a view to our getting together in order to take proper advantage of Marshall's offer. I saw Bidault this morning. I hadn't very much to say except to suggest that Alphand, who was in any case going to London next week, should be authorised to discuss the question. Bidault was most forthcoming and helpful. He had already given the matter some thought and had useful suggestions to make.

The next week Bevin arrived with a formidable host of Civil Servants representing half-a-dozen government departments. I gave a dinner-party that evening of thirty men, including the British delegation and French Ministers and Civil Servants.

We had a good dinner and some discussion afterwards. There was almost entire agreement on the line that we should take. The important thing is the approach to the Russians. They must be invited to participate and at the same time they must be given no opportunity to cause delay and obstruction. This will not be easy.

The next day was a very full and successful one. We had a meeting of our delegation in the Embassy at ten, which was followed by a full meeting of both sides at the Quai d'Orsay at eleven.

Then there was a short meeting of officials between 12.30 and 1.30. Rather to my surprise the Secretary of State said I was to take part in this. He explained later that he thought the representatives of the Treasury were too disposed to raise unnecessary difficulties. It is true, but it is a fault on the right side. I, on the contrary, am too slapdash.

Lunch at the Quai d'Orsay—men only and Madame Bidault. This was followed by speeches by Bevin and Bidault. Then another meeting of us officials at the Embassy from 3.30 to 4.30—then a further meeting of French and British officials at the Quai d'Orsay which I attended. This went on until six, when there was a full meeting with the two Foreign Ministers. This went very well. Bevin wiped away some of the small points for which the officials had been standing out, and complete agreement was reached. The situation was somewhat complicated by the French Minister of Information having given out in the morning some completely inaccurate as well as indiscreet communiqués. I was much annoyed, as it was just the sort of thing the English say the French always do. The result was that it was decided to communicate the message for the Soviets to their Chargé d'Affaires here, as well as to our respective Embassies at Moscow. So Bevin had to receive the Chargé d'Affaires here at the Embassy before dinner. He also received the American Ambassador and gave him a copy of the invitation we are sending to Moscow. I was present at both interviews which went on until dinner-time. I think it was a good day's work.

I had the principal members of our delegation to dinner. It went quite well. Bevin talked and talked and we all listened. This was the day of the visit of the B.B.C. orchestra. Diana had to give a large luncheon and a cocktail party for Adrian Boult and the rest of them, and went to their concert this evening. She and John Julius came back after the guests had gone, while Bevin and I were still sitting in the green drawing-room. He soon went to bed. I found Louise in the library translating my Lille speech and we worked at it until past midnight.

My visit to Lille was on the same pattern as those I had paid to Lyons and Bordeaux. Once again I received an honorary degree. On my return there followed the second stage in the negotiations concerning the Marshall offer. Molotov arrived, and adopted the line that the United States should say how much money they would give us before we told them what we were going to do with it. The answer was simple. What they gave us depended upon their approval of our plan, and if we produced no plan we should get no money. Molotov replied that the Soviets had made their plans and were not going to change them at the bidding of the United States. This took longer to say than it does to write. It took in fact a week, at the end of which the Russians, without saying good-bye to anybody, went home, leaving the British and the French to pursue their own plans and to invite other nations to participate.

During this visit I was glad to find Bevin more than ever inclined towards my views.

He is now entirely in favour of the western bloc, of customs union with France, common currency etc.—everything in fact which I advocated in my despatch from Algiers in May 1944. How long it has taken!

How much longer it was to take!

August 10th. The question of the possibility of a customs union is causing difficulty. It would please the Americans, the French are for it and our Ministers are willing, but the officials of the Treasury and the Board of Trade—pig-headed as ever—won't hear of it. We need only accept the principle. The thing itself would not come about for years.

When I wrote "Nunc dimittis" after signing the Treaty of Dunkirk, I did not know how soon my prayer was to be granted.

September 3rd. This morning I received a letter from the Secretary of State informing me that I am to leave this Embassy at the end of the year. It was a very civil letter, saying that the service I had rendered "was of the highest order," that I would "certainly be remembered as one of the outstanding British representatives to hold this important post," and that it had been very largely due to me "personally that in these difficult times the position of H.M. Ambassador in France has been fully restored to its recognised place in French life." He ends by saying that he owes me a debt of gratitude for my help and loyalty and that he is sad that this happy association should come to an end. No reason is given for the change except the fact that I have been here for three years. It came as a shock and all shocks are unpleasant. I am sad to go but perhaps it is better now than later. I am sad to leave the house, but not the pomp and circumstance which I have always felt as a hindrance and have never enjoyed. I shall have time now to do something else before I pack up. Diana took it superbly, as she always takes bad news, and said that so long as we can make sure of Chantilly she doesn't mind.

On the following day we left for our holiday and drove to San Vigilio, a small place on the Lake of Garda which we had long known and loved. On the way there I recorded:

September 5th. I slept badly last night. I remember how when I resigned at the time of Munich, although I was quite happy and sure I had done right, I used to dream that I was very unhappy and, waking, would remain so for a while. So last night I was wretched in my sleep to be leaving the Embassy, and waking about four in the morning I began to worry, to think that I had been very ill-treated, and to compose letters and speeches on the subject. Everything is out of perspective at 4 a.m. which is, in fact, the middle of the night. I turned on the light, read for a little and fell asleep. When I woke again "my untroubled mind came back to me."

Later that month Bevin had to come to Paris for twenty-four hours to sign the report of the Marshall planners. My trusted and most capable Minister, Ashley Clarke, thought that there was no need for me to return. In ordinary circumstances I should probably have taken his advice, but I wanted to show that I was not neglecting my duties because they were shortly coming to an end, nor feeling pique because I had been dismissed. So at some inconvenience, the nearest aerodrome being the other side of Genoa, I flew back, and met the Secretary of State on his arrival. He made no reference whatever to the fact that I was going. Nor did I.

September 22nd. I had a busy morning. At twelve I went with the Secretary of State to call on Ramadier. The conversation went very well and I was glad to have been present. As we came away Bevin said to me "We've made the union of England and France this morning." He would certainly like to, and I believe if it were not for other government departments he might bring it off. We lunched at the Quai d'Orsay and came back to the Embassy for half an hour before the final meeting of the

Marshall Conference. There were no hitches. The speeches were short and good. Everything went like a marriage bell. I came back and dictated an account of this morning's Bevin–Ramadier conversation. Oliver Franks called to say good-bye to me, which was very civil. I like him.

October 11th. Ashley came back from London this afternoon. He said that everybody in the Foreign Office was aware of my coming departure and regretted it. He doesn't think that anyone in the Office was responsible. They all attribute it to political pressure. He had been present at a discussion—inter-departmental—on how to implement the Bevin–Ramadier conversation. In the face of determined opposition by the Treasury and the Board of Trade nothing had been accomplished.

October 13th. I went to see Bidault this afternoon and after discussing one or two other matters with him informed him of my coming departure. He was genuinely distressed and quite eloquent in his expression of regret at my going and gratitude for what I had done. He spoke, he said, not only for himself but for the French Government and the French people. He insisted on accompanying me not only to the door but down the steps to my car and stood by it, at attention, until I drove away. He did it with great dignity. It was almost dramatic and I felt moved.

I said when the Treaty of Dunkirk was signed that if it were the end of a long chapter it was of little importance, but that if it proved to be the beginning of a new one it was a great event. I hoped that it might lead to closer relations between the two countries, with integration as the final aim, and that the solidarity of this north-west corner of Europe might become the nucleus of a great international combine, larger and more powerful than the Soviet Union or the United States.

I hoped that this policy would be pursued upon three planes, the military, the economic and the colonial. The first step on the military plane must be staff conversations. The French wanted them, but in spite of my advocacy they had not started before I left the Embassy. I did, however, succeed in setting up an Anglo-French economic committee, which I hoped would meet regularly at fixed intervals and at which representatives of the Treasury and the Ministry of Finance would frankly exchange information and discuss problems. It was in being when I left the Embassy, and I am told that it continued to function, but when the British Government devalued the pound the French financial authorities were given no previous information, although they were sitting by the side of their British colleagues in Washington when the decision was taken.

During my last months of office I did not diminish but increased my efforts to get support for the policy in which I believed. I adopted the method of the personal letter rather than the official despatch. I wrote on October 16th:

My dear Secretary of State, As I shall shortly be leaving the service I hope you will forgive me if I write to you in terms that would hardly be proper as coming from a subordinate to his chief.

I then reminded him of the despatches I had written both to his predecessor and to himself, how they had both agreed with me "in principle," but how it had always seemed that the moment was unsuitable to take any action of the kind desired. How Léon Blum had at first made the same objection, with better reason than most, for his Government was doomed to fall in a fortnight, how I had persuaded him none the less to come to London, and how his two days' visit had produced the Treaty of Dunkirk.

Last month I thought another stride forward had been taken in the conversation that you had with Ramadier. I have just seen an advance copy of the record of the Foreign Office discussion which took place on the 8th October on the subject of that conversation, and I must say that it is a most melancholy document. The total outcome is zero—or rather a minus quantity. I hardly think that you will have found time to look at it, but when I tell you that a third of the time was devoted to talking about Eire you will understand how unrealistic the discussion was. But the usefulness of this report lies in the fact that it demonstrates beyond all doubt that, as I have always believed, certain departments, and especially the Treasury and the Board of Trade, are opposed in principle to any closer collaboration between Great Britain and France.

I think their motives may be traced to two main principles. They believe:

First, while we are both very poor, Great Britain is still richer than France and, therefore, if we combine our resources, we shall be giving more than we get;

Secondly, they are convinced that nothing in the world matters except dollars, and that therefore no country counts except the United States.

The first of these objections is the more fundamental and I believe it to be the more profoundly wrong. It betrays not only a narrow and parochial outlook but an economic and political error. Unity is strength.

Banks would never have come into being if the rich had not thought it worth their while to collaborate with those who were less rich. Trade Unions could not have existed if the better paid, more successful and more robust workers had allowed, as for long they did, their weaker brethren to go to the wall. The nations who from time to time have led the world would never have done so if they had thought it worth their while to make alliances only with those who were richer and stronger than themselves.

I went on to deal at some length with the desirability of increasing the volume of trade between the two countries, of joint economic planning to cover not only our metropolitan but also our respective colonial territories, especially in Africa, and of encouraging our tour- ist traffic. I suggested that the Chancellor of the Exchequer and the President of the Board of Trade should be persuaded to inform their departments that the policy of closer Anglo-French integration had been decided upon and that it was their business to suggest the best way of carrying it out. I concluded:

Civil servants, like most mature human beings, have both an innate and an acquired antipathy to radical change. It is their duty, which they ad- mirably perform, to point out to Ministers the dangers and difficulties in- separable from any new departure in policy. It is also their duty, and I have never known them to fail in it, once Ministers have taken a decision, to do their utmost to implement that decision successfully. Let the instruc- tions be given, and they will be carried out.

I wrote again the following month, deploring the fact that my Military Attaché had received a letter from the War Office in which it was stated that "the Foreign Office is anxious that you should do your best to discourage any suggestion of staff talks as wholly pre- mature."

Having received no reply to either letter from the Secretary of State, I wrote to his Private Secretary on November 26th, enquiring whether they had been received. I added:

One-way traffic in letters is always discouraging and, if it is a question of giving advice, one likes to know whether one is making the mistake of pushing on an open door, or else of putting forward views which are so unacceptable that it is a waste of time to advance them. As my days draw to their close I wish to pass out preaching the gospel; but not if its accept- ance is likely to be prejudiced by my advocacy.

The result was that I received a letter which might have been drafted in the Board of Trade, although my Commercial Minister detected one or two inaccuracies in it. But what could it profit me to argue with the Board of Trade? The excuses put forward in another letter for postponing staff conversations were so feeble that they provoked me to write yet once more and for the last time.

After dealing with the immediate issue and expatiating on the evils of postponement and delay, I ended:

After the former war Great Britain and France were, in 1919, the strongest and best armed Powers in Europe. If they had then maintained their strength and concluded an alliance, they could have preserved the peace of the world. But they threw away their weapons and drifted apart, and by their criminal folly permitted the second catastrophe to occur. Yet the men who were responsible for the government of the two countries during that period were neither criminals nor fools. Their fault was that they did not want to be hurried, they did not want to take premature decisions, they did not want to commit themselves, they did not want to spend too much money, they did not want to alarm public opinion, they did not want to antagonise other nations, and they did not—the British and the French—quite trust one another; so everything was put off until it was too late—until neither country could face with confidence the enemy whom they had utterly defeated and crushed twenty years before.

This, my dear Secretary of State, is probably the last letter that I shall write you as Ambassador in Paris. I have been happy to serve under you because I have felt from the first that upon the great issues we were agreed. You may think that I am making a lot of fuss about nothing, and that it matters little whether staff conversations start in January or in June or in the year after next. But, to my mind, this is just one of those many small matters upon the settlement of which depends the fate of great nations. I watched the process in operation during the twenty years that separated the wars. During that period I served in the Foreign Office, the Treasury, the War Office and the Admiralty. The attitude of the Government at every turn was always defensible, logical, and supported by sound arguments, but it lacked one thing—a guiding policy behind it—and so, in the end, it landed us in a ghastly war without a previously pledged ally or an agreed scheme of defence. We came within an ace of losing that war. For God's sake, and for the sake of humanity, don't let that happen again.

This was my final exhortation to the Secretary of State, and I am content that these words should remain my last official utterance. They contain a warning, the need for which has not passed.

Part of the regret with which I left the Embassy was due to the fondness that I had come to feel for the house. Built in the first half of the eighteenth century, it is a perfect example of what a rich gentleman's house should be. Neither palatial nor imposing, but commodious and convenient, central and quiet. I sometimes felt that it was gently haunted by the spirits of the pleasant people who had sat in its comfortable rooms. Of the Dukes of Charost for whom it was built I know little save that the last one died of the smallpox caught while he was nursing the poor. They were followed by Pauline Borghese, youngest and loveliest of Napoleon's sisters, who, whatever her faults, was always loyal to her brother and was leaving for St. Helena when she learnt of his death. The house is very much as she left it and her plate still adorns the dinner-table on great occasions. In 1814 Wellington bought it for our Embassy, which it has remained ever since. I liked to think of Talleyrand calling there on Lady Granville, when he impressed her as being, to her surprise, "so gentle, so kind, so simple and so grand." I liked also to think of Dickens performing theatricals and of Thackeray getting married there. It was not until after I had left that I discovered that my own grandparents, on my mother's side, were also married there, he being at the time an honorary attaché.

When I first arrived I found some precious volumes lying about which had been presented by Stephen Gaselee, formerly librarian to the Foreign Office. Knowing the habits of book-borrowers and the lack of respect that government property inspires, I said that they should be put away in the library, only to learn that there was no library in the house.

Buying books was always my weakness, and I have left a trail of them wherever I have been. When we gave up living at the Admiralty we moved to my mother-in-law's house in Chapel Street which she had left to Diana. She had built out into the garden one very large room, which we converted into a library designed for us by Rex Whistler. For the first time in my life I had all my books in one room. It was hardly finished before the war broke out, and it seemed foolish to leave my treasures exposed to the bombs. So we sent them to lie in the security of Belvoir's cellars.

When therefore I arrived at the Embassy I had not seen my books for five years; and I had missed them. I proposed to the Office of Works that they should pay for the conversion of one of the rooms into a library, worthy of the house, and I undertook that I would leave it adequately stocked with books when I went away. I received the inevitable Civil Service reply that the suggestion was admirable but the time was not suitable. I replied that the time was not likely to recur when they would have an Ambassador who would be willing to bequeath them a library. With the help of the Minister of Works I overcame official objections. A great deal of trouble was taken over that library, and when I left I thought it was the most agreeable room in the world, and I was glad to leave in it some memorial of my sojourn.

We gave a ball before we left and by great good fortune Winston Churchill happened to be passing through Paris that night, on the way to spend his Christmas holiday in Morocco. So that he who had appointed me to the post was present at my farewell party, where his presence lent lustre to the occasion. It was a gay evening. Many of our English friends came over for it and our French friends were profuse in expressions of enjoyment of the party, and regret at our departure. Léon Blum very kindly wrote an article in praise of me, giving me full credit for the Treaty of Dunkirk.

I was now nearly fifty-eight, which is two years under the Civil Service age of retirement. It was suggested that I should return to the House of Commons and I was assured that I should be able to get a seat. But a parliamentary candidate must either attack or defend the Government. I felt that it would be a graceless action on my part to turn and bite the hand that had been feeding me for the last two and a half years. I thought also that it would be improper for one who had enjoyed the Government's confidence during that period to attack them immediately on quitting their service. I therefore postponed a decision, and such appetite as I had left for party politics died away.

Journalism and business provided an income and gave me more leisure than I had enjoyed before. Nor, although living in France, did I feel that I was altogether neglecting my civic responsibilities. Chairmanship of the local branches of the British Legion and the St. George's Society, the presidency of the Travellers Club, and work on the Managing Committee of the British Hospital provided me with the kind of duties which old men are best fitted to perform.

As I said at the beginning of this book, I find that old age has many compensations, and I still feel, as I felt in my youth, that the old should make way for the young and give them their opportunity while they yet have vision to inspire them, energy to perform and time to achieve.

I have never felt that the contemplation of the past, with the knowledge that it cannot come again, need be a source of sorrow. The emotion is like that aroused by looking through an album of old photographs which recall happy days, and if we find among them the faces of friends who are no more we are glad to be reminded of the affection we felt for them. I have written this book, and enjoyed writing it, because I wanted to set down some of these memories before they faded. Nor can the dearest and the most sacred of them be included. Life has been good to me and I am grateful. My delight in it is as keen as ever and I will thankfully accept as many more years as may be granted. But I am fond of change and have welcomed it even when uncertain whether it would be for the better; so, although I am very glad to be where I am, I shall not be too distressed when the summons comes to go away. Autumn has always been my favourite season, and evening has been for me the pleasantest time of day. I love the sunlight but I cannot fear the coming of the dark.

INDEX

FINE WORKS OF NON-FICTION
AVAILABLE IN QUALITY
PAPERBACK EDITIONS FROM
CARROLL & GRAF

- ☐ Anderson, Nancy/WORK WITH PASSION $8.95
- ☐ Berton, Pierre/KLONDIKE FEVER $10.95
- ☐ Blanch, Lesley/THE WILDER SHORES OF LOVE $8.95
- ☐ Conot, Robert/JUSTICE AT NUREMBURG $10.95
- ☐ Cooper, Lady Diana/AUTOBIOGRAPHY $12.95
- ☐ Elkington, John/THE GENE FACTORY $8.95
- ☐ Gill, Brendan/HERE AT THE NEW YORKER $12.95
- ☐ Lansing, Alfred/ENDURANCE: SHACKELTON'S
  INCREDIBLE VOYAGE $8.95
- ☐ McCarthy, Barry & Emily/SEXUAL AWARENESS $9.95
- ☐ Moorehead, Alan/THE RUSSIAN REVOLUTION $10.95
- ☐ Poncins, Gontran de/KABLOONA $9.95
- ☐ Pringle, David/SCIENCE FICTION: THE 100 BEST
  NOVELS $7.95
- ☐ Rowse, A.L./HOMOSEXUALS IN HISTORY $9.95
- ☐ Roy, Jules/THE BATTLE OF DIENBIENPHU $8.95
- ☐ Werth, Alexander/RUSSIA AT WAR 1941–1945 $15.95

Available from fine bookstores everywhere or use this coupon for ordering:

Carroll & Graf Publishers, Inc., 260 Fifth Avenue, N.Y., N.Y. 10001

Please send me the books I have checked above. I am enclosing
$_____ (please add $1.75 per title to cover postage and handling.) Send check or money order—no cash or C.O.D.'s please.
N.Y. residents please add 8¼% sales tax.

Mr/Mrs/Miss _____

Address _____

City _____ State/Zip _____

Please allow four to six weeks for delivery.